John Obadiah Justamond

A Philosophical and Political History of the Settlements and Trade of

the Europeans

in the East and West Indies

John Obadiah Justamond

A Philosophical and Political History of the Settlements and Trade of the Europeans
in the East and West Indies

ISBN/EAN: 9783337318628

Printed in Europe, USA, Canada, Australia, Japan

Cover: Foto ©ninafisch / pixelio.de

More available books at **www.hansebooks.com**

A

PHILOSOPHICAL AND POLITICAL

HISTORY

OF THE

SETTLEMENTS AND TRADE

OF THE

EUROPEANS

IN THE

EAST AND WEST INDIES.

Tranſlated from the French of the

ABBÉ RAYNAL,

By J. JUSTAMOND, M. A.

THE THIRD EDITION:
REVISED AND CORRECTED.
WITH MAPS ADAPTED TO THE WORK,
AND A COPIOUS INDEX.

IN FIVE VOLUMES.

VOLUME THE FIRST.

LONDON:
Printed for T. CADELL, in the Strand.
M DCC LXXVII.

CONTENTS

OF THE

FIRST VOLUME.

BOOK I.

INTRODUCTION   Page 1

BOOK II.

The settlements, wars, policy, and trade, of the Dutch in the East Indies   161

BOOK III.

Settlements, trade, and conquests of the English in the East Indies   302

A
PHILOSOPHICAL AND POLITICAL
HISTORY
OF THE
SETTLEMENTS AND TRADE
OF THE
EUROPEANS
IN THE
EAST AND WEST INDIES.

BOOK I.
INTRODUCTION.

NO event has been so interesting to mankind in general, and to the inhabitants of Europe in particular, as the discovery of the new world, and the passage to India by the Cape of Good Hope. It gave rise to a revolution in the commerce, and in the power of nations; and in the manners, industry, and government of the whole world. At this period, new connections were formed by the inhabitants of the most distant regions, for the supply of wants they had never before experienced. The productions of climates situated under the equator, were consumed in countries bordering on the pole; the industry of the north was transplanted to the south; and the

BOOK I.

The discoveries, wars, and conquests of the Portuguese in the East Indies.

Vol. I. B inhabitants

inhabitants of the weſt were cloathed with the manufactures of the eaſt; a general intercourſe of opinions, laws and cuſtoms, diſeaſes and remedies, virtues and vices, was eſtabliſhed among men.

EVERY thing has changed, and muſt change again. But it is a queſtion, whether the revolutions that are paſſed, or thoſe which muſt hereafter take place, have been, or can be of any utility to the human race? Will they ever add to the tranquillity, the happineſs, and the pleaſures of mankind? Can they improve our preſent ſtate, or do they only change it?

THE Europeans have founded colonies in all parts, but are they acquainted with the principles on which they ought to be formed? They have eſtabliſhed a commerce of exchange, of the productions of the earth and of manufactures. This commerce is transferred from one people to another. Can we not diſcover by what means, and in what ſituations this has been effected? Since America and the paſſage by the Cape has been known, ſome nations that were of no conſequence are become powerful: others, that were the terror of Europe, have loſt their authority. How has the condition of theſe ſeveral people been affected by theſe diſcoveries? How comes it to paſs that thoſe to whom Nature has been moſt liberal, are not always the richeſt and moſt flouriſhing? To throw ſome light on theſe important queſtions, we muſt take a view of the ſtate of Europe before theſe diſcoveries were made; we muſt trace circumſtantially the events they have given riſe to; and conclude

IN THE EAST AND WEST INDIES.
conclude with examining it, as it prefents itfelf at this day.

The commercial ftates have civilized all others. The Phœnicians, whofe extent of country and influence were extremely limited, acquired by their genius for naval enterprifes, an importance which ranked them foremoft in the hiftory of the antient nations.

They are mentioned by writers of every clafs. They were known to the moft diftant climes, and their fame has been tranfmitted to fucceeding ages.

Situated on a barren coaft, feparated from the continent by the Mediterranean on the one fide, and the mountains of Libanus on the other; they feem to have been deftined by Nature for the dominion of the fea. Fifhing taught them the art of navigation, and furnifhed them with the purple dye which they extracted from the murex: at the fame time the fea-fand led them to difcover the fecret of making glafs. Happy in poffeffing fo few natural advantages, fince the want of thefe awakened that fpirit of invention and induftry, which is the parent of arts and opulence!

It muft be confeffed, that the fituation of the Phœnicians was admirably adapted to extend their commerce to every part of the world. By inhabiting, as it were, the confines of Africa, Afia, and Europe, if they could not unite the inhabitants of the globe in one common intereft, they at leaft had it in their power, by a commercial intercourfe, to communicate to every nation the enjoyments of all climates. But the antients whom we have so often excelled, though we have derived much useful knowledge from them, had not means sufficient to enable them to establish an universal commerce. The Phœnicians had no shipping except gallies; they only carried on a coasting trade, and their sailing was confined to the Mediterranean. Though this state was the model upon which other maritime powers were formed, it is not so easy to determine what they have, as what they might have performed. We may form a conjecture of their population by their colonies. It is said that their numbers extended along the coasts of the Mediterranean, particularly on the shores of Africa.

TYRE or Sidon, the queen of the ocean, gave birth to Carthage. While the opulence of Tyre invited tyrants to rivet its fetters, Carthage, the offspring of Tyre, notwithstanding its riches, had this happy advantage over the parent state, that it enjoyed its liberty. It commanded the coasts of Africa, and had possession of Spain, which in those days was the richest country in Europe, and famous for gold and silver mines of its own, though destined, at the expence of so much bloodshed, to acquire others in the new world.

HAD the Roman power never existed, Carthage would in all probability have been nothing more than a commercial state; but the ambition of one nation excited all the rest to relinguish the arts of commerce for those of war, and either to conquer or to perish. Carthage, after a long and glorious contest for the empire of the world, was forced to submit to the all-subduing genius of Rome. The subversion

IN THE EAST AND WEST INDIES.

subverfion of a republic, which gloried in its induftry, and owed its power to its skill in useful arts, was, perhaps, a misfortune to Europe, and to the world in general.

GREECE, interfected every where by seas, must necessarily flourish by commerce. Its position in the Archipelago, and its distance from any large continent, seemed to make it unlikely that it should either conquer or be conquered. Situated between Asia and Europe, it contributed to civilize both the one and the other, and enjoyed a deserved share of prosperity, as the reward of its services. As almost all the Greeks came either from Egypt or Phœnicia, they brought along with them the knowledge and industry of those countries; but of all the Asiatic colonies, those were the most flourishing and happy, that had a turn for commerce.

ATHENS employed her first ships either in carrying on a trade with Asia, or in planting as many colonies as Greece in her infancy might have received from thence: but these emigrations involved them in wars. The Persians, living under an arbitrary government, would not even suffer any free people to settle on the confines of the sea; and the Satraps inculcated into the great king, the doctrine of universal slavery. This was the source of all the wars in Asia Minor, where the Athenians found means to make all the insular and maritime states either their allies or their subjects. Athens enlarged her commerce by her victories, and her power by her commerce. All the arts made their appearance in Greece at the same time, together with the luxury of Asia.

COMMERCE,

COMMERCE, agriculture, and the means of population, were introduced into Sicily by the Greeks and the Carthaginians. Rome, who beheld their progress with a jealous eye, seized upon that island which was destined to supply it with subsistence; and having driven out the two nations that contended for the sovereignty of it, attacked first one, and then the other. From the moment that Carthage was destroyed, Greece trembled for her fate. But it was Alexander who marked the way for the Romans; nor was it possible, perhaps, that the Greeks could have been subdued by a foreign power, if they had not first conquered each other. Commerce is finally destroyed by the riches it accumulates, as power is by its own conquests; and when the commerce of the Greeks had failed in the Mediterranean, it no longer subsisted in any part of the known world.

THE Greeks, by improving upon all the sciences and arts they had received from the Egyptians and Tyrians, elevated human reason to a high degree of perfection: but it has been reduced so low by the subsequent revolutions of empires, that in all probability it will never rise again to the same standard. Their admirable institutions were superior to the best we have at this day. The plan upon which they founded their colonies does honour to their humanity. As all the arts owed to them their rise, and perfection, they did not survive the fate of their protectors: It is evident from some works of Xenophon, that the Greeks were better acquainted with the principles of trade, than most modern nations are at present.

IF

IF we confider that the Europeans have the advantage of all the knowledge of the Greeks, that their commerce is infinitely more extenfive, that fince the improvements in navigation, their ideas are directed to greater, and more various objects; it is aftonifhing that they fhould not have the moft palpable fuperiority over them. But it muft be obferved, that when thefe people arrived at the knowledge of the arts and of trade, they were juft produced as it were from the hands of nature, and had all the powers neceffary to improve the talents fhe had given them: whereas the European nations had the misfortune to be reftrained by laws, by government, and by an exclufive and imperious religion. In Greece the arts of trade met with men, in Europe with flaves. Whenever the abfurdities of our inftitutions have been pointed out, we have taken pains to correct them, without ever daring totally to overthrow the edifice. We have remedied fome abufes, by introducing others; and, in our efforts to fupport, reform and palliate, we have adopted more contradictions and adfurdities in our manners, than are to be found among the moft barbarous people. For this reafon, if the arts fhould ever gain admiffion among the Tartars and Iroquois, they will make an infinitely more rapid progrefs among them, than they can ever do in Ruffia and Poland.

THE Romans, formed for conqueft, though they dazzled the world with an appearance of grandeur, fell fhort of the Greeks in their improvements in philofophy, and the arts. They promoted an intercourfe between different nations, not by uniting them by the ties of commerce, but by impoſing upon them the ſame yoke of ſubordination. They ravaged the globe, which, when reduced to ſubjection, they left in a ſtate rather of lethargy than tranquillity. Their deſpotiſm and military government oppreſſed the people, extinguiſhed the powers of genius, and degraded the human race.

CONSTANTINE paſſed two laws, which, though Monteſquieu has not ventured to reckon them among the cauſes of the declenſion of the empire, threw every thing into ſtill greater diſorder. The firſt, dictated by imprudence and fanaticiſm, though it appeared to be the effect of humanity, affords a proof that great innovations are often attended with great danger; and that the original rights of mankind cannot always be made the ſtandard of government. By this law, all ſlaves who ſhould embrace chriſtianity, were allowed their freedom. Thus, while thoſe who had hitherto dragged on a precarious exiſtence were reinſtated in their primitive rights, the ſtate was weakened; becauſe the proprietors of large tracts of land were deprived of the number of hands neceſſary for their improvement, and were for ſome time reduced to the extremeſt indigence. On the other hand, the new converts, having no property themſelves, or any certain means of ſubſiſtence, were not in a condition to aſſiſt the government, in repairing the injury it had done to their maſters. It is equally impoſſible that they ſhould have any attachment to a ſtate which did not afford them ſubſiſtence, or to a religion, which the irreſiſtible deſire of liberty alone induced them to embrace.

IN THE EAST AND WEST INDIES.

embrace. By another edict, paganism was prohibited throughout the whole empire; and thus these extensive dominions were inhabited by men, whose attachment to each other, and to the state, was no longer secured by the solemn sanctions of religion: having no priests, no temples, no public morals, they had no motives to excite them to repel an enemy who should attack a government with which they were no longer connected.

THE inhabitants of the north, therefore, when they fell upon the empire, found every thing ready to favour their invasion. Harassed in Poland and in Germany by some nations who had migrated from Great Tartary, they took a temporary possession of certain provinces already ruined, till they were expelled by succeeding conquerors of a still more ferocious disposition than themselves. When these barbarians determined to settle in the regions they had laid waste, they divided countries which the Romans had formerly united. From that moment, all communication between those states established by accident, necessity or caprice, was at an end. The swarms of pirates that infested the seas, together with the fierce disposition of the inhabitants of the frontiers, discouraged every connection that mutual convenience might render necessary. The subjects of each state, however small in extent, were separated from each other by insurmountable obstacles; for the banditti who infested the roads, made a journey of any length a dangerous expedition. The nations of Europe, thus plunged a second time by slavery and despair into that state of

insensibility

insensibility and indolence, which must for many ages have been the state of the human race, derived little advantage from the fertility of their soil; and their industry was exhausted in the employments of a savage life; tracts of country at no great distance, were to them of as little importance, as if they had not existed: nor had they any further knowledge of their neighbours, than as they happened to excite their fears or their enmity.

THE accounts given by some authors of the wealth and splendour of the seventh century, are as fabulous as all the other miraculous things we read of in the history of those times. The cloathing then in use was of skin and coarse woollen, the conveniences of life were not known; buildings indeed were erected with strength and solidity, but which conveyed no idea, either of the affluence or taste of the age. Neither much money, nor much knowledge of the arts is required to pile up heaps of stone by the hands of slaves. One incontestible proof of the indigence of the people was, that taxes were levied in kind; and that even the contributions which the inferior clergy paid to their superiors, consisted of provisions.

THE superstition that prevailed increased the general darkness. In the eighth, and the beginning of the ninth century, Rome, no longer the capital of the masters of the universe, attempted to exercise her authority as before, in deposing or making kings. Deprived of inhabitants and soldiers, by dint of opinions and religious tenets alone, she aspired to universal monarchy. By her management princes

were

were excited to take up arms againſt each other, people againſt their kings, and kings againſt their people. All merit confiſted in making war, and all virtue in obeying the church. The dignity of monarchs was degraded by the claims of Rome, which inſpired a contempt for princes, without exciting the love of liberty. Literature was then compriſed in a few abſurd romances, and ſome melancholy tales, the offspring of cloiſtered indolence. This contributed to entertain that dejection of ſpirit, and that propenſity to the marvelous, ſo favourable to the intereſts of ſuperſtition.

THE face of the globe was again changed by two other nations. A people pouring in from Scandinavia and the Cimbrian Cherſoneſus ſpread themſelves to the north of Europe, which on the ſouthern ſide was haraſſed by the Arabs. The former were diſciples of Wodin, the latter of Mohammed; men who had equally diffuſed the fanaticiſm of conqueſt with that of religion. Charlemagne ſubdued one of theſe nations, and maintained his ground againſt the other. Theſe inhabitants of the north, called Saxons or Normans, were indigent, ill armed, and undiſciplined, of ſavage manners, and driven to combat and to death by miſery and ſuperſtition. Charlemagne was deſirous of compelling them to change that religion which rendered them ſo terrible, for another which would diſpoſe them to obedience. He was obliged to wade through ſeas of blood, and the croſs was erected on heaps of ſlain. He was leſs ſuccefsful againſt the Arabs, conquerors of Aſia, Africa and Spain, and could

could not gain a footing beyond the Pyrenean mountains.

The neceffity of repulfing the Arabs, but efpecially the Normans, occafioned the revival of naval fkill in Europe. Charlemagne in France, Alfred the Great in England, and fome cities of Italy, built fhips; and thefe firft attempts towards navigation revived for a fhort time maritime commerce. Charlemagne eftablifhed great fairs, the principal of which was at Aix-la-Chapelle. This is the method of trading among people where commerce is ftill in its infancy.

The Arabs, however, laid the foundations of the moft extenfive commerce that had been known fince the times of Athens and Carthage. It is true, this was not fo much owing to the lights of cultivated reafon, and to the progrefs of a good adminiftration, as to the extent of their power, and the nature of the country they poffeffed. Mafters of Spain, of Africa, of Afia Minor, of Perfia, and part of India, they introduced reciprocal exchanges, from one region to another, of the commodities in different parts of their vaft empire. They extended themfelves gradually as far as the Moluccas and to China, fometimes as traders, fometimes as miffionaries, frequently as conquerors.

Soon after this, the Venetians, Genoefe and Arabs of Barcelona went to Alexandria to buy up the merchandife of Africa and India, and difpofed of it in Europe. The Arabs, enriched by commerce, and fated with conqueft, were no longer the fame people who burnt the Alexandrian library. They

IN THE EAST AND WEST INDIES.

They cultivated the arts and polite literature, and are diſtinguiſhed from other conquering nations by their improvements of the reaſon and induſtry of men. To them we owe the ſciences of algebra and chymeſtry, new diſcoveries in aſtronomy, new improvements in mechanics and medicine, unknown to the ancients. But among the fine arts, poetry is the only one they have cultivated with ſuccefs.

AT the fame period, the ſubjects of the Greek empire imitated the manufactures of Aſia; and had, through various channels, monopolized the riches of India. But the advantages they derived from both theſe circumſtances, could not ſurvive the fate of their empire; which had nothing to oppoſe to the heroic and daring enthuſiaſm of the Arabs, but the weak and unmanly weapons of ſcholaſtic logic, and the controverſial armour of monks; who had gained ſuch an aſcendant, that the Emperor uſed to aſk God pardon for the time he employed in affairs of ſtate. Painting and ſculpture were no longer known, and it was matter of eternal diſpute whether images ought, or ought not, to be worſhipped. The Greeks, ſurrounded by the ocean, and in poſſeſſion of ſeveral iſlands, had yet no maritime forces; they defended themſelves againſt the naval power of Egypt and of the Saracens by wild fire; the vain and precarious defence of a degenerate people. Conſtantinople, not being in a condition to protect her maritime trade at a diſtance, reſigned it to the Genoeſe, who ſeized upon Caffa, which they made a flouriſhing city.

The nobility of Europe acquired a tincture of the manners of the Greeks and Arabs in their ridiculous expeditions of the crufades. They became acquainted with their arts and their luxury; which were afterwards almoſt neceſſary to their happineſs. The Venetians had a more extenſive demand for the goods they brought from the eaſt; and the Arabs themſelves carried ſome of them into France, England, and even into Germany.

These powers had at that period neither ſhipping nor manufactures: they laid reſtraints upon commerce, and the character of a merchant was held in contempt. This uſeful ſet of men were never reſpected among the Romans. They treated their merchants with as much contempt as their players, courteſans, baſtards, ſlaves and gladiators. The political ſyſtem, eſtabliſhed throughout Europe by the power and ignorance of the northern nations, muſt neceſſarily have confirmed a prejudice which owed its riſe to a barbarous pride. Our anceſtors had the abſurdity to adopt, as the baſis of their government, a principle deſtructive of all ſociety; a contempt for uſeful labour. The only perſons held in any degree of eſtimation were the lords of manors, or ſuch as had diſtinguiſhed themſelves in battle. The nobles, it is well known, were ſo many petty ſovereigns who abuſed their own power, and oppoſed that of the monarch. The barons were fond of parade, avaritious, whimſical and poor. Sometimes they invited the merchants into their little ſtates and at others, extorted money from them. In theſe barbarous times were eſtabliſhed the ſeveral duties of tolls,

IN THE EAST AND WEST INDIES.
tolls, of export and import, of paſſage, of quarters, of eſcheat, and other oppreſſions without number. All the bridges and highways were opened or ſtopped up at the will of the prince or his vaſſals. The firſt elements of commerce were ſo totally unknown, that it was cuſtomary to fix the price of commodities. The merchants were often pillaged, and always ill paid by the knights and barons. Trade was carried on in caravans or companies, which went armed to the places where the fairs were kept. At theſe marts the merchants omitted nothing that might engage the favour of the people. They were generally accompanied by jugglers, muſicians and buffoons. As there were then no large towns, and neither public ſpectacles and meetings, nor the ſedentary pleaſures of private ſociety were known, the fair time was the ſeaſon for diverſions, which, degenerating into diſſoluteneſs, gave a ſanction to the invectives and ſeverities of the clergy. The traders were frequently excommunicated. The people held thoſe ſtrangers in abhorrence, who ſupplied their tyrants with ſuperfluities, and aſſociated with men, whoſe manners were ſo repugnant to their prejudices and rude auſterity of life. The Jews, who ſoon engaged in all the branches of commerce, did not bring it into repute. They were then conſidered in the ſame light throughout all Europe, as they are at this day in Poland and Turky. As their fortunes were increaſing every day, they were enabled to advance money to merchants and tradeſmen; for which they demanded intereſt equivalent to the riſque they ran in veſting their capital

capital in other hands. The fchoolmen were violent in oppofing this neceffary meafure, which their rude prejudices had taught them to condemn. This theological determination of a point of a civil and political nature, was attended with ftrange confequences. The magiftrates, blinded by an authority, againft even the unjuft exercife of which no one dared to appeal, denounced fentence of confifcation and ignominious penalties againft ufury, which, in thofe dark ages, the laws did not diftinguifh from the moft moderate intereft. It was at this juncture, that to make themfelves amends for the dangers and mortifications they were expofed to in carrying on a commerce, which was looked upon as odious and unlawful, the Jews abandoned themfelves to the moft exceffive rapacity. They were held in univerfal deteftation. Perfecuted, pillaged, and profcribed, they invented bills of exchange, which fecured the remains of their fortunes. The clergy declared the exchange ufurious, but it was of too great utility to be abolifhed. One of the effects it produced was to make the merchants more independent of the prince, who treated them better, apprehending that they might tranfport their riches into foreign countries.

THE Italians, who are better known by the name of Lombards, were the firft who took advantage of this early change of ideas. They formed fmall communities, and procured the protection of fome ftates, who, on their account, difpenfed with the laws againft ftrangers, which had been made in the barbarous ages. By virtue
of

IN THE EAST AND WEST INDIES.

of this indulgence, they became agents for all the southern parts of Europe.

The inhabitants of the north began likewife to awake from their lethargy: but their recovery was later, and effected with greater difficulty. Hamburgh and Lubec having attempted to open a trade in the Baltic, were obliged to unite for their mutual defence againft the pirates who infefted thofe latitudes. The fuccefs of this little combination encouraged other towns to enter into the confederacy; in a fhort time, this was compofed of fourfcore cities, which had either obtained or purchafed the privilege of being governed by their own laws, and formed a line of communication from the Baltic to the Rhine. This affociation, which was the firft modern one that adopted a regular fyftem of commerce, fupplied the Lombards with naval ftores and other merchandife of the north, in exchange for the produce of Afia, Italy, and the other fouthern countries.

Flanders was the fcene of thefe happy tranfactions; but it was not to its fituation alone that it owed a diftinction fo favourable to its interefts: this muft likewife be attributed to its numerous manufactures of fine cloth, and particularly of tapeftry; which laft affords a convincing proof how little the arts of drawing and perfpective were then known. By thefe advantageous circumftances, the Low-Countries became the richeft, the moft populous, and the beft cultivated part of Europe.

Vol. I. C The

The flourishing condition of the inhabitants of Flanders, the Hanse Towns, and some republics, who owed their prosperity to their freedom, engaged the attention of most of the reigning monarchs, in whose dominions the rights of citizens had hitherto been confined to the nobility and clergy; the rest of their subjects were slaves. But as soon as the cities were declared free, and had large immunities granted them, the merchants and mechanics entered into associations, which rose in estimation as they acquired riches. The sovereigns opposed these associations to the barons. Thus anarchy and feudal tyranny gradually decreased. The tradesmen became citizens, and the third state was restored to the privilege of being admitted to the national assembly.

MONTESQUIEU attributes to Christianity the honour of having abolished slavery; but we venture to differ from him. When industry and riches prevailed among the people, the princes began to hold them in some estimation; when the sovereign could avail himself of the riches of the people to gain advantages over the barons, laws were framed to put the people in a better condition. It was through that sound policy, which commerce always introduces, and not through the spirit of the Christian Religion, that kings were induced to bestow freedom upon the slaves of their vassals, because those slaves, when made free, became subjects. It is true, that Pope Alexander III. declared that Christians were to be exempt from servitude; but this declaration was made merely to please the kings of France and England,

England, who were defirous of humbling their vaffals.

In Italy one might perceive the dawning of more profperous days. The republics of Pifa, Genoa and Florence, were eftablifhed on the wifeft principles; the factions of the Guelphs and Gibbelines, which had for fo many ages laid wafte thefe delightful countries, were at length appeafed; trade flourifhed, and confequently learning would foon be introduced. Venice was in the height of its glory; its navy, which eclipfed that of its neighbours, checked the progrefs of the maritime power of the Mammelucs, and the Turks; in commerce it was fuperior to all the European ftates taken together; its inhabitants were numerous, and its riches immenfe; the revenues were well managed, and the people were content; the republic borrowed money of the richer fubjects, from motives not of neceffity, but of policy. The Venetians were the firft people who found out the fecret of attaching rich individuals to the intereft of government, by inviting them to veft fome part of their fortune in the public funds. At Venice there were manufactures of filk, gold and filver; it fupplied foreigners with fhips: its works in gold and filver were the beft, and almoft the only ones of that time. The inhabitants were even accufed of extravagance in having gold and filver plate, and other utenfils of the fame materials. They were not, however, without fumptuary laws; but thefe laid no reftraint on a fpecies of luxury by which the fums expended were preferved to the ftate.

state. . The noblemen united œconomy with splendour; the opulence of Venice revived the architecture of Athens, and upon the whole there was magnificence as well as elegance in their luxury; the people were ignorant, but the nobles were enlightened; the government opposed the attempts of the popes with firmness and prudence: *Siamo Veneziani, poi Christiani*, said one of their senators, who expressed in these words the sense of the whole senate; for at that early period they debased the priesthood, though they should rather have made it useful to morality; which, however, was more rigid and pure among the Venetians than among the other people of Italy. Their troops were very different from those miserable *Condottieri*, whose name was so much more terrible than their arms. Venice was the seat of politeness; and society was then under less restraint from the spies of government, than it has been since the republic began to be jealous of the power of its neighbours, and to be diffident of its own strength.

In the fifteenth century, Italy far surpassed the other states of Europe. Religious zeal, which supplied the place of merit, and occasioned so many trifling ceremonies and cruel oppressions, was, however, the means of releasing Spain from the Arabian yoke; its several provinces had lately been united by the marriage of Ferdinand and Isabella, and the conquest of Granada; and its power was even equal to that of France. The fine wool of Castile and Leon was manufactured at Segovia, and their cloths were sold all over Europe, and even in Asia; the perpetual efforts
the

IN THE EAST AND WEST INDIES.

the Spaniards were obliged to make to preserve their liberty, infpired them with refolution and confidence; their fuccefs had elevated their minds, and, being ignorant, they abandoned themfelves to all the enthufiafm of chivalry and religion. Confined to a peninfula, and having no immediate intercourfe with other nations, they entertained that contempt for them, which, either among indi‑ viduals or communities, is ufually the chara&eriftic of ignorance. They were the only people that maintained a ftanding body of infantry, which was excellent. As the Spaniards for many ages had been involved in war, their foldiery was indifputably fuperior to that of the other ftates of Europe.

THE Portuguefe had much the fame difpofitions; but their monarchy was better regulated than that of Caftile, and the adminiftration was conducted with more eafe after the reduction of the Moors by the conqueft of Algarva.

IN France, Lewis XI. had juft lowered the power of the great vaffals, raifed that of the ma- giftracy, and made the nobles fubject to the laws. The people of France growing lefs dependent on their lords, muft neceffarily become, in a fhort time, more induftrious, more active, and more refpectable; but induftry and commerce could not flourifh on a fudden. Reafon muft of courfe make but a flow progrefs in the midft of thofe commo- tions which were ftill excited by the great, and under the reign of a prince devoted to the moft abominable fuperftition. The barons were dif- tinguifhed only by their favage haughtinefs; their revenues were scarce sufficient to entertain in their suite a train of gentlemen without employment, who defended them against the sovereign and the laws. The expences of their table were immoderate; and this savage luxury, of which there are still too many remains, afforded no encouragement to any of the useful arts. But neither the manners nor the language of those times partook of that decency which distinguishes the superior ranks of citizens, and procures them respect from the rest. Notwithstanding the courtesy enjoined to the knights, coarse and rough manners still prevailed among the great; the nation had then the same character of inconsistence it has since preserved, and which a nation will ever have, whose morals and customs are not conformable to the laws. The councils issued innumerable, and frequently contradictory edicts, but the prince readily dispensed with the observance of them. By this easy disposition of the sovereign, the inconveniences which would have arisen from a multitude of laws inconsiderately made by the French ministry, have been happily prevented.

ENGLAND, less opulent, and less industrious than France, was composed of insolent barons, despotic bishops, and a people who were tired of their yoke; a certain restless disposition prevailed in the nation, which must necessarily sooner or later introduce liberty. This character owed its rise to the absurd tyranny of William the Conqueror, and the cruel disposition of several of his successors. The intolerable abuse of power had made the English

IN THE EAST AND WEST INDIES.

English extremely jealous of their sovereigns; the very name of king carried with it the idea of terror; and these sentiments, transmitted from father to son, afterwards laid the foundations of that form of government they now have the happiness to enjoy. The long contention between the houses of York and Lancaster, while it raised a martial spirit and an impatience of slavery, involved the nation, at the same time, in poverty and confusion. The English wool was then manufactured in Flanders, and was exported, as well as its lead and tin, in vessels belonging to the Hanse Towns. The principles of navigation, of internal policy, jurisprudence, luxury, and the fine arts were entirely unknown in England; at the same time that it was overburthened with a multitude of rich convents and hospitals. These convents were the usual resort of the distressed nobles, as the hospitals were of the common people; idleness and barbarous manners were encouraged by these superstitious institutions.

GERMANY, which had long been harassed by quarrels between the emperors and the popes, and by intestine wars, had at this time begun to enjoy a state of tranquillity; order had taken place of anarchy, and the inhabitants of this extensive country, who, though strangers to wealth and commerce, were versed in the arts of war and agriculture, had nothing to fear from their neighbours, neither could they be formidable to them. The feudal system, so fatal to mankind in other countries, here assumed a milder aspect; the princes presiding over this vast extent of territory, generally speaking, governed their respective states with a good deal of moderation; they seldom abused their authority, and if the peaceable possession of their estates could compensate the want of liberty, the Germans were happy; commerce and industry were entirely confined to the free cities, and to the towns included in the Hanseatic league; the mines of Hanover and Saxony were not yet discovered; silver was scarce; the farmer sold a few horses to strangers, nor had the princes yet introduced the traffic of the human species; the expences of the table, and a variety of equipages were the only articles of luxury; the nobles and the clergy intoxicated themselves, without disturbing the government; it was with some difficulty that the gentry were dissuaded from amusing themselves with robbing on the highways; their manners were savage, and during the two succeeding centuries the German troops were more distinguished by their cruelties than by their discipline and bravery.

The northern countries had made less progress than Germany. Oppressed by the nobles and priests, the inhabitants no longer retained that enthusiastic love of glory with which the religion of Wodin had formerly inspired them; nor were they yet acquainted with those wise institutions which some of them have since borrowed from better forms of government. Their power was so inconsiderable, that a single Hanse Town was capable of intimidating the three potentates of the north. They recovered their national importance after

after the reformation, and under the auspices of Frederic and Gustavus Vasa.

The Turks were strangers to the science of government: they had no knowledge of the arts, nor taste for commerce: but the Janissaries were the best troops in the world. These attendants of a despot whom they kept in awe, at the same time that they insured respect to him whom they placed upon the throne or strangled at pleasure, had at that time some great men for their leaders. They subverted the empire of the Greeks, who were infatuated with theology, and stupified by superstition. Some of the inhabitants of this mild climate, who cultivated literature and the arts, abandoned their country after it was subdued, and took refuge in Italy; whither they were followed by artists and traders. Tranquillity, peace, prosperity, the ambition of excelling in every accomplishment, and the desire of new pleasures, which is inspired by good governments, favoured the revival of letters in the country of the ancient Romans; and it was from the Greeks that the Italians derived a better knowledge of good models, and a taste for antiquity. The art of printing was invented; and though for a long time the discovery was of little use while the people continued in a state of poverty and indolence, yet when commerce and the arts had made some progress, books became more common. A love of study prevailed, and the ancients were universally admired: but they had no rivals except in Italy.

Rome, which in every century has almost always assumed a character the best adapted to the

present

present moment, seemed disposed no longer to encourage that ignorance which had so long and so materially been subservient to her interests. She protected polite literature, and such of the arts as depended more on imagination than reason. The most ignorant priest is well aware, that representations of a terrible divinity, mortification, self-denial, austerity, melancholy and terror, are so many expedients to gain an ascendant over the minds of men, by engaging them deeply in religious matters. But there are times when these expedients have but little effect. Men who have grown rich in peaceful states, are fond of enjoying themselves; they dislike the dull road of life, and are eager in their pursuit of pleasures. When fairs began to be established, with entertainments of sports, dancing, and other recreations, the clergy, who observed, that the love of festivity made the people less religious, prohibited these sports, and excommunicated those who bore a part in them. But finding that no regard was paid to their censures, they changed their plan, and determined to take these amusements into their own hands. This was the origin of sacred comedy. The death of St. Catherine, acted by the monks of St. Denys, rivalled the success of the players. Music was introduced into the churches; and even farces were exhibited there. The festivals called *la Fête des foux & de L'Ane, & des Innocens*, proved as entertaining to the people as the farces that were acted in the public places. It often happened, that attracted by the mere love of amusement, they left the Egyptian dances to join in the procession for the

festival

festival of St. John. As the Italians improved in politeness, their pleasures became more refined; and the decency that was introduced into their common feasts and public entertainments, afforded less pretence for the censures of the priests, and procured them a toleration. The merit of being able to read had been long confined to this class of men; but when it became a more general accomplishment, they could no longer avail themselves of this distinction: and finding that learning was the road to fame, they were ambitious of shining in literary pursuits. The popes, who enjoyed an opulent and peaceful sovereignty in the voluptuous region of Italy, laid aside their austerity. Their court became an agreeable one. The encouragement of literature was considered as a new expedient to establish their authority over the minds of men. Genius was cherished, and marks of honour were conferred upon great artists. Raphael died but a short time before he was to have been created a cardinal; and Petrarch had the honours of a triumph. As little conformable as this good taste, these fine arts, and new amusements, may appear to the spirit of the gospel, they were evidently calculated to promote the interest of the papal throne. The belles lettres serve to ornament this ecclesiastical structure; but philosophy demolishes it. Thus, while the church of Rome favoured polite literature and the fine arts, it discountenanced the severer sciences. The poets were crowned with laurel; but the philosophers were persecuted. Galileo from his prison might have beheld Tasso carried in triumph to the capitol, if those men of great genius had been cotemporaries.

It was now time that philosophy and learning should lend their support to morality and reason. The church of Rome had taken all imaginable pains to subvert those principles of justice which nature had implanted in all mankind. The single maxim, that the pope had a right to the sovereignty of all empires, sapped the foundation of all society and public virtue: this maxim, however, had for a long time prevailed, together with that horrid doctrine, which not only permitted but enjoined hatred and persecution towards all whose religious opinions were not agreeable to those of the Romish church. Indulgences, a species of expiation which might be purchased for all crimes, or if any thing can be still more monstrous, for crimes to be committed in future; dispensations for breaking faith with the enemies of the pontiff, though they were of the same religion; that article of belief which teaches, that the merit of the just may be transferred to the wicked; vices of all kinds exemplified in the lives of the popes, and other religious persons, who ought to have been models to the people; above all, that greatest reproach to humanity, the inquisition: all these horrid enormities made Europe appear to be rather the haunt of tygers and serpents, than a vast country inhabited or cultivated by men.

Such was the situation of Europe, when the Portuguese monarch, at the head of an active, generous and intelligent people, surrounded by neighbours who still preyed upon each other, formed a plan of extending his dominions by sea and land.

John

JOHN I. had several sons, who, being ambitious of signalizing themselves, undertook, at first, some expeditions to Barbary. Henry, whose genius was superior to that of the others, resolved to make discoveries in the west. This young prince availed himself of the little knowledge of astronomy which was preserved among the Arabs. At Sagrés, a city of Algarva, he established an observatory, and made it the place of education for all the nobility who composed his train; he had a considerable share in the invention of the Astrolabe, and was the first who was sensible of the advantages that might be drawn from the compass, which, though already known in Europe, had never been applied to the purposes of navigation.

THE pilots, who studied under his direction, discovered Madeira in the year 1418. Two years after this, one of his ships took possession of the Canaries; he doubled the Cape of Sierra-Leona, and the river Zara led him into the interior parts of Africa as far as Congo. He made an easy conquest of those countries, and established an advantageous commerce. The inconsiderable nations who inhabited those parts, being separated from each other by impassable deserts, were strangers both to the value of their riches, and the art of defending themselves. These voyages raised great expectations; the revenues that might in future arise from the coast of Guinea, were farmed. An instance of avidity so premature, shews, that the princes, who undertook these discoveries, were more solicitous to increase their finances, than to promote the commerce of their subjects.

IN the reign of John II. an intelligent prince, who firſt declared Liſbon a free port, and under whoſe auſpices a new method was adopted of applying aſtronomy to navigation, ſome of his ſubjects, whom he ſent out upon an expedition, doubled the Cape which is at the extremity of Africa. The Cape was then called the Cape of Storms; but the prince, who foreſaw that it would open a paſſage to India, gave it the name of the Cape of Good Hope.

EMANUEL purſued the plan marked out by his predeceſſors. In 1497 he equipped a fleet conſiſting of four ſhips, and gave the command of it to *Vaſco de Gama*. This admiral, having weathered ſeveral ſtorms in his cruiſe along the eaſtern coaſts of Africa, and attempted ſeas before unknown, landed at length in Indoſtan, after a voyage of thirteen months.

A geographical deſcription of Aſia.

ASIA, of which Indoſtan is one of the richeſt parts, is a vaſt continent, lying, according to the obſervations of the Ruſſians, the truth of which has been juſtly doubted, between the 43d and the 207th degree of longitude. It extends, between the two poles, from the 77th degree of northern to the 10th degree of ſouthern latitude. That part of this large continent which is ſituated in the temperate zone, between the 35th and the 50th degree of latitude, appears to be higher than the reſt: it is bordered both towards the north and ſouth by two vaſt chains of mountains, which run almoſt from the weſtern extremity of Aſia Minor and the coaſts of the black ſea, to the ocean that waſhes the coaſts of China and Tartary towards the eaſt. Theſe two chains are united

IN THE EAST AND WEST INDIES.

united by other intermediate chains, in a direction from south to north; they branch out towards the northern, the Indian, and eastern oceans, and appear like so many bulwarks raised between the beds of the large rivers which roll through these immense regions.

Such is the great basis which nature has raised to support the fabric of Asia. In the inland parts of this vast country, the earth, parched by the heat of the sun, becomes so light, that it is carried about by the winds; there is not the least appearance either of stone or marble; no petrified shells, or other fossils, are to be found; the beds of minerals lie upon the surface. All these phœnomena, joined to the observations made with the barometer, are proofs of the great elevation of the central part of Asia, to which the moderns have given the name of the less Bucharia.

From these heights, which form a kind of girdle, surrounding this immense and unfruitful region, several large streams arise, that run in different channels. The fragments of barren earth, which are perpetually carried down by these rivers towards the several extremities of Asia, form so many barriers against the sea, and promise a stability and duration to this continent, superior to that of any other. Perhaps it will be its fate to see the rest repeatedly buried under the waters, before it suffers any encroachment itself.

The Caspian sea alone has preserved its station within the limits of this vast tract of land, which has been emerging from the deep through a series of ages. It is undoubtedly the reservoir of those large

large rivers that fall into it, and poffibly may alfo have fome fmall communication, by fubterraneous paffages, with the ocean and the Mediterranean; if it be true, as it appears to be from obfervations made with the barometer at Aftracan, that its furface is below the level of both thofe feas.

The frozen ocean, which extends along the northern coafts of Siberia, renders them inacceffible, if we may believe the accounts given by the Ruffians. They tell us, that it is in vain to expect to find a new paffage by this fea from Europe to America; and that the ice will always prevent the doubling of the Cape of Schalaginfkoi, which feparates the old from the new world, though this paffage has once been croffed. But the Ruffians are probably not fincere enough, or not fufficiently informed, to deferve entire credit; and either tell us more or lefs than the truth.

The Indian ocean, which bears towards the fouth of Afia, is divided from the great fouth fea by a chain of mountains, which begins at the ifland of Madagafcar, and extending under water as far as Sumatra, (as is evident from the fhallows and rocks which are fcattered in thofe parts) unites again at Van Diemen's Land and New Guinea. M. Buache, a geographer, who has examined the earth as a natural philofopher, and has laid down a chart of the world according to this hypothefis, is of opinion, that the fea between this long chain of iflands and the fouthern coafts of Afia, fhould be divided into three great bafons; the limits of which feem to have been circumfcribed or drawn by the hand of nature.

The

IN THE EAST AND WEST INDIES.

THE firſt, wich lies towards the weſt, between Arabia and Perſia, is bounded towards the ſouth by that chain of iſlands, which extends from Cape Comorin and the Maldivia Iſlands to Madagaſcar. This baſon, which runs into the land, is inceſſantly enlarging the gulph of Perſia and the red ſea. The ſecond of theſe baſons forms the gulph of Bengal. The third includes the great Archipelago, which contains the Sunda, the Moluccas, and the Philippine Iſlands. This joins Aſia to the ſouthern continent, and ſerves as a boundary to the pacific ocean. Between this ſea and the great Archipelago, a kind of new baſon is formed by a chain of mountains under water towards the eaſt, which extends from the Ladrone to the Japan Iſlands. When we have paſſed theſe celebrated iſlands, we come to a chain of iſlands called Kuriles, which touch the ſouthern point of the Peninſula of Kamtſchatka; and form a fifth baſon into which the river Amur empties itſelf; but as its entrance is obſtructed by the Bamboos, which grow there in great abundance, it is imagined that this ſea has very little depth.

THESE geographical details, far from being foreign to our purpoſe, are in a manner neceſſary to direct and engage our attention to the richeſt and fineſt continent upon the globe. We will begin with Indoſtan.

THOUGH by the general name of the Eaſt Idies is commonly underſtood that immenſe tract of land which lies beyond the Arabian ſea, and the Perſian empire; yet by Indoſtan is properly meant a country lying between two celebrated rivers, the Indus and

Natural hiſtory of Indoſtan.

the

the Ganges, which fall into the Indian ocean, at the diſtance of four hundred leagues from each other. A ridge of high mountains runs acroſs this long tract from north to ſouth, and dividing it into two equal parts, extends as far as Cape Comorin, where it forms the boundary between the coaſts of Malabar and Coromandel.

It is a remarkable circumſtance, and perhaps the only one of the kind, that this ridge ſeems to be a barrier, erected by nature, to ſeparate one ſeaſon from another. The mere breadth of theſe mountains divides ſummer from winter, that is to ſay, the ſeaſon of fine weather from the rainy; for it is well known there is no winter between the tropics: all that is meant by winter in India is that time of the year when the clouds, which the ſun attracts from the ſea, are driven violently by the winds againſt the mountains, where they break and diſſolve in rain, accompanied with frequent ſtorms. From hence torrents are formed, which ruſh from the hills, ſwell the rivers, and overflow the vallies; dark vapours, that obſcure the day, and ſpread a thick and impenetrable gloom over the deluged country: but, as the chaos which brooded over the principles of things before the creation, this cloudy ſeaſon promotes fertility; for at this time the plants and flowers appear in full ſtrength and beauty, and the fruits in general come to maturity.

The ſummer may naturally be expected to preſerve its uſual temperature better than the winter, in a climate ſo immediately under the influence of the ſun: the ſky, without a cloud to intercept its

rays

rays, seems to be all on fire; but the sea-breezes which spring up in the day-time, and the land-breezes that blow during the night, alternately alleviate the heat of the atmosphere; yet the calms, that now and then intervene, stifle these refreshing gales, and the inhabitants are reduced to suffer the inconveniencies of excessive drought.

THE effect of the two different seasons is still more remarkably felt in the two Indian oceans, where they are distinguished by the name of the dry and rainy monsoons. While the sea that washes the coasts of Malabar is agitated by storms, which the returning sun introduces with the spring, the slightest vessels sail securely along the coast of Coromandel upon a smooth surface, and require neither skill nor precaution in their pilots; but in the autumn, which, in its turn, changes the face of the elements, the western coast enjoys a perfect calm, while the eastern Indian ocean is tossed by tempests; each experiencing, as it were, the alternatives of peace and war. An inhabitant of the island of Ceylon, who contemplates the equatorial region at the two equinoxes, beholds the seas on the right hand and on the left alternately agitated with storms, or lulled into tranquillity; as if the Author of Nature, in these two instants of equilibrium, turned at once the scales of good and evil, which he holds perpetually in his hands. It is not improbable that the doctrine of the Manichees, concerning the two principles, might take its rise in India, where the two empires of good and evil are divided only by a partition of mountains; since pain and pleasure seem to be as much the origin of the different forms of worship, as they are of the ideas of mankind. There is so infinite a connection between natural and moral principles, that all systems of importance to the happiness of the human species have taken their colour from the nature of the climate: accordingly it is observable, that the Indians, whose imaginations receive the deepest impression of nature from the more forcible operation of good and evil, and the view they constantly have of the discord of the elements, are placed in a situation most fertile in revolutions, events and transactions of every kind.

HENCE it is, that the celebrated countries of India have long engaged the attention of the philosopher and the historian, whose conjectures have assigned to their earliest inhabitants an æra of the most extraordinary antiquity. To say the truth, whether we consult historical records, or consider the position of Indostan upon the globe, taking it for granted, that the ocean has a progressive motion from east to west, we must allow that this part of the earth was the first that was inhabited. We may trace the origin of most of the sciences in the history of that country. Even before the age of Pythagoras, the Greeks travelled to India for instruction; the trade carried on by them with the oldest commercial nations, in exchange for their cloth, is a proof of their great progress in the arts of industry.

UPON the whole, it should seem reasonable to conclude, that a part of the globe, the best adapted to the human species, would be peopled the earliest; and that the first men would fix their abode

in

in a delicious climate, pure air, and a soil too fertile to require much cultivation. If the human race could be supposed to multiply and extend themselves in those horrid regions, where they must maintain a perpetual struggle with nature: if they could inhabit burning sands, impracticable morasses, and regions of perpetual ice; or frequent deserts and forests, where they must defend themselves against the violence of the elements, and the attacks of wild beasts: how easily might they not form themselves into societies in these delightful countries, where mankind, exempt from necessity, has nothing to pursue but pleasure; where enjoying without labour or anxiety the choicest productions, and the most glorious prospect of the great scene of nature, they might justly assume the distinguishing title of Lords of the Creation! These beautiful scenes present themselves on the banks of the Ganges, and in the plains of Indostan. The air is perfumed with the most delicious fruits, which afford a wholesome and refreshing nourishment; the trees form a shade impenetrable to the rays of the sun. While the living animals that are disperfed over the globe, cannot subsist in other parts without devouring each other, they share in India, in common with their master, the sweets of plenty and security. Even at this day, when the earth may be supposed to have been exhausted by the productions of so many ages, and their consumption in foreign countries, Indostan, if we except a few sandy and barren districts, is still the most fruitful country in the world.

HISTORY OF SETTLEMENTS AND TRADE

Religion, government, and cuſtoms of Indoſtan.

The ſyſtem of morals in this country is no leſs extraordinary than the ſyſtem of nature. When we fix our eyes on this vaſt region, where nature hath exerted her utmoſt efforts for the happineſs of man, we cannot but regret that man hath done all in his power to oppoſe her. The rage of conqueſt, and what is no leſs deſtructive an evil, the greedineſs of traders have, in their turns, ravaged and oppreſſed the fineſt country on the face of the globe.

Notwithstanding the numbers of ſavage banditti, and other ſtrangers, whom war or the deſire of gain has invited to India, it is eaſy to diſtinguiſh the antient inhabitants. There is not, however, ſo much difference in the caſt of complexion and outward appearance of theſe people, as in the particularities of their character; oppreſſed as they have been with the yoke of tyranny, or rather of the wildeſt anarchy, they have not adopted either the manners, the laws, or the religion of their maſters. Their continual experience of all the horrors of war, all the exceſſes and vices of which human nature is capable, has not tainted their character. Nothing has ever been able to reconcile the tender, humane and timorous Indian to ſcenes of blood, or to animate him with the courage and ſpirit of rebellion. His vices ariſe ſolely from a weak mind.

The judicious traveller, who paſſing over the plains of Egypt, ſees trunks of columns, mutilated ſtatues, broken entablatures, and immenſe pyramids that have eſcaped the ravages of war and time diſperſed about the country, is loſt in admiration at the

the view of the ruins of a nation which no longer exists. He cannot now find out the situation of Thebes, that city so celebrated in antiquity for its hundred gates; but the venerable remains of its temples and of its tombs, give him a higher idea of its magnificence than the descriptions of Herodotus and Diodorus Siculus.

WHEN we attentively examine the accounts given by travellers of the manners of the natives of India, we seem to wander among heaps of ruins, the remains of an immense fabric. The original form is lost, but enough is preserved to convince us of the magnificence and regularity of the plans. Amidst a variety of absurd superstitions, puerile and extravagant customs, strange ceremonies and prejudices, we may discover the traces of sublime morality, deep philosophy, and refined policy; but when we attempt to trace the religious and civil institutions to their origin, we find that is lost in the maze of antiquity. By the most antient traditions, the Indians appear to have been the first who received the rudiments of science, and the polish of civilization. But their legislative system has never been discovered; and the antients themselves seem only to have been acquainted with the remains of it.

IN India are found the traces of a multitude of superstitious observances, arts, sports, errors and truths of all kinds, which have been adopted by almost all nations.

THE Indians themselves are ignorant of the origin of their religion and policy: they have to this day preserved customs which must certainly have

have owed their rife to a fyftem that no longer exifts: the fpirit of their political conftitution is loft, and every branch of it either changed or corrupted. Their religion, which was of the allegorical and moral kind, hath degenerated into a heap of extravagant and obfcene fuperftitions, owing to their having realized thofe fictions which were intended merely as fo many fymbols and emblems.

WERE it poffible to obtain a fight of their facred books, the only remains there are of the Indian antiquities, we might, in fome meafure, be enabled to remove the veil that envelops thefe numerous myfteries; but we have little reafon to hope that we fhall ever be intrufted with fuch a communication.

THE emperor Mahmoud Akbar had an inclination to make himfelf acquainted with the principles of all the religious fects throughout his extenfive provinces. Having difcarded the fuperftitious notions with which he had been prepoffeffed by his education in the Mohammedan faith, he refolved to judge for himfelf. It was eafy for him to be acquainted with the nature of thofe fyftems, that are formed upon the plan of making profelytes; but he found himfelf difappointed in his defign, when he came to treat with the Indians, who will not admit any perfon whatever to the participation of their myfteries.

NEITHER the authority nor promifes of Akbar could prevail with the Bramins to difclofe the tenets of their religion; he was therefore obliged to have recourfe to artifice. The ftratagem he

made

IN THE EAST AND WEST INDIES.

made ufe of was, to caufe an infant, of the name of Feizi, to be committed to the care of thefe priefts, as a poor orphan of the facerdotal line, who alone could be initiated into the facred rites of their theology. Feizi, having received the proper inftructions for the part he was to act, was conveyed privately to Benares, the feat of knowledge in Indoftan; he was received into the houfe of a learned Bramin, who educated him with the fame care as if he had been his fon. After the youth had fpent ten years in ftudy, Akbar was defirous of recalling him; but he was ftruck with the charms of the daughter of his preceptor.

The women of the facerdotal tribe are looked upon as the greateft beauties in Indoftan. The old Bramin laid no reftraint on the growing paffion of the two lovers; he was fond of Feizi, who had gained his affection by his addrefs and docility, and offered him his daughter in marriage. The young man, divided between love and gratitude, refolved to conceal the fraud no longer; and falling at the feet of the Bramin, difcovered the impofture, and afked pardon for his offence.

The prieft, without reproaching him in the leaft, feized a poniard which hung at his girdle, and was going to plunge it in his breaft, if Feizi had not prevented him by taking hold of his arm. The young man ufed every means to pacify him, and declared himfelf ready to do any thing to expiate his treachery. The Bramin burfting into tears, promifed to pardon him on condition that he fhould fwear never to tranflate the *Bedas,* or facred sacred volumes, or disclose to any person whatever the symbol of the Bramin creed. Feizi readily promised all that the Bramin required: how far he kept his word is not known; but the sacred books of the Indians have never been translated by him, or any one else, to this day.

As the Bramins are the only persons who understand the language of the sacred book, their comments on the text are the same as those which have ever been made on religious books; all the maxims which fancy, interest, passion or false zeal can suggest, are to be found in these volumes. These exclusive pretensions of the interpreters of religion have given them that unbounded influence over the people, which impostors and fanatics will not fail to exert over men who have not the courage to consult either their own reason, or their own feelings.

From the Indus to the Ganges, the *Vedam* is universally received as the book that contains the principles of religion; but the generality differ on several points relative to faith and practice. That spirit of debate and refinement, which for so many ages has infected the philosophy of our schools, has made still further progress among the Bramins, and caused more absurdities in their doctrines than it has introduced into ours, by a mixture of Platonism which is perhaps itself derived from the doctrines of the Bramins.

Throughout all Indostan, the laws of government, customs and manners make a part of religion; being all derived from Brama, a being far superior in dignity to the human race, the interpreter

preter of the divinity, the author of the sacred books, and the great law-giver of India.

THERE is some reason to believe that Brama was possessed of the sovereign authority; as his religious institutions were evidently designed to inspire the people with a profound reverence and great love for their country, and are particularly levelled against the vices incident to the climate. Few religions seem to have been so well adapted to the countries for which they were calculated.

IT is from Brama that the Indians derive their religious veneration for the three capital rivers of Indostan, the Indus, the Cristina, and the Ganges. It was he who consecrated the animal that is most serviceable in the cultivation of land, as well as the cow, whose milk is so wholesome a nourishment in hot countries. To him they ascribe the division of the people into tribes or *castes*, distinguished from each other by their political and religious principles. This institution is antecedent to all traditions and known records, and may be considered as the most striking proof of the great antiquity of the Indians. Nothing appears more contrary to the natural progress of social connections, than this distribution of the members of the same community into distinct classes. Such an idea could only be the result of a studied plan of legislation, which pre-supposes a great proficiency in civilization and knowledge. Another circumstance still more extraordinary is, that this distinction should continue so many ages, after the leading idea and connecting tie was forgotten; and affords us a remarkable example of the strength of national prejudices, when sanctified by religious ideas.

The nation is divided into four classes, the Bramins, the soldiery, husbandmen and mechanics: these classes have their subdivisions. There are several orders of Bramins: those who mix in society are, for the most part, very corrupt in their morals; they believe that the water of the Ganges will wash away all their crimes; and as they are not subject to any civil jurisdiction, live without either restraint or virtue, excepting that character of compassion and charity which is so commonly found in the mild climate of India.

The others who live abstracted from the world, are either weak-minded men or enthusiasts, and abandon themselves to laziness, superstition, and the dreams of metaphysics. We find in their disputes the very same ideas that occur in the writings of our most celebrated metaphysicians; such as, substance, accident, priority, posteriority, immutability, indivisibility, the vital and sensitive soul; but with this difference, that in India these fine discoveries are very ancient, though it is but a very short time since father Lombard, Thomas Aquinas, Leibnitz, and Mallebranche astonished all Europe with their dexterity in raising these visionary systems. As this abstracted manner of reasoning was derived to us from the Greek philosophers, whose refinements we have far exceeded, it is not improbable that the Greeks themselves might have borrowed this ridiculous knowledge from the Indians; unless we rather chuse to suppose, that as the principles of metaphysics lie open to the capacities of all nations, the indolence of the Bramins may have produced the same effect in India, as that of our monks has done in Europe: notwithstanding the inhabitants of one country had never communicated their doctrines to those of the other.

SUCH are the descendants of the ancient Brachmans, whom antiquity never speaks of but with admiration; because the affectation of austerity and mystery, and the privilege of declaring the will of heaven have imposed upon the vulgar in all ages. The Greeks ascribe to them the doctrine of the immortality of the soul, and certain notions concerning the nature of the Supreme Being, and future rewards and punishments.

To this species of knowledge, which is the more flattering to the curiosity of man in proportion as it transcends his weak capacity, the Brachmans added an infinite number of religious observances, which were adopted by Pythagoras in his school; such as, fasting, prayer, silence, and contemplation; virtues of the imagination, which have a more powerful effect upon the vulgar than those of a useful and benevolent tendency. The Brachmans were looked upon as the friends of the gods, because they affected to pay them so much regard; and as the protectors of mankind, because they paid them no regard at all. No bounds were therefore set to the respect and gratitude that were shewn them; princes themselves did not scruple to consult these recluses upon any critical conjuncture, from a supposition, no doubt, that they were inspired; since it was impossible to imagine that they

they had the advantages of experience. We can scarcely, however, deny that there might be among them some men of real virtue, whose minds relished the pure and ingenuous delights of study and science; and who, by nobly raising their thoughts to the contemplation of the first Being, must have had more powerful incitements to render themselves worthy of his care, and none to justify them in deceiving, and tyrannizing over their fellow-creatures.

The military class consists of the Rajas on the coast of Coromandel, and the Nairs on the coast of Malabar. There are likewise whole nations, the Canarins and the Marattas for instance, who assume the profession, either because they are the descendants of some tribes originally devoted to arms, or because times and circumstances have introduced a change in their primitive institutions.

The third class consists entirely of husbandmen, and there are few countries where this set of men have a better title to the gratitude of their fellow-subjects; they are laborious and industrious, perfectly acquainted with the art of distributing their rivulets, and of making the burning soil they inhabit as fertile as possible. They are in India what they would be every where else, if not corrupted or oppressed by government, the most honest and virtuous of men. This class, which was formerly much respected, was free from tyranny, and the ravages of war ; never were the husbandmen obliged to bear arms ; their lands and their labours were held equally sacred ; they ploughed their fields within view of contending armies, who

suffered

suffered them to purfue their peaceful toil without moleftation; their corn was never fet on fire, nor their trees cut down; religion too, that all-powerful principle, lent her affiftance to reafon, which, though it inculcates indeed the propriety of protecting ufeful occupations, has not of itfelf fufficient influence to enforce the execution of its own laws.

The tribe of mechanics was branched out into as many fubdivifions as there are trades; no one was allowed to relinquifh the profeffion of his parents; for which reafon induftry and vaffalage have ever gone hand in hand, and carried the arts to as high perfection as they can poffibly attain without the affiftance of tafte and imagination, which feldom unfold themfelves but under the kind influences of emulation and liberty.

Besides thefe tribes, there is a fifth, which is the outcaft of all the reft; the members of it are employed in the meaneft offices of fociety; they bury the dead, carry away dirt, and live upon the flefh of animals that die natural deaths; they are held in fuch abhorrence, that if any of their fociety dares to touch any perfon belonging to the other claffes, he has a right to kill him on the fpot; they are called Parias.

In Malabar there is another race of men, called Poulichees, who fuffer ftill greater injuries and hardfhips; they inhabit the forefts, where they are not permitted to build huts, but are obliged to make a kind of neft upon the trees: when they are preffed with hunger, they howl like wild beafts to excite the compaffion of the paffengers. The
moft

most charitable among the Indians deposit some rice or other food at the foot of a tree, and retire with all possible haste, to give the famished wretch an opportunity of taking it without meeting with his benefactor, who would think himself polluted by coming near him.

The Europeans, by living with these unhappy people upon terms of common humanity, at length made themselves almost equally the objects of detestation among the Indians. This detestation prevails even to this day in the inland parts of the country, where the want of intercourse keeps alive those rooted prejudices, which wear off gradually near the seacoasts, where the interests and mutual wants of commerce unite men with each other, and consequently introduce juster notions of human nature.

All these classes are for ever separated from each other by unsurmountable barriers; they are not allowed to intermarry, live, or eat together. Whoever transgresses this rule, is banished as a disgrace to his tribe.

But it is quite otherwise when they go in pilgrimage to the temple of Jagrenat, or the Supreme Being. At these seasons the Bramins, the Raja or Nair, the husbandman and mechanic carry their offerings, and eat and drink promiscuously; they are there admonished that the distinctions of birth are of human institution, and that all men are brethren and children of the same God.

The religious system which has given a sanction to the subordination of rank among the Indians, has not had sufficient influence to prevent them

them entirely from afpiring to thofe marks of diftinction which are appropriated to the fuperior claffes. Ambition, fo natural to mankind, has fometimes exerted itfelf, and fingular expedients have been tried by men jealous of fuperiority to fhare with the Bramins the veneration of the multitude ; this has given rife to a race of monks known in India by the name of Fakirs.

MEN of all the tribes or caftes are permitted to follow this clafs of life; nothing more is required than to emulate the Bramins in abftracted contemplation and indolence; but at the fame time they are obliged to furpafs them in exceffive aufterities, which ftrike the mildeft people in the world with religious horror. The appearance of thefe fanatics exceeds imagination; fome of them wallow in the dirt, others accuftom themfelves to painful poftures, extending their arms over their head till they are unable to recover their natural pofition ; and a third fort continue ftanding feven or eight days together, which occafions prodigious fwellings in their legs; they all of them enter into an engagement never to wafh their bodies, or comb their hair ; and to oppofe and difgrace nature, with a view of recommending themfelves to its author. The refpect paid them by the people is their only recompenfe for thefe facrifices, which infinitely exceed all the mortifications practifed by the European monks; if thofe may be called mortifications, which are nothing more than fingular ceremonies practifed at an early age, when to get rid of fcruples concerning the gratification of natural and forbidden paffions, the youthful

youthful imagination ardently embraces any syftem of life, however extravagant, provided it has received the public fanction, and is calculated to adminifter to their pleafures.

Though in the facred books of the Indians we do not meet with thofe inftances of the marvellous, which fometimes ftrike fo forcibly in the Greek theology, their mythology is as irregular as that of almoft any other people. We do not find, in particular, any connection between their religious principles and the feveral claffes that form the bafis of their government. The fhaftah is looked upon by fome as a commentary on the vedam, and by others as an original work, an extract of which has been lately publifhed in England, and has thrown fome light upon this fubject. This book teaches, that the Eternal Being abforbed in the contemplation of his own effence, formed the refolution of created beings, who might partake of his glory. He fpoke, and angels rofe into exiftence; they fang in concert the praifes of their Creator, and harmony reigned in the celeftial regions, when two of thefe fpirits having revolted, drew a legion after them. The Supreme Being drove them into a place of torment, from whence they were releafed at the interceffion of the faithful angels, upon conditions, which at once infpired them with joy and terror. The rebels were fentenced, under different forms, to undergo punifhments in the loweft of the fifteen planets, in proportion to the enormity of their firft offence; accordingly each angel underwent eighty-feven tranfmigrations upon earth, before

before he animated the body of a cow, which holds the higheſt rank among the animal tribes. Theſe different tranſmigrations are confidered as ſo many ſtages of expiation, preparatory to a ſtate of probation, which commences as ſoon as the angel tranſmigrates from the body of the cow into a human body: in this fituation the Creator enlarges his intellectual faculties, and conſtitutes him a free agent; and his good or bad conduct haſtens or retards the time of his pardon. The good are at their death, re-united to the Supreme Being, and the wicked begin anew the æra of their expiation.

HENCE it appears, from this tradition of the ſhaſtah, that the metempſychofis is an actual puniſhment, and that the fouls which animate the generality of the brute creation, are nothing more than wicked ſpirits. This explanation is certainly not univerſally adopted in India. It was probably invented by ſome devotee of a melancholy and rigid caſt, as the doctrine of the tranſmigration of ſouls ſeems originally to have been founded rather on hope than fear.

IN fact, it is natural to ſuppoſe that it was only adopted at firſt as an idea that flattered and foothed mankind, and would eaſily be embraced in a country where men, living under the influence of a delicious climate and a mild government, began to be ſenſible of the ſhortneſs of life. A ſyſtem, therefore, which extended it beyond its natural limits could not fail to be well received. It is a confolation to an old man, who fees himſelf deferted by all that is dear to him, to imagine

gine that his enjoyments will still remain, and that his diffolution only opens a paffage to another fcene of exiftence. At the fame time, it is equally a matter of confolation to the friends who attend him in his laft moments, to think, that in leaving the world he does not relinquish the hopes of rifing once more into life. Hence was the rife and progrefs of the doctrine of tranfmigration. Reafon, diffatisfied with this illufion, may urge in vain, that without recollection there can be no continuance or identity of being; and that if a man does not remember that he has exifted, he is in the fame fituation as if he had never exifted before:—Sentiment adopted what reafon difallowed.

The fhaftah, no doubt, has given a greater air of feverity to the doctrine of the metempfychofis, with a view of making it more inftrumental in fupporting the fyftem of morality neceffary to be eftablifhed. In fact, upon this idea of tranfmigration confidered in the light of a punifhment, the fhaftah explains the duties which the angels were required to perform. The principal ones were charity, abftinence from animal food, and a fcrupulous adherence to the profeffion of their anceftors. This laft-mentioned prejudice, in which all thefe people agree, notwithftanding they differ in their opinions concerning its origin, is without example, unlefs it be among the ancient Egyptians, whofe inftitutions and thofe of the Indians have certainly fome hiftorical relation to each other, which is now unknown to us. But though the Egyptian laws eftablifhed a

diftinction

distinction of ranks, none were held in contempt; while, on the contrary, the laws of Brama, by the introduction, perhaps, of some abuses, seem to have condemned one part of the nation to pain and infamy.

There is reason to believe that the Indians were almost as civilized when Brama instituted his laws, as they are at present. Whenever a community begins to assume a certain form, it naturally divides into several classes, according to the variety and extent of those arts that are necessary to supply its demands.

It was doubtless the intention of Brama, by confirming these different professions by sanctions of religion, and confining the exercise of them perpetually to the same families, to give them a lasting establishment on political principles; but he did not foresee that by these means he should obstruct the progress of discoveries, which, in the end, might give rise to new occupations. Accordingly, if we may judge by the scrupulous attention paid by the Indians at this day to the laws of Brama, we may affirm that industry has made no advances among this people, since the time of this legislator; and that they were almost as civilized as they are at present, when they first received his laws. This remark is sufficient to give us an idea of the antiquity of these people, who have made no improvements in knowledge since an æra which seems to be the most ancient in history.

Brama prescribed different kinds of food for these respective tribes. The military, and some other

other ranks, were permitted to eat venison and mutton. Fish was allowed to some husbandmen and mechanics. Others lived upon milk and vegetables. None of the Bramins ate any thing that had life. Upon the whole, these people are extremely sober; but their abstinence varies in proportion to the greater or less labour required in their professions.

They marry in their infancy, and their wives maintain a character of fidelity unknown in other countries. Some of the superior ranks are allowed the privilege of having several wives. It is well known that the wives of the Bramins burn themselves on the death of their husbands, and they seem to be the only persons who are obliged to it by the laws. Others, however, have been disposed to follow their example, led by that point of honour to which so many victims are sacrificed in all countries. This cruel injunction is confined to widows who have no issue. Those who have children are expected to take care of their education and settlement in the world. Were it not for this precaution, the state, which ought to be the guardian of these orphans, would be laden with a very oppressive burthen.

Since the Moguls became masters of Indostan, these horrible spectacles have been much less frequent, as it costs a sum too considerable for any but the rich to obtain a licence for that purpose. But this obstacle has sometimes made their inclinations the stronger. Some women have been known to devote themselves for several years to the lowest and most laborious employments, in

order

order to raife money to defray the expences of this extravagant fuicide. Others have been more eagerly ambitious of facrificing themfelves, in proportion as fcenes of this kind became lefs common.

A FEW years ago a young, beautiful, and rich widow of Surat afpired to this high honour. The governor refufed to grant her permiffion to confign herfelf, with all her valuable accomplifhments, to the flames. The lady, full of indignation, took a handful of burning coals, and, feemingly regardlefs of the pain, faid in a firm tone to the governor: *Confider not alone the tendernefs of my age; fee with what infenfibility I hold this fire in my hands; and know that with equal conftancy I fhall throw myfelf into the flames.*

ALL the women, however, are not animated with this enthufiaftic intrepidity. Many of them, who were ambitious of devoting themfelves to the manes of their hufbands, have been feized with an involuntary tremor when their approaching fate appeared in all its horrors. To encourage them to this great action, fo contrary to reafon and nature, a mixture is given them, which, by ftupifying the fenfes, removes the apprehenfions which the preparation for death muft unavoidably occafion. The moment the intoxication takes place, thefe unfortunate widows are directly thrown upon the fatal pile; and to this ftratagem, invented by the advocates for fanaticifm, are to be attributed thofe feeming figns of joy and fatisfaction, which appear in their countenances at the fight of thofe devouring flames that are ready to reduce them to afhes.

This inftitution is not attributed to Brama, but rather feems to be the invention of fome Bramin, who carried his jealoufy beyond the grave. It is a piece of refinement, dictated by a barbarous and over-ftrained affection, and fuitable to the character of thofe fuperftitious mortals, who think there is an effential merit in rigid morality, and what they call a fuperior purity.

These people are of a mild, humane difpofition, and are almoft ftrangers to the paffions that prevail among us. What motive of ambition can there be among men who are deftined to continue always in the fame ftate? They love peaceable labour and an indolent life, and often quote this paffage of one of their favourite authors: *'Tis better to fit ftill than to walk; better to fleep than to awake; But death is beft of all.*

Their temperance, and the exceffive heats of the climate, reftrain the violence of their paffions, and weaken their propenfity to amorous pleafures. Avarice, which reigns chiefly in people of weak bodies, and little minds, is almoft their only paffion.

We may judge of their ingenuity in arts by the fpecimens that are brought from India. They are not to be made without much difficulty, but they are deftitute of tafte and elegance. The fciences are ftill more neglected, nor have they the leaft notion of mechanics; before they were acquainted with the Mohammedans, no bridges had ever been erected. The Pagodas are in general nothing more than miferable ftructures of a fquare form, admitting no light but at the entrance, which always fronts the eaft; this defect is fupplied by tapers, which

which are kept burning by the pious and devout. It is afferted, however, that their great Pagodas are regularly built, and that the ornaments both within and without are of confiderable value. The idol is placed in the center of the building, fo that the Parias who are not admitted into the temple, may have a fight of it through the gates. In thefe Pagodas there are cifterns of water for the purification of the Indians. Thefe fuperftitious ceremonies are chiefly obferved by the people. It is faid that there are ftill fome of the Bramins who know how to calculate eclipfes; but it is not very eafy to difcover whether this is done by means of fome of their tables derived from their anceftors, or whether they are really acquainted with the theory previoufly neceffary towards the folution of fuch problems.

The military clafs have chofen to fix their refidence in the northern provinces, and the peninfula is chiefly inhabited by the inferior tribes. Hence it has happened, that all the powers who have attacked India by fea, have met with fo little refiftance. It may not be amifs to remind thofe philofophers who maintain that man is an animal deftined to fubfift upon the fruits of the earth, that the military people who indulge in animal food, are more robuft, courageous and fprightly, and live longer than thofe of the other claffes who feed upon vegetables; at the fame time it muft be owned, that the difference between the inhabitants of the north and fouth, is of too uniform a caft to be attributed entirely to the particular kind of nourifhment; the cold of the north, the elafticity of
the

the air, less fertility and more labour and exercise, with a more varied kind of life; all these circumstances whet the appetite, brace the nerves, raise a spirit of resolution and activity, and give a firmer tone to the organs: on the other hand, the heats of the south, together with great quantities of fruit, an active life, a constant perspiration, a more free and more lavish use of the means conducive to population, more indulgence in effeminate pleasures, and a sedantry and uniform course of life, while they increase the number of births, occasion a speedier dissolution. Upon the whole it should seem, that though man was not by nature designed to consume the flesh of animals, he is endued with a power of accommodating himself to the various modes of life that prevail in every different climate, and either hunts and lives upon flesh or vegetables; or turns shepherd or husbandman according to the fertility or barrenness of the soil.

The religion of Brama was antiently, and still continues to be, divided into eighty-three sects, which agree in some fundamental points, and have no disputes about the rest; they live in amity with men of all persuasions, as their own does not oblige them to make proselytes. The Indians seldom admit strangers to their worship, and always with the greatest reluctance. This was in some measure the spirit of the ancient superstition, as it appears among the Egyptians, the Jews, the Greeks, and the Romans: and though it has occasioned fewer ravages than the zeal of making converts, it prevents the intercourses of society, and raises an additional barrier between one people and another. WHEN

IN THE EAST AND WEST INDIES.

When we confider how bounteoufly nature has provided for the happinefs of thefe fertile countries, where every want is eafily fupplied; and that the compaffionate temper and morals of the Indians render them equally averfe from perfecution and the fpirit of conqueft, we cannot help lamenting that a barbarous inequality fhould have diftinguifhed one part of the nation by power and privileges, while the reft of the inhabitants are loaded with mifery and contempt. What can be the caufe of this ftrange illufion? It muft doubtlefs be traced to that principle which has been the conftant fource of all the calamities that have befallen the inhabitants of this globe.

We need only fuppofe that a powerful people, with few lights to direct them, adopt an original error, which ignorance brings into fafhion: as foon as this error becomes general, it is made the bafis of an intire fyftem of politics and morality; and men begin to find that their innocent propenfities run counter to their duty. In order to conform to this new plan of morality, they muft perpetually be offering violence to the order of nature. This continual ftruggle will introduce a moft amazing contrariety into their manners; and the nation will be compofed of a fett of wretches, who will pafs their lives in mutually tormenting each other, and accufing nature. Such is the picture of all the people upon earth, excepting, perhaps, a few focieties of favages. Abfurd prejudices have perverted human reafon, and even ftifled that inftinct which teaches animals to refift oppreffion and tyranny. Multitudes of the human race

race implicitly submit to be a sort of vassals to a small number of men who oppress them.

Such is the fatal progress of that original error, which imposture has either produced or kept up in the mind of man. May true knowledge revive those rights of reasonable beings, which to be recovered, want only to be known! Ye sages of the earth, philosophers of every nation, it is yours alone to make laws by pointing them out to your countrymen. Take the glorious resolution to instruct your fellow creatures, and be assured that it is much easier to propagate truth than error. Mankind, animated by the desire of happiness, to which you will point the way, will listen to you with attention. Make those millions of hireling slaves blush, who are always ready, at the command of their masters, to destroy their fellow-citizens. Rouse all the powers of human nature to oppose this subversion of social laws. Teach mankind that liberty is the institution of God; authority that of man. Expose those mysterious arts which hold the world in chains and darkness: let the people be sensible how far their credulity has been imposed upon; let them re-assume with one accord the use of their faculties, and vindicate the honour of the human race.

Besides the natives, the Portuguese found Mohammedans in India, some of whom came from the borders of Africa. The greatest part of them were descendants of the Arabs, who either settled here or made incursions. They had possessed themselves of all the countries as far as the Indus, by

IN THE EAST AND WEST INDIES.

the force of arms. The moſt enterprizing among them paſſed this river, and ſucceſſively penetrated into the extremities of the eaſt. On this immenſe continent they became the factors of Arabia and Egypt, and were treated with diſtinguiſhed reſpect by all the ſovereigns who wiſhed to keep up an intercourſe with theſe countries. Here they multiplied to a great degree; for as their religion allowed poligamy, they married in every place where they made any ſtay.

THEIR ſuccefs was ſtill more rapid and laſting in the iſlands that lie ſcattered in this ocean. The want of commerce procured them the beſt reception both from princes and their ſubjects. They ſoon roſe to the higheſt dignities in theſe petty ſtates, and became the arbiters of government. They took advantage of the ſuperiority of their knowledge, and the ſupport they received from their country, to eſtabliſh an univerſal dominion. The deſpots and their vaſſals, in order to ingratiate themſelves with them, abandoned a religion to which they had no great attachment, for new opinions which might procure them ſome advantages. This ſacrifice coſt them the lefs, as the preachers of the Koran made no ſcruple of mixing ancient ſuperſtitions among thoſe they wiſhed to eſtabliſh.

THESE Mohammedan Arabs, who were apoſtles and merchants at the ſame time, had already propagated their religion by purchaſing a great number of ſlaves, to whom, after they had been circumciſed and inſtructed in their doctrine, they gave their freedom; but as a certain pride prevented

vented them from mixing their blood with that of these freedmen, the latter have in time become a distinct people, inhabiting the coast of the Indian peninsula from Goa to Madrafs; they are at present known in Malabar by the name of Pooliahs, and by that of Coolies in Coromandel; they understand neither the Persian, the Arabian, nor the Moorish language, and confine themselves to that of the countries in which they live; the generality are addicted to commerce, and profess a species of Mohammedism extremely corrupted by the Indian superstitions.

INDOSTAN, which has since been almost entirely reduced by war under a foreign yoke, was, at the time of the arrival of the Portuguese, divided between the kings of Cambaya, Delhi, Bifnagar, Narzingua and Calicut, each of which reckoned several sovereigns, more or less powerful, among their tributaries. The last of these monarchs, who is better known by the name of Zamorin, which answers to that of emperor, than by the name of his capital city, possessed the most maritime states, and his empire extended over all Malabar.

THERE is an ancient tradition, that when the Arabs began to establish themselves in India in the eighth century, the king of Malabar took so great a fancy to their religion, that he not only embraced it, but determined to end his days at Mecca. Calicut, where he embarked, became a place so dear and respectable to the Moors, that they were insensibly led to make it the constant rendezvous of their ships. Thus by the sole effect of this superstition,

perſtition, this harbour, incommodious and dangerous as it was, became the richeſt ſtaple of theſe countries. Precious ſtones, pearls, amber, ivory, china-ware, gold and ſilver, ſilks and cottons, indigo, ſugar, all kinds of ſpices, valuable woods, perfumes, beautiful varniſh, and whatever conduces to the elegance of life, were carried thither from all parts of the eaſt. Some of theſe rich commodities came by ſea; but as navigation was neither ſo ſafe nor purſued with ſo much ſpirit as it is now, a great deal was brought by land by buffaloes and elephants.

GAMA, having informed himſelf of theſe particulars, when he touched at Melinda, hired an able pilot to conduct him to that port in which trade was the moſt flouriſhing. Here he fortunately met with a Moor of Tunis, who underſtood the Portugueſe language, and having ſeen with admiration the great atchievements of this nation on the coaſts of Barbary, conceived a fondneſs for it which overcame his prejudices. This predilection engaged the Moor to uſe all his intereſt in favour of theſe ſtrangers, who put themſelves entirely under his direction. He procured Gama an audience of the Zamorin, who propoſed an alliance, and a treaty of commerce with the king his maſter. This was upon the point of being concluded, when the Muſſulmen found means to throw a ſuſpicion upon a rival power, whoſe courage, activity and knowledge they dreaded. The reports they made to him of its ambition and reſtleſſneſs, made ſuch an impreſſion on the mind of the prince, that he reſolved to deſtroy thoſe adventurers

venturers to whom he had juſt before given ſo favourable a reception.

Gama being informed of this change by his faithful guide, ſent his brother on board the fleet, telling him, *If you ſhould hear that I am thrown into priſon, or put to death, I forbid you, as your commander, either to come to my aſſiſtance, or revenge my death; ſet ſail immediately, and inform the king of the particulars of our voyage.*

They were happily not reduced to theſe extremities. The Zamorin, who wanted neither power nor inclination, wanted courage to put his deſign in execution; and the admiral had leave to return to his fleet. After making ſome well timed repriſals, which procured a reſtitution of the merchandiſe he had left as a pledge in Calicut, he ſailed for Europe.

It is impoſſible to deſcribe the joy that prevailed at Liſbon on his return. The inhabitants beheld themſelves on the point of eſtabliſhing the richeſt commerce in the world, and being not only avaritious, but ſuperſtitious at the ſame time, flattered themſelves with the hopes of propagating their religion either by perſuaſion, or by the force of arms. The popes, who omitted no opportunity of confirming the opinion of their ſupreme authority upon earth, gave the Portugueſe all the coaſts they ſhould diſcover in the eaſt, and inſpired this little ſtate with all the folly of conqueſt.

Numbers were eager to embark on board the new fleet that was fitted out for an expedition to India. Thirteen veſſels that ſailed from the Tagus,

gus, under the command of Alvares Cabral, arrived at Calicut, and reſtored ſome of the Zamorin's ſubjects whom Gama had carried away with him. Theſe Indians ſpoke highly of the treatment they had received; but it was a long time before the Zamorin was reconciled to the Portugueſe; the Mooriſh party prevailed, and the people of Calicut, ſeduced by their intrigues, maſſacred fifty of the adventurers. Cabral, in revenge, burnt all the Arabian veſſels in the harbour, cannonaded the town, and then ſailed firſt to Cochin and afterwards to Cananor.

THE kings of both theſe towns gave him ſpices, offered him gold and ſilver, and propoſed an alliance with him againſt the Zamorin, to whom they were tributaries. The kings of Onor, Culan, and ſeveral other princes, made the ſame overtures; flattering themſelves that they ſhould all be relieved from the tribute they paid to the Zamorin, extend the frontiers of their ſtates, and ſee their harbours crouded with the ſpoils of Aſia. This general infatuation procured to the Portugueſe ſo great an aſcendant over the whole country of Malabar, that wherever they appeared they gave the law. No ſovereign was ſuffered to enter into an alliance with them, unleſs he would acknowledge himſelf dependent on the court of Liſbon, give leave that a citadel ſhould be built in his capital, and ſell his merchandiſe at the price fixed by the buyer. The foreign merchant was obliged to wait till the Portugueſe had completed their lading; and no perſon was ſuffered to navigate theſe ſeas without producing paſſports

ports from them. The wars in which they were unavoidably engaged, gave little interruption to their trade; with a small number of men they defeated numerous armies; their enemies met with them every where, and always fled before them; and, in a short time, the ships of the Moors, of the Zamorin and his dependents, no longer dared to make their appearance.

THE Portuguese, thus become the conquerors of the east, were perpetually sending rich cargoes to their own country, which refounded with the fame of their exploits. The port of Lisbon gradually became the resort of all the traders in Europe, and the grand mart of Indian commodities; for the Portuguese, who brought them immediately from India, sold them at a lower rate than the merchants of other nations.

To secure and extend these advantages, it became necessary to call in the aid of reflection to correct and strengthen what had hitherto been the offspring of chance, a singular intrepidity, and a happy concurrence of circumstances. It was necessary to establish a system of power and commerce, which, at the same time, that it was extensive enough to take in all objects, should be so well connected, that all the parts of the grand structure they meant to raise, should mutually strengthen each other. Notwithstanding the information the court of Lisbon had received from the accounts transmitted from India, and the testimony of those who had hitherto been intrusted with the management of her interests in that quarter; it wisely reposed

IN THE EAST AND WEST INDIES.

pofed all its confidence in Alphonfo Albuquerque, the moft difcerning of all the Portuguefe who had been in Afia.

THE new viceroy acquitted himfelf beyond expectation: he found it neceffary that Portugal fhould have an eftablifhment which might eafily be defended, where there was a good harbour and a wholefome air, and where the Portuguefe might refrefh themfelves, after the fatigues of their paffage from Europe. With this view he caft his eyes upon Goa, which he forefaw would be an important acquifition to Lifbon.

GOA, which rifes in the form of an amphitheatre, is fituated near the middle of the coaft of Malabar, upon an ifland feparated from the continent by the two branches of a river which falls into the fea at fome diftance from the city, forming under its walls one of the fineft harbours in the world. This ifland is reckoned to be ten leagues in circumference. Within this little fpot are to be feen hills, vallies, woods, canals, fprings of excellent water, a city magnificently built, market-towns and large villages. Before the entrance into the port, we obferve the two peninfulas Salfet and Barda, which equally ferve the purpofes of defence and fhelter. They are guarded by forts lined with artillery, where all fhips are obliged to ftop before they come to an anchor in the harbour.

GOA, though not fo confiderable at that time as it has been fince, was looked upon as the moft advantageous poft in India. It belonged to the king of the Decan; but Idalcan, who was intrufted with
the

the government of it, had aſſumed an independency, and endeavoured to extend his power in Malabar. While this uſurper was purſuing his ſchemes on the continent, Albuquerque appeared before the gates of Goa, took the city by ſtorm, and acquired this valuable advantage with very little loſs.

IDALCAN, apprized of the loſs the king had ſuſtained, did not heſitate a moment what meaſures he ſhould take. In conjunction even with the Indians his enemies, who were almoſt as much intereſted in this matter as himſelf, he marched towards the capital, with a degree of expedition never known before in that country. The Portugueſe having no firm footing, and finding themſelves unable to preſerve their conqueſt, retreated to their ſhips which kept their ſtation in the harbour, and ſent to Cochin for a reinforcement. While they were waiting for it, their proviſions failed. Idalcan offered them a ſupply, giving them to underſtand, *That he choſe to conquer by arms, and not by famine*. It was cuſtomary at that time, in the Indian wars, for the armies to ſuffer proviſions to be carried to their enemies. Albuquerque rejected the offer made him, with this reply, *That he would receive no preſents from Idalcan till they were friends*. The ſuccour he hourly expected never arrived.

THIS diſappointment determined him to retreat, and to poſtpone the execution of his darling project to a more favourable opportunity, which preſented itſelf a few months after. Idalcan being obliged to take the field again to preſerve his dominions from abſolute deſtruction, Albuquerque
made

IN THE EAST AND WEST INDIES. made a sudden attack upon Goa, which he carried by storm, and fortified himself in the place. As the harbour of Calicut was good for nothing, and ceased to be frequented by the Arabian vessels, all its trade and riches were transferred to this city, which became the metropolis of all the Portuguese settlements in India.

THE natives of the country were too weak, too dispirited, and too much at variance, to put a stop to the success of this enterprizing nation. Nothing remained to be done but to guard against the Egyptians, nor was the least precaution either omitted or neglected.

EGYPT, which is considered as the parent of all historical antiquities, the source of policy, and the nursery of arts and sciences, after having remained for ages in a state of separation from the rest of the world, who were held in contempt by this wise country, understood and practised navigation. The inhabitants had long neglected the Mediterranean, where they did not certainly expect any great advantages, and directed their course towards the Indian ocean, which was the true channel of wealth.

STRUCK with the situation of this country between two seas, one of which opens the road to the east, and the other to the west, Alexander formed the design of fixing the seat of his empire in Egypt, and of making it the centre of trade to the whole world. This prince, who had more discernment than any other conqueror, saw that if it were possible to form an union between his present and future acquisitions, he must make choice of a country

The manner of carrying on trade in India before the conquests of the Portuguese.

try which nature seems to have placed, as it were, in contact with Africa and Asia to connect them with Europe. The premature death of the greatest commander that history and fable have held forth to the admiration of mankind, would for ever have annihilated these vast projects, had they not been in part pursued by Ptolemy, one of his lieutenants; who, upon the division of the most magnificent spoil ever known, claimed Egypt for his share.

In the reign of this new sovereign and his immediate successors, commerce made prodigious improvements. Alexandria was the mart of the merchandise that came from India, by the red sea, to the port of Berenice.

A writer, who has entered deeply into this subject, and whose accounts we follow, tells us, that some of the numerous vessels that were built in consequence of these connections, traded only in the gulph with the Arabians and Abyssinians. Among those which ventured out into the main ocean, some of them sailed southward to the right along the eastern coasts of Africa, as far as the island of Madagascar; and others steering to the left towards the Persian gulph, went even as far as the Euphrates, to trade with the people on its banks, particularly with the Greeks, whom Alexander had brought there with him in his expeditions. Others, grown still more enterprising from the hopes of gain, penetrated as far as the mouths of the Indus, traversed the coast of Malabar, and touched at the island of Ceylon, known by the ancients under the name of Taprobane. A very small

small number passed through the Coromandel to go up the river Ganges, as far as Palybotra, a town the most celebrated in India on account of its riches. Thus, industry proceeded by gradual advances, from one river or coast to another, to appropriate the productions of those countries that abound most in fruits, flowers, perfumes, precious stones, and all the delicacies of voluptuous luxury.

The boats made use of in these expeditions were long and flat, not unlike those that are seen upon the Nile. Before the invention of the compass, in consequence of which, larger vessels carrying more sail were fitted out for the main ocean; it was necessary to row close to the shore, and to follow the windings of the coast from one point of land to another. The sides of the ships were also made less, in order to weaken the power of the wind over them; and the ships less deep, for fear of striking against rocks, sands, or shallows. Thus a voyage not so long by one-third as those which are now performed in less than six months, sometimes lasted five years or more. What their vessels wanted in size, was supplied by their numbers; and the disadvantages of their slow sailing were compensated by the frequent squadrons that were fitted out.

The Egyptians exported to India, as has been done ever since, woollen manufactures, iron, lead, copper, some small pieces of workmanship in glass and silver, in exchange for ivory, ebony, tortoiseshell, white and printed linens, silks, pearls, precious stones, cinnamon, spices, and particularly

F 4 frankincense;

frankincense; which was a perfume the most in esteem, on account of its being used in divine worship, and contributing to the gratification of princes. It sold at so high a price, that the merchants adulterated under pretence of improving it. So apprehensive is avarice of being defrauded by poverty, that the workmen who were employed in making it were naked; having only a girdle about their loins, the ends of which were sealed by the superintendant of the manufacture.

ALL the sea-faring and trading nations in the Mediterranean resorted to the ports of Egypt to purchase the produce of India. When Carthage and Corinth became the victims of the vices introduced by their opulence, the Egyptians were themselves obliged to export the riches with which these cities formerly loaded their own vessels. As their maritime power increased, they extended their navigation as far as Cadiz. They could scarcely supply the demands of Rome, whose luxury kept pace with its conquests; at the same time that they were arrived at such a pitch of extravagance themselves, that the accounts given of it have the air of romance. Cleopatra, with whom their empire and history expired, was as profuse as she was voluptuous. But notwithstanding these incredible expences, the advantages they derived from the Indian trade were so great, that after they were subdued and spoiled, lands, provisions, and merchandise, bore double the price at Rome. If Pliny may be credited, the conqueror, by reinstating the conquered in this source of opulence, which was calculated rather to flatter their vanity than

IN THE EAST AND WEST INDIES. 73

than to aggrandize their power, gained twenty thousand per cent. Though it is eafy to fee that this calculation is exaggerated, we may from thence form a conjecture what profits muft have been reaped in thofe diftant ages, when the Indians were not fo well acquainted with their own intereft.

WHILE the Romans had virtue enough to preferve the power acquired by their anceftors, Egypt very much contributed to fupport the dignity of the empire by the riches it brought thither from India. But the fulnefs of luxury, like the corpulency of the body, is a fymptom of approaching decay. This vaft empire funk under its own weight, and, like levers of wood or metal whofe exceffive length contributes to their weaknefs, broke into two parts.

EGYPT was annexed to the eaftern empire, which lafted longer than that of the weft; not being attacked fo foon, or with fo much vigour. If riches could have fupplied the place of courage, its fituation and refources would even have made it invincible. But the inhabitants of this empire had nothing except ftratagem to oppofe againft an enemy, who, befide the enthufiafm of a new religion, were animated with all the ftrength of an uncivilized people. A torrent thus increafing, as it deftroyed every thing in its paffage, was not to be ftopped by fo flight a barrier. In the feventh century it laid wafte feveral provinces, and Egypt amongft the reft; which after having been one of the principal empires of antiquity, and the model of all modern monarchies, was at length deftined

to

to sink into a state of languor and oblivion, in which it remains to this day.

The Greeks comforted themselves under this misfortune, on finding that the wars of the Saracens had diverted the stream of the Indian commerce from Alexandria to Constantinople, by two well-known channels. One of these was the Euxine or black sea, where it was usual to embark to go up the Phasis. Large vessels were at first employed, and afterwards smaller ones were introduced, which sailed as far as Serapanna; from whence, in four or five days, the merchants conveyed their commodities by land-carriage to the river Cyrus, which falls into the Caspian sea. Having crossed this tempestuous ocean, they arrived at the mouth of the Oxus, which extended almost as far as the source of the Indus, and from whence they returned the same way, laden with the treasures of Asia. Such was one of the means of communication between this continent, always naturally rich, and that of Europe, which was then poor, and ruined by its own inhabitants.

The other channel of communication was more easy. The Indian vessels, sailing from different coasts, passed the Persian gulph, and arrived at the banks of the Euphrates, where they unloaded their cargo; which, from this river, was in one day sent by land-carriage to Palmyra. This city, the ruins of which still preserve an idea of its opulence, transported this merchandise through the deserts to the confines of Syria. By this rich commerce, it became more flourishing than could have been expected from its sandy situation. Since its destruction,

IN THE EAST AND WEST INDIES.

deftruction, the caravans, after fome changes, conftantly took the road of Aleppo, which, by means of the port of Alexandretta, turned the current of wealth to Conftantinople, that was at length become the general market of the productions of India.

THIS advantage might alone have retarded the fall of the empire, and, perhaps, have reſtored it to its ancient grandeur: but that grandeur had been acquired by its arms, its virtues, and its frugal manners; and it was now deftitute of all thofe means of maintaining its profperity. The Greeks, corrupted by the prodigious acceffion of wealth, which their exclufive commerce poured in upon them almoft without any care or activity of their own, abandoned themfelves to an indolent and effeminate way of life, which infallibly leads to luxury; fond only of the trivial amufements of glittering fhows, and the voluptuous refinements of art; of futile, obfcure, and fophiftical difquifitions on matters of tafte, fentiment, and even religion and politics. They could fuffer themfelves to be oppreffed, but knew not how to affert their right to be properly governed; and alternately made their court to tyrants by the moft abject adulation, or irritated them by a faint refiftance. Thefe people were bought by the emperors, who fold them to all the monopolizers who aimed to enrich themfelves by the ruin of the ftate. The government, ftill more corrupted than its fubjects, fuffered its navy to decay, and placed its whole dependence on the treaties it entered into with the

the ſtrangers, whoſe ſhips frequented its ports. The Italians had inſenſibly engroſſed the article of tranſportation, which the Greeks had for a long time kept in their own hands. This branch of buſineſs, which is rather laborious than profitable, was doubly uſeful to a trading nation, whoſe chief riches conſiſt in maintaining their vigour by labour. Indolence haſtened the deſtruction of Conſtantinople, which was preſſed and ſurrounded on all ſides by the conqueſts of the Turks. The Genoeſe fell into the precipice which their perfidy and avarice had digged for them. Mohammed the ſecond drove them from Caffa, to which place they had, of late years, drawn the greateſt part of the Aſiatic trade.

THE Venetians did not wait for this event to give them an opportunity of reviving their connections with Egypt. They had experienced more indulgence than they expected from a government eſtabliſhed ſince the laſt cruſades, and nearly reſembling that of Algiers. The Mammelucs, who at the time of theſe wars had taken poſſeſſion of a throne they had hitherto ſupported, were for the moſt part ſlaves brought from Circaſſia in their infancy, and trained up early to a military life. The ſupreme authority was veſted in a chief, and a council compoſed of four-and-twenty principal perſons. This military corps, which eaſe would unavoidably have enervated, was recruited every year, by a multitude of brave adventurers, who flocked from all parts, with a view of making their fortune. Theſe needy people were prevailed upon, by a ſum of money and promiſes, promifes, to confent that their country fhould be made the mart of Indian merchandife. Thus they were bribed into a meafure, which the political intereft of their ftate always required them to adopt. The inhabitants of Pifa and Florence, the Catalans, and the Genoefe, received fome benefit from this change; but it was of fignal advantage to the Venetians, by whofe management it was effected. Affairs were in this fituation when the Portuguefe made their appearance in India.

This great event, and the confequences that immediately followed it, occafioned much uneafinefs at Venice. This republic, fo celebrated for its wifdom, had lately been difconcerted by a league which it could not oppofe, and certainly did not forefee. Several princes of different interefts who were rivals in power, and had pretenfions of an oppofite nature, united, in defiance of all the rules of juftice and policy, to deftroy a ftate which had not given any of them the leaft umbrage; and even Lewis the XIIth, whofe intereft was moft concerned in the prefervation of Venice, brought it to the brink of ruin by the victory of Aignadelle. The quarrels which muft neceffarily arife among fuch allies, joined to the prudence of the republic, faved it from this danger; which, though more imminent in appearance, was, in fact, not fo great nor fo immediate as that they were now expofed to by the difcovery of a paffage to India by the Cape of Good Hope.

Venice soon perceived that her commerce, and consequently her power, was on the point of being transferred to the Portuguese. Every expedient was tried that an able administration could suggest. Some of the skilful emissaries, which the state took care to retain and employ dexterously in all places, persuaded the Arabs settled in their country, and those that were dispersed over India, or the eastern coast of Africa, that as their interest was equally concerned with that of Venice, they ought to unite with her against a nation, which had made itself mistress of the common source of their riches.

THE rumour of this league reached the Sultan of Egypt, whose attention was already awakened by the misfortunes he felt, as well as those he foresaw. The customs, which constituted a principal branch of his revenue, and by which five per cent. was levied on the importation, and ten on the exportation of Indian goods, began to bring in little or nothing. The frequent bankruptcies, which were the necessary consequence of the embarrassment of affairs, exasperated men's minds against the government, which is always responsible to the people for the calamities they endure. The militia, which was ill paid, fearing that their pay would be still more precarious, raised mutinies, which are more to be dreaded on the decline of a state, than in the time of its prosperity. Egypt was equally a sufferer by the trade carried on by the Portuguese, and by the obstructions their own was exposed to by their encroachments.

IN THE EAST AND WEST INDIES. 79

The Egyptians might have extricated themselves from these inconveniencies by fitting out a fleet; but the red sea afforded no materials for the building of ships. The Venetians removed this obstacle by sending wood, and other materials to Alexandria. They were conveyed by the Nile to Cairo, from whence they were carried by camels to Suez. From this celebrated port, in the year 1508, four large vessels, one galleon, two gallies, and three galliots, sailed to India.

The Portuguese, who foresaw this confederacy, had the preceding year laid a scheme to prevent it, by making themselves masters of the red sea: secure, that with this advantage they should have nothing to fear from this connection, nor from the combined forces of Egypt and Arabia. With this view, they formed a plan to seize upon the island of Socotora, well known by the name of Dioscorides to the ancients, from the abundance and excellence of its aloes. It lies in the gulph of the red sea, a hundred and eighty leagues from the straits of Babelmandel formed by the Cape of Guardafui on the African side, and by the Cape of Fartack on the side of Arabia.

Tristan d'Acugna sailed from Portugal with a considerable armament to attack this island. Upon his landing, he was encountered by Ibrahim, son of the king of the people of Fartack, who was sovereign of part of Arabia and Socotora. This young prince was killed in the engagement; the Portuguese besieged the only town that was in the island, and carried it by storm, though it was defended to the

the laſt extremity by a garriſon ſuperior in number to their ſmall army. The ſoldiers that compoſed this garriſon determined not to ſurvive the ſon of their ſovereign, refuſed to capitulate, and were all, to the laſt man, put to the ſword. D'Acugna's troops, by their intrepidity, proved an over-match for their bravery.

This ſucceſsful enterpriſe was not attended with the advantages that were expected from it. It was found that the iſland was barren, that it had no port, and that the ſhips that came from the red ſea never touched there, though they could not enter the gulph without taking an obſervation of it. Accordingly, the Egyptian fleet found a ſafe paſſage into the Indian ocean, where it joined that of Cambaya. Theſe united armaments had the advantage of the Portugueſe, who were conſiderably weakened by the great number of veſſels they had lately fitted out to carry merchandiſe to Europe. This triumph, however, did not laſt long; the conquered party got reinforcements, and regained their ſuperiority, which they ever after preſerved. The armaments, which continued to come from Egypt, were always beaten and diſperſed by the ſmall Portugueſe ſquadrons that cruized at the entrance of the gulph.

As, however, theſe ſkirmiſhes kept up a conſtant alarm, and occaſioned ſome expence, Albuquerque thought it incumbent on him to put an end to them by the deſtruction of Suez. But a thouſand obſtacles oppoſed the execution of this project.

The red fea, which takes its name from the corals, madrepores, and marine plants, which cover the bottom of it almoft throughout; or, perhaps, only from the fand which difcolours its waters, is bordered on one fide by Arabia, and on the other by Upper Ethiopia and Egypt. It meafures fix hundred and eighty leagues from the ifland of Socotora to the famous Ifthmus, which unites Africa to Afia. As its length is very confiderable, and its breadth fmall, and no river falls into it of fufficient force to counteract the influence of the tide, it is more affected by the motions of the great ocean, than any of the inland feas nearly in the fame latitude. It is not much expofed to tempefts; the winds ufually blow from the north and fouth, and being periodical like the monfoons in India, invariably determine the feafon of failing into or out of this fea. It may be divided into three parts; the middle divifion is open and navigable at all times, its depth being from twenty-five to fixty fathoms. The other two, which lie nearer the land, though they abound in rocks, are more frequented by the neighbouring nations; who being obliged to keep clofe to the fhore on account of the fmallnefs of their veffels, never launch out into the principal channel, unlefs they expect a fquall of wind. The difficulty, not to fay impoffibility, of landing in the harbours on this coaft, makes the navigation dangerous for veffels of large burthen, not to mention the great number of defert iflands they meet with in their paffage, which are barren, and afford no frefh water.

ALBUQUERQUE, notwithstanding his abilities, experience, and resolution, could not surmount so many obstacles. After entering a considerable way into the red sea, he was obliged to return with his fleet, which had suffered perpetual hardships, and been exposed to the greatest dangers. He was prompted by a restless and cruel spirit of enterprize, to employ methods for the accomplishment of his designs, which, though of a still bolder cast, he thought could not fail of success. He wanted to prevail with the emperor of Ethiopia, who solicited the protection of Portugal, to turn the course of the Nile so as to open a passage for him into the red sea. Egypt would then have become in a great measure uninhabitable, or at least unfit for commerce. In the mean time he proposed to transport into Arabia, by the gulph of Persia, three or four hundred horse, which he thought would be sufficient to plunder Medina and Mecca. He imagined that by so bold an expedition, he should strike terror into the Mohammedans, and put a stop to that prodigious concourse of pilgrims which was the chief support of a trade he wanted totally to extirpate.

OTHER enterprizes of a less hazardous nature, and attended with more immediate advantage, led him to postpone the ruin of a power, whose influence as a rival was the only circumstance necessary to be guarded against at the present juncture. The conquest of Egypt by the Turks, a few years after, made it requisite to act with the greatest precaution. Those men of genius, who were well qualified to pursue the series of events which had preceded

IN THE EAST AND WEST INDIES.

ceded and followed the difcovery of the paffage by the Cape of Good Hope, and to form deep conjectures concerning the revolutions which this new track of navigation muft neceffarily prevent, could not help confidering this remarkable tranfaction as the moft important æra in the hiftory of the world.

EUROPE began to recover its ftrength by flow degrees, and to fhake off the yoke of flavery, which had difgraced its inhabitants from the time of the Roman conquefts down to the inftitution of the feudal laws. Innumerable tyrants, who kept multitudes in a ftate of oppreffion and flavery, had been ruined by the folly of the crufades. To defray the expences of thefe wild expeditions, they were obliged to fell their lands and caftles, and for a pecuniary confideration to allow their vaffals fome privileges, which at length almoft re-inftated them in the order of human beings. From that time the right of property began to be introduced among private perfons, and gave them that kind of independence, without which, property itfelf is a mere illufion. Thus the firft dawnings of liberty in Europe were, however unexpectedly, owing to the crufades; and the rage of conqueft for once contributed to the welfare of mankind.

IF Vafco de Gama had not made his difcoveries, the fpirit of liberty would have been again extinguifhed, and probably without hopes of a revival. The Turks had lately expelled thofe favage nations, who, pouring from the extremities of the globe, had driven out the Romans, to become, like them, the scourges of human kind; and our barbarous inftitutions would have been followed by oppreffions ftill more intolerable. This muft inevitably have been the cafe, if the favage conquerors of Egypt had not been repulfed by the Portuguefe in their feveral expeditions to India. Their poffeffion of the riches of Afia would have fecured their claim to thofe of Europe. As the trade of the whole world was in their hands, they muft confequently have had the greateft maritime force that ever was known. What oppofition could our continent then have made to the progrefs of a people whofe religion and policy equally animated them to conqueft?

Dissentions prevailed in England on account of its liberties; France contended for the interefts of its fovereigns; Germany for thofe of its religion; and Italy was employed in adjufting the mutual claims of a tyrant and an impoftor. Europe, overrun with fanatics and armies, refembled a fick perfon, who falling into a delirium, in the tranfport of madnefs opens his veins till he faints with lofs of blood and fpirits. In this ftate of weaknefs and anarchy, it was ill prepared to refift the inroads of the Turks.

As the calm which fucceeds the violence of civil wars makes a nation formidable to its neighbours; fo the diffentions which divide it as certainly expofe it to ravage and oppreffion. The depraved morals of the clergy would likewife have favoured the introduction of a new worfhip; and we fhould have been condemned to a ftate of flavery without any hopes of relief. In truth, there is not one among all

all the political and religious syſtems that oppreſs mankind, which allows ſo little ſcope to liberty as that of the Muſſulmen. Throughout almoſt all Europe, a religion foreign to government, and introduced without its patronage; rules of morality diſperſed without order or preciſion in obſcure writings, capable of an endleſs variety of interpretations; authority engroſſed by prieſts and princes, who are perpetually conteſting their right to rule over their fellow-creatures; political and civil inſtitutions daily formed in contradiction to the prevailing religion, which condemns ambition and inequality of rank; a turbulent and enterpriſing adminiſtration, which, in order to tyrannize with a higher hand, is perpetually ſetting one part of the ſtate at variance with the other: all theſe principles of diſcord muſt neceſſarily keep the minds of men in conſtant agitation. Is it ſurpriſing that on the view of this tumultuous ſcene, nature alarmed ſhould riſe up in our hearts, and cry out, " Is " man born free?"

But when men once became ſlaves to a religion which conſecrates tyranny by eſtabliſhing the throne upon the altar; which ſeems to check the ſallies of ambition by encouraging voluptuouſneſs, and cheriſhes a ſpirit of indolence by forbidding the exerciſe of the underſtanding: there is no reaſon to hope for any conſiderable revolutions. Thus the Turks, who frequently ſtrangle their maſter, have never entertained a thought of changing their government. This is an idea beyond the reach of minds enervated and corrupted like theirs. Hence it appears, that the whole world would have loft its liberty, had not the moft fuperftitious, and, perhaps, the moft enflaved nation in Chriftendom checked the progrefs of the fanaticifm of the Mohammedans, and put a ftop to the career of their victories, by depriving them of thofe fources of wealth which were neceffary to the fuccefs of their enterprizes. Albuquerque went ftill further; not fatisfied with having taken effectual meafures to prevent any veffel from paffing from the Arabian fea to the Indian ocean, he attempted to get the command of the Perfian gulph.

The Portuguefe make themfelves mafters of the Perfian gulph.

AT the mouth of the ftrait of Mocandon, which leads into the Perfian gulph, lies the ifland of Gombroon. In the eleventh century an Arabian conqueror built upon this barren rock the city of Ormus, which afterwards became the capital of an empire, comprehending a confiderable part of Arabia on one fide, and of Perfia on the other. Ormus had two good harbours, and was large and well fortified; its riches and ftrength were entirely owing to its fituation. It was the center of trade between Perfia and India; which was very confiderable, if we remember that the Perfians at that time caufed the greateft part of the merchandife of Afia to be conveyed to Europe from the ports of Syria and Caffa. At the time of the arrival of the foreign merchants, Ormus afforded a more fplendid and agreeable fcene than any city in the eaft. Perfons from all parts of the globe exchanged their commodities, and tranfacted their bufinefs, with an air of politenefs and attention

attention which are feldom feen in other places of trade.

These manners were introduced by the merchants belonging to the port, who engaged foreigners to imitate their affability. Their addrefs, the regularity of their police, and the variety of entertainments which their city afforded, joined to the interefts of commerce, invited merchants to make it a place of refort. The ftreets were covered with mats, and in fome places with carpets; and the linen awnings which were fufpended from the tops of the houfes prevented any inconvenience from the heat of the fun. Indian cabinets ornamented with gilded vafes, or china filled with flowering fhrubs, or aromatic plants, adorned their apartments. Camels laden with water were ftationed in the public fquares. Perfian wines, perfumes, and all the delicacies of the table were furnifhed in the greateft abundance, and they had the mufic of the eaft in its higheft perfection. Ormus was crouded with beautiful women from all parts of Afia, who were inftructed from their infancy in all the arts of varying and heightening the pleafures of voluptuous love. In fhort, univerfal opulence, an extenfive commerce, a refined luxury, politenefs in the men, and gallantry in the women, united all their attractions to make this city the feat of pleafure.

Albuquerque, on his arrival in India, began to ravage the coafts, and to plunder the towns that belonged to the jurifdiction of Ormus: though thefe inroads, which fhewed more of the robber than of the conqueror, were naturally repugnant to Albuquerque's querque's character, he thought himself obliged to have recourse to them, in order to induce a power he was not in a condition to subdue by force, to submit voluntarily to the yoke he wanted to impose. As soon as he imagined the alarm was spread sufficiently to favour his design, he appeared before the capital, and summoned the king to acknowledge himself tributary to Portugal, as he was to Persia. This proposal was received in the manner it deserved. A fleet composed of ships from Ormus, Arabia, and Persia, came to an engagement with Albuquerque's squadron, who with five vessels destroyed the whole armament. The king, discouraged by his ill success, consented that the conqueror should erect a fort which might command the city and both its harbours.

ALBUQUERQUE, who knew the importance of seizing the present conjuncture, carried on the work with the utmost expedition. He laboured as hard as the meanest of his followers; but this spirit of activity could not prevent the enemy from taking notice of the smallness of his numbers. Atar, who, in consequence of the revolutions so frequent in the east, had been raised from the condition of a slave to that of a prime minister, was ashamed of having sacrificed the state to a handful of adventurers. As his talent lay rather in the arts of policy than of war, he determined to repair the ill consequences of his timidity by stratagem. By the arts of insinuation and bribery, he succeeded so far in sowing dissentions among the Portuguese, and prejudicing them against their leader, that they were frequently ready

ready to take arms againſt each other. This animoſity, which increaſed every day, determined them to reimbark at the inſtant they were informed that a plot was concerted to maſſacre them. Albuquerque, whoſe ſpirit roſe ſuperior to oppoſition and diſcontent, reſolved to ſtarve the place, and deprive it of ſuccours by cutting off all communication. It muſt certainly have fallen into his hands, had not three of his captains ſhamefully abandoned him, and gone off with their ſhips. To juſtify their deſertion, they were guilty of ſtill blacker perfidy, in accuſing their general of the moſt atrocious crimes.

This treachery obliged Albuquerque to defer the execution of his deſign for ſome time, till he he had all the national troops at his command. As ſoon as he was appointed viceroy, he appeared before Ormus with ſo ſtrong an armament, that a debauched court and an effeminate people, finding it in vain to make any reſiſtance, were obliged to ſubmit. The ſovereign of Perſia had the confidence to demand tribute of the conqueror. Albuquerque ordered ſome bullets, grenades, and ſabres to be produced to the envoy, telling him, that this was the kind of tribute paid by the king of Portugal.

After this expedition, the power of the Portugueſe was ſo firmly eſtabliſhed in the Arabian and Perſian gulphs, and on the Malabar coaſt, that they began to think of extending their conqueſts into the eaſtern parts of Aſia.

Albu-

BOOK I.

The Portuguese form a settlement at Ceylon.

ALBUQUERQUE's first attempt was on the island of Ceylon, which is eighty leagues long, and thirty at its greatest breadth. It was anciently known by the name of Taprobane. We have no accounts transmitted to us of the revolutions it has undergone. All that history relates worthy of remark is, that the laws were formerly held in so high esteem, that the monarch was under the same obligation of observing them as the meanest of his subjects. If he violated them, he was condemned to death; with this mark of distinction, however, that he did not suffer in an ignominious manner. He was denied all intercourse, all the comforts and supports of life: and, in this kind of excommunication, miserably ended his days.

WHEN the Portuguese landed in Ceylon they found it well peopled, and inhabited by two nations, who differed from each other in their manners, their government, and their religion. The Bedas, who were settled in the northern parts of the island, where the country was less fertile, were distinguished into tribes, which considered themselves as so many families headed by a chief, whose power was not absolute. They go almost naked, and, upon the whole, their manners and government are the same with that of the Highlanders in Scotland. These tribes, who unite for the common defence, have always bravely fought for their liberty, and have never invaded that of their neighbours. Their religion is little known, and it is uncertain whether they have any form of worship. They have little intercourse with strangers; keep
a watchful

a watchful eye over thofe who travel through the diftrict they inhabit; treat them well, and fend them away as foon as poffible. This caution is owing in part to the jealoufy the Bedas entertain of their wives, which contributes to eftrange them from all the world. They feem to be the firft inhabitants of the ifland.

The fouthern part is poffeffed by a more numerous and powerful people, called Cinglaffes. This nation is polite, in comparifon of the other. They wear clothes, and live under an arbitrary government. They have a diftinction of cafts, as well as the Indians; but their religion is different. They acknowledge one fupreme being, and in fubordination to him divinities of the fecond and third order : all which have their priefts. Among the deities of the fecond order, particular honours are paid to Buddou, who defcended upon earth to take upon himfelf the office of mediator between God and mankind. The priefts of Buddou are perfons of great confequence in Ceylon. They are never punifhable by the prince, even for an attempt againft his life. The Cinglaffes underftand the art of war. They know how to take advantage of the natural fecurity their mountains afford againft the attacks of the Europeans, whom they have often conquered. Like all people in arbitrary ftates, they are deceitful, felfifh, and full of compliment. They have two languages : one peculiar to the people, the other to the learned. Wherever this cuftom prevails, it furnifhes priefts and princes

with

with a further opportunity of impofing upon mankind.

Both thefe nations enjoyed the benefits of the fruits, the corn, and the pafture which abounded in the ifland. They had elephants without number; precious ftones, and the only kind of cinnamon that was ever efteemed. On the northern coaft, and on the fifhing coafts which borders upon it, was carried on the greateft pearl fifhery in the eaft. The harbours of Ceylon were the beft in India, and its fituation was fuperior to all its other advantages.

It fhould feem to have been the intereft of the Portuguefe to have placed all their ftrength in this ifland. It lies in the center of the eaft; and is the paffage that leads to the richeft countries. All the fhips that come from Europe, Arabia and Perfia, cannot avoid paying a kind of homage to Ceylon; and the monfoons, which alternately blow from different points, make it eafy for veffels to come in and go out at all feafons of the year. It might have been well peopled and fortified with a fmall number of men, and at very little expence. The numerous fquadrons that might have been fent out from every port in the ifland would have kept all Afia in awe; and the fhips that might cruize in thofe latitudes, would have intercepted the trade of other nations.

The viceroy overlooked thefe advantages. He alfo neglected the coaft of Coromandel, though richer than that of Malabar. The merchandife of the latter was of an inferior quality: it produced plenty of provifions, a fmall quantity of bad cinnamon,

namon, fome pepper and cardamon, a kind of fpice much ufed by the eaftern people. The coaft of Coromandel furnifhed the fineft cottons in the world. Its inhabitants, who for the moft part were natives of the country, and had lefs intercourfe with the Arabians and other nations, were the moft humane and induftrious of all the people in Indoftan. To this we may add, that the paffage along the coaft of Coromandel towards the north, leads to the mines of Golconda: befides that, this coaft is admirably fituated for the trade of Bengal and other countries.

NOTWITHSTANDING this, Albuquerque made no fettlement there. The fettlements of St. Thomas and Negapatan were not formed till afterwards. He knew that this coaft was deftitute of harbours, and inacceffible at certain periods of the year, when it would be impoffible for the fleets to protect the colonies. In fhort, he thought that when the Portuguefe had made themfelves mafters of Ceylon, a conqueft begun by his predeceffor d'Almeyda, and afterwards completed, they might command the trade of Coromandel, if they got poffeffion of Malacca. He therefore determined to make the attempt.

THE country, of which Malacca is the capital city, is a narrow tract of land, about a hundred leagues in length. It joins to the continent towards the northern coaft, where it borders on the ftate of Siam, or, more properly, the kingdom of Johor, which has been feparated from it. The reft is furrounded by the fea, and divided from the ifland

The Portuguefe conquer Malacca.

of Sumatra by a channel which is called the ſtraits of Malacca.

NATURE had amply provided for the happineſs of the Malays, by placing them in a mild, healthy climate, where refreſhing gales and cooling ſtreams allay the fervour of the torrid zone; where the ſoil pours forth an abundance of delicious fruits to ſatisfy the wants of a ſavage life; and where it is capable of anſwering, by cultivation, all the neceſſary demands of ſociety; where the trees wear an eternal verdure, and the flowers bloom in a perpetual ſucceſſion; where the moſt delicate and fragrant odours breathing from aromatic plants, perfume the air, and infuſe a ſpirit of voluptuous delight into all living beings.

BUT while nature has done every thing in favour of the Malays, ſociety has done them every poſſible injury. Such has been the influence of a tyrannical government, that the inhabitants of the happieſt country in the univerſe have become remarkable for the ferocity of their manners. The feudal ſyſtem, which was firſt planned among the rocks and woods of the north, has extended itſelf even to the foreſts and mild regions of the equator, where every thing conſpires to promote the enjoyment of a long life of tranquillity, which can only be ſhortened by a too frequent and exceſſive indulgence in pleaſures. This enſlaved nation is under the dominion of an arbitrary prince, or rather of twenty tyrants, his repreſentatives. Thus the deſpotiſm of a ſultan ſeems to extend its oppreſſive influence to multitudes, by being divided among a number of powerful vaſſals. THIS

IN THE EAST AND WEST INDIES.

THIS turbulent and oppreſſive ſcene gave riſe to an univerſal ſavageneſs of manners. In vain did heaven and earth ſhower their bleſſings upon Malacca; theſe bleſſings only ſerved to make its inhabitants ungrateful and unhappy. The maſters let out their ſervices, or rather thoſe of their dependents, for hire, to the beſt bidder, regardleſs of the loſs that agriculture would ſuſtain for want of hands. They preferred a wandering and adventurous life, either by ſea or land, to induſtry. This people had conquered a large Archipelago, well known in the eaſt by the name of the Malayan Iſlands. The numerous colonies that were tranſplanted thither, carried with them their laws, their manners, their cuſtoms, and, what is ſomething remarkable, the ſofteſt language in all Aſia.

THE ſituation of Malacca had, however, made it the moſt conſiderable market in India; its harbour was conſtantly crouded with veſſels either from Japan, China, the Philippine and Molucca Iſlands, and the adjacent part of the eaſtern coaſt; or from Bengal, Coromandel, Malabar, Perſia, Arabia, and Africa. Theſe merchants carried on a ſafe trade among themſelves, or with the inhabitants: the paſſion of the Malays for plunder had at length given way to advantages of a more certain nature than the precarious and doubtful ſucceſs of piratical expeditions.

THE Portugueſe were deſirous of having a ſhare in the general commerce of Aſia. At firſt they appeared at Malacca in the character of merchants; but their uſurpations in India rendered their deſigns

signs so much suspected, and the animosity of the Arabians had circulated reports so much to their disadvantage, that measures were taken to destroy them. They fell into the snares that were laid for them; several of them were massacred, and others thrown into prison. Those who escaped got back to their ships, and retreated to the Malabar coast.

Though Albuquerque did not intend to wait for a rupture to afford him a pretence of seizing Malacca, he was not displeased at this incident, since it gave his enterprize an appearance of justice that might lessen the odium which such a step must naturally have drawn upon the Portuguese name. As an impression so favourable to his views might be weakened by delay, he did not hesitate a moment to take his revenge. The enemy expected a sudden blow; and accordingly, when he appeared before the place, in the beginning of the year 1511, he found every thing in readiness to receive him.

But formidable as these preparations appeared, there was a still greater obstacle, which for some days damped the valour of the christian general; his friend Araûjo had been taken prisoner in the first expedition, and the enemy threatened to put him to death the moment the siege should begin. Albuquerque, who did not want sensibility, paused at the prospect of his friend's danger, when he received the following billet: *Think of nothing but the glory and advantage of Portugal; if I cannot contribute towards your victory, at least let me not be the means of preventing it.* The place was attacked and carried after several doubtful, bloody, and obstinate engagements.

gagements. They found in it immense treasure, vast magazines, and whatever could contribute to the elegancies and pleasures of life; and a fort was erected there to secure the conquest.

As the Portuguese contented themselves with the possession of the city, the inhabitants, who professed a kind of corrupt Mohammedism, and were unwilling to submit to their new masters, either retired into the inland parts, or dispersed themselves along the coast. Having lost the spirit of commerce, they relapsed into all the excesses of their violent character. These people never go without a poniard, which they call *crid*. The invention of this murderous weapon seems to have exhausted all the powers of their sanguinary genius. Nothing is more to be dreaded than such men armed with such an instrument. When they get on board a vessel, they stab all the crew at the time when no harm is suspected. Since their treachery has been known, all the Europeans take care never to employ a Malayan sailor; but these barbarians, who always made it a rule to attack the weaker party, have now changed this ancient custom, and, animated by an unaccountable resolution to kill or be killed, come in boats with thirty men to board our vessels, and sometimes succeed in carrying them off: if they were repulsed, they have the satisfaction, at least, of having imbrued their hands in blood.

People who derive from nature such inflexible bravery, may be exterminated, but cannot be subdued by force. They are only to be civilized by humane treatment, by the allurements of riches or liberty, by the

Vol. I. H influence

influence of virtue and moderation, and by a mild government. They muſt be reſtored to their rights, or left to themſelves, before we can hope to eſtabliſh any intercourſe with them. To attempt to reduce them by conqueſt, is, perhaps, the laſt method that ſhould be tried; as it will only increaſe their abhorrence of a foreign yoke, and diſcourage them from entering into any ſocial engagements. Nature has placed certain people in the midſt of the ocean, like lions in the deſerts, that they may enjoy their liberty. Tempeſts, ſands, foreſts, mountains and caverns, are the places of refuge and defence to all independent beings. Civilized nations ſhould take care how they invade the rights, or rouze the ſpirits of iſlanders and ſavages: as they may be aſſured that they will become cruel and barbarous to no purpoſe; that their ravages will make them deteſted; and that diſgrace and revenge are the only laurels they can expect to obtain.

AFTER the reduction of Malacca, the kings of Siam, Pegu, and ſeveral others, alarmed at a conqueſt ſo fatal to their independence, ſent ambaſſadors to congratulate Albuquerque, to make him an offer of their trade, and to deſire an alliance with Portugal.

Settlement of the Portugueſe in the Molucca iſlands.

AFFAIRS being in this ſituation, a ſquadron was detached from the fleet to the Moluccas. Theſe iſlands, which lie in the Indian ocean near the equinoxial, are ten in number, including as uſual thoſe of Banda. The largeſt is not more than twelve leagues in circumference, and the others are much ſmaller.

It is not known who were the first inhabitants; but it is certain that the Javans and the Malays have succeffively been in poffeffion of them. At the beginning of the fixteenth century they were inhabited by a kind of favages, whofe chiefs, though honoured with the title of kings, poffeffed only a limited authority, totally dependent on the caprice of their fubjects. They had of late years joined the fuperftitions of Mohammedifm to thofe of Paganifm, which they had profeffed for a confiderable time. Their indolence was exceffive. Their only employment was hunting and fifhing; and they were ftrangers to all kind of agriculture. They were encouraged in their inactivity by the advantages they derived from the cocoa tree.

The cocoa is a tree whofe roots are fo flender and fo fuperficial, that it is frequently blown down by the wind. Its trunk, which rifes to the height of thirty or forty feet, is ftraight, of a middling thicknefs, and every where of the fame diameter. It is of fo fpongy a nature, that it is unfit for fhip-timber, or for any building that requires folidity. The tuft is compofed of ten or twelve leaves, which are large, long, and thick, and are made ufe of in covering the roofs of houfes. From this tuft, which is renewed thrice every year, at every renewal there arife very large buds, from each of which hang ten or twelve cocoas, which, including their fhells, are more than half a foot in diameter. The outer coat of the nut confifts of filaments, which are ufed for coarfe ftuffs, and fhip cables. Of the next coat, which

is

is very hard, are made small cups, and other domestic utensils. The inside of this shell is filled with a white firm pulp, from which is expressed an oil much used in India. It is sweet, as long as it continues fresh, but it contracts a bitter taste when it is kept long, and is then only proper for burning. The sediment that remains in the press, affords nourishment for cattle, poultry, and even the lower kind of people in times of scarcity. The pulp of the cocoa contains a liquid which is extremely refreshing, and quenches the thirst of labouring p ple both at sea and land. This liquor is very wholesome, but has a sweet insipid taste.

WHEN these buds are cut at the extremity, vessels are placed to receive the white liquor that distils from them; which if drawn off before sunrise, and drunk while it is fresh, has the flavour of sweet wine. It afterwards turns sour, and makes good vinegar. When distilled in its highste perfection, it produces a strong brandy: and boiled with quick-lime, yields a middling kind of sugar. The trees from which this liquor has been extracted, bear no fruit; the juices being exhausted, which serve to produce and nourish the kernel.

BESIDES this tree, which is common in all parts of India, the Moluccas produce a singular plant, which is called sago. This tree affords a nutriment from its trunk and vital substance, its fruit being a superfluous and useless part. It grows wild in the forests, and multiplies itself by seeds and suckers. It rises to the height of thirty feet, and

IN THE EAST AND WEST INDIES.

and is about six in circumference. The bark is an inch thick. The inner rind is compofed of an affemblage of long fibres which are interwoven with each other. This double coat contains a kind of fap or gum, which falls into meal. The tree, which feems to grow merely for the ufe of man, points out the meal by a fine white powder which covers its leaves, and is a certain fign of the maturity of the fago. It is then cut down to the root, and fawn into featlings, which are divided into four quarters, for the better extracting of the fap or meal they contain. After this fubftance has been diluted in water, it is ftrained through a kind of fieve, which retains the groffer particles; the reft is thrown into earthen moulds, where it dries and hardens for fome years. The Indians eat the fago diluted with water, and fometimes baked or boiled. Through a principle of humanity, they referve the fineft part of this meal for the aged and infirm. A jelly is fometimes made of it, which is white and of a delicious flavour.

TEMPERATE, independent, and averfe from labour, thefe people had lived for ages upon the meal of the fago, and the milk of the cocoa, when the Chinefe landing by accident at the Moluccas, difcovered the clove and the nutmeg, with which valuable fpices the ancients were entirely unacquainted. They were foon admired all over India, from whence they were tranfported to Perfia and Europe. The Arabians, who at that time engroffed almoft all the trade of the univerfe, did not overlook fo lucrative a part of it. They repaired in crowds to the

celebrated

celebrated iflands, whofe productions they had already monopolized, had not the Portuguefe, who purfued them every where, deprived them of this branch of trade. Notwithftanding the fchemes that were laid to fupplant thefe conquerors, they obtained permiffion to build a fort. From this time the court of Lifbon ranked the Moluccas among the number of their provinces, and it was not long before they became fuch in reality.

WHILE Albuquerque's lieutenants enriched their country with the new productions of the eaft, that general completed the conqueft of Malabar, which would have taken advantage of his abfence to recover its liberty. After his late fuccefs, he employed the leifure he enjoyed in the midft of his conquefts, in fuppreffing the licentioufnefs of the Portuguefe; eftablifhing order in all the colonies, and regulating the difcipline of the army; in the courfe of which he difplayed an activity, fagacity, wifdom, juftice, humanity, and difintereftednefs, which did honour to his character. His good qualities made fo deep an impreffion on the minds of the Indians, that, for a long time after his death, they continued to repair to his tomb to demand juftice for the outrages committed by his fucceffors. He died at Goa in the year 1515, without riches, and out of favour with Emanuel, who had been prevailed upon to entertain fufpicions of his conduct.

The caufes of the enterprifing fpirit of the Portuguefe.

IF our aftonifhment is raifed at the number of Albuquerque's victories, and the rapidity of his conquefts, how defervedly do thofe brave men claim

claim our admiration, whom he had the honour to command in thefe expeditions! Did any nation, with fo flender a force, ever perform fuch great actions? The Portuguefe, with lefs than forty thoufand troops, ftruck terror into the empire of Morocco, the barbarous nations of Africa, the Mammelucs, the Arabians, and all the eaftern countries from the ifland of Ormus to China. With a force in the proportion of one to a hundred, they engaged troops, which, when attacked by an enemy of equal ftrength, would frequently defend their lives and poffeffions to the laft extremity. What kind of men then muft the Portuguefe have been, and what extraordinary caufes muft have confpired to produce fuch a nation of heroes!

They had been at war with the Moors near a century, when Henry of Burgundy, with feveral French knights, landed in Portugal with a defign to ferve in Caftile under the famous Cid, whofe reputation had drawn them thither. The Portuguefe invited them to lend their affiftance againft the infidels; the knights complied, and the greateft part of them fettled in Portugal. Chivalry, which has contributed as much as any other inftitution to exalt human nature, fubftituting the love of glory to the love of our country; that refined fpirit, drawn from the dregs of the barbarous ages, and calculated to repair or leffen the errors and inconveniences of the feudal government from whence it took its rife, was then revived on the banks of the Tagus, in all the fplendour it had at its firft appearance in France and England. The princes endeavoured to keep it alive, and to extend its influence by eftablifhing feveral orders formed upon the plan of the ancient ones, and calculated to infufe the fame fpirit, which was a mixture of heroifm, gallantry, and devotion.

The fovereigns raifed the fpirit of the nation ftill higher by treating the nobility in fome meafure upon a footing of equality, and by fetting bounds to their own authority. They frequently affembled their ftates general, without which properly fpeaking, there can be no nation. By thefe ftates Alphonfo was invefted with the regal authority after the taking of Lifbon; and in conjunction with them, his fucceffors, for a long time, excreifed the power of making laws. Many of thefe laws were calculated to infpire the love of great actions. The order of nobility was conferred upon thofe who had diftinguifhed themfelves by fignal fervices; by killing or taking prifoner the enemy's general, or his fquire: or by refufing to purchafe their liberty, when in the hands of the Moors, by renouncing their religion. On the other hand, whoever infulted a woman, gave falfe evidence, broke his promife, or " difguifed the truth to his fovereign," was deprived of his rank.

The wars waged by the Portuguefe in defence of their rights and liberties, were at the fame time religious wars. They partook of that fierce yet enterprifing fanaticifm, which the popes had encouraged at the time of the crufades. The Portuguefe,

Portuguese, therefore, were knights armed in defence of their properties, their wives, their children, and their kings, who were knights as well as themselves. Besides these, they were the heroes of the crusade, who in defending christianity were fighting for their country. To this may be added, that the nation was small, and its power extremely limited; it being chiefly in little states that we find that enthusiastic fondness for their country, which is utterly unknown in larger communities, that enjoy a greater security.

The principles of activity, vigour, and a noble elevation of mind, which united in the character of this nation, were not lost after the expulsion of the Moors. They pursued these enemies of their religion and government into Africa. They were engaged in several wars with the kings of Castile and Leon; and during the interval that preceded their expeditions to India, the nobility lived at a distance from cities and the court, and preserved in their castles the virtues of their ancestors, together with their portraits.

When the plan of extending conquest in Africa and Asia became the object of attention among the Portuguese; a new passion co-operated with the principles just mentioned, to give additional energy to the Portuguese spirit. This passion, which, however it might animate all the rest for the present, would soon destroy the generosity of their temper, was avarice. The vessels were crouded with adventurers, who wanted to enrich themselves,

selves, serve their country, and make profelytes. They appeared in India to be fomething more than men till the death of Albuquerque. Then riches, which were the object and reward of their conquests, introduced an univerfal corruption. The nobler paffions gave way to the pleafures of luxury, which never fail to enervate the body, and to deftroy the virtues of the mind. The weak fucceffors of the illuftrious Emanuel, and the men of mean abilities, which he himfelf fent as viceroys to India, gradually contributed to the degeneracy of the Portuguefe.

Lopez Soarez, however, who fucceeded Albuquerque, purfued his defigns. He abolifhed a barbarous cuftom that prevailed in the country of Travancor, in the neighbourhood of Calicut. The inhabitants of this region confulted forcerers concerning the deftiny of their children: if the magician promifed a happy deftiny, they were fuffered to live; if he foretold any great calamities that were to befal them, they were put to death. Soarez interpofed to preferve thefe children. He was for fome time employed in preventing the oppofition with which the Portuguefe were threatened in India; and as foon as he was relieved from his anxiety, he refolved to attempt a paffage to China.

Arrival of the Portuguefe at China. State of this empire.

The great Albuquerque had formed the fame defign. He had met with Chinefe fhips and merchants at Malacca, and conceived a high opinion of a nation whofe very failors had more politenefs, a better a better fenfe of decorum, more good nature and humanity, than were, at that time, to be found among the European nobility. He invited the Chinefe to continue their commerce with Malacca. From them he procured a particular account of the ſtrength, riches, and manners of their extenſive empire, and communicated his intelligence to the court of Portugal.

THE Chinefe nation was utterly unknown in Europe. Mark Paul, a Venetian, who had travelled to China by land, had given a defcription of it which was looked upon as fabulous. It correfponded, however, with the particulars fince tranfmitted by Albuquerque. Credit was given to this officer's teftimony, and to his account of the lucrative trade that might be carried on with this country.

IN the year 1518 a fquadron failed from Lifbon to convoy an ambaffador to China. As foon as it arrived at the iflands in the neighbourhood of Canton, it was furrounded by Chinefe veffels, which came to reconnoitre it. Ferdinand Andrada, who commanded it, did not attempt to defend himfelf: he fuffered the Chinefe to come on board; communicated the object of his voyage to the Mandarins that prefided at Canton, and fent his ambaffador on fhore, who was conducted to Pekin.

THE ambaffador was every moment prefented with fome new wonder, that ftruck him with amazement. If we confider the largenefs of the towns, the multitude of villages, the variety of canals, of which fome are navigable acrofs the empire,

empire, and others contribute to the fertility of the foil; the art of cultivating their lands, and the abundance and variety of their productions; the fagacious and mild afpect of the inhabitants, the perpetual interchange of good offices which appeared in the country and on the publick roads, and the good order preferved among thofe numberlefs crouds who were engaged in the hurry of bufinefs; we fhall not wonder at the furprize of the Portuguefe ambaffador, who had been accuftomed to the barbarous and ridiculous manners of Europe.

LET us take a tranfient view of this people. The hiftory of a nation fo well governed, is the hiftory of mankind: the reft of the world refembles the chaos of matter before it was wrought into form. After a long feries of devaftation, fociety has at length rifen to order and harmony. States and nations are produced from each other, like individuals, with this difference, that in families nature brings about the death of fome, and provides for the births of others, in a conftant and regular fucceffion: but in ftates, this rule is violated and deftroyed by the diforders of fociety, where it fometimes happens that ancient monarchies ftifle rifing republics in their births, and that a rude and favage people, rufhing like a torrent, fweep away multitudes of ftates, which are difunited and broken in pieces.

CHINA alone has been exempted from this fatality. This empire, bounded on the north by Ruffian Tartary, on the fouth by India, by Thibet on the weft, and by the ocean on the eaft,
comprehends

comprehends almoſt all the eaſtern extremity of the continent of Aſia. It is eighteen hundred leagues in circumference. It is ſaid to have laſted through a ſucceſſive ſeries of four thouſand years; nor is this antiquity in the leaſt to be wondered at. The narrow bounds of our hiſtory, and the ſmall extent of our kingdoms, which riſe and fall in a quick ſucceſſion, are the conſequence of wars, ſuperſtition, and the unfavourable circumſtances of our ſituation. But the Chineſe, who are encompaſſed and defended on all ſides by ſeas and deſerts, have, like the ancient Egyptians, given a laſting ſtability to their empire. Since their coaſts and the inland parts of their territories have been peopled and cultivated, this happy nation muſt of courſe have been the center of attraction to all the ſurrounding people; and the wandering or cantoned tribes muſt neceſſarily have gradually attached themſelves to a body of men, who ſpeak leſs frequently of the conqueſts they have made, than of the attacks they have ſuffered; and are happier in the thought of having civilized their conquerors, than they could have been in that of having deſtroyed their invaders.

In a country where the government is ſo ancient, we may every where expect to find deep traces ofe the continued force of induſtry. Its roads have been levelled with the exacteſt care; and, in general, have no greater declivity than is neceſſary to facilitate the watering of the land, which they conſider, with reaſon, as one of the greateſt helps in agriculture. They have but few, even of the moſt uſeful trees, as their fruits would

rob

rob the corn of its nourishment. There are gardens, it is true, interspersed with flowers, fine turf, shrubberies, and fountains; but however agreeable these scenes might be to an idle spectator, they seem to be concealed and removed from the public eye, as if the owners were afraid of shewing how much their amusements had encroached upon the soil that ought to be cultivated for the support of life. They have no parks or extensive forests, which are not near so serviceable to mankind by the wood they furnish, as prejudicial by preventing agriculture; and while they contribute to the pleasure of the great by the beasts that range in them, prove a real misfortune to the husbandman. In China, the beauty of a country-seat consists in its being happily situated, surrounded with an agreeable variety of cultivated fields, and interspersed with trees planted irregularly, and with some heaps of a porous stone, which at a distance have the appearance of rocks or mountains.

The hills are generally cut into terraces, supported by dry walls. Here there are reservoirs, constructed with ingenuity, for the reception of rain and spring water. It is not uncommon to see the bottom, summit and declivity of a hill watered by the same canal, by means of a number of engines of a simple construction, which save manual labour, and perform with two men what could not be done with a thousand in the ordinary way. These heights commonly yield three crops in a year. They are first sown with a kind of radish, which produces an oil; then with cotton, and
after

after that with potatoes. This is the common method of culture; but the rule is not without exception.

Upon moſt of the mountains which are incapable of being cultivated for the ſubſiſtence of man, proper trees are planted for building houſes or ſhips. Many of them contain iron, tin, and copper mines, ſufficient to ſupply the empire. The gold mines have been neglected, either becauſe their produce did not defray the expence of working them, or becauſe the gold duſt, waſhed down by the torrents, was found ſufficient for the purpoſes of exchange.

The ſandy plains, ſaved from the ravages of the ocean, (which changes its bed as rivers do their courſe, in a ſpace of time ſo exactly proportioned to their different moments, that a ſmall encroachment of the ſea cauſes a thouſand revolutions on the ſurface of the globe) form, at this day, the provinces of Nankin and Tchekiang, which are the fineſt in the empire. As the Egyptians checked the courſe of the Nile, the Chineſe have repulſed, reſtrained, and given laws to the ocean. They have re-united to the continent, tracts of land which had been disjoined by this element. They ſtill exert their endeavours to oppoſe that over-ruling effect of the earth's motion, which in conformity with the celeſtial ſyſtem drives the ocean from eaſt to weſt. To the action of the globe the Chineſe oppoſe the labours of induſtry: and while nations, the moſt celebrated in hiſtory, have, by the rage of conqueſt, increaſed the ravages that time is perpetually

petually making upon this globe; they exert such efforts to retard the progress of universal devastation, as might appear supernatural, if daily experience did not afford us strong evidence to the contrary.

To the improvements of land this nation adds, if we may be allowed the expression, the improvement of the water. The rivers, which communicate with each other by canals, and run under the walls of most of the towns, present us with the prospect of floating cities, composed of an infinite number of boats filled with people, who live constantly upon the water, and whose sole employment is fishing. The sea itself is covered with numberless vessels, whose masts, at a distance, appear like moving forests. Anson mentions it as a reproach to the fishermen belonging to these boats, that they did not give themselves a moment's intermission from their work to look at his ship, which was the largest that had ever anchored in those latitudes. But this inattention to an object, which appeared to a Chinese sailor to be of no use, though it was in the way of his profession, is, perhaps, a proof of the happiness of a people, who prefer business to matters of mere curiosity.

THE manner of culture is by no means uniform throughout this empire, but varies according to the nature of the soil and the difference of the climate. In the low countries towards the south they sow rice, which being always under water, grows to a great size, and yields two crops in a year. In the inland parts of the country, where
the

IN THE EAST AND WEST INDIES. the situation is lofty and dry, the soil produces a species of rice, which is neither so large, so well-tasted, or so nourishing, and makes the husbandman but one return in the year for his labour. In the northern parts the same kinds of grain are cultivated as in Europe, which grow in as great plenty, and are of as good a quality as in any of our most fertile countries. From one end of China to the other, there are large quantities of vegetables, particularly in the south, where together with fish they supply the place of meat, which is the general food of the other provinces. But the improvement of lands is universally understood and attended to. All the different kinds of manure are carefully preserved, and skilfully distributed to the best advantage; and that which arises from fertile lands, is applied to make them still more fertile. This grand system of nature, which is sustained by destruction and re-production, is better understood and attended to in China than in any other country in the world.

A PHILOSOPHER, whom the spirit of observation has led into their empire, has found out and explained the causes of the rural œconomy of the Chinese.

THE first of these causes is that character of industry by which these people are particularly distinguished, who in their nature require a less share of repose. Every day in the year is devoted to labour, except the first, which is employed in paying and receiving visits among relations; and the last, which is sacred to the memory of their ancestors.

ceftors. The firft is a focial duty, the latter a part of domeftic worfhip. In this nation of fages, whatever unites and civilizes mankind is religion; and religion itfelf is nothing more than the practice of the focial virtues. Thefe fober and rational people want nothing more than the controul of civil laws to make them juft; their private worfhip confifts in the love of their parents whether living or dead; and their public worfhip in the love of labour; and that labour which is held in the moft facred veneration is agriculture.

THE generofity of two of their emperors is much revered, who, preferring the interefts of the ftate to thofe of their family, kept their own children from the throne to make room for men taken from the plough. They revere the memory of thefe hufbandmen, who fowed the feeds of the happinefs and ftability of the empire in the fertile bofom of the earth; that inexhauftible fource of whatever conduces to the nourifhment, and confequently to the increafe of mankind.

IN imitation of thefe royal hufbandmen, the emperors of China become hufbandmen officially. It is one of their public functions to break up the ground in the fpring; and the parade and magnificence that accompanies this ceremony, draws together all the farmers in the neighbourhood of the capital. They flock in crouds to fee their prince perform this folemnity in honour of the firft of all the arts. It is not, as in the fables of Greece, a god, who tends the flocks of a king; it is the father of his people, who, holding the

plough

plough with his own hands, shews his children what are the true riches of the state. In a little time he repairs again to the field he has ploughed himself, to sow the seed that is most proper for the ground. The example of the prince is followed in all the provinces; and at the same seasons, the viceroys repeat the same ceremonies in the presence of a numerous concourse of husbandmen. The Europeans, who have been present at this solemnity at Canton, never speak of it without emotion; and make us regret that this festival, whose political aim is the encouragement of labour, is not established in our climate, instead of that number of religious feasts, which seem to be invented by idleness to make the country a barren waste.

It is not to be imagined, however, that the court of Pekin is really engaged in the labours of a rural life. The arts of luxury are grown to so great a height in China, that these performances can only pass for mere ceremonies. But the law which obliges the prince to shew this token of respect to the profession of husbandmen, has a tendency to promote the advantage of agriculture. The deference paid by the sovereign to public opinions contributes to perpetuate them; and the influence of opinion is the principal spring that actuates the political machine.

This influence is preserved in China by conferring honours on all husbandmen, who excel in the cultivation of the ground. When any useful discovery is made, the author of it is called to court to communicate it to the prince; and is sent by the government into the provinces, to inftruct them in his method. In a word, in this country, where nobility is not hereditary, but a mere perfonal reward indifcriminately beftowed upon merit; feveral of the magiftrates and perfons raifed to the higheft employments in the empire are chofen out of families who are folely employed in the cultivation of land.

THESE encouragements which belong to their mannners, are further feconded by the beft political inftitutions. Whatever is in its nature incapable of being divided, as the fea, rivers, canals, &c. is enjoyed in common, and is the property of no individual. Every one has the liberty of going upon the water, fifhing, and hunting; and a fubject who is in poffeffion of an eftate, whether acquired by himfelf or left by his relations, is in no danger of having his right called in queftion by the tyrannical authority of the feudal laws.

THE fmallnefs of the taxes is ftill a further encouragement to agriculture. Till lately, the proportion paid to government out of the produce of the lands, was from a tenth down to a thirtieth part of the income, according to the quality of the foil. This was the only tribute levied in China. The leading men never entertained a thought of increafing it; they would not have ventured to act in fuch direct oppofition to cuftom and opinion, which determine every thing in this empire. Some emperors and minifters, no doubt, would have been glad to attempt an innovation of this kind; but as fuch an undertaking would require time, and they

could

could not hope to live to fee its fuccefs, they did not choofe to engage in it. Men of bad principles aim at immediate enjoyment, while the virtuous fubject, extending his benevolence beyond the prefent generation, contents himfelf with forming defigns, and propagating ufeful truths, without expecting to reap any advantage from them in his own perfon.

It is but lately that conqueft and commerce have introduced new taxes into China. The Tartar emperors have laid a duty upon certain articles of provifions, metals, and merchandife. In fhort, if we may believe the Jefuit Amyot, cuftoms are eftablifhed there as well as in Europe.

It were to be wifhed, that the Europeans would imitate the Chinefe in the mode of levying their taxes; which is juft, humane, and not expenfive. Every year, at the time of harveft, the fields are meafured, and rated in proportion to their actual produce. Whether the Chinefe are as difhoneft as they are reprefented, or whether, like feveral nations among the ancients, they are only faithlefs and deceitful in their dealings with ftrangers, I fhall not take upon me to determine; but it fhould feem that government repofes fufficient confidence in them, not to vex and moleft them by thofe fearchings and troublefome vifits, fo common in the mode of taxation in Europe. The only penalty inflicted on perfons liable to be taxed, and who are too flow in the payment of the tribute demanded by the public, is to quarter old, infirm, and poor people upon them, to be maintained at their expence, till they have difcharged the debt due to government. This manner of proceeding has a tendency to awaken pity and humanity in the breast of a citizen, when he sees miserable objects and hears the cries of hunger; instead of giving him disgust, and exciting his resentment by forcible seizures and the menaces of an insolent soldiery, who come to live at discretion in a house exposed to the numberless extortions of the treasury.

In China, the taxes are levied without having recourse to those oppressive methods that are practised in Europe. The mandarins take the tenth part of the produce of the earth in kind. The officers in the municipal towns give in their account of this tribute and all other taxes to the receiver-general of the province; and the whole is lodged in the public treasury. The use that is made of this revenue prevents all frauds in collecting it; as it is well known, that a part of these duties is allotted for the maintenance of the magistrates and soldiers. The money arising from the sale of this proportion of the product of the lands is never issued from the treasury but in public exigencies. It is laid up in the magazines against times of scarcity, when the people receive what they had lent, as it were, in times of plenty.

It may naturally be expected that a nation, enjoying so many advantages, will be extremely populous; especially in a climate where, whatever reason may be assigned for it, the women are remarkably prolific, and the men do no injury to the natural vigour of their constitution by the use of strong liquors; where the climate is wholesome and tem-

temperate, and few children die in proportion to the numbers born; where the foil overpays the labour of cultivating it, not to mention the fimple and plain manner of living in ufe there, which is regulated by the ftricteft œconomy.

The Jefuits, however, who were employed by the court of Pekin to make charts of the empire, in the courfe of their undertaking difcovered fome confiderable tracts of defert land, which had efcaped the notice of the merchants who frequented only the fea-ports, and of travellers who went only by the road of Canton to the capital.

It would be impoffible to account for the want of population in fome parts of China diftant from each other, if it were not known, that, in thefe extenfive ftates, a great number of children are deftroyed foon after they are born; that feveral of thofe who efcape this cruel fate, fuffer the moft fhameful mutilation; and that of thofe who are not thus barbaroufly robbed of their fex, many are reduced to a ftate of flavery, and deprived of the comforts of marriage by tyrannical mafters; that polygamy, fo contrary to reafon and the fpirit of fociety, is univerfally practifed; that the vice which nature rejects with the utmoft abhorrence, is very common; and that the convents of the Bonzes contain little lefs than a million of perfons devoted to celebacy.

But if a few fcattered *diſtricts*, which are hardly known even in China, be deftitute of hands to cultivate them; are there not many more in which men are crouded together in fuch numbers as to incommode each other? This inconvenience is obfervable in the neighbourhood of great cities and public roads, and particularly in the southern provinces. Accordingly it appears, by the records of the empire, that a bad harvest has seldom failed to produce an insurrection.

We need go no further to find the reasons which prevent despotism from making any advances in China. It is evident from these frequent revolutions, that the people are fully sensible that a regard to the rights of property, and submission to the laws, are duties of a lower class, subordinate to the original rights of nature, and that communities are formed for the common benefit of those who enter into them. Accordingly, when the more immediate necessaries of life fail, the Chinese cease to acknowledge an authority which does not provide for their subsistence. The right of kings is founded on the regard they pay to the preservation of the people. Neither religion nor morality teach any other doctrine in China.

The emperor is well aware, that he presides over a people who submit to the laws no longer than while they promote their happiness. He is sensible, that if the spirit of tyranny, which is so common and infectious in other countries, should seize him but for a moment, such a violent opposition would be raised, that he would be expelled from the throne. Accordingly, finding himself invested with the supreme authority by a people who observe and criticise his conduct, he is far from attempting to erect himself into an object of religious superstition, and doing just as he pleases. He does not violate the sacred contract, by virtue of which he holds the sceptre,

tre. He is convinced that the people are so well acquainted with their rights, and the manner of defending them, that whenever a province complains of the mandarin who governs it, he recalls him without examination, and delivers him up to a tribunal, which proceeds against him if he is in fault; but should he even prove innocent, he is not reinstated in his employment, as it is deemed a crime to have drawn upon himself the resentment of the people. He is considered as an ignorant tutor, who should attempt to deprive a father of the love his children bear him. This compliance, which, in other countries, would nourish perpetual discontent, and occasion an infinite number of intrigues, is not attended with any inconvenience in China, where the inhabitants are naturally disposed to be mild and just, and the constitution of the state is so ordered, that its delegates have seldom any rigorous commands to execute.

The necessity of justice in the prince tends to make him more wise and intelligent. He is in China what one would gladly believe princes in all countries were, the idol of his people. It should seem that their manners and laws conspired to establish this fundamental principle, that China is a family of which the emperor is the patriarch. He does not possess his authority as a conqueror, or a legislator, but as a father: as a father he governs, rewards, and punishes. This pleasing sentiment gives him a greater power than the tyrants of other nations can possibly derive from the number of their troops, or the artifices of their ministers. It is not to be imagined what esteem and affection the Chinese

nese have for their emperor, or, as they exprefs it, their common, their univerfal father.

This public veneration is founded upon that which is eftablifhed by private education. In China, the father and mother claim an abfolute right over their children at every period of life, even when raifed to the higheft dignity. Paternal authority and filial affection are the fources of every thing in this empire: by thefe the manners are regulated, and they are the grand tie that unites the prince to his fubjects, the fubjects to their prince, and citizens to one another. The Chinefe government has gradually arrived at that point of perfection, from which all others feem to have finally and irrevocably degenerated: I mean the patriarchal governmennt, a government eftablifhed by nature itfelf.

Notwithstanding this fublime fyftem of morals, that for fo many ages has contributed to the profperity of the Chinefe empire, it would probably have experienced an infenfible change, if the chimerical diftinctions allowed to birth had deftroyed that original equality eftablifhed by nature among mankind, and which ought only to give place to fuperior abilities and fuperior merit. In all the ftates of Europe, one clafs of men affume from their infancy a pre-eminence independent of their moral character. The attention paid them from the moment of their birth, gives them the idea that they are formed for command; they foon learn to confider themfelves as a diftinct fpecies, and being fecure of a certain rank and ftation, take no pains to make themfelves worthy of it.

This

This system, to which we owe so many indifferent ministers, ignorant magistrates, and bad generals has no place in China, where nobility does not descend by hereditary right. The figure any citizen makes, begins and ends with himself. The son of the prime minister of the empire has no advantages at the moment of his birth, but those he may have derived from nature. The rank of nobility is sometimes conferred upon the ancestors of a man who has done signal services to his country; but this mark of distinction, which is merely personal, dies with its possessor, and his children derive no other advantage from it than the memory and example of his virtues.

In consequence of this perfect equality, the Chinese are enabled to establish an uniform system of education, and to inculcate correspondent principles. It is no difficult task to persuade men who are upon an equal footing by birth, that they are all brethren. This opinion gives them every advantage which would be lost if a contrary idea prevailed. A Chinese, who should abstract himself from this common fraternity, would become a solitary and miserable being, and wander as a stranger in the heart of his country.

Instead of those frivolous distinctions which are allotted to birth in almost every other country, the Chinese substitute real ones, founded entirely on personal merit. A sett of wise and intelligent men, who are honoured with the title of the learned mandarins, devote themselves to the study of all sciences necessary to qualify them for the administration of

public

public affairs. None can be admitted into this respectable society, who are not recommended by their talents and knowledge: for riches give no claim to this honour. The mandarins are at their option to fix upon proper perfons to affociate with them; and they never chufe any perfon without a previous and ftrict examination. There are different claffes of mandarins, the fucceffion to which is regulated by merit, and not by feniority.

Out of the clafs of mandarins, the emperor, according to a cuftom as ancient as the empire, elects minifters, magiftrates, governors of provinces, and officers of every denomination who are called to any employment in the ftate. As his choice can only fall upon men of tried abilities, the welfare of the people is always lodged in the hands of thofe who are worthy of fuch a truft.

In confequence of this inftitution, no dignity is hereditary except that of the crown; and even that does not always devolve to the eldeft fon; but to him whom the emperor and the council of mandarins judge moft worthy. By this method, a fpirit of virtuous emulation prevails even in the imperial family. The throne is given to merit alone, and it is affigned to the heir only in confideration of his abilities. The emperors rather chufe to appoint a fucceffor from a different family, than to intruft the reins of government to unfkilful hands.

The viceroys and magiftrates enjoy the affection of the people, at the fame time that they partake of the authority of the fovereign; and any miftakes in their adminiftration meet with the fame indulgence

dulgence that is shewn to those of the supreme legislator. They have not that tendency to sedition which prevails in this part of the world. In China there is no sett of men to form or manage a faction: as the mandarins have no rich and powerful family connections, they can derive no support but from the crown, and their own prudence. They are trained up in a way of thinking that inspires humanity, the love of order, beneficence, and respect for the laws. They take pains to iuculcate these sentiments into the people, and secure their attachment to every law, by shewing them its useful tendency. The sovereign passes no edict that does not convey some moral or political instruction. The people necessarily become acquainted with their interests, and the measures taken by government to promote them; and the better informed they are, the more likely they will be to remain quiet.

SUPERSTITION, which excites disturbances in all other countries, and either establishes tyranny, or overthrows government, has no influence in China. It is tolerated, injudiciously, perhaps, by the laws: but, at least, it never makes laws itself. No person can have any share in the government who does not belong to the class of literati, which admits of no superstition. The bonzes are not allowed to ground the duties of morality upon the doctrines of their sects, nor consequently to dispense with them. If they impose upon some part of the nation, their artifices do not affect those whose example and authority are of the greatest importance to the state.

CONFUCIUS,

Confucius, in whose actions and discourses precept was joined to example, whose memory is equally revered, and whose doctrine is equally embraced by all classes and sects whatsoever, was the founder of the national religion of China. His code contains a system of natural law, which ought to be the ground-work of all religions, the rule of society, and standard of all governments. He taught that reason was an emanation of the Deity; and that the supreme law consisted in the harmony between nature and reason. The religion that runs in opposition to these two guides of human life, does not come from heaven.

As the Chinese have no term for God, they say that heaven is God. *But,* says the emperor Chang-chi, in an edict published in 1710, *it is not to the visible and material heaven that we offer our sacrifices, but to the Lord of heaven.* Thus atheism, though not uncommon in China, is not publicly professed. It is neither the characteristic of a sect, nor an object of persecution; but is tolerated as well as superstition.

The emperor, who is sole pontiff, is likewise the judge in matters of religion; but as the national worship was made for the government, not the government for it; and as both were designed to be subservient to the ends of society; it is neither the interest nor inclination of the sovereign to employ the two-fold authority lodged in his hands, for the purposes of oppression. If on the one hand the doctrines and ceremonies of the hierarchy do not prevent the prince from making an ill use of absolute authority; he is more powerfully restrained on

IN THE EAST AND WEST INDIES.

the other, by the general influence of the national manners.

Any attempt to change thefe manners would be attended with the greateft difficulty, becaufe they are inculcated by a mode of education which is, perhaps, the beft we are acquainted with. The Chinefe do not make a point of inftructing their children till they are five years old. They are then taught to write words or hieroglyphics, which reprefent fenfible objects, of which at the fame time they endeavour to give them clear ideas. Afterwards their memory is ftored with fententious verfes containing precepts of morality, which they are taught to reduce to practice. As they advance in years they are inftructed in the philofophy of Confucius. This is the manner of education among the ordinary ranks. The children who are defigned for pofts of honour, begin in the fame manner; but intermix other ftudies relative to human conduct in the different ftations of life.

In China, the manners take their complexion from the laws, and are preferved by common ufage, which is likewife prefcribed by the laws. The Chinefe have a greater number of precepts, relating to the moft common actions, than any other people in the world. Their code of politenefs is very voluminous; the loweft citizen is inftructed in it, and obferves it with the fame exactnefs as the mandarins and the court.

The laws in this code, like all the reft, are formed with a view of keeping up the opinion that China is but one great family, and of promoting that

that regard and mutual affection in the citizens, which is due to each other as brethren. These rights and customs tend to preserve the manners. Sometimes, indeed, ceremonies are substituted for sentiment; but how often are they the means of reviving it! They compose a kind of constant homage that is paid to virtue; and is calculated to engage the attention of youth. This homage preserves the respect due to virtue herself; and if it sometimes leads to hypocrisy, it encourages at least a laudable zeal. Tribunals are erected to take cognizance of transgressions against the customs; as well as to punish crimes, and reward merit. Moderate penalties are inflicted upon crimes, and virtue is distinguished by marks of honour. Honour is accordingly one of the principles that actuate the Chinese government: and though it is not the leading one, operates more strongly than fear, and more feebly than affection.

UNDER the influence of such institutions, one should expect, that China would be the country in the whole world, where men would be most humane. Accordingly the humanity of the Chinese is conspicuous on those occasions, where it should seem, that virtue could have no other object but justice; and that justice could not be executed without severity. Their prisoners are confined in neat and commodious apartments, where they are well taken care of even to the moment when they suffer. It frequently happens, that the only punishment inflicted on a rich man amounts to no more than obliging him for a certain time to maintain or

clothe

clothe some old men and orphans at his own expence. Our moral and political romances form the real history of the Chinese, who have regulated all the actions of men with such an exact nicety, that they have scarcely any need of sentiment. Yet they do not fail to cultivate the latter, in order to give a proper estimation to the former.

The spirit of patriotism, that spirit, without which states are mere colonies, and not nations, is stronger, perhaps, and more active among the Chinese than it is found in any republic. It is common to see them voluntarily contributing their labour to repair the public roads: the rich build places of shelter upon them for the use of travellers; and others plant trees there. Such actions, which are proofs of a beneficent humanity rather than an ostentation of generosity, are far from being uncommon in China.

There have been times, when they have been frequent; and others, when they have been less so; but the corruption which was the cause of the latter, brought on a revolution, and the manners of the people were reformed. They suffered by the late invasion of the Tartars: they are now recovering, in proportion as the princes of that victorious nation lay aside the superstitions of their own country, to adopt the principles of the nation they have conquered; and in proportion as they improve in the knowledge of those books, which the Chinese call canonical.

It cannot be long before we see the amiable character of this nation entirely revived; that fraternal, and kindred principle; thofe enchanting focial ties, which foften the manners of the people, and attach them inviolably to the laws. Political errors and vices cannot take deep root in a country where no perfons are ever promoted to public employments, but fuch as are of the fect of the learned, whofe fole occupation is to inftruct themfelves in the principles of morality and government. As long as real knowledge fhall be held in eftimation, as long as it fhall continue to lead to public honours, there will exift among the people of China a fund of reafon and virtue, which will not be found among other nations.

If this picture of the manners of the Chinefe fhould be different from that drawn by other writers, it is not, peahaps, impoffible to reconcile opinions fo feemingly contradictory. China may be confidered in two diftinct points of view. If we ftudy the inhabitants as they appear in the fea-ports and great towns, we fhall be difgufted at their cowardice, knavery and avarice: but in the other parts of the empire, particularly in the country, we fhall find their manners domeftic, focial and patriotic. It would be difficult to point out a more virtuous, humane, and intelligent people.

It muft, however, be acknowledged, that the greateft part of thofe improvements, which depend upon theories at all complicated, are not fo far advanced there, as might naturally be expected from that ancient, active, and diligent people, who have fo long had a clue to them. But this riddle is not inexplicable. The Chinefe language requires a long and laborious ftudy, fcarcely to be comprehended

within

within the term of a man's life. The rights and ceremonies which they obferve upon every occafion, afford more exercife for their memory than their fenfibility. Their manners are calulated to check the impulfes of the foul, and weaken its operations. Too affiduous in the purfuit of what is ufeful, they have no opportunity of launching out into the extenfive regions of imagination. An exceffive veneration for antiquity, makes them the flaves of whatever is eftablifhed. All thefe caufes united, muft neceffarily have ftifled, among the Chinefe, the fpirit of invention. It requires ages with them to bring any thing to perfection; and whoever reflects on the ftate, in which arts and fciences were found among them three hundred years ago, muft be convinced of the extraordinary antiquity of their empire.

THE low ftate of learning, and of the fine arts in China, may perhaps be further owing to the very perfection of its government, and fyftem of policy. This paradox has its foundation in reafon. Where the ftudy of the laws holds the firft rank in a nation, and is rewarded with an appointment in the adminiftration, inftead of a poft in the academy; where learning is applied to the regulation of manners, or the maintenance of the public weal; where the fame nation is exceedingly populous, and requires a conftant attention in its learned members to make fubfiftence keep an equal pace with population; where every individual, befides the duties he owes to the public, which take a confiderable time to be well underftood, has particular duties arising from the claims of his family or profession: in such a nation the speculative and ornamental parts of science cannot be expected to arrive at that height of splendour they have attained in Europe. But the Chinese, who are only our scholars in the arts of luxury and vanity, are our masters in the science of good government. They study how to increase, not how to diminish the number of inhabitants.

One of the arts in which the Chinese have made the least progress, is that of war. It is natural to imagine, that a nation, whose whole conduct, like that of infants, is influenced by ceremonies, precepts, and customs either of private or public institution, must consequently be pliant, moderate, and inclined to tranquillity both at home and abroad. Reason and reflection, while they cherish sentiments like these, leave no room for that enthusiasm, which constitutes the hero and the warrior. The spirit of humanity, which they imbibe in their tender years, makes them look with abhorrence on those sanguinary scenes of rapine and massacre, that are so familiar to nations of a warlike turn. With such dispositions, can we wonder that the Chinese are not warriors? They have soldiers without number, but totally undisciplined, except in the single article of obedience, being still more deficient in military manœuvres than in courage. In their wars with the Tartars, the Chinese knew not how to fight, and only stood to be killed. Their attachment to their government, their country, and their laws, may supply the want of a warlike spirit,

IN THE EAST AND WEST INDIES.

rit, but will never fupply the want of good arms, and military fkill. When a nation has found the art of fubduing its conquerors by its manners, it has no occafion to overcome its enemies by force of arms.

Such is the empire of China fo much talked of, and fo little known. Such it was, when the Portuguefe landed there. They might have learned in it leffons of wifdom and government, but they thought of nothing but enriching themfelves, and propagating their religion. Thomas Perez, their ambaffador, found the court of Pekin difpofed to favour his nation, whofe fame had fpread itfelf throughout Afia. It had already attracted the efteem of the Chinefe, which the conduct of Ferdinand Andrada, who commanded the Portuguefe fquadron, tended ftill further to increafe. He vifited all the coafts of China, and traded with the natives. When he was on the point of departure, he made proclamation in the ports he had put into, that if any one had been injured by a Portuguefe, and would make it known, he fhould receive fatisfaction. The ports of China were now upon the point of being opened to them : Thomas Perez was juft about concluding a treaty, when Simon Andrada, brother to Ferdinand, appeared on the coafts with a frefh fquadron. This commander treated the Chinefe in the fame manner as the Portuguefe had, for fome time, treated all the people of Afia. He built a fort without permiffion, in the ifland of Taman, from whence he took opportunities of pillaging, and extorting money from all the ships bound from or to the ports of China. He carried off young girls from the coast; he seized upon Chinese men, and made them slaves; he gave himself up to the most licentious acts of piracy, and the most shameful dissoluteness. The sailors and soldiers under his command, followed his example. The Chinese enraged at these outrages fitted out a large fleet: the Portuguese defended themselves courageously, and escaped by making their way through the enemy's fleet. The emperor imprisoned Thomas Perez, who died in confinement, and the Portuguese nation was banished from China for some years. After this, the Chinese relaxed, and gave permission to the Portuguese to trade at the port of Sancian, to which place they brought gold from Africa, spices from the Molucca islands, and from Ceylon elephants teeth, and some precious stones. In return they took silks of every kind, china, gums, medicinal herbs, and tea, which is since become so necessary a commodity to the northern nations of Europe.

THE Portuguese contented themselves with the huts and factories they had at Sancian, and the liberty granted to their trade by the Chinese government, till an opportunity offered of establishing themselves upon a footing more solid, and less dependent upon the mandarins, who had the command of the coast.

A PIRATE, named Tokang-fi-loo, whose successes had made him powerful, had seized upon the island of Macao, from whence he blocked up the ports of China, and even proceeded so far as to lay siege to Canton.

IN THE EAST AND WEST INDIES.

Canton. The neighbouring mandarins had recourse to the Portuguese, who had ships in the harbour of Sancian; they haftened to the relief of Canton, raifed the fiege, and obtained a complete victory over the pirate, whom they purfued as far as Macao, where he killed himfelf.

THE emperor of China being informed of the fervice the Portuguefe had rendered him on this occafion, beftowed Macao on them, as a mark of his gratitude. They received this grant with joy, and built a town which became very flourifhing, and was advantageoufly fituated for the trade they foon after entered into with Japan.

IN the year 1542, it happened that a Portuguefe veffel was fortunately driven by a ftorm on the coaft of thofe celebrated iflands. The crew were hofpitably received, and obtained of the natives every thing they wanted to refrefh, and refit them for the fea. When they arrived at Goa, they reported what they had feen, and informed the viceroy, that a new country, not lefs rich than populous, prefented itfelf to the zeal of miffionaries, and the induftry of merchants. Both miffionaries and merchants embarked without delay for Japan.

THEY found a great empire, which is, perhaps, the moft ancient of any in the world, except that of China; its annals are not without a great mixture of fable, but it appears beyond a doubt, that in the year 660, Sin-chu founded the monarchy, which has ever fince been continued in the fame family. Thefe fovereigns called Dairos, were at the fame time the kings, and the pontiffs of the nation; and

The beginning of the Portuguefe trade in Japan. The ftate of the Japanefe iflands.

by virtue of thefe united powers got the whole extent of the fupreme authority into their hands. The perfon of the Dairos was facred, they were confidered as the defcendents, and reprefentatives of the gods. The leaft difobedience to the moft trifling of their laws, was looked upon as a crime fearcely to be expiated by the fevereft punifhments; nor were they confined to the offender alone, his whole family was involved in the confequences of his crime.

About the eleventh century thefe princes, who, no doubt, were more jealous of the pleafing prerogatives of priefthood, than of the troublefome rights of royalty, divided the ftate into feveral governments, and intrufted the adminiftration of them to fuch of the nobility as were diftinguifhed for their knowledge and wifdom.

By this means the unlimited power of the Dairos fuffered a confiderable change. The affairs of the empire were left to fluctuate at all adventures. The reftlefs and quick-fighted ambition of their viceroys took advantage of this inattention to bring about a variety of revolutions. By degrees they began to depart from the allegiance they had fworn to preferve. They made war upon each other, and even upon their fovereign. An abfolute independence was the confequence of thefe commotions; fuch was the ftate of Japan, when it was difcovered by the Portuguefe.

The great iflands, of which this empire is compofed, being fituated in a tempeftuous climate furrounded by ftorms, agitated by volcanos, and fubject to thofe great natural events which imprefs terror on the human mind, were inhabited by a people entirely

entirely addicted to superstition, but divided into several sects. That of Xinto is the ancient established religion of the country: it acknowledges a supreme being, and the immortality of the soul; and pays adoration to a multitude of gods, saints, or camis, that is to say, the souls of great men, who have been the support and ornament of their country. It is by the authority of this religion, that the Dairo, high-priest of the gods from whom he claimed his descent, had long reigned over his subjects with that despotic sway, with which superstition governs the mind. Being both emperor and high-priest, he had rendered religion, in some respects, useful to his people, which is not absolutely impossible in countries where the sacerdotal and civil power are united in the same person.

It does not appear that the sect of Xinto has had the madness, which of all others is the most dangerous to morality, to fix a criminal stigma on actions innocent in themselves. Far from encouraging that gloomy fanaticism and fear of the gods, which is inspired by almost all other religions, the Xinto sect had applied itself to prevent, or at least to moderate this disorder of the imagination, by instituting festivals, which were celebrated three times in every month. They were dedicated to friendly visits, feasts, and rejoicings. The priests of Xinto taught, that the innocent pleasures of mankind are agreeable to the deity, and that the best method of paying devotion to the camis is to imitate their virtues, and to enjoy in this world that happiness they enjoy in another. In consequence of this tenet, the Japanese,

nese, after having put up their prayers in the temples, which are always situated in the midst of groves, resorted to courtezans, who commonly inhabited places consecrated to love and devotion, and composed a religious community under the direction of an order of monks, who received a share of the profits arising from this pious compliance with the dictates of nature.

The Budzoists are another sect in Japan, of which Budzo was the founder. Their doctrine was nearly the same with that of the sect of Xinto; over which they hoped to gain a superiority by the severity of their morals. Besides Amida, the deity of the Xintoists, the Budzoists worshipped a kind of mediator between God and mankind. They likewise worshipped other mediatorial divinities between men and Amida. The professors of this religion flattered themselves, that they should prevail over the religion of Xinto by the multitude of their precepts, the excess of their austerity, their devotions and mortifications.

The spirit of Budzoism is dreadful. It breathes nothing but penitence, excessive fear, and cruel severity. Of all fanaticisms it is the most terrible. The monks of this sect oblige their disciples to pass one half of their lives in penance, to expiate imaginary sins; and inflict upon them the greatest part of that penance themselves, with a tyranny and cruelty, of which one may conceive an idea, from the inquisitors in Spain; with this difference, that the Japanese fathers are themselves the butchers of these voluntary victims to superstition;

whereas

IN THE EAST AND WEST INDIES.

whereas the inquisitors are only the judges of those sins and punishments, which they have themselves devised and invented. The Budzoist priests keep the minds of their followers in a continual state of torture, between remorse and expiations. Their religion is so over-loaded with precepts, that it is not possible to observe them. They represent their gods as always desirous to punish, and always offended.

It may be readily imagined, what effects so horrible a superstition must have on the character of the people, and to what degree of ferocity it hath brought them. The lights of a sound morality, a little philosophy, and a prudent system of education might have remedied these laws, this government, and this religion; which conspire to make mankind more savage in society with his own species, than if he lived in the woods, and had no companions but the monsters that roam about the deserts.

In China, they put into the hands of children books of instruction, which contain a detail of their duties, and teach them the advantages of virtue. The Japanese children are made to get by heart poems in which the actions of their forefathers are celebrated, a contempt of life is inculcated, and suicide is set up as the most heroic of all actions. These songs and poems, which are said to be full of energy and beauty, beget enthusiasm. The Chinese education tends to regulate the soul, and keep it in order: the Japanese, to inflame and excite it to heroism. These are guided through life by sentiment; the Chinese by reason and custom.

The Chinese aim only at truth in their writings, and place their happiness in a state of tranquillity. The Japanese have a quick relish of pleasures, and would rather suffer, than be without feeling. In fine, the Chinese seem to wish to counteract the violence and impetuosity of the soul; the Japanese to keep it from sinking into a state of languor and inactivity.

It is natural to imagine that people of this character must be fond of novelty. The Portuguese were accordingly received with all possible demonstrations of joy. All the ports were open to them. All the petty princes of the country invited them to their provinces: each contending who should give them the most valuable advantages, grant them the most privileges, and shew them the greatest civilities. These merchants established a prodigious trade. The Portuguese carried thither the commodities of India which they brought from different markets; and Macao served as a repository for their European goods. Immense quantities of the productions of Europe and Asia were consumed by the Dairo, the usurpers of his rights, the nobles, and the whole nation. But what had they to give in return?

The country of Japan is in general mountainous, stony, and by no means fertile. Its produce in rice, barley, and wheat, which are the only crops it admits of, is not sufficient for the maintenance of its numerous inhabitants; who, notwithstanding their activity, foresight, and frugality, must perish with famine, if the sea did not supply them with

great

IN THE EAST AND WEST INDIES.
great quantities of fish. The empire affords no productions proper for exportation; nor do the mechanic arts furnish any article of trade except works in steel, which are the best we are acquainted with.

WERE it not for the advantages it derives from its mines of gold, silver, and copper, which are the richest in Asia, and perhaps in the whole world, Japan could not support its own expences. The Portuguese every year carried off quantities of these metals, to the amount of fourteen or fifteen millions of livres *. They married also the richest of the Japanese heiresses, and allied themselves to the most powerful families.

WITH such advantages, the avarice, as well as the ambition of the Portuguese might have been satisfied. They were masters of the coast of Guinea, Arabia, Persia, and the two peninsulas of India. They were possessed of the Moluccas, Ceylon, and the isles of Sunda, while their settlement at Macao infured to them the commerce of China and Japan.

Extent of the Portuguese dominions in India.

THROUGHOUT this immense tract, the will of the Portuguese was the supreme law. Earth and sea acknowledged their sovereignty. Their authority was so absolute, that things and persons were dependent upon them, and moved entirely by their directions. No nation or private person dared to make voyages, or carry on trade, without obtaining their permission and passport. Those who had this liberty granted them, were prohibited

* Upon an average, about 634,000l.

from

from trading in cinnamon, ginger, pepper, timber, iron, steel, lead, tin, and arms, of which the conquerors referved to themfelves the exclufive benefit. A number of valuable articles, by which fo many nations have fince enriched themfelves, and which then bore a higher price on account of their novelty, were entirely ingroffed by the Portuguefe. In confequence of this monopoly, the prices of the produce and manufactures both in Europe and Afia were regulated at their difcretion.

In the midft of fo much glory, wealth, and conqueft, the Portuguefe had not neglected that part of Africa, which lies between the cape of Good Hope and the Red fea, and has in all ages been famed for the richnefs of its productions. The poffeffion of this country was on many accounts an important object: the Arabians had been fettled there for feveral ages, and their numbers were greatly increafed. They had formed along the coaft of Zanguebar feveral fmall independent fovereignties, fome of which made a confiderable figure, and almoft all of them were in good condition. The flourifhing ftate of thefe fettlements was owing to mines of gold and filver, which they found within their refpective territories, the produce of which enabled them to purchafe the commodities of India. To poffefs themfelves of this treafure, and to deprive their competitors of it, was looked upon by the Portuguefe as an indifpenfable duty. Agreeable to this principle, thefe Arabian merchants were attacked, and without much difficulty fubdued, about the year 1508.

Upon

IN THE EAST AND WEST INDIES.

Upon their ruin was established an empire, extending from Sofala as far as Melinda, of which the island of Mosambique was made the center. This island is separated from the continent only by a narrow channel, and is no more than two leagues in circumference. Its port, which is excellent, and wants no advantage but a purer air, was fixed upon as a place for the vessels of the conqueror to put in at, and as a staple for all their merchandise. Here they used to wait for those settled winds, which at certain times of the year blow without intermission from the African to the Indian coasts, as at other times of the year they blow in an opposite direction from the coasts of India to those of Africa.

THESE successes properly improved might have formed a power so considerable, that it could not have been shaken; but the vices and folly of some of their chiefs, the abuse of riches and of power, the wantonness of victory, the distance of their own country, changed the character of the Portuguese. Religious zeal, which had added so much force and activity to their courage, now produced in them nothing but ferocity. They made no scruple of pillaging, cheating, and enslaving the idolaters. They supposed that the Pope, in bestowing the kingdoms of Asia upon the Portuguese monarchs, had not with-holden the property of individuals from their subjects. Being absolute masters of the eastern seas, they extorted a tribute from the ships of every country; they ravaged the coasts, insulted the princes, and became

Degeneracy of the Portuguese in India.

became in a short time the terror and scourge of all nations.

The king of Sidor was carried off from his own palace, and murdered with his children, whom he had intrusted to the care of the Portuguese.

At Ceylon, the people were not suffered to cultivate the earth, except for their new masters, who treated them with the greatest barbarity.

At Goa they had established the inquisition, and whoever was rich became a prey to the ministers of that infamous tribunal.

Faria, who was sent out against the pirates from Malacca, China, and other parts, made a descent on the island of Calampui, and plundered the sepulchres of the Chinese emperors.

Souza caused all the pagodas on the Malabar coast to be destroyed, and his people inhumanly massacred the wretched Indians, who went to weep over the ruins of their temples.

Correa terminated an obstinate war with the king of Pegu, and both parties were to swear on the books of their several religions to observe the treaty. Correa swore on a collection of songs, and thought by this vile stratagem to elude his engagement.

Nuno d'Acughna resolved to make himself master of the island of Daman on the coast of Cambaya; the inhabitants offered to surrender it to him, if he would permit them to carry off their treasures. This request was refused, and Nuno put them all to the sword.

Diego de Silveira was cruizing in the Red sea. A vessel richly laden saluted him. The captain

IN THE EAST AND WEST INDIES.

captain came on board and gave him a letter from a Portuguefe general, which was to be his paffport. The letter contained only thefe words: *I defire the captains of fhips belonging to the king of Portugal to feize upon this moorifh veffel, as lawful prize.*

In a fhort time the Portuguefe preferved no more humanity or good faith with each other than with the natives. Almoft all the ftates, where they had the command, were divided into factions.

There prevailed every where in their manners a mixture of avarice, debauchery, cruelty and devotion. They had moft of them feven or eight concubines, whom they kept to work with the utmoft rigour, and forced from them the money they gained by their labour. Such treatment of women was very repugnant to the fpirit of chivalry.

The chiefs and principal officers admitted to their table a multitude of thofe finging and dancing women, with which India abounds. Effeminacy introduced itfelf into their houfes and armies. The officers marched to meet the enemy in palanquins. That brilliant courage, which had fubdued fo many nations, exifted no longer among them. The Portuguefe were with difficulty brought to fight, except where there was a profpect of plunder. In a fhort time the king of Portugal no longer received the produce of the tribute, which was paid him by more than one hundred and fifty eaftern princes. This money was loft in its way from them to him. Such corruption prevailed in the finances, that the tributes of fovereigns, the revenues of provinces, which ought to have been immenſe, the taxes levied in gold, ſilver, and ſpices, on the inhabitants of the continent and iſlands, were not ſufficient to keep up a few citadels, and to fit out the ſhipping that was neceſſary for the protection of trade.

It is a melancholy circumſtance to contemplate the fall of nations. Let us haſten to the adminiſtration of Don Juan da Caſtro, who reſtored to the Portugueſe ſome part of their virtue.

Castro was a man of much knowledge, confidering the age he lived in. He poſſeſſed a noble and elevated ſoul; and the ſtudy of the ancients had preſerved in him that love of glory and of his country, which was ſo common among the Greeks and Romans.

In the beginning of his wiſe and glorious adminiſtration, Cojé-Sophar, miniſter of Mahmoud king of Cambaya, had inſpired his maſter with a deſign of attacking the Portugueſe. This man, whoſe father is ſaid to have been an Italian, and his mother a Greek, had raiſed himſelf from ſlavery to the conduct of the ſtate, and the command of armies. He had embraced Mohammediſm, and, though he had really no religion, he knew how to avail himſelf of the averſion the people had conceived againſt the Portugueſe, on account of the contempt they ſhewed for the religions of the country. He engaged in his ſervice experienced officers, veteran ſoldiers, able engineers, and even founders, whom he procured from Conſtantinople. His preparations ſeemed intended againſt the Mogul or the Patans,

IN THE EAST AND WEST INDIES.

tans, and when the Portuguese least expected it, he attacked and made himself master of Diu, and laid siege to the citadel.

This place, which is situated on a little island upon the coast of Guzarat, had always been considered as the key of India in those times, when navigators never launched beyond the coast; and Surat was the great staple of the east. From the arrival of Gama, it had been constantly an object of ambition to the Portuguese, into whose hands it fell at length in the time of d'Acughna. Mascarenhas, who was governor of it at the juncture we are speaking of, and should have had nine hundred men, had only three: the rest of his garrison, by an abuse very common in those days, were employed in trade at the different towns upon the coast. He must have surrendered, if he had not received immediate assistance. Castro sent him a reinforcement under the command of his son, who was killed in the attack. Cojé-Sophar shared the same fate; but his death did not slacken the operations of the siege.

Castro instituted funeral games in honour of those who fell in defence of their country. He congratulated their parents in the name of the government, and received congratulations himself on the death of his eldest son. His second presided at the funeral games, and marched immediately after for Diu, to deserve, as it were, the honours he had just been paying to his brother. The garrison repulsed the enemy in every attack, and signalized themselves every day by extraordinary actions. In the eyes of the Indians the Portuguese were more than men. *Happily,* faid they, *providence has decreed that there fhould be but as few of them as there are of tygers and lions, leaft they fhould exterminate the human fpecies.*

CASTRO himfelf headed a larger reinforcement than thofe he had fent. He threw himfelf into the citadel with provifions, and above four thoufand men. It was debated, whether they fhould give battle. The reafons on both fides were difcuſſed. Garcias de Sâ, an old officer, commanded filence; *Ye have all fpoken,* faid he, *now let us fight.* Caftro was of the fame opinion. The Portuguefe marched out to the enemy's intrenchments, and gained a fignal victory. After having raifed the fiege, it was neceffary to repair the citadel. They were in want of money, and Caftro borrowed it on his own credit.

AT his return to Goa, he wifhed to give his army the honours of a triumph after the manner of the ancients. He thought that fuch honours would ferve to revive the warlike fpirit of the Portuguefe, and that the pomp of the ceremony might have a great effect on the imagination of the people. At his entry the gates of the city were ornamented with triumphal arches; the ftreets were lined with tapeftry; the women appeared at the windows in magnificent habits, and fcattered flowers and perfumes upon the conquerors; while the people danced to the found of mufical inftruments. The royal ftandard was carried before the victorious foldiers, who marched in order. The viceroy crowned with branches of palm rode on a fuperb car: the generals

generals of the enemy followed it, and after them the foldiers that had been made prifoners. The colours that had been taken from them, were carried in proceffion reverfed and dragging on the ground, and were followed by their artillery and baggage. Reprefentations of the citadel they had delivered, and of the battle they had gained, enhanced the fplendour of the fpectacle. Verfes, fongs, orations, firing of cannon, all concurred to render the feftival magnificent, agreeable, and ftriking.

Accounts of this triumph were brought to Europe. The wits condemned it as ridiculous, the bigots as profane. The queen of Portugal faid upon the occafion, *That Caftro had conquered like a chriftian hero, and triumphed like a pagan one.*

The vigour of the Portuguefe, which Caftro had re-animated, did not long continue. Corruption made daily advances among the citizens of every clafs. One of the viceroys fet up boxes in the principal towns, in which any perfon might put memorials and articles of intelligence. Such a method might be very ufeful, and tend to a reformation of abufes in an enlightened country, where the morals of the inhabitants were not totally fpoiled, but among a fuperftitious and corrupt people of what fervice could it be?

The original conquerors of India were none of them now in being, and their country exhaufted by too many enterprizes and colonies was not in a capacity to replace them. The defenders of the Portuguefe fettlements were born in Afia; their opulence, the foftnefs of the climate, the manner of living, and, perhaps, the nature of the food, had taken from them much of the intrepidity of their forefathers. At the fame time that they gave themfelves up to all thofe exceffes which make men hated, they had not courage enough left to make themfelves feared. They were monfters; poifon, fire, affaffination, every fort of crime was become familiar to them; nor were they private perfons only who were guilty of fuch practices; men in office fet them the example! They maffacred the natives; they deftroyed one another. The governor, who was juft arrived, loaded his predeceffor with irons, that he might deprive him of his wealth. The diftance of the fcene, falfe witneffes and large bribes fecured every crime from punifhment.

The ifland of Amboyna was the firft to avenge itfelf. A Portuguefe had at a public feftival feized upon a very beautiful woman, and regardlefs of all decency, had proceeded to the greateft of outrages. One of the iflanders, named Genulio, armed his fellow-citizens; after which he called together the Portuguefe, and addreffed them in the following manner: " To revenge affronts of fo cruel a na-
" ture as thofe we have received from you, would
" require actions, not words: yet we will fpeak to
" you. You preach to us a deity, who delights,
" you fay, in generous actions; but theft, murder,
" obfcenity, and drunkennefs, are your common
" practice; your hearts are inflamed with every
" vice. Our manners can never agree with yours:
" nature forefaw this, when fhe feparated us by im-
" menfe feas, and ye have overleaped her barriers.
" This

IN THE EAST AND WEST INDIES.

" This audacity, of which ye are not afhamed to
" boaft, is a proof of the corruption of your
" hearts. Take my advice; leave to their repofe
" thefe nations that refemble you fo little; go, fix
" your habitations among thofe who are as brutal as
" yourfelves; an intercourfe with you would be more
" fatal to us than all the evils which it is in the
" power of your God to inflict upon us. We re-
" nounce your alliance for ever : your arms are fu-
" perior to ours; but we are more juft than you,
" and we do not fear you. The Itons are from this
" day your enemies; fly from their country, and
" beware how you approach it again."

THIS harangue, which thirty years before would have brought on the deftruction of Amboyna, was liftened to with a degree of patience that fully demonftrated what change had taken place among the Portuguefe.

EQUALLY detefted in every quarter, they faw a confederacy forming to expel them from the eaft. All the great powers of India entered into the league, and for two or three years carried on their preparations in fecret. The court of Lifbon was informed of them; and the reigning king Sebaftian, who, if it had not been for his fuperftition, would have been a great prince, difpatched Ataida and all the Portuguefe, who had diftinguifhed themfelves in the wars of Europe, to India.

THE general opinion on their arrival was to abandon the diftant fettlements, and affemble their forces on the Malabar coaft, and in the neighbourhood of Goa. Although Ataida was of opinion that

that too great a number of settlements had been formed, he did not like the appearance of sacrificing them. *Comrades,* said he, *I mean to preserve all, and so long as I live, the enemy shall not gain an inch of ground.* Immediately upon this he sent succours to all the places that were in danger, and made the necessary dispositions for defending Goa.

The Zamorin attacked Manjalor, Cochin, and Cananor. The king of Cambaya attacked Chaul, Daman, and Baichaim. The king of Achem laid siege to Malacca. The king of Ternate made war upon the Portuguese in the Moluccas. Agalachem, a tributary to the Mogul, imprisoned the Portuguese merchants at Surat. The queen of Gareopa endeavoured to drive them out of Onor.

Ataida, in the midst of the care and trouble attending the siege of Goa, sent five ships to Surat, which obliged Agalachem to set the Portuguese, whom he had seized, at liberty. Thirteen ships were dispatched to Malacca; upon which the king of Achem and his allies abandoned the siege. Besides these, Ataida fitted out even the vessels which were employed every year to carry tribute and merchandise to Lisbon. It was represented to him, that instead of depriving himself of the assistance of men who were to go on board this fleet, he should preserve them for the defence of India. *We shall be enough without them,* said he; *the state is in distress, and its hopes must not be disappointed.* This reply surprised his opponents, and the fleet sailed. At the time when the place was most vigorously pressed by Idalcan, Ataida sent troops to the succour of Cochin, and ships to Ceylon. The archbishop, whose authority was unlimited, interposed to prevent it. *Sir*, replied Ataida, *you understand nothing of these affairs; content yourself with recommending them to the blessing of God.* The Portuguese, who came from Europe, exhibited prodigies of valour during this siege. It was oftentimes with difficulty, that Ataida could restrain them from throwing away their lives. Many of them would sally out in the night, contrary to his orders, to attack the besiegers in their lines.

The viceroy did not depend so entirely on the force of his arms, as to reject the assistance of policy. He was informed, that Idalcan was governed by one of his mistresses, and that she was in the camp with him. Women who devote themselves to the pleasures of princes are generally slaves to ambition, and unacquainted with those virtues which love inspires. The mistress of Idalcan suffered herself to be corrupted, and sold to Ataida her lover's secrets. Idalcan was aware of the treason, but could not discover the traitor. At last, after ten months spent in toil and action, his tents destroyed, his troops diminished, his elephants killed, and his cavalry unable to serve; this prince, overcome by the genius of Ataida, raised the siege, and retreated in shame and despair.

ATAIDA marched without delay to the assistance of Chaul, which was besieged by Nizam-al-Muluck, king of Cambaya, at the head of more than a hundred thousand men. The defence of Chaul had been conducted with as much intrepidity as that of Goa. It was followed by a great victory, which

which Ataida, with a handful of men, obtained over a numerous army, difciplined by a long fiege.

ATAIDA, after this, marched againſt the Zamorin, defeated and obliged him to ſign a treaty, by which he engaged never to maintain any ſhips of war.

THE Portugueſe became throughout the eaſt what they were under the immediate conduct of Ataida. A ſingle ſhip, commanded by Lopez Carafco, fought for three days ſucceſſively againſt the whole fleet of the king of Achem. In the middle of the engagement word was brought to Lopez's ſon, that his father was killed: *we have one brave man the leſs*, ſaid he; *we muſt conquer, or deſerve to die like him.* Saying this, he took the command of the ſhip, and forcing his way in triumph through the enemy's fleet, anchored before Malacca.

NOR was courage the only virtue that revived among the Portugueſe at this period, ſo powerful is the aſcendant of a great man, even over the moſt corrupt nations. Thomas de Sofa had got as a ſlave a beautiful girl, who had not long before been promiſed to a young man that was in love with her. Hearing of the misfortune of his miſtreſs, he flew to throw himſelf at her feet, and partake of her chains. Sofa was preſent at their interview; they embraced, and melted into tears. *I give you your liberty*, ſaid the Portugueſe general; *go and live happy elſewhere.*

The management of the public money was likewiſe reformed by Ataida, who reſtrained thoſe abuſes, which are moſt injurious to ſtates, and moſt

difficult

IN THE EAST AND WEST INDIES.

difficult to be reftrained. But this good order, this returning heroifm, this glorious moment, did not furvive his adminiftration.

AT the death of Sebaftian, Portugal funk into a kind of anarchy, and was by degrees reduced under the dominion of Philip the Second. From this æra the Portuguefe in India ceafed to confider themfelves as of the fame country. Some made themfelves independent, others turned pirates, and paid no refpect to any flag. Many entered into the fervice of the princes of the country, and thefe almoft all became minifters or generals, fo great were the advantages this nation ftill maintained over thofe of India. No Portuguefe purfued any other object than the advancement of his own intereft: there was no zeal, no union for the common good. Their poffeffions in India were divided into three governments, which gave no affiftance to each other, and even clafhed in their projects and interefts. Neither difcipline, fubordination, nor the love of glory, animated either the foldiers or the officers. Men of war no longer ventured out of the ports, or whenever they appeared were badly equipped. Manners became more and more depraved. Not one of their commanders had power enough to reftrain the torrent of vice, and the majority of thefe commanders were themfelves corrupted. The Portuguefe at length loft all their former greatnefs, when a free and enlightened nation, actuated with a proper fpirit of toleration, appeared in India, and contended with them for the empire of that country.

It

It may be affirmed, that at the time when Portugal firſt made its diſcoveries, the world was very little acquainted with the political principles of trade, the real power of different ſtates, the advantages of conqueſt, the manner of eſtabliſhing and preſerving colonies, and the benefits the mother country might derive from them.

It was a wiſe project to endeavour to find a paſſage by Africa to go to India, and to bring merchandiſe. The benefits which the Venetians derived by leſs direct roads, had juſtly excited the emulation of the Portugueſe; but it was proper there ſhould be ſome limits to ſo laudable an ambition.

This ſmall nation becoming on a ſudden miſtreſs of the richeſt and moſt extenſive commerce of the globe, ſoon conſiſted of nothing elſe but merchants, factors, and ſailors, who were deſtroyed by long voyages. Thus the Portugueſe loſt the foundation of all real power, which conſiſts in agriculture, natural induſtry, and population; and there was conſequently no proportion between their commerce and the means of keeping it up.

They carried theſe deſtructive meaſures ſtill further; and, animated with the rage of conqueſt, extended themſelves over a vaſt tract of land, which no European nation would have been able to preſerve, without impairing its own ſtrength.

Thus this ſmall country, which of itſelf was not very populous, conſtantly exhauſted itſelf in ſoldiers,

IN THE EAST AND WEST INDIES.
foldiers, failors, and inhabitants, fent to fupply the colonies.

THE fpirit of religious intoleration that prevailed amongft them, would not allow them to admit into the clafs of their own citizens the people of the eaft end of Africa, and they were therefore obliged to be perpetually at war with their new fubjects.

As the government foon changed its fchemes of trade into projects of conqueft; the nation, which had never been guided by the true commercial fpirit, foon affumed that of rapine and plunder.

TIME-PIECES, fire-arms, fine cloths, and other articles, which have been fince carried into India, not being then brought to that degree of perfection they have lately acquired, the Portuguefe could not carry any thing there but money. They foon grew tired of this, and took away from the Indians by force what they had before obtained by purchafe.

THEN was to be feen throughout the kingdom of Portugal the utmoft profufion of riches, joined to the moft extreme poverty. The only opulent perfons were thofe who had held fome employment in India; while the hufbandman, who found no one to affift him in his toil, and the artifts, who were unable to procure workmen, being foon compelled to forego their feveral occupations, were reduced to the loweft ftate of mifery.

ALL thefe misfortunes had been forefeen. When the difcovery of India engaged the attention of
Portugal,

Portugal, that court flattered itself that the bare appearance of its ships in that mild climate, would infure the poffeffion of it; that the trade of thefe countries would prove as inexhauftible a fource of riches to the nation, as it had been to thofe people who had hitherto been mafters of it; and that by the treafure arifing from it, the ftate, notwithftanding its fmall extent of territory, would become equal in ftrength and grandeur to the moft formidable powers. There were fome, however, who were not mifled by thefe delufive hopes. The moft penetrating and moderate of the minifters ventured to affirm, that the confequence of running in fearch of rich minerals, and glittering merchandife, would be an inattention to objects of real advantage, agriculture, and manufactures; that wars, shipwrecks, epidemical difeafes, and other accidents, would weaken the whole empire beyond recovery; that the ftate thus carried out from its center by the impulfe of an extravagant ambition, would either by force or art attract the fubjects to the moft diftant parts of Afia; that even if the enterprize fucceeded, it would raife a powerful confederacy, which it would be impoffible for the crown of Portugal to defeat. Attempts were in vain made, fome time after this, to convince thefe difcerning men of their error, by fhewing them that the Indians were fubdued, the Moors repulfed, and the Turks defeated; and by exhibiting the tide of wealth that flowed into Portugal. Their opinions were too well grounded in experience to be fhaken by the report of thefe these flattering successes. They still insisted that a few years would discover the folly of pushing these pursuits to extremity, and that they must inevitably lead to a corruption of morals, and end in ravages and universal confusion. Time, the great arbiter of political matters, has since confirmed their predictions.

OF all the conquests which the Portuguese had made in India, they possess none at present but Macao, Diu, and Goa; and the united importance of these three settlements, in their intercourse with India and Portugal, is very inconsiderable.

MACAO annually sends two vessels to Goa laden with China and other goods, that are rejected at Canton; the owners of which are generally Chinese merchants. These ships bring back as much of the sandal, Indian saffron, ginger and pepper, as one of the frigates belonging to Goa has been able to procure on the southern coast. The vessel which trades to the north carries a part of the cargo that comes from China to Surat, where it takes in some linens, and completes its lading at Diu, which is not what it was formerly. A ship arrives every year from Europe, which procures at Goa a small and indifferent cargo, consisting of goods picked up from China, Guzarat, and a few English factories, and sells them at Mosambique, Brasil, Angola, or the capital.

SUCH is the declining state into which the Portuguese affairs in India are fallen, from that pinacle of glory to which they had been raised by the

Present state of the Portuguese affairs in India.

the bold adventurers who difcovered, and the intrepid heroes who conquered that country. The fcene of their glory and opulence is become that of their ruin and difgrace. Their fituation, however, is not fo defperate as it may appear. Their remaining poffeffions are more than fufficient to entitle them to a large fhare in the affairs of India. But this change can only be effected by the aids of philofophy and a fpirit of liberty. If the Portuguefe knew their true interefts, if their ports were declared free, and thofe who fettled in them had their fortunes and the liberty of confcience fecured to them ; Indians who are now oppreffed by their government, and Europeans who are injured by their monopolizing companies, would refort to their fettlements in great numbers, and their flag, which has long been defpifed, would again become refpectable. Their power cannot, however, be equal to that of the Dutch, a perfevering and confiderate people, whofe enterprizes we now proceed to relate.

BOOK II.

The settlements, wars, policy, and trade of the Dutch in the East-Indies.

THE republic of Holland has, from its first rise, been an object of universal admiration, and cannot fail to engage the curiosity and attention of the remotest posterity. Its inhabitants have on all occasions distinguished themselves by their industry and enterprizing genius; but are particularly celebrated for their knowledge of maritime affairs, and their expeditions to the continent of India. Before we attend them in their progress to these opulent and extensive regions, let us trace their history to its earliest æra. Such a retrospect is peculiarly proper in a work of this nature, as it will comprehend at one glance, all those characteristic marks by which the genius of a nation is distinguished. It is necessary that a reader who reflects may be enabled to judge of himself, if the original state of this nation were such as afforded a presage of its future power; and whether the heroic associates of Civilis, who defied the Roman power, did not transfuse their spirit into those brave republicans, who, under the auspices of Nassau,

opposed

opposed the dark and odious tyranny of Philip the Second.

Ancient revolutions in Holland.

It is a fact established by the best historical authority, that in the century preceding the christian æra, the Battæ, dissatisfied with their situation in Hesse, settled upon the island formed by the Naal and the Rhine; which was marshy, and had few or no inhabitants. They gave the name of Batavia to their new country. Their government was a mixture of monarchy, aristocracy, and democracy. Their chief was, properly speaking, nothing more than a principal citizen, whose office was rather to advise than to command. The principal men who exercised jurisdiction, and commanded the troops in their respective districts, were chosen, as well as the kings, in a general assembly. A hundred persons, selected from among the people, presided over every country, and acted as chiefs in the different hamlets. The whole nation was, in some measure, an army always in readiness. Each family composed a body of militia, which served under a captain of its own chusing.

Such was the state of Batavia when Cæsar passed the Alps. This Roman general defeated the Helvetians, several tribes of the Gauls, the Belgæ and Germans, who had crossed the Rhine, and extended his conquests beyond that river. In consequence of this expedition, the boldness and success of which were equally astonishing, the protection of the conqueror was courted on all sides.

Some writers, too zealous for the honour of their country, affirm that the Batavians entered

into

IN THE EAST AND WEST INDIES.

into an alliance with Rome: but the truth is, they fubmitted, on condition that they fhould be governed by their own laws, pay no tribute, and be obliged only to perform military fervices.

CÆSAR foon diftinguifhed the Batavians from the other nations that were fubdued by the Romans. This conqueror of the Gauls, when by Pompey's influence he was recalled to Rome, and refufed to obey the fenate's orders; when relying on the abfolute authority which his conduct had at length given him over the legions and auxiliaries, he attacked his enemies in Spain, Italy, and Afia: at this juncture, fenfible that the Batavians had a principal fhare in his victories, he gave them the glorious appellation of *the friends and brethren of the Roman people*.

AFTER this, irritated by the unjuft proceedings of certain governors, they obeyed the dictates of that noble impulfe, fo becoming men of fpirit, which prompts them to take arms to revenge an infult. They fhewed themfelves as formidable enemies, as they were faithful allies; but thefe troubles fubfiding, the Batavians were pacified, but not fubdued.

WHEN Rome, after having rifen to a pitch of greatnefs unknown before, and which has never fince been equalled by any ftate, no longer retained thofe manly virtues and ftrict principles which were the ground-work of that noble fuperftructure; when her laws had loft their force, her armies their difcipline, and her citizens the love of their country: the barbarians, who by the terror of the Roman name had been driven to the north, where they had been confined by force to remain, poured like a torrent into the fouthern countries. The empire was torn in pieces, and the fineft provinces became a prey to thofe whom the Romans had always either degraded or oppreffed. The Franks, in particular, feized upon the countries belonging to the Gauls; and Batavia became a part of that extenfive and famous kingdom, which was founded by thefe conquerors in the fifth century.

The new monarchy experienced thofe inconveniences which are almoft infeparable from rifing ftates; and are indeed too frequently felt in the beft eftablifhed governments. It was fometimes under the dominion of a fingle perfon; and at others was fubject to the caprice of a number of tyrants. It was conftantly engaged either in foreign wars, or expofed to the rage of inteftine diffentions. Sometimes it made the neighbouring ftates tremble for their fafety; but much more frequently fuffered from the incurfions of the northern people who ravaged its provinces. It was equally the victim of the weaknefs of feveral of its princes, and of the unbounded ambition of their favourites and minifters. The overbearing fpirit of the pontiffs undermined the power of the throne, and their infolence brought both the laws and religion into difgrace. Anarchy and tyranny followed each other fo clofe, that the moft fanguine defpaired of ever feeing affairs put upon a tolerable footing. The glorious æra of Charlemagne's government was only a tranfient gleam of light. As his great action were

were the effect of his genius, and not in the least owing to the influence of any good inſtitutions; after his death, affairs returned to that ſtate of confuſion from which they had been retrieved by his father Pepin, and more particularly by his own endeavours. The French monarchy, the limits of which he had extended too far, was divided. Germany, to which the Rhine ſerved as a natural barrier, fell to the ſhare of one of his grandſons: and, by an unaccountable arrangement, Batavia, to which the Normans in their excurſions had a little before given the name of Holland, was included in that allotment.

IN the beginning of the tenth century, the German branch of the Carlovinians became extinct. As the other princes of France had neither courage nor power to aſſert their rights, the Germans eaſily diſengaged themſelves from a foreign yoke. Thoſe of the nation, who, by virtue of a delegated power from the monarch, governed the five circles of which the ſtate was compoſed, choſe a chief out of their own body. This chief, fearing leſt theſe powerful men might be tempted to throw off their dependence, if any ſeverer conditions were required of them, contented himſelf with their fidelity and homage, and exacted only ſuch ſervices as they were obliged to by the feudal laws.

AT this memorable juncture, the counts of Holland, who, as well as the reſt of the provincial chiefs, had hitherto exerciſed a precarious and dependent authority, obtained the ſame rights as the other great vaſſals of Germany: and as they afterwards enlarged their territories by conqueſt, marriages, and grants from the emperors, they in time became totally independent of the empire. They were not equally ſuccefsful in their unjuſt attempts againſt the public liberty. Their ſubjects were not to be intimidated by force, cajoled by flattery, or corrupted by profuſion. War and peace, taxes, laws, and treaties were managed by the three united powers of the count, the nobles, and the towns. The republican ſpirit ſtill prevailed in the nation, when by ſome extraordinary events it fell under the dominion of the houſe of Burgundy, whoſe former power, though before confiderable, was greatly ſtrengthened by this union.

Those who had the fagacity to inveſtigate probabilities, foreſaw, that this ſtate, which was formed as it were by the gradual accretion of many others, would one day be of great weight in the political ſyſtem of Europe. The genius of its inhabitants, its advantageous ſituation, and its real ſtrength, afforded moſt a certain proſpect of its future greatneſs. Theſe projects and expectations, which were juſt ripening into realities, were diſappointed by an event, which, though it happens every day, never fails to baffle the deſigns of ambition. The male line in that houſe became extinct; and Mary, who was ſole heireſs to its dominions, by her marriage in 1477, transferred to the houſe of Auſtria the advantages that had been gained by ſeveral ſuccefsful ſtruggles, a great number of intrigues, and ſome acts of injuſtice.

At this æra, fo famous in hiftory, each of the feventeen provinces of the low countries had particular laws, extenfive privileges, and almoft a diſtinct government. The excellent principle of union which equally contributes to the welfare and fecurity both of empires and republics, was univerfally difregarded. The people having been, from time immemorial, accuftomed to this ftate of confufion, had no idea that it was poffible to enjoy a more rational form of government. This prejudice was of fo long a ftanding, fo generally adopted, and fo firmly eftablifhed, that Maximilian, Philip and Charles, the three Auftrian princes who firft inherited the dominions of the houfe of Burgundy, thought it prudent not to attempt any innovation. They flattered themfelves, that fome happier conjuncture might enable their fucceffors to execute with fafety, a plan, which they could not even attempt without danger.

At this time a great change was preparing in the minds of men in Europe. The revival of letters, the extenfion of commerce, the invention of printing, and the difcovery of the compafs, brought on the æra when human reafon was to fhake off the yoke of fome of thofe prejudices which had gained ground in the barbarous ages.

The intelligent part of the world were for the moft part cured of the Romifh fuperftitions. They were difgufted at the abufe the popes made of their authority; the contributions they raifed upon the people; the fale of indulgences; and more particularly at thofe abfurd refinements with which

which they had difguifed the plain religion of Jefus Chrift.

But thefe difcerning people were not the firft who attempted a revolution. This honour was referved for a turbulent monk, whofe barbarous eloquence rouzed the northern nations. The moft enlightened men of the age contributed to undeceive the reft. Some of the European princes embraced the reformed religion; others held communion with the church of Rome. The former found no difficulty in bringing over their fubjects to their opinions; while the latter had much difficulty to prevent theirs from embracing the new doctrines. They had recourfe to a variety of meafures, which were too often purfued with rigour. That fpirit of fanaticifm, which had deftroyed the Saxons, the Albigenfes, and the Huffites, was revived. Gibbets were erected and fires kindled anew, to check the progrefs of the new doctrine.

No fovereign was fo ready to make ufe of thefe expedients as Philip II. His tyranny was felt in every part of his extenfive monarchy; and his zeal for his religion prompted him to perfecute all thofe who fell under the denomination of heretics or infidels. Defigns were formed to deprive the inhabitants of the low countries of their privileges; and millions of citizens were condemned to the fcaffold. The people revolted: and the fame fcene was renewed which the Venetians had fhewn the world many centuries before, when flying from oppreffion, and finding no retreat upon land, they fought an afylum upon the waters. Seven fmall provinces lying on the northern fide of

Brabant

Brabant and Flanders, which were rather overflowed than watered by large rivers, and often covered by the sea, whose violence was with difficulty restrained by dikes; having no wealth but what accrued from a few pasture lands, and a little fishing; formed one of the richest and most powerful republics in the world; and which may, perhaps, be considered as the model of commercial states. The first efforts of this united people had not the desired success; but though they were frequently defeated, they ended with victories. The Spanish troops they had to encounter, were the best in Europe, and at first gained several advantages. But by degrees the new republicans recovered their losses. They resisted with firmness; and gaining experience from their own miscarriages, as well as from the example of their enemies, they at length became their superiors in the art of war: and the necessity they lay under of disputing every inch of ground in so confined a country as Holland, gave them opportunities of improving the art of fortifying a country or a town in the best manner.

THE weak state of Holland, at its first rise, obliged it to seek for arms and assistance from every quarter where there was any prospect of obtaining them. It granted an asylum to pirates of all nations, with a view of employing them against the Spaniards; and this was the foundation of their naval strength. Wise laws, an admirable order, a constitution which preserved equality among mankind, an excellent police and a spirit of toleration, soon erected this republic

into

into a powerful state. In the year 1590, the Hollanders more than once humbled the pride of the Spanish flag. They had already established a kind of trade, the most suitable that could be to their situation. Their vessels were employed, as they are still, in carrying the merchandise of one nation to another. The Hanse Towns, and some towns in Italy, were in possession of these transports: and the Hollanders, in competition with them, by their frugality soon gained the advantage. Their ships of war protected their merchantmen. Their merchants grew ambitious of extending their commerce, and got the trade of Lisbon into their hands, where they purchased Indian goods, which they sold again to all the states of Europe.

PHILIP II. having made himself master of Portugal, enjoined his new subjects in 1594, to hold no correspondence with his enemies. This arbitrary prince did not foresee that this prohibition, which he thought must weaken the Hollanders, would in fact render them more formidable. Had not these discerning navigators been excluded from a port, upon which the whole success of their naval enterprises depended, there is reason to believe that they would have contented themselves with the large commerce they carried on in the European seas, without thinking of sailing to remoter climates. But as it was impossible to preserve their trade without the productions of the east, they were forced to go beyond a sphere which was, perhaps, too confined for a situation like theirs;

IN THE EAST AND WEST INDIES.

theirs; and refolved to feek their riches at the fountain head.

It appeared to be the beft plan to fit out fhips, and fend them to India: but the Hollanders wanted pilots who were acquainted with the feas, and factors who underftood the commerce of Afia. They were alarmed at the danger of making long voyages, where the enemy was mafter of the coafts, and of having their veffels intercepted during a paffage of fix thoufand leagues. It was judged more advifeable to attempt the difcovery of a paffage to China and Japan through the northern feas, which would be fhorter, as well as more wholefome and fecure. The Englifh had made the attempt in vain; and the Hollanders renewed it with no better fuccefs.

The firft voyages of the Hollanders to India.

While they were engaged in this enterprife, Cornelius Houtman, a merchant of that nation, a man of a penetrating and daring genius, being detained at Lifbon for debt, gave the merchants at Amfterdam to underftand, that if they would procure his enlargement, he would communicate to them many difcoveries he had made, which might turn to their advantage. He had in fact informed himfelf of every particular relating to the paffage to India, and the manner of carrying on trade in thofe parts. His propofals were accepted, and his debts difcharged. The information he gave proving anfwerable to the expectations he had raifed, thofe who had releafed him from his confinement, formed an affociation under the name of the Company of diftant Countries, and gave him the command

mand of four veffels to conduct them to India by the cape of Good Hope.

THE principal object of this voyage was to obferve the coafts, the inhabitants and the trade of different places, avoiding, as much as poffible, the Portuguefe fettlements. Houtman reconnoitred the coafts of Africa and Brazil; made fome ftay at Madagafcar, touched at the Maldives, and vifited the iflands of Sunda: where finding the country abounding in pepper, he bought a quantity of it, together with fome others of the moft valuable fpices. His prudence procured him an alliance with the principal fovereign of Java; but the Portuguefe, notwithftanding they were hated, and had no fettlement upon the ifland, created him fome enemies. Having got the better in fome fkirmifhes he was unavoidably engaged in, he returned with his fmall fquadron to Holland; where, though he brought little wealth, he raifed much expectation. He brought away fome negroes, Chinefe, and inhabitants of Malabar, a young native of Malacca, a Japanefe, and Abdul, a pilot of the Guzarat, a man of great abilities, and perfectly well acquainted with the coaft of India.

THE account given by Houtman, and the difcoveries made in the courfe of the voyage, encouraged the merchants of Amfterdam to form the plan of a fettlement at Java, which, at the fame time that it would throw the trade of pepper into their hands, place them near the iflands that produce more valuable fpices, and facilitate their communication with China and Japan, would fix them at a diftance from the center of that European

ropean power, which they had the moſt reaſon to dread in India. Admiral Van Neck, who was ſent upon this important expedition with eight veſſels, arrived at the iſland of Java, where he found the inhabitants prejudiced againſt his nation. They fought and negociated by turns. Abdul the pilot, the Chineſe, and above all, the hatred that prevailed againſt the Portugueſe, proved of ſervice to the Dutch. They were permitted to trade, and, in a ſhort time, fitted out four veſſels laden with ſpices and ſome linens. The admiral, with the reſt of his fleet ſailed to the Moluccas, where he learnt that the natives of the country had forced the Portugueſe to abandon ſome places, and that they only waited for a favourable opportunity of expelling them from the reſt. He eſtabliſhed factories in ſeveral of theſe iſlands, entered into treaty with ſome of the ſovereigns, and returned to Europe laden with riches.

It is impoſſible to deſcribe the joy that prevailed at his return. The ſucceſs of his voyage raiſed a freſh emulation. Societies were formed in moſt of the maritime and trading towns in the low countries. Theſe aſſociations ſoon became ſo numerous, that they injured each other; as the rage of purchaſing raiſed the value of commodities to an exorbitant degree in India, and the neceſſity of ſelling them made them bear a low price in Europe. They were on the point of being ruined by their own efforts, and by the want of power in each of them to reſiſt a formidable enemy, fully bent upon their deſtruction, when the government, which is

ſome-

sometimes wiser than individuals, opportunely stepped in to their assistance.

Establishment of the India company.

IN 1602 the states-general united these different societies into one body, to which they gave the name of the East India Company. It was invested with authority to make peace or war with the eastern princes, to erect forts, chuse their own governors, maintain garrisons, and to nominate officers for the conduct of the police, and the administration of justice.

THIS company, which had no parallel in antiquity, and was the pattern of all succeeding societies of the same kind, set out with great advantages. The private associations which had been previously formed, proved of service to it by their misfortunes, and even by their mistakes. The great number of vessels which they fitted out had contributed to make all the branches of trade perfectly understood; to form many officers and seamen; and to encourage citizens of repute to undertake these foreign expeditions; persons only of no estimation or fortune having been exposed in the first voyages.

So many united assistances could not fail of being improved to advantage, when prosecuted with vigour; and, accordingly, the new company soon acquired a considerable degree of power. It was a new state, erected within the state itself, which enriched it, and increased its strength abroad; but might, in time, weaken the influence of the democratical principle, which inspires the love of equality and œconomy, of the laws, and of one's own countrymen.

Soon after its establishment, the company fitted out for India fourteen ships and some yachts, under the command of Admiral Warwick, whom the Hollanders look upon as the founder of their commerce, and of their powerful colonies in the east. He built a factory in the island of Java, and secured it by fortifications; he likewise built another in the territories of the king of Johor; and formed alliances with several princes in Bengal. He had frequent engagements with the Portuguese, in which he had almost always the advantage. In those parts where the Portuguese had appeared in the character of merchants only, he found it necessary to remove the prejudices they had raised against his countrymen, whom they had represented as a set of banditti, avowed enemies to all regal authority, and addicted to all manner of vice. The behaviour of the Hollanders and the Portuguese speedily convinced the people of Asia which of these nations had the advantage in point of manners. A bloody war soon ensued between these two powers.

THE Portuguese had on their side the advantage of a thorough knowledge of these seas; they were accustomed to the climate, and had the assistance of several nations, which, though they hated them, were compelled through fear to fight for their oppressors. The Hollanders were animated by the critical situation of their affairs; by the hopes of procuring an absolute and lasting independency,

Wars of the Hollanders and Portuguese.

pendency, which at prefent they could not boaft of; by the ambition of eftablifhing a vaft commerce upon the ruins of that of their old mafters; and by the hatred which a difference in religious opinions had rendered implacable. Thefe paffions, at the fame time that they infpired all the activity, ftrength, and perfeverance neceffary for the execution of great defigns, did not hinder them from taking their meafures with precaution. Their humanity and honefty attached the people to their caufe; and many of them foon declared againft their ancient oppreffors.

The Hollanders were continually fending over frefh colonifts, fhips, and troops, while the Portuguefe were left without any forces but their own. Spain did not fend them any fleets of merchantmen, or grant them the protection of the fquadron which had hitherto been kept in India; fhe neither repaired their places of ftrength, or renewed their garrifons. It fhould feem that fhe wanted to humble her new fubjects, whom fhe thought not fo fubmiffive as might be wifhed, and to perpetuate her authority by expofing them to repeated loffes. She proceeded ftill further; and to prevent Portugal from having any refources in itfelf, fhe feized upon its inhabitants, and fent them to Italy, Flanders, and other countries where fhe was at war.

Notwithstanding this, the fcale continued even for a long time, and the fuccefs was various on both fides. Nor is this in the leaft furprizing. The Portuguefe, on their arrival in India,

India, had nothing to encounter at sea but a few weak vessels, ill built, ill armed, and ill defended; nothing by land but effeminate men, voluptuous princes, and dastardly slaves: whereas those who came to wrest the sceptre of Asia out of their hands, had vessels to board of the same construction as their own; regular fortresses to assault, and Europeans to conquer and subdue, who were grown haughty by a long series of victories, and by being the founders of an immense empire.

THE time was now come, when the Portuguese were to expiate their perfidy, their robberies, and their cruelties: and the prediction of one of the kings of Persia was fulfilled, who asking an ambassador just arrived at Goa, how many governors his master had beheaded since the establishment of his power in India; received for answer, *None at all. So much the worse,* replied the monarch; *his authority cannot be of long duration in a country where so many acts of outrage and barbarity are committed.*

IT does not, however, appear, in the course of this war, that the Hollanders possessed that daring rashness, that unshaken intrepidity, which had marked the enterprizes of the Portuguese; but there was a consistency and unremitting perseverance observable in all their designs. Often repulsed, but never discouraged, they renewed their attack with fresh vigour, and on a better plan. They never exposed themselves to the danger of a total defeat. If, in any engagement, their ships had suffered, they sheered off; and as they never lost sight of their commercial interest, the vanquished fleet, while it was repairing on the coasts belonging to some of the Indian princes, purchased merchandife, and returned to Holland. By this method the company acquired a new fund, which enabled them to undertake fresh enterprizes. If the Hollanders did not always perform great actions, they never attempted useless ones. They had neither the pride nor the vain glory of the Portuguese, who had frequently engaged in war rather perhaps through the love of fame than of power. The Hollanders steadily pursued their first plan, without suffering themselves to be diverted from it either by motives of revenge, or projects of conquest.

In the year 1607, they endeavoured to open a communication with the ports belonging to the vast empire of China, which, at that time, was cautious of admitting strangers. The Portuguese found means, by bribery, and the intrigues of their missionaries, to get the Hollanders excluded. They resolved to extort by force what they could not obtain by treaty, and determined to intercept the vessels belonging to the Chinese. This piratical proceeding did not answer their expectations. A Portuguese fleet sailed from Macao to attack the pirates who thought proper to retire. The inequality of their numbers, the impossibility of refitting in seas where they had no shelter, and the fear of disgracing their nation in the eyes of a great empire, whose good opinion it was their interest to preserve; all these considerations determined

mined them to decline the fight; but this was only for a short time.

Some years after the Hollanders laid siege to a place, the importance of which they had become acquainted with. The enterprize did not succeed; but as they never lost any advantage that could be gained by their armaments, they sent that which they had employed against Macao to form a colony in the Piscadore-isles. These are rocks where no water is to be had in dry seasons, and no provisions at any time. These inconveniencies were not counterbalanced by any solid advantages, because the people of the neighbouring continent were forbidden, on the severest penalties, to hold any correspondence with strangers who might become dangerous so near the coasts. The Hollanders had determined to abandon a settlement which they despaired of making useful, when, in the year 1624, they were invited to fix at Formosa, and had assurances given them that the Chinese merchants would be allowed full liberty to go there and trade with them.

This island, though it lies opposite to the province of Fokien, at the distance of only thirty leagues from the coast, was not subject to the dominion of the Chinese, whose genius does not incline them to conquest, and who, through an inhuman and ill-judged policy, would rather suffer a decrease of population, than transplant their supernumerary subjects to the neighbouring countries. Formosa was found to be a hundred and thirty or forty leagues in circumference. Its inhabitants,

The Hollanders form a settlement at Formosa.

bitants, if we may judge from their manners and their appearance, feemed to be defcended from the Tartars in the moft northern part of Afia: and probably found their way through the country of Corea. They lived chiefly by fifhing and hunting, and fcarce wore any covering.

The Hollanders, having without difficulty informed themfelves of every particular that prudence fuggefted, thought it moft advifeable to fix their fettlement on a fmall ifland that lay contiguous to the larger one. This fituation afforded them three confiderable advantages; they could eafily defend themfelves if hatred or jealoufy fhould incline their neighbours to give them any difturbance; the two iflands afforded them a harbour, and they might carry on a fafe communication with China during the monfoons, which they could not have done in any other pofition they could have chofen.

The new colony infenfibly gained ftrength without attracting any notice, 'till it rofe at once to a degree of confequence that aftonifhed all Afia. This unexpected profperity was owing to the conqueft of China by the Tartars. Thus it is that torrents enrich the vallies with the ftores they carry down from the defolated mountains. Above a hundred thoufand Chinefe, who refolved not to fubmit to the conqueror, fled for refuge to Formofa. They carried with them that activity which is peculiar to their character, the manner of cultivating rice and fugar, and were the means of drawing thither from their own nation an infinite number of vefſels.

IN THE EAST AND WEST INDIES.

veffels. In a fhort time the ifland became the centre of all the correfpondence that was carried on between Java, Siam, the Philippine iflands, China, Japan, and the reft of thofe countries; and in a few years was confidered as the firft mart in India. The Hollanders flattered themfelves with the profpect of ftill greater advantages; but fortune deceived their expectations.

A CHINESE, called Equam, of obfcure birth, whofe turbulent difpofition had made him turn pirate, had attained, by the greatnefs of his talents, to the rank of high-admiral. He defended his country againft the Tartars for a confiderable time, but feeing his mafter obliged to fubmit, he endeavoured to make terms for himfelf with the conquerors. He was decoyed to Pekin, where he was feized, and condemned by the ufurper to perpetual imprifonment, in which he is fuppofed to have died of poifon. Coxinga faved himfelf on board his father's fleet, vowed eternal enmity to the oppreffors of his family and country, and concluded that he fhould be able to take the fevereft revenge upon them, if he made himfelf mafter of Formofa. He made a defcent upon it, and the minifter Hambroeck was taken prifoner in the attack.

HAMBROECK, being appointed with fome other prifoners to be fent to the fort of Zealand to prevail with his countrymen to capitulate, called to mind the example of Regulus; he exhorted them to be firm, and ufed every argument to perfuade them, that if they ftrenuoufly perfevered,

they

they would oblige the enemy to retire. The garrison being aware that this generous man would, on his return to the camp, fall a sacrifice to his magnanimity, used their utmost efforts to detain him. Their remonstrances were seconded by the tenderest solicitations of two of his daughters, who were in the citadel. His answer was, *I have pledged my honour to return to my confinement; I hold myself obliged to perform my promise. My memory shall never be sullied with the reproach, that out of regard to my own safety I was the cause of severer treatment, or perhaps of death, to the companions of my misfortune.* After this heroic speech he calmly returned to the Chinese camp, and the siege began.

NOTWITHSTANDING the fortifications were in a bad condition, and the fort ill stored with ammunition and provisions; notwithstanding the garrison was weak, and the succours sent to attack the enemy had retreated with disgrace, Coyet the governor made an obstinate defence. In the beginning of the year 1662, being forced to capitulate, he repaired to Batavia, where his superiors had recourse to those iniquitous state-intrigues which are frequently practised in all governments. They cast reflections upon his conduct, to prevent any suspicion that the loss of so important a settlement was owing to their own folly, or negligence. The attempts made to recover it, proved unsuccessful; and the Hollanders were at last reduced to the necessity of carrying on a trade with Canton on the same conditions,

IN THE EAST AND WEST INDIES.

ditions, and under the same restrictions as other nations.

It may appear somewhat singular, that since the year 1683, when Formosa fell under the dominion of China, no Europeans have ever attempted to form any settlement there, upon the same conditions at least, as that of the Portuguese at Macao. But besides that the suspicious temper of the nation to whom that island belongs, gives no room to expect such an indulgence from them, one may venture to pronounce that such an enterprise would be a bad one. Formosa was a place of importance only so long as the Japanese had a communication with it, and its produce was allowed a free importation into Japan.

The Hollanders seemed to be for ever excluded from this empire. After some unsuccessful attempts, they began to despair of getting any footing there; when one of their captains, who was thrown upon the coasts of Japan by a storm in 1609, informed them that the people were favourably disposed towards them.

About a century before this, the government of Japan had been changed. A magnanimous people had been made furious by a tyrant. Taycosama, who from a soldier became a general, and from a general an emperor, had usurped the whole power, and abolished all the rights of the people. Having stripped the Dairo of the little remains of his authority, he had reduced all the petty princes of the country under his subjection. Tyranny is arrived at its height when it establishes

Trade of the Hollanders to Japan.

despotism

despotism by law. Taycosama went still further, and confirmed it by sanguinary laws. His civil legislation was actually a code of criminal prosecutions, exhibiting nothing but scaffolds, punishments, criminals, and executioners.

The Japanese, alarmed at this prospect of slavery, had recourse to arms. Torrents of blood were shed throughout the empire: and though liberty might be supposed to be superior in courage to tyranny, the latter triumphed over it. Tyranny became still more ferocious, when animated by the spirit of revenge. An inquisition, public as well as private, dismayed the citizens; they became spies, informers, accusers, and enemies to each other. An error in the administration of the police was construed into a crime against the state; and an unguarded expression was made high-treason. Prosecution assumed the character of legislation. Three successive generations were doomed to welter in their own blood; and rebel parents gave birth to a proscribed posterity.

During a whole century, Japan resembled a dungeon filled with criminals, or a place of execution. The throne, which was raised upon the ruins of the altar, was surrounded with gibbets. The subjects were become as cruel as their tyrant. They sought, with a strange avidity, to procure death, by committing crimes which were readily suggested under a despotic government. For want of executioners, they punished themselves for the loss of liberty, or revenged themselves of tyranny, by putting an end to their own
existence.

IN THE EAST AND WEST INDIES.

exiftence. To enable them to face death, and to affift them in fuffering it, they derived new courage from chriftianity, which the Portuguefe had introduced amongft them.

THE oppreffions the Japanefe laboured under afforded an opportunity for the profeffors of this new worfhip to make numerous profelytes. The miffionaries who preached a fuffering religion, were liftened to with attention. In vain did the doctrine of Confucius try to gain reception among a people who bordered upon China. Some erroneous tenets of chriftianity, which bore a confiderable affinity to thofe of the Budzoifts, and the penances equally enjoined by the two fyftems, procured the Portuguefe miffionaries feveral profelytes. But fetting afide this refemblance, the Japanefe would have chofen to embrace chriftianity merely from a motive of hatred to the prince.

IF the new religion was difcountenanced at court, it could not fail to meet with a favourable reception in the families of the dethroned princes. It added frefh fuel to their refentment: they were fond of a ftrange God whom the tyrant did not love. Taycofama ruled with a rod of iron, and perfecuted the chriftians as enemies to the ftate. He profcribed the doctrines imported from Europe, and this profcription made them ftrike the deeper root. Piles were kindled, and millions of victims threw themfelves into the flames. The emperors of Japan tranfcended thofe of Rome in the art of perfecuting the chriftians. During the fpace of forty years the fcaffolds were ftained with the innocent blood of martyrs. This proved the feed of chriftianity, christianity, and of sedition also. Near forty thousand christians in the kingdom or province of Darima took up arms in the name, and for the name of Christ; and defended themselves with such fury, that not a single person survived the slaughter occasioned by persecution.

The navigation, trade, and factories of the Portuguese were preserved during this great crisis. The court and people had, however, for a long time, been jealous of them; they had incurred the suspicion of government by their ambition, their intrigues, and perhaps by their secret conspiracies; and had rendered themselves odious to the people by their avarice, their pride, and their treachery. But as the merchandise they brought was grown into fashion, and could not be procured by any other channel, they were not excluded from Japan till the end of the year 1638; when other merchants were in a situation to supply their place.

The Hollanders, who had, for some time, entered into competition with them, were not involved in the disgrace. As these republicans had never shewn themselves ambitious of interfering with the government; as they had suffered their artillery to be employed against the christians; as they were at war with the proscribed nations; as their strength was not thoroughly known, and they appeared to be reserved, pliant, modest, and entirely devoted to commerce; they were tolerated, though at the same time they were subjected to great restraints. Three years after, whether it was that the spirit of intrigue and dominion seized them, or, which is more probable, that no conduct

whatever

whatever could prevent the Japanese from harbouring suspicions, they were deprived of the liberty and the privileges they enjoyed.

EVER since the year 1641, they have been confined to the artificial island of Disnia, raised in the harbour of Nangasaque, and which has a communication with the city bridge. As soon as they arrive, their ships are stripped, and their powder, muskets, swords, guns, and even rudder, carried ashore. In this kind of imprisonment they are treated with a degree of contempt which is beyond conception; and can transact no business but with commissaries appointed to regulate the price and the quantity of their merchandise. It is impossible that the tameness with which they have endured this treatment more than a century, should not have lessened them in the eyes of the nation who is witness of it; and that the love of gain should have produced such an extreme insensibility to insults, without tarnishing their character.

THE chief commodities which the Dutch carry to Japan are European cloths, silks, spices, printed linens, sugar, and wood for dying. These articles were formerly of considerable importance. In the very year of the company's disgrace, its returns amounted to sixteen millions * : but the shackles, which from time to time have been imposed upon it, have gradually reduced their once flourishing trade to nothing. The cargo of the two vessels they send annually, cannot be sold for more than a million †. They receive in payment eleven thousand chests of copper, at forty-one livres four sols ‡ per

* 700,000l.   † 43,750l.   ‡ 1l. 16s. od. ⅘.

chest,

188   HISTORY OF SETTLEMENTS AND TRADE

BOOK II.

cheſt, which weighs one hundred and twenty pounds. Their expences, including preſents and the charge of the embaſſy they ſend every year to the emperor, generally amount to two hundred and eighty thouſand livres *, and their profits do not exceed three hundred and ten thouſand †; ſo that if the company gains forty thouſand livres ‡, it is reckoned a good year.

The trade of the Chineſe, who, except the Hollanders, are the only foreigners admitted into the empire, is not more extenſive than theirs, and ſubjected to the ſame reſtrictions. Ever ſince the year 1688 they are confined during the continuance of the ſale of their goods, without the walls of Nangaſaqué, in a kind of priſon, which is divided into ſeveral huts, ſurrounded with a paliſade, and defended by a good ditch, and a guard placed at all the gates. Theſe precautions have been taken in conſequence of a diſcovery that ſome works, in favour of chriſtianity, had been ſold together with ſome books of philoſophy and morality. The European miſſionaries had ordered ſome people of Canton to circulate them, and the deſire of gain betrayed them into a piece of chicanery, which has coſt them very dear.

It is natural to ſuppoſe, that thoſe who have changed the ancient government of the country into the moſt arbitrary tyranny upon earth, would look upon all intercourſe with ſtrangers as dangerous to their authority. There is the more reaſon for this conjecture, as the inhabitants are all

* 12,250l.   † About 131,687l.   ‡ 1,750l.

forbidden,

IN THE EAST AND WEST INDIES.

forbidden, on pain of death, to go out of their country. This rigorous edict is become the fundamental maxim of the empire.

THUS the inhuman policy of the state has deprived it of the only means of acquiring a milder temper, by softening the national character. The Japanese, fiery as his climate, and restless as the ocean that surrounds him, required that the utmost scope should be given to his activity, which could only be done by encouraging a brisk trade. To prevent the necessity of restraining him by punishments, it was necessary to keep him in exercise by constant labour; and to allow his vivacity an uninterrupted career abroad, when it was in danger of kindling the flame of sedition at home. That energy of mind which has degenerated into fanaticism, would have been improved into industry; contemplation would have changed into action; and the fear of punishment into the love of pleasure. That hatred of life, which torments the Japanese, while he is enslaved, oppressed and kept in continual fears by the rigour of the laws, against which he is perpetually struggling, would have given way to the spirit of curiosity, that would have induced him to traverse the ocean, and visit foreign nations. By a frequent change of place and climate, he would insensibly have changed his manners, opinions, and character; and this change would have been as happy for him as it is for the generality of people. What he might chance to lose by this intercourse as a citizen, he would gain as a man; but the Japanese are become tygers, through the cruelty of their tyrants.   WHATEVER

WHATEVER may be said in praise of the Spartans, the Egyptians, and other distinct nations, who have owed their superior strength, grandeur, and permanency to the state of separation in which they kept themselves; mankind has received no benefit from these singular institutions. On the contrary, the spirit of intercourse is useful to all nations, as it promotes a mutual communication of their productions and knowledge. In a word, if it were useless or pernicious to some particular people, it was necessary for the Japanese. By commerce they would have become enlightened in China, civilized in India, and cured of all their prejudices among the Europeans.

The Moluccas submit to the Dutch.

THE Dutch had the good fortune to meet with resources which indemnified them for the loss they had sustained at Japan. They had not yet entered into commerce with these, the most remarkable islands in the torrid zone, when they attempted to secure to themselves the trade of the Moluccas. The Portuguese, who had long been in possession of them, were obliged to share their advantages with their masters the Spaniards; and, at length, to give up the trade almost entirely to them. The two nations, divided in their interests, and perpetually at war with each other, because the government had neither leisure nor skill to remove their mutual antipathy, joined to oppose the subjects of the United Provinces. The latter, assisted by the natives of the country, who had not yet learned to fear or hate them, by degrees gained the superiority. The antient conquerors were driven out about the year 1627; and their place was supplied by others

equally

equally avaritious, though lefs turbulent, and more enlightened.

As foon as the Dutch had eftablifhed themfelves firmly at the Moluccas, they endeavoured to get the exclufive trade of fpices into their own hands: an advantage, which the nation they had juft expelled was never able to procure. They fkilfully availed themfelves both of the forts they had taken fword in hand, and thofe they had imprudently been fuffered to erect, to draw the kings of Ternate and Tidor, who were mafters of this Archipelago, into their fcheme. Thefe princes found themfelves obliged to confent, that the clove and nutmeg trees fhould be rooted up in the iflands that were ftill under their dominion. The firft of thefe fceptered flaves, in confideration of this great facrifice, received a penfion of 64,500 livres*; and the other, one of about 12,000†. A garrifon of feven hundred men was appointed to fecure the performance of this treaty: and to fo low an ebb is the power of thefe kings reduced by war, tyranny, and misfortunes, that thefe forces would be more than fufficient to keep them in this ftate of dependence, if it were not neceffary to have an eye upon the Philippine iflands, whofe vicinity conftantly occafions fome alarm. Notwithftanding the inhabitants are prohibited from carrying on any navigation, and that no foreign nation is admitted among them, the Dutch trade there is in a languifhing ftate; as they have no means of exchange, nor any filver but what they carry over to pay their troops, their commiffioners

---

* About 2,3811. † 525L.

sioners and pensions. This government, deducting the small profits, costs the company 140,000 livres * a year.

THIS loss is fully compensated at Amboyna, where they have engrossed the cultivation of cloves. The tree that produces them is, as to its bark, very much like the olive-tree, and resembles the laurel in its height, and the shape of its leaves. It produces at the extremity of its numerous branches, a prodigious quantity of flowers, which are white at first, then green, and at last grow red and pretty hard. When they arrive at this degree of maturity, they are, properly speaking, cloves. As it dries, the clove assumes a dark yellowish cast; when gathered, it becomes of a deep brown. No verdure is ever seen under this plant, which is doubtless owing to its exhausting all the nutritious juices of the soil that produces it.

THE season for gathering the cloves is from October to February. The boughs of the tree are strongly shaken, or the cloves beat down with long reeds. Large cloths are spread to receive them, and they are afterwards either dried in the sun, or in the smoke of the bamboo cane.

THE cloves which escape the notice of those who gather them, or are purposely left upon the tree, continue to grow till they are about an inch in thickness; and these falling off, produce new plants, which do not bear in less than eight or nine years. These cloves which they call mother-cloves, though inferior to the common sort, are not with-

* 6,125l.

out

out their value. The Dutch preserve them in sugar, and, in long voyages, eat them after meals to promote digestion; or make use of them as an agreeable remedy for the scurvy.

THE clove, to be in perfection, must be full sized, heavy, oily, and easily broken; of a fine smell, and a hot aromatic taste, so as almost to burn the throat; it should make the fingers smart when handled, and leave an oily moisture upon them when pressed. The principal use of it is for culinary purposes. In some parts of Europe, and in India in particular, it is so much admired as to be thought an indispensible ingredient in almost every dish. It is put into their food, liquors, wines, and enters likewise into the composition of perfumes. It is little used in medicine; but there is an oil extracted from it which is in considerable repute.

THE company have allotted the inhabitants of Amboyna four thousand parcels of land, on each of which they were at first allowed, and about the year 1720 compelled, to plant a hundred and twenty-five trees, amounting in the whole to five hundred thousand. Each of these parcels produces annually, on an average, upwards of two pounds of cloves: and consequently the collective produce must weigh more than a million.

THE cultivator is paid with the specie that is constantly returned to the company, and receives some blue and unbleached cottons which are brought from Coromandel. This small trade might, in some measure, be increased, if the inhabitants of Amboyna, and the small islands that depend

pend upon it, would have attended to the culture of pepper and indigo, which has been tried with fuccefs. Miferable as thefe iflanders are, fince they are not tempted by an adequate reward for their labours, they remain in a ftate of indolence.

The adminiftration is fomewhat different in the iflands of Banda, which are thirty leagues diftant from Amboyna. There are five of thefe iflands, two of which are uncultivated and almoft uninhabited; and the other three claim the diftinction of being the only iflands in the world that produce the nutmeg.

The nutmeg grows to the fame height as the pear-tree. It has a pithy wood, an afh-coloured bark, and flexible branches. The leaves are produced in pairs upon one fingle ftem, and when bruifed, emit an agreeable odour. The fruit fucceeds the flowers, which refemble thofe of the cherry-tree. It is of the fize of an egg, and of the colour of an apricot. The outer rind is very thick, and refembles that of our nuts as they hang upon the tree, opening in the fame manner when ripe, and difcovering the nutmeg covered with its mace. It is then time to gather it, to prevent the mace or flower of the nutmeg from growing dry, and the nutmeg from lofing that oil which preferves it, and in which its excellence confifts. Thofe that are gathered before they are perfectly ripe are preferved in vinegar or fugar, and are admired only in Afia.

It is nine months before this fruit comes to perfection. After it is gathered, the outer rind is ftripped off, and the mace feparated from it, and laid in the fun to dry. The nuts require more preparation.

preparation. They are spread upon hurdles, or dried for six weeks by a slow fire, in sheds erected for that purpose. They are then separated from the shell, and thrown into lime-water, which is a necessary precaution to preserve them from worms.

THE nutmeg differs in goodness according to the age of the tree, the soil, the exposition, and method of culture. It is most esteemed when it is fresh, moist, and heavy, and when it yields an oily juice upon being pricked. It helps digestion, expels wind, and strengthens the bowels.

IF we except this valuable spice, the islands of Banda, like all the Moluccas, are barren to a dreadful degree. What they produce in superfluities they want in necessaries. The land will not bring forth any kind of corn: and the pith of the sago serves the natives of the country instead of bread.

As this food is not sufficient for the Europeans who settle in the Moluccas, they are allowed to fetch provisions from Java, Macassar, or the extremely fertile island of Bali. The company itself carries some merchandise to Banda.

THIS is the only settlement in the East Indies that can be considered as an European colony; because it is the only one where the Europeans are proprietors of lands. The company finding that the inhabitants of Banda were savage, cruel, and treacherous, because they were impatient under their yoke, resolved to exterminate them. Their possessions were divided among the white people, who got slaves from some of the neighbouring islands to cultivate the lands. These white people are for the

the moſt part Creoles or malecontents, who have quitted the ſervice of the company. In the ſmall iſle of Roſinging, there are likewiſe ſeveral banditti, whom the laws have branded with diſgrace, and young men of abandoned principles, whoſe families wanted to get rid of them : ſo that Banda is called the *iſland of correction*. The climate is ſo unhealthy, that theſe unhappy men live but a ſhort time. It is on account of the loſs of ſo great a number of hands, that attempts have been made to transfer the culture of the nutmeg to Amboyna; and the company were likewiſe probably influenced by two other ſtrong motives of Intereſt, as their trade could be carried on with leſs expence and greater ſafety. But the experiments that have been made have proved unſucceſsful, and matters remain in their former ſtate.

To ſecure to themſelves an excluſive title to the produce of the Moluccas, which are, with good reaſon, ſtiled the *gold mines* of the company, the Dutch have been under a neceſſity of forming two ſettlements, one at Timor, and the other at Celebes.

The Dutch form a ſettlement at Timor. The firſt of theſe iſlands is ſixty leagues long, and fifteen or eighteen broad. It is divided into ſeveral ſovereignties ; in which there are numbers of Portugueſe. Theſe conquerors, who at their firſt arrival in India had advanced with the utmoſt intrepidity and moſt amazing celerity, and had purſued a long and dangerous career with a rapidity which nothing could ſtop ; who were ſo well accuſtomed to acts of heroiſm, that they performed the moſt arduous enterpriſes with eaſe ; theſe conquerors, I ſay, when they were attacked by the Dutch, when their whole empire,

empire, grown too large and tottering under its own weight, was ready to fall, difplayed none of thofe virtues, which had laid the foundation of their power. When they were difpoffeffed of a fort, driven out of a kingdom, difperfed in confequence of a defeat, they fhould have fought an afylum among their brethren, and fhould have rallied under ftandards that had hitherto been invincible; either to put a ftop to the progrefs of the enemy, or to recover their fettlements: but fo far were they from forming a refolution fo generous, that they folicited fome employment, or fome penfion, from thofe very Indian princes they had fo often infulted. Thofe who had contracted a habit of effeminacy, and idlenefs above the reft, retreated to Timor, which, being a poor ifland, where no works of induftry were carried on, would fkreen them they thought from the purfuit of an enemy intent upon ufeful conquefts. They were, however, deceived. In the year 1613 they were driven from the town of Kupan by the Dutch, who found a fort there, which they have ever fince garrifoned with fifty men. The company fends fome coarfe linens thither every year, and receives in return wax, tortoife-fhell, fanders wood, and cadiang, a fmall fpecies of bean, commonly ufed by the Dutch on fhip-board, by way of variety of food for the crew. All thefe objects employ one or two floops, which are difpatched from Batavia: nothing is either gained or loft by this fettlement; the profits juft anfwer the expences. The Dutch would have abandoned Timor long ago, if they had not been apprehenfive that fome active nation might fix there and avail themselves of the opportunities that situation would give them to difturb the trade of the Moluccas. It was the fame cautious principle which drew them to Celebes.

The Dutch make themselves mafters of Celebes.

THIS ifland, which is about a hundred and thirty leagues in diameter, is very habitable, though it lies in the center of the torrid zone. The heats are allayed by the copious rains, and cooling breezes. The inhabitants are the braveft people in the fouth of Afia; they make a furious onfet, but, after a conteft of two hours, a total want of courage takes place of this ftrange impetuofity: the intoxicating fumes of opium, which are doubtlefs the caufe of this terrible ferment, go off, when their ftrength is exhaufted by tranfports that approach to madnefs. The *crid*, which is their favourite weapon, is a foot and a half long; it is fhaped like a poniard, and the blade is ferpentine. They never carry more than one to battle; but in private quarrels two are neceffary; they parry with that in the left hand, and attack the adverfary with the other. The wounds made by this weapon are very dangerous, and the duel moft commonly ends in the death of both the combatants.

THE inhabitants of Celebes are rendered active, induftrious, and robuft, by a rigid education. Every hour in the day their nurfes rub them with oil, or water juft warm. Thefe repeated unctions encourage nature to exert herfelf freely. They are weaned at a year old, an idea prevailing, that if they continued to fuck any longer, it would hurt their underftandings. When they are five or fix years

years old, the male children of any diſtinction are intruſted to the care of ſome relation or friend, that their courage may not be weakened by the careſſes of their mothers, and a habit of reciprocal tenderneſs. They do not return to their families till they arrive at the age of fifteen or ſixteen, when the law allows them to marry: a liberty they ſeldom make uſe of, before they are thoroughly verſed in the exerciſe of arms.

FORMERLY theſe people acknowledged no other gods but the ſun and the moon. They ſacrificed to them in the public ſquares, having no materials which they thought valuable enough to be employed in raiſing temples. According to the creed of theſe iſlanders, the ſun and moon were eternal as well as the heavens, whoſe empire they divided between them. Ambition ſet them at variance. The moon, flying from the ſun, miſcarried, and was delivered of the earth; ſhe was big with ſeveral other worlds which ſhe will ſucceſſively bring forth, but without violence, in order to repair the loſs of thoſe whom the fire of her conqueror will conſume.

THESE abſurdities were univerſally received at Celebes; but they had not ſo laſting an influence over either the nobles or the people as is found in the religious doctrines of other nations. About two centuries ago, ſome Chriſtians and Mohammedans having brought their opinions hither, the principal king of the country took a total diſlike to the national worſhip. Alarmed at the terrible cataſtrophe, with which he was equally threatened by both the new ſyſtems of religion, he convened a general aſſembly. On the day appointed he aſcended

ascended an eminence; where spreading out his hands towards heaven, and, in a standing posture, he addressed the following prayer to the Supreme Being.

" Great God, I do not, at this time, fall
" down before thee, because I do not implore
" thy clemency. I have nothing to ask of thee
" which thou oughtest not in justice to grant.
" Two foreign nations whose mode of worship is
" widely different, are come to strike terror into
" me, and my subjects. They assure me that
" thou wilt punish me eternally if I do not obey
" thy laws: I have therefore a right to require
" that thou wouldest make them known to me.
" I do not ask thee to reveal the impenetrable
" mysteries which surrounded thy essence, and
" which to me are useless. I am come hither to
" inquire, together with my people, what those
" duties are which thou intendest to prescribe
" to us. Speak, O my God; since thou art
" the Author of nature, thou canst discern the
" bottom of our hearts, and knowest that it is
" impossible they should entertain any thoughts
" of disobedience. But if thou condescendest
" not to make thyself understood by mortals; if
" it is unworthy of thine essence to employ the
" language of man to dictate the duties re-
" quired of man; I call my whole nation, the sun
" which enlightens me, the earth that supports
" me, the waters that encompass my dominions,
" and thyself to witness, that in the sincerity of
" my heart I seek to know thy will: and I de-
" clare to thee this day, that I shall acknow-
" ledge,

"ledge, as the depofitaries of the oracles, the mi-
"nifters of either religion whom thou fhalt caufe
"to arrive the firft in our harbours. The winds
"and the waves are the minifters of thy power;
"let them be the fignals of thy will. If, with
"thefe honeft intentions, I embrace an error, my
"confcience will be at eafe; and the blame will
"lie upon thee."

THE affembly broke up, determined to wait the orders of heaven, and to follow the firft miffionaries that fhould arrive at Celebes. The apoftles of the coran were the moft active, and the fovereign and his people were circumcifed: the other parts of the ifland foon followed their example.

THIS unfortunate circumftance did not hinder the Portuguefe from gaining a footing at Celebes. They maintained their ground there, even after they were driven out of the Moluccas. The motive which induced them to ftay, and which attracted the Englifh to this place, was, the facility of procuring fpices, which the natives of the country found means to get, notwithftanding the precautious that were taken to keep them at a diftance from the places where they grew.

THE Dutch, who by this competition were prevented from monopolizing the articles of cloves and nutmegs, attempted in 1660, to put a ftop to this trade, which they called contraband. To favour this defign, they had recourfe to means repugnant to all principles of morality, but which an infatiable avarice had familiarized in Afia. By perfevering in these infamous proceedings, they succeeded so far as to drive out the Portuguese, keep off the English, and to take possession of the harbour and fort of Macassar. From that time they were absolute masters of the island without having conquered it. The princes among whom it was divided, reunited in a kind of confederacy. They hold assemblies, from time to time, on affairs that concern the general interest. The result of their determinations becomes a law to each state. When any contest arises, it is decided by the governor of the Dutch colony, who presides at this diet. He observes these different sovereigns with a watchful eye, and keeps them in perfect equality with each other, to prevent any of them from aggrandizing himself to the prejudice of the company. They have disarmed them all, under pretence of hindering them from injuring each other; but in reality with a view of depriving them of the power of breaking their chains.

The Chinese, who are the only foreigners permitted to come to Celebes, carry thither tobacco, gold wire, china and unwrought silks. The Dutch sell opium, spirituous liquors, gum lac, fine and coarse linens. They get but little gold from thence, but great quantities of rice, wax, slaves, and tripam, a species of mushroom, which the rounder and blacker it is, the more excellent it is esteemed. The customs bring in 80,000 livres [*] to the company: but it receives a much larger profit from its trade, and the tenth part of the territory

[*] 3,500l.

ritory which it holds in full right of sovereignty. Thefe advantages, however, taken altogether, do not counterbalance the expences of the colony, which arife to 150,000 livres * more. It would certainly be given up, if it were not with good reafon looked upon as the key of the fpice iflands.

The fettlement at Borneo was formed with a lefs interefting view. It is one of the largeft, if not actually the largeft ifland hitherto known. The ancient inhabitants live in the inland parts. The coafts are peopled with inhabitants from Macaffar, with Javanefe, Malayans, and Arabs, who, to the vices that are natural to them, have added a ferocity hardly to be met with elfewhere. The moft ufeful production of this large country is camphire, which is a volatile, fubtile oil, or refinous fubftance. The tree from which it is produced, grows in feveral of the Afiatic iflands; and it has lately been difcovered that this fingular fubftance may be obtained in a greater or lefs quantity from all the trees that are of the laurel tribe.

To procure this camphire, the tree is cut into fmall pieces, like matches, which are put into a veffel fhaped like a bladder: they are boiled in water, and the camphire forms a glutinous mafs at the top. The Dutch are the only people in Europe who poffefs the fecret of refining it in the grofs.

The Dutch open a communication with Borneo.

---

* About 6,562*l*.

HISTORY OF SETTLEMENTS AND TRADE

The camphire from Borneo is unqueſtionably the beſt of any. Its ſuperior excellence is ſo well known, that the Japaneſe give five or ſix quintals of their own for one pound of that from Borneo; and the Chineſe, who look upon it as the beſt medicine in the world, give us no leſs than eight hundred livres* a pound for it. The Pagans in all the eaſtern countries uſe common camphire in their fireworks, and the Mohammedans put it into the mouth of the dead at the time of burial.

About the year 1526 the Portugueſe attempted to ſettle at Borneo. Too feeble to make their arms reſpected, they tried to gain the good-will of one of the ſovereigns of the country by offering him ſome pieces of tapeſtry. This weak prince took the figures wrought in it for inchanted men, who would ſtrangle him in the night-time, if he ſuffered them to come near his perſon. The explanations they gave to remove his apprehenſions had no effect; he obſtinately refuſed to let the preſent be brought into his palace, and prohibited the donors from entering his capital.

However, theſe adventurers afterwards gained admiſſion; but it proved their misfortune, for they were all maſſacred. A factory which the Engliſh eſtabliſhed ſome years after ſhared the ſame fate. The Dutch, who had met with no better treatment, appeared again, in the year 1748, with a ſquadron, which, though very inconſiderable, ſo far impoſed upon the prince, who has the pepper entirely in his hands, that he determined to grant

* 35l.

them

IN THE EAST AND WEST INDIES.
them the privilege of trading for it exclusively: with this single reserve, that he should be allowed to deliver five hundred thousand pounds of this article to the Chinese, who had always frequented his ports. Since this treaty, the company sends rice, opium, salt, and coarse linens to Bendermassen, from whence they bring some diamonds, and about six hundred thousand weight of pepper, at one and thirty livres * a hundred weight. The profits arising from the goods they export are scarce sufficient to answer the expences of the colony, though they amount to no more than 32,000 livres†. Sumatra proves of greater advantage to them.

Though this island, before the arrival of the Europeans in India, was divided into several kingdoms, Achen was the center of all trade. Its harbour was frequented by all the Asiatic states, and afterwards by the Portuguese and other nations, who raised themselves upon their ruins. Here all the productions of the east were bartered for gold, pepper, and other articles of merchandise with which this more opulent than healthy climate abounded. The disturbances which threw this famous emporium into confusion, put a stop to all industry, and drove the foreign merchants away.

When this declension happened, the Dutch formed the project of making settlements in other parts of the island, which enjoyed more tranquility. Those that were allowed to fix in the empire of Indrapore are much reduced, since the English established themselves on the same coast. The factory

Settlements of the Dutch at Sumatra.

* 1l. 7s. 0d. ¾   † 1,400l.

of

of Iambay is still of less use, as the neighbouring kings have stript the prince of this district of his possessions. The company makes itself amends for these misfortunes at Palinban, where, for sixty thousand livres*, it maintains a fort, a garrison of eighty men, and two or three sloops, which keep continually cruising. It purchases annually two million weight of pepper, at one and twenty livres† a hundred, and a million and a half of calin at fifty-seven livres ten sols‡ a hundred. This, though it seems to be a moderate price, is of advantage to the king, who buys it from his subjects at a still lower rate. Though he takes some part of the provision and cloathing for his states from the merchants at Batavia, they are obliged to settle accounts with him in piastres. The treasures he has amassed of the silver and of the gold found in his rivers, are known to be immense. A single European vessel might take possession of all these riches; and, with some troops for landing, maintain a post, which would be won without difficulty. It seems very extraordinary, that avarice should never have prompted any adventurer to undertake so lucrative and easy an enterprise.

CIVILIZED nations, who, to make themselves masters of the universe, have trampled upon all the rights, and stifled all the dictates of nature will scarcely shrink at one additional act of injustice or cruelty. There is not a nation in Europe which does not think it has a just right to seize the treasures of the east. Setting aside religion which it is no longer fashionable to plead, since it

* 2,625 l.   † 18s. 4d.½   ‡ 2 l. 10s. 3d.¾

ver

IN THE EAST AND WEST INDIES. very ministers have brought it into disrepute, by their unbounded avarice and ambition; how many pretences are still remaining to justify the rage of invasion! They who live under a monarchy are desirous of extending the glory and empire of their master beyond the seas. These happy people are ready to venture their lives in the extreme parts of the globe, to increase the number of fortunate subjects, who live under the laws of the best of princes. A free nation, which is its own master, is born to command the ocean; it cannot secure the dominion of the sea, without seizing upon the land, which belongs to the first possessor; that is, to him who is able to drive out the ancient inhabitants; they are to be enslaved by force or fraud, and exterminated in order to get their possessions. Moreover, the interests of commerce, the national debt, and the majesty of the people, require it. Republicans, who have happily shaken off the yoke of foreign tyranny, must impose it on others in their turn. If they have broken their chains, it is to forge new ones. They detest monarchy, but they are in want of slaves. They have no lands of their own: why should they not seize upon those of others?

The trade of the Dutch at Siam was at first very considerable. A tyrannic prince, who oppressed this unhappy country, having, about the year 1660, shewn a want of respect to the company, it punished him by abandoning the factories it had established in his dominions, as if it would have been a favour to have continued them. These republicans, who af-

Trade of the Dutch at Siam.

fected

fected an air of grandeur, chofe at that time to have their prefence looked upon as a favour, a fecurity, and an honour: and they inculcated this fingular prejudice with fo much fuccefs, that in order to engage them to return, a pompous embaffy was fent, afking pardon for what had paft, and giving the ftrogeft affurances of a different conduct for the future.

There was a time, however, when this defèrence was to ceafe, and it was haftened by the naval enterprifes of other powers. The affairs of the company at Siam have always been in a declining ftate. Having no fort, it has never been in a condition to keep up the exclufive privilege. The king, notwithftanding the prefents he requires, fells merchandife to traders of all nations, and takes goods from them on advantageous terms: with this difference only, that they are obliged to ftop at the mouth of the Menan, whereas the Dutch go up the river as far as the capital of the empire, where their agent conftantly refides. Their trade derives no great activity from this privilege. They fend only one veffel which tranfports Javanefe horfes, and is freighted with fugar, fpices and linens; for which they receive in return calin, at 70 livres* a hundred weight; gum lac, at 52†, fome elephants teeth, at five livres fix fols‡ a pound; and a fmall quantity of gold, at 175 livres 10 fols§ a mark. One may venture to affert, that their connections here are kept up merely on account of the fappan wood which is neceffary for the ftowing of their fhips

* 3l. 1s. 3d. † 2l. 5s. 6d. ‡ 4s. 7d. ½ § 7l. 13s. 1d. ½

IN THE EAST AND WEST INDIES.

and for which they give no less than five livres * per hundred weight. Were it not for this want, they would long ago have given up a trade where the expence exceeds the profits; because the king, who is the only merchant in his dominions, sets a very low price upon the commodities that are imported. A more interesting object turned the ambitious views of the Dutch towards Malacca.

THESE republicans, who knew the importance of this place, used their utmost efforts to make themselves masters of it. Having miscarried in two attempts, they had recourse at last, if we may believe a satirical writer, to an expedient which a virtuous people will never employ; but which frequently answers the purpose of a degenerate nation. They endeavoured to bribe the Portuguese governor, whom they knew to be covetous. The bargain was struck, and he introduced the enemy into the city in 1641. The besiegers hastened to his house and massacred him, to save the payment of the 500,000 livres † they had promised him. But truth obliges us to declare, for the honour of the Portuguese, that they did not surrender till after a most obstinate defence. The commander of the victorious party asked the commander of the other, in a boasting strain which is not natural to his nation, when he would come back again to the place? *When your crimes are greater than ours,* replied the Portuguese gravely.

THE conquerors found a fort, which, like all the works of the Portuguese, was built with a de-

Situation of the Dutch at Malacca.

* 4s. 4d. ½   † 21,875l.

VOL. I.   P   gree

gree of strength that has never since been imitated by any nation. They found the climate very healthy, though hot and damp: but the trade there was entirely decayed; the continual exactions having deterred all nations from resorting thither. It has not been revived by the company, either on account of some insuperable difficulties, or the want of moderation, or the fear of injuring Batavia. The business is confined at present to the sale of a small quantity of opium, and a few blue linens, and to the purchase of elephants teeth, calin, which costs 70 livres * per hundred weight, and a small quantity of gold, at 180 livres † a mark. Their affairs would be carried on with more spirit and to a greater amount, if the princes adhered more faithfully to the exclusive treaty subsisting between them. Unfortunately for their interests, they have formed connections with the English, who furnish them with the commodities they want at a cheaper rate, and give a greater price for their merchandise. Their farms and customs make them some little amends, bringing in 200,000 livres‡ a year. These revenues, however, and the advantages of commerce taken together, are not sufficient to maintain the garrison and people employed; which costs the company 40,000 livres§.

This might for a long time appear to be a small sacrifice. Before the Europeans doubled the cape of Good Hope, the Moors, who were the only maritime people in India, sailed from Su-

* 3l. 1s. 3d.   † 7l. 17s. 6d.   ‡ 8,750.   § 1,750l.

rat

IN THE EAST AND WEST INDIES.

rat and Bengal, to Malacca, where they found ships from the Molucca iſlands, Japan, and China. When the Portugueſe became maſters of this place, they went themſelves to Bantam for pepper, and to Ternate for ſpices. To make their return the ſhorter, they attempted a paſſage by the Sunda iſlands, and ſucceeded. The Dutch, who had got poſſeſſion of Malacca and Batavia, were maſters of the two only ſtraits that were then known. They cruiſed there in times of war, and intercepted the enemy's veſſels. This ſituation has ceaſed to be reſpectable, ſince the ſtrait of Bali was diſcovered by the French at the end of the war in 1744, and that of Lomboc by the Engliſh in the laſt war. Batavia will always continue to be the ſtaple of an immenſe trade; but Malacca loſes the only advantage that gave it any importance.

THOUGH the company did not foreſee this event, yet at the ſame time that they were enlarging and ſtrengthening their power in the eaſtern parts of Aſia, they formed the project of ſecuring to themſelves that part of India, where the Portugueſe continued to counteract their operations, and of taking from them the iſland of Ceylon. It is obſervable that this nation, ſo diſtinguiſhed for the juſtneſs of its commercial views, endeavoured to get thoſe productions into its hands, which were either abſolutely neceſſary or nearly ſo, before it turned its attention to articles of luxury. It owes its grandeur in Aſia to the ſpice trade, and in Europe to the herring fiſhery. The Moluccas ſupply

Settlement of the Dutch at Ceylon.

it with nutmegs and cloves; and Ceylon furnishes it with cinnamon.

SPILBERG, the firſt of their admirals who had the courage to diſplay his colours on the coaſt of this delicious iſland, found the Portugueſe employed in ſubverting the government and the religion of the country; in exciting the ſovereigns, among whom it was divided, to deſtroy each other; and in raiſing themſelves upon the ruins of the ſtates that were thus ſucceſſively demoliſhed. He offered the court of Candy the aſſiſtance of his country, which was joyfully accepted. *You may aſſure your maſters*, ſaid the monarch, *that if they will build a fort, myſelf, my wife, and children will be foremoſt in bringing the neceſſary materials.*

THE people of Ceylon looked upon the Dutch in no other light than as the enemies of their oppreſſors, and joined them. By their united forces, the Portugueſe were, in the year 1658, entirely diſpoſſeſſed, after a long, bloody, and obſtinate war. All their ſettlements fell into the hands of the company, who ſtill keep poſſeſſion of them, excepting a ſmall diſtrict on the eaſtern coaſt, without any port, from whence the ſovereign of the country had his ſalt; theſe ſettlements formed a regular ſtring, extending from two to twelve leagues into the inland parts of the iſland.

THE fort of Jaffranapatam, as well as thoſe erected on the iſlands of Manar and Calpentine, were deſtined to prevent all correſpondence with the inhabitants of the neighbouring continent. At Negombo, deſigned to comprehend the diſtrict in which

which the beft cinnamon is produced, there is a harbour large enough to admit floops: but it is not frequented, on account of a navigable river that leads from it to Columbo. This place, which the Portuguefe had fortified with the greateft care, as the center of opulence, is become the principal ftation in the colony. It is not improbable, that, independent of the fums which had been expended upon it, the badnefs of its road might have determined the Dutch to fix the ftrength of their government at the promontory of Galla, where there is a harbour; which, though the entrance is indeed difficult, and the bafon very confined, has every other advantage that can be wifhed. It is here that the company take in their cargoes for Europe.

MATARAN is the magazine for coffee and pepper, the culture of which has been introduced by the company. It has no other fortification than a redoubt built upon a river that is only navigable for boats. Trinquimale is the fineft and beft harbour in India. It is compofed of feveral bays, where the moft numerous fleets may anchor in fecurity. No trade is carried on there. The country furnifhes no one article of merchandife; and even provifions are very fcarce : in fhort, it is protected by its barrennefs. Other fettlements of inferior note that are fcattered upon the coaft, ferve to make the communication eafy, and to keep off ftrangers.

By thefe wife precautions, the company have appropriated all the productions of the ifland. The feveral articles which conftitute fo many branches of trade are; 1. Amethyfts, fapphires, topazes, and rubies which are very small, and very different. The Moors, who come from the coast of Coromandel, buy them, paying a moderate tax; and, when they are cut, sell them at a low price in the different countries of India.

2. PEPPER, which the company buy for eight sols* a pound; coffee, for which they only pay four †; and cardamom, which has no fixed price. The natives of the country are so indolent, that these productions, which are all of an inferior quality, will never turn to any great advantage.

3. A HUNDRED bales of handkerchiefs, pagnes and ginghams, of a fine red colour, which are fabricated by the Malabars at Jafranapatan, where they have long been settled.

4. A SMALL quantity of ivory, and about fifty elephants, which are carried to the coast of Coromandel. Thus this gentle and peaceful animal, which is too useful to mankind to be suffered to remain upon an island, is transported to the continent, to aggravate and bear a part in the dangers and horrors of war.

5. ARECA, which the company buys at the rate of ten livres ‡ the ammonan, and sells upon the spot at thirty-six or forty livres § to the merchants of Bengal, Coromandel, and the Maldives; who give in return rice, coarse linens, and cowries. The areca, which grows upon a species of palm-tree, is a fruit not uncommon in most parts of Asia, and is in great plenty at Ceylon. It is oval, and would not be much unlike the date, if its extremities

* About 4d.   † About 2d.   ‡ 8s. 9d.   § About 1l. 13s.

were

were lefs pointed. The bark is thick, fmooth, and membranaceous, and covers a kernel of a whitifh caft, fhaped like a pear, and of the bignefs of a nutmeg. When eaten by itfelf, as it fometimes is by the Indians, it impoverifhes the blood, and caufes the jaundice. It is not attended with thefe inconveniencies when mixed with betel.

The betel is a creeping and climbing plant like the ivy, but does no injury to the agoti, which it embraces as its fupport, and is remarkably fond of. It is cultivated in the fame manner as the vine. Its leaves a good deal refemble thofe of the citron, though they are longer and narrower at the extremity. The betel grows in all parts of India, but flourifhes beft in moift places.

At all times of the day, and even in the night, the Indians chew the leaves of the betel, the bitternefs of which is corrected by the areca that is wrapped up in them. There is conftantly mixed with it the chinam, a kind of burnt lime made of fhells. The rich frequently add perfumes, either to gratify their vanity or their fenfuality.

It would be thought a breach of politenefs among the Indians to take leave for any long time, without prefenting each other with a purfe of betel. It is a pledge of friendfhip that relieves the pain of abfence: No one dares to fpeak to a fuperior unlefs his mouth is perfumed with betel; it would even be rude to neglect this precaution with an equal. The women of gallantry are the moft lavifh in the ufe of betel, as being a powerful incentive to love. Betel is taken after meals; it is chewed during a

visit;

visit; it is offered when you meet, and when you separate; in short, nothing is to be done without betel. If it is prejudicial to the teeth, it assists and strengthens the stomach. At least, it is a general fashion that prevails throughout India.

6. The pearl fishery, which is also one of the sources of the revenue of Ceylon. It is no improbable conjecture, that this island, which is only fifteen leagues from the continent, was at some distant period separated from it by some great convulsion of nature. The tract of sea, which at present divides it from the land, is so full of shallows, that no ships can sail upon it; and there are only a few places where small boats may pass in four or five feet water. The Dutch, who assume the sovereignty here, have always two armed sloops to enforce the payment of the taxes they have imposed. In this strait the pearl fishery is carried on, which was formerly of so much importance; but this source of wealth has been so much exhausted, that it is but rarely resorted to. The bank, indeed, is visited every year, to see how it is replenished with oysters; but, in general, it is five or six years before a sufficient quantity is to be found. The fishery is then farmed out; and, every thing computed, it may produce to the revenues of the company 200,000 livres*. Upon the same coasts is found a shell-fish called xanxus, of which the Indians at Bengal make bracelets. The fishery is free, but the trade is exclusive.

After all, the great object of the company is cinnamon. The root of the tree that produces it

* 8,750l.

is large, and divides it into several branches covered with a bark, which on the outer side is of a greyish brown, and on the inner of a reddish cast. The wood of this root is hard, white, and has no smell. The body of the tree, which grows to the height of eight or ten toises, is covered as well as its numerous branches, with a bark which at first is green, and afterwards red. The leaf, if it were not longer and narrower, would not be much unlike that of the laurel. When first unfolded it is of a flame colour: but after it has been for some time exposed to the air, and grows dry, it changes to a deep green on the upper surface, and to a lighter on the lower. The flowers are small and white, and grow in large bunches at the extremity of the branches; they have an agreeable smell, something like that of the lily of the valley. The fruit is shaped like an acorn, but is not so large. It is commonly ripe in September. When boiled in water, it yields an oil which swims at top, and takes fire. If left to cool, it hardens into a white substance, of which candles are made, which have an agreeable smell, and are reserved for the use of the king of Ceylon. No part of the tree that produces the cinnamon is valuable except the under bark. The best season for raising and separating it from the outer bark, which is grey and rugged, is the spring, when the sap flows in the greatest abundance. It is cut into thin slices, and exposed to the sun; and curls up in drying.

The old trees produce a coarse kind of cinnamon, which is in perfection only when the trees are

are not older than three or four years. When the trunk has been stripped of its bark it receives no further nourishment, but the root is still alive, and continues to throw out fresh shoots. Besides this, the fruit of the cinnamon-tree contains a seed from which it is raised.

There are some of the company's territories where this tree does not grow. It is only to be found in those of Negombo, Columbo, or the promontory of Galla. The prince's forests supply the deficiency which sometimes prevails in the magazines. The mountains inhabited by the Bedas abound with the tree: but neither the Europeans nor the Cinglasses are allowed access to them, and there is no way of sharing the riches of the Bedas but by declaring war against them.

As the Cinglasses, as well as the Indians upon the continent, are divided into casts which never make any alliances with one another, each constantly adhering to the same profession; the art of barking the cinnamon-trees is a distinct occupation, and the meanest of all others, and is confined to the cast of the Cooleys. Every other islander would look upon it as a disgrace to be employed in this trade.

The cinnamon is not reckoned excellent unless it be be fine, smooth, brittle, thin, of a yellow colour inclining to red, fragrant, aromatic, and of a poignant, yet agreeable taste. The connoisseurs give the preference to that, the pieces of which are long but slender. It adds to the delicacies of the table, and is of sovereign use in medicine.

The

IN THE EAST AND WEST INDIES.

THE Dutch purchase the greatest part of their cinnamon of the Indians who are subject to them. They have engaged to take a limited quantity of the king of Candy, at an advanced price. Setting one against the other, it does not cost them twelve sols * a pound. It would not be impossible for the ships that frequent the ports of Ceylon, to procure the tree that produces the cinnamon; but it has degenerated at Malabar, Batavia, the isle of France, and in all parts where it has been transplanted.

FORMERLY the company thought it necessary to maintain four thousand black or white soldiers, to secure the advantages they derived from Ceylon. The number is now reduced to fifteen or sixteen hundred. Their annual expences, nevertheless, amount to 2,200,000 livres †; and their revenues, and small branches of commerce, produce no more than 2,000,000 of livres ‡. This deficiency is supplied out of the profits arising from cinnamon. They are likewise obliged to provide for the expence attending the wars they are from time to time engaged in with the king of Candy, who is at present the sole sovereign of the island.

THE Dutch freely own that these ruptures are fatal to them. As soon as they break out, most of the people who inhabit the coasts retire into the inland parts of the country. Notwithstanding the despotism that awaits them, they look upon the yoke of the Europeans as an evil still more insupportable. The Cooleys are so far from

* About 6d.   † 96,250l.   ‡ 87,500l.

always

always waiting for the commencement of hostilities as a signal for their removal, that they sometimes resolve to take this desperate step as soon as they perceive the least misunderstanding between the king and the Dutch. On these occasions, besides the loss of a harvest, a long train of expence and fatigue follows, to enable them to penetrate, sword in hand, into a country, encompassed on all sides by rivers, woods, hollow vales, and mountains.

These important considerations had determined the company to engage the good will of the king of Candy, by shewing him all imaginable civilities. Every year they sent an ambassador laden with rich presents. They offered their ships to convey his priests to Siam, to be instructed in the religion of that country, which is the same with his own. Notwithstanding they had taken the forts and the lands which were occupied by the Portuguese, they contented themselves with receiving from this prince the appellation of *guardians of his coasts.* They also made him several other concessions.

These singular instances of management have not, however, been always sufficient to maintain good harmony, which has several times been interrupted. The war which ended on the 14th of February, 1766, had been the longest and the most active of any that had been occasioned by distrust, and the clashing of interests. As the company prescribed terms to a monarch who was driven from his capital, and obliged to wander in the woods, they made a very advantageous treaty

IN THE EAST AND WEST INDIES.

treaty. Their sovereignty was acknowledged over all the countries they were in poffeffion of before the troubles broke out; and that part of the coafts which remained in the occupation of the natives was ceded to them. They are to be allowed to gather cinnamon in all the plains, and he court is to fell them the beft fort that is produced in the mountainous parts at the rate of forty-one livres five fols * for eighteen pounds. Their commiffaries are authorifed to extend their trade to all parts where they think it can be carried on with advantage. The government engages to have no connection with any other foreign power; and even to deliver up any Europeans who may happen to ftray into the ifland. In return for fo many conceffions, the king is to receive annually the value of the produce of the ceded coafts: and from thence his fubjects are to be furnifhed gratis with falt fufficient for their confumption. It fhould feem that the company may derive great advantages from fo favourable a fituation.

THE property of the lands in Ceylon belongs more of right to the fovereign than in any other part of India. This pernicious fyftem has in that ifland been attended with fatal confequences infeparable from it. The people are in a ftate of total inactivity. They live in huts, have no furniture, and fubfift upon fruits; and thofe who are the moft affluent, have no other covering than a piece of coarfe linen wrapped about

* 1L. 16s. 1d.

their

their waift. It were to be wifhed that the Dutch would purfue a fcheme, which all the nations who have eftablifhed colonies in Afia, are to blame never to have attempted, and that is, to diftribute the lands among the families, and make them their own property. They would forget, and perhaps hate their former foveriegn; they would attach themfelves to a government that confulted their happinefs; they would become induftrious, and occafion a greater confumption. Under fuch circumftances the ifland o Ceylon would enjoy that opulence which was defignec it by nature: it would be fecure from revolutions and be enabled to fupport the fettlements of Mala bar and Coromândel, which it is bound to protect

Trade of the Dutch on the coaft of Coromandel.

THE Portuguefe, in the time of their profpe rity, had formed fome tolerable fettlements o the coaft of Coromandel. That at Negapata was taken from them by the Dutch in 1658. gradually increafed to ten or twelve village which were all inhabited by weavers. In 169(it was thought proper to build a fort to fecu their tranquillity, and in 1742 the tower was fu rounded by walls. This is the central place in which all the white, blue, painted, printed, fi and coarfe linens are brought, which the cor pany collects for the confumption of Europe India: and which come either from Bimilip: nam, Pellicate, Sadrafpatan, or from its facl· ries on the fifhing coaft. Their inveftmen, which commonly amount to four or five thc· fand bales, are carried to Negapatan, by t,) floops ftationed in thefe feas for that purpofe.

IN THE EAST AND WEST INDIES.

The Dutch fell, on the coaſt of Coromandel, iron, lead, copper, calin, tutenague, pepper, and ſpices. Theſe united articles produce a million of livres *, to which we may add eighty thouſand † ariſing from the cuſtoms. The expences of their ſeveral eſtabliſhments amount to eight hundred thouſand livres ‡; and we may venture to aſſert without fear of being accuſed of exaggeration, that the freight of the ſhips ſwallows up the reſt of the profits. The net produce therefore of the Coromandel trade to the company, is the profit ariſing from the linens they export from thence. Their trade on the Malabar coaſt is ſtill leſs advantageous to them. It commenced pretty nearly at the ſame period, and was eſtabliſhed at the expence of the ſame nation.

It appears to be no difficult taſk to gueſs at the motives that led to this new enterpriſe. After the Portugueſe had loſt Ceylon, they ſold the wild cinnamon of Malabar in Europe nearly for the ſame price as they had always ſold the right ſort. Though this rivalſhip could not continue long, it gave uneaſineſs to the Dutch, who, in 1662, ordered Vaugoens, their general, to attack Cochin.

Trade of the Dutch on the coaſt of Malabar

The place was no ſooner inveſted, than intelligence was received of a peace being concluded between Holland and Portugal. This news was kept ſecret. The operations were carried on with vigour; and the beſieged, harraſſed by conti-

* 43,750l.   † 3,500l.   ‡ 35,000l.

nual

nual assaults, surrendered on the eighth day. The next day a frigate arrived from Goa with the articles of peace. The conquerors gave themselves no further trouble to justify their treachery, than by saying, that those who complained in so haughty a stile, had observed the same conduct at Brazil a few years before.

AFTER this conquest, the Dutch thought themselves firmly established in Malabar. Cochin seemed to be necessary to protect Cananor, Cranganor, and Quillon, of which they had just before made themselves masters, and the factory of Porcat, which they had formed the plan of at that time, and have since actually established. The event has not answered their expectation. The company have not succeeded in their hopes of excluding other European nations from this coast. They procure no kind of merchandise there, but what they are furnished with from their other settlements; and being rivalled in their trade they are obliged to give a higher price here, than in the markets where they enjoy an exclusive privilege.

THEIR articles of sale consist of a small quantity of alum, benzoin, camphire, tutenague, sugar, iron, calin, lead, copper, and quicksilver. The vessel that carries this slender cargo returns to Batavia laden with caire, or cocoa-tree bark, for the use of the port. By these articles the company gain, at most, 360,000 livres *, which, with 120,000 † arising from the customs, make

* 15,750 l.   † 5,250 l.

IN THE EAST AND WEST INDIES.

the sum of 480,000 livres *. In times of profound peace the maintenance of these settlements costs 464,000 livres †, so that 16,000 ‡ only, remain to defray the expences of their shipping, for which that sum is certainly not sufficient.

It is true, the company gets two millions weight of pepper from Malabar, which is carried in sloops to Ceylon, where it is put aboard the ships fitted out for Europe. It is likewise true, that, by virtue of these capitulations, they pay only 192 livres § the candil, which weighs five hundred pounds, for which other companies give 240 **, and private merchants 288 ††; but whatever advantage may be made of this article, it is reduced to nothing by the bloody wars it occasions.

These observations had doubtless escaped the notice of Golonefs, the director-general of Batavia, when he ventured to affirm that the settlement of Malabar which he had long superintended, was one of the most important settlements belonging to the company. " I am so far from being of your " opinion, said general Moffel, that I could wish " the sea had swallowed it up about a century ago."

Be this as it may, the Dutch, in the height of their success, felt the want of a place where their vessels might put in to get refreshments, either in going to, or returning from India. They were undetermined in their choice, when Van-Riebeck the surgeon, in 1650, proposed the Cape of Good Hope, which the Portuguese had imprudently

The Dutch form a settlement at the Cape of Good Hope.

* 21,000l. † 20,300l. ‡ 700l.
§ 8l. 8s.   ⁎⁎ 10l. 10s.   †† 12l. 12s.

despised.

despised. This jdicious man, during a stay of some weeks, was convinced that a colony might be placed to advantage on this southern extremity of Africa, which might serve as a staple for the commerce of Europe and Asia. The care of forming this settlement was committed to him; and his measures were concerted upon a good plan. He caused it to be stipulated that every man who chose to fix there should have sixty acres of land allotted him. Corn, cattle, and utensils were to be provided for those who wanted them. Young women taken from alms-houses were given them as companions to soften, and to share their fatigues. All those, who after three years found the climate did not agree with them, had liberty to return to Europe, and to dispose of their possessions in what manner they pleased. Having settled these arrangements he set sail.

The large tract of country which it was proposed to cultivate, was inhabited by the Hottentots, who, according to a French traveller, are divided into several clans, each of which forms an independent village. Their habitations are huts covered with skins, which cannot be entered without creeping upon their hands and knees, and are disposed in a circle. These huts are hardly of any other use than to hold a few provisions and household furniture. The Hottentots never enter them but in the rainy season. They are always found lying at their doors; and if they interrupt their repose it is to smoke a strong herb which serves them instead of tobacco.

IN THE EAST AND WEST INDIES.

THE management of cattle is the fole employment of thefe favages. As there is but one herd in each town which is common to all the inhabitants, each of them is appointed to guard it in his turn. This poft requires conftant vigilance, the country being full of wild beafts, which are more voracious at this extremity of Africa than in any other part. The fhepherd fends out fcouts every day. If a leopard or tyger is feen in the neighbourhood, the whole town takes up arms, and flies to the enemy, who feldom efcapes from fo many poifoned arrows, and fharp ftakes hardened in the fire.

As the Hottentots neither have, nor appear to have riches, and that their oxen and fheep, which is all the property they have, are in common; it is natural to imagine that there is little occafion for difputes among them. They are accordingly united to each other by the clofeft ties of friendfhip: nor do they ever engage in any war, even with their neighbours; fetting afide the quarrels between the fhepherds on account of cattle that may have ftrayed, or been carried off.

IT has often been remarked that public cuftoms gave rife to the firft colonies. Marks of diftinction were adopted to make men unite and recognize one another. A broken nofe, a flat head, bored ears, paintings, burnings, head-dreffes, are the uniform characteriftics of the favage world. As no plan of morality or education prevails among them, it follows of courfe, that univerfal cuftoms muft with them fupply the place of policy and government. Thefe uncivilized men,

the

the children of nature, depend entirely on the temper of the climate: and hence the Hottentots have the manners of ploughmen.

WHEN the Dutch arrived, the Hottentots were, like all people who lead a paftoral life, full of benevolence; and partook in fome degree of the uncleanlinefs and ftupidity of the animals they kept. They had inftituted an order, with which they honoured thofe who had fubdued any of the monfters that were deftructive to their fheepfolds: and they revered the memory of the heroes who had done fervice to mankind. The apotheofis of Hercules had the fame origin.

RIEBECK, in conformity to the notions unhappily prevailing among the Europeans, began to take pofleffion of the moft commodious part of the territory; and he afterwards defigned to fix himfelf there. This behaviour difpleafed the natives. *On what pretence,* faid their envoy to thefe ftrangers, *have you fown our lands? Why do you employ them to feed your cattle? How would you behave if you faw your own fields invaded in this manner? You fortify yourfelves with no other view than to reduce the Hottentots to flavery.* Thefe remonftrances were followed by fome hoftilities, which brought the founder of the colony back to thofe principles of juftice and humanity, that where agreeable to his natural character. he purchafed the country he wanted to occupy for the fum of 90,000 livers * which was paid in merchandife. All parties were reconciled, and from

---
* 3,937 l. 10 s.

that

that period to the prefent time, there has been no further difturbance.

It has been proved that the company have expended 46,000,000 of livres* in raifing the colony to its prefent ftate. A few particulars will enable us to judge how fo confiderable a fum has been employed.

It is computed that there are at the Cape of Good Hope about twelve thoufand Europeans, Dutch, Germans, and French refugees. Some part of thefe numbers refide in the capital, and two confiderable towns: the reft are difperfed along the coaft, which extends fifty leagues into the country. The foil of the Hottentots being fandy, and only good by intervals; the hufbandmen chufe to confine themfelves to thofe places where they meet with water, wood, and fertile lands; three advantages feldom found together.

The company formerly procured flaves from Madagafcar, who alleviated the burthen of the white people. Since the French appeared as rivals, this communication has been difcontinued. The prefent planters confift of a few Malays, who are unaccuftomed to that climate, and are fcarce fit for the work that is required of them.

If it were practicable to make the Hottentots fteady, great advantages might accrue, which cannot be hoped for from their prefent character. All that has yet been done, has been to prevail with the pooreft of them to engage in their fervice for one, two, or three years. They are of a

* 2,012,500 l.

docile temper, and perform the work that is expected from them; but, at the expiration of their agreement, they take the cattle that are allowed them for wages, rejoin their clan, and never make their appearance again till they have oxen or sheep to barter for knives, tobacco, and brandy. They find an inexpreffible charm in the independent and indolent life they lead in their deferts. Nothing can wean them from this attachment. One of their children was taken from the cradle, and inftructed in our manners and religion; he made a progrefs anfwerable to the pains that where beftowed upon his education; he was fent to India, and ufefully employed in trade. Happening, by accident, to revifit his country, he went to fee his relations in their hut. He was ftruck with the fimplicity that appeared there; he clothed himfelf with a fheep-fkin, and went to the fort to carry back his European habiliments. *I am come,* faid he to the governor, *to renounce for ever the mode of life you have taught me to embrace. I am refolved to follow, till death, the manners and religion of my anceftors. As a token of my affection, I will keep the collar and fword you have given me: all the reft you will permit me to leave behind.* He did not wait for an anfwer, but ran away, and was never heard of after.

Though the character of the Hottentots is not fuch as the Dutch could wifh, the company derive folid advantages from this colony. Indeed, the tenth part of the corn and wine, together with their cuftoms and other duties, does

not

IN THE EAST AND WEST INDIES.

not exceed 240,000 livres*. They gain no more than 40,000 † by their thick cloths, common thread and cotton pieces, hardware, coals, and other confiderable articles, which they vend at this place.

They receive a ſtill ſmaller profit from ſixty lecques of red wine, and eighty or ninety of white, which they carry to Europe every year. The lecque weighs about twelve hundred pounds. There are only two places in the neighbourhood of Conſtantia that produce this wine. The company might have it entirely genuine, and at a very low rate. Happily the governor finds it his intereſt to allow the cultivators to mix it with the produce of the adjacent vineyards. By this management what remains of this celebrated wine, the genuine excellent Cape wine, is ſold to foreign veſſels that happen to touch at the coaſts at four livres ‡ a bottle. It is generally preferable to that which is extorted by tyranny; nothing good being to be expected where it is not voluntarily obtained.

As the expences neceſſary for the ſupport of ſo large a ſettlement, ſwallow up, at leaſt, all theſe profits taken together, its utility muſt reſt upon ſome other foundation.

The Dutch ſhips that ſail to and from India find a ſafe aſylum at the Cape; a delightful, ſerene, and temperate ſky, and learn every thing of importance that happens in both thoſe parts of the globe. Here they take in butter, meal,

* 10,500 l. † 1,750 l. ‡ 3s. 6d.

wine,

wine, large quantities of pickled vegetables for their voyage, and for the use of the colonies. They might derive much greater advantages from hence, if the company, blinded by their avidity, were not perpetually checking the induftry of the planters. They oblige them to part with their provifions at fo low a price, that they have not, for a long time, been able to procure cloathing and other abfolute neceffaries.

This tyrannical conduct might, perhaps, be borne with, if the victims of it where authorifed to fell their fuperfluous produce to foreign navigators, whom the convenience of their fituation, or other reafons, might invite into their ports. But a fpirit of jealoufy in trade, which is one of the greateft evils that can befal mankind, has deprived them of this refource. The Dutch have long flattered themfelves, that by with-holding this convenience from other trading nations, they fhould make them abandon India in difguft. Notwithftanding they have experienced the reverfe of this, their conduct is not altered; though it was eafy to difcern, that all the wealth which flowed into the colony would, fooner or later, return to the company. The governor only is authorifed to fupply the moft preffing neceffities of thofe who touch at the Cape. Thefe wrong meafures, have been, as they muft neceffarily be, the fource of a thoufand inconveniences.

We muft, however, do juftice to M. Tolbac, who at prefent prefides over this colony. This generous man, during the laft war, fet an example

ample of benevolence and difintereftednefs, which was not to be found in any of his predeceffors. As his underftanding raifed him above prejudice, and that he had a fufficient degree of firmnefs to deviate from the abfurd orders he received, he encouraged the nations who endeavoured to fupplant one another to repair to his colony for fubfiftence. The price was fo regulated by fo juft a ftandard, that while it was fo moderate as to invite purchafers, it was high enough to animate the cultivators to induftry. May this wife magiftrate long enjoy the pleafing confcioufnefs of having made the fortune of his fellow-citizens, and the glory of having neglected his own!

If the company fhould adopt his plan, they will imitate the fpirit of their founders, who did nothing by chance; and, without waiting for the happy events we have been defcribing, they will fet themfelves to find out a place, which they may make the center of their power. They had caft their eyes upon Java as early as the year 1609.

The people of this ifland, which is two hundred leagues in length, and thirty or forty in breadth, traced their origin from China, though they retained nothing either of its religion or its manners. A very fuperftitious fpecies of Mohammedifm conftituted the prevailing worfhip. Some idolaters were ftill remaining in the interior part of the country; and thefe were the only inhabitants of Java that where not arrived at the laft ftage of depravity. This ifland which was formerly under the dominion of a fingle monarch,

Dominions of the Dutch in the Ifland of Java.

narch, was at that time divided among several sovereigns, who were perpetually at war with each other. These eternal diffensions, while they kept up a military spirit among the people, made them neglect manners. Their enmity to strangers, and want of confidence in each other, would lead one to conclude, that they breathed no sentiment but hatred. Here men were wolves to each other, and seemed to unite in society more for the sake of committing mutal injuries, than of receiving mutal assistances. A Javanese never accosted his brother without having a poniard in his hand; ever watchful to prevent, or prepared to commit some act of violence. The nobles had a great number of slaves, either bought, taken in war, or detained for debt, whom they treated with the utmost inhumanity. They cultivated the lands, and performed all kinds of hard labour; while the Javanese was employed in chewing betel, smoking opium, passing his life with his concubines, fighting or sleeping. These people possessed a cosiderable share of understanding, but retained few traces of any moral principle. They had not so much the character of an unenlightened, as of a degenerated nation: in short, they were a sett of men, who from a regular government had fallen into a kind of anarchy; and gave full scope to the impetuous emotions which nature excites in these climates

This depraved character of the inhabitants did not alter the views of the Dutch with respect to Java. Their company might, indeed, be

thwarted

thwarted by the English, who were then in poffeffion of a part of the trade of this ifland. But
this obftacle was foon removed. The weaknefs
of James the Firft, and the corruption of his
council, had fo damped the fpirits of thefe haughty
Britons, that they fuffered themfelves to be fup-
planted, without making thofe efforts that might
have been expected from their bravery. The natives of the country, deprived of this fupport,
were forced to fubmit; but it required time,
addrefs, and policy, to accomplish that fcheme.

It was one of the fundamental maxims of the
Portuguefe to perfuade thofe princes they wanted to
engage or retain inaftate of dependence, to fend their
children to Goa to be educated at the expence of
the court of Lifbon, and initiated early into its manners and principles. But this, which was in itfelf a
good project, was fpoiled by the conquerors, who
admitted thefe young people to a participation of the
moft criminal pleafures, and the moft fhameful
fcences of debauchery. The confequence was, that
when thefe Indians arrived at maturity, they could
not help detefting, or, at leaft, defpifing fuch
abandoned inftructors. The Dutch adopted the
fame plan, and improved upon it. They endeavoured to convince their pupils of the weaknefs,
inconftancy, and treachery of their fubjects; and
ftill more of their power, wifdom, and good faith
of the company. By this method they ftrength-
ened their ufurpations: but we are obliged to fay,
that the Dutch employed means that were treacherous and cruel.

The

The government of the ifland, which was founded entirely on the feudal laws, feemed calculated to promote difcord. Fathers and fons turned their arms againft each other. They fupported the pretenfions of the weak againft the ftrong, and of the ftrong againft the weak, as they faw occafion. They fometimes took the monarch's part, and fometimes that of his vaffals. If any perfon afcended the throne, who was likely to become formidable by his talents, they raifed up rivals to oppofe him. Thofe who were not to be feduced by gold or promifes, were fubdued by fear. Every day was productive of fome revolution which was always begun by the intrigues of the tyrants, and always ended to their advantage, At length they became mafters of the moft important pofts in the inland parts of the country; and of the forts that were built upon the coafts.

This plan of ufurpation was but juft ready to be carried into execution, when a governor was appointed at Java, who had a palace and guards, and appeared in great pomp. The company thought proper to depart from the principles of œconomy they had hitherto adopted; from a perfuafion, that the Portuguefe had derived a great advantage from the brilliant court kept by the viceroy of Goa: that the people of the Eaft were to be dazzled in order to be the more eafily fubdued: and that it was neceffary to ftrike the imagination and the eyes of the Indians, who are guided more by their fenfes than the inhabitants of our climates.

THE

The Dutch had another reason for assuming an air of dignity. They had been represented in Asia as pirates, without a country, without laws, and without a ruler. To silence these calumnies, they endeavoured to prevail with several states adjoining to Java to send ambassadors to prince Maurice of the house of Orange.

The execution of this project procured them a double advantage, as it gave them credit with the eastern nations, and flattered the ambition of the Stadtholder, whose protection was necessary to be obtained, for reasons which we are going to explain.

When the company obtained their exclusive privilege, the straits of Magellan, which could have no connection with the East Indies, were improperly enough included in the grant. Isaac Lemaire, one of those rich and enterprising merchants, who ought every where to be cosidered as the benefactors of their country, formed the project of penetrating into the South Sea by the southern coasts. Access being denied by the only track that was known at that time; he fitted out two ships which passed a strait, since called by his name, running between Cape Horn and Staten land; and were driven by accidents to the coast of Java, where they were condemned, and the crew sent prisoners to Europe.

This tyrannical proceeding gave offence to the people, already prejudiced against an exclusive commerce. It was thought absurd, that instead of giving those who attempted discoveries the encouragement they deserved, a state purely commercial should forge shackles to confine their industry. The monopoly, which the avarice of individuals had endured with impatience, became more odious when the company stretched the concessions that had been made them beyond their due bounds. It was found, that as their pride and influence increased with their power, the interest of the nation would at length be sacrificed to the interest, or even to the caprice of this formidable body. It is probable, that they must have sunk under the publick resentment; and that the charter which was near expiring, would not have been renewed, if they had not been supported by prince Maurice, favoured by the States-General, and encouraged to brave the storm by the strength they derived from their settlement at Java.

Though the tranquillity of this island may have been disturbed by various commotions, several wars, and some conspiracies, it continues to be as much in subjection to the Dutch as they wish it to be.

Bantam comprehends the western part. One of its sovereigns having resigned the crown to his son, was restored to the throne in 1680 by the natural restlessness of his temper, the bad conduct of his successor, and a powerful faction. His party was on the point of prevailing, when the young monarch, besieged in his capital by an army of thirty thousand men, without any adherents, except the companions of his debaucheries, implored the protection of the Dutch. They flew to his assistance, beat his enemies, delivered him from his rival, and re-established his authority. Though

IN THE EAST AND WEST INDIES.

the expedition was fpeedy, fhort, and rapid, and confequently could not be expenfive; they contrived to make the charges of the war amount to a prodigious fum. The fituation of things would not admit of a fcrutiny into the fum demanded for fo great a piece of fervice, and the exhaufted ftate of the finances made it impoffible to difcharge it. In this extemity this weak prince determined to entail flavery on himfelf and his defcendants, by granting to his deliverers the exclufive trade of his dominions.

THE company maintain this great privilege with three hundred and fixty-eight men, who are ftationed in two bad forts, one of which ferves as a habitation for the governor, and the other as a palace for the king. The expences of this fettlement amount to no more than 100,000 livres *, which are regained upon the merchandife fold there. Their clear profits confift of what they gain upon three millions weight of pepper, which they oblige the inhabitants to fell at twenty-five livres twelve fols † a hundred.

THESE profits are inconfiderable in comparifon of what the company receives from Tfieribon, which it fubdued without any efforts, without intrigues, and without expence. The Dutch were fcarce fettled at Java, when the fultan of this narrow but very fertile ftate put himfelf under their protection, to avoid fubmitting to a neighbouring prince more powerful than himfelf. He fells them annually a thoufand lafts of rice, each weighing three thoufand three hundred pounds, at feventy-

* 4,375 l.   † 1 l. 2 s. 4 d. ¾:

fix livres fixteen fols * a laft; a million weight of fugar, the fineft of which coft thirteen livres nine fols † a hundred; one million two hundred thoufand pounds of coffee, at four fols ‡ a pound; a hundred quintals of pepper, at four fols eight deniers § a pound; thirty thoufand pounds of cotton, the fineft of which cofts no more than one livre eight fols ‖ a pound; fix hundred thoufand pounds of areca, at twelve livres ** a hundred. Though fixing thefe prices fo low is a manifeft impofition upon the weaknefs of the inhabitants, the people of Tfieribon, who are the moft gentle and civilized of any in the ifland, have never been provoked by this injuftice to take up arms. A hundred Europeans are fufficient to keep them in fubjection. The expences of this fettlement amount to no more than 41,000 livres ††, which is gained by linens imported thither.

THE empire of Mataram, which formerly extended over the whole ifland, and at prefent takes up the greateft part of it, was the laft that was reduced to fubjection. Often vanquifhed, and fometimes vanquifhing, it continued its ftruggles for independency, when the fon and brother of a fovereign who died in 1704, difputed the fucceffion. The nation was divided between the two rivals. He who was entitled to the crown by orde of fucceffion, had fo vifibly the advantage, that he muft foon have got the fupreme power entirel into his hands, if the Dutch had not declared i favour of his rival. The party efpoufed by thef

* About 3 l. 7 s. 2 d. ¾.   † About 11 s. 9 d.   ‡ 2 d.   § About 2 d.
‖ About 1 s. 2 d. ⅖   ** 10 s. 6 d.   †† 1,793 l. 15 s.

republican

republicans, at length prevailed after a series of contests, more active, frequent, well conducted, and obstinate, than could have been expected. The young prince, whom they wanted to deprive of his succession to the king his father, displayed so much intrepidity, prudence and firmness, that he would have triumphed over his enemies, had it not been for the advantage they derived from their magazines, forts, and ships. His uncle usurped his throne; but shewed himself unworthy to fill it.

WHEN the company restored him to the crown, they dictated laws to him. They chose the place where his court was to be fixed, and secured his attachment by a citadel in which a guard was maintained, with no other apparent view than to protect the prince. After all these precautions, they employed every artifice to lull his attention by pleasures, to gratify his avarice by presents, and to flatter his vanity by pompous embassies. From this æra, the prince and his successors, who were educated suitably to the part they were to act, were nothing more than the despicable tools of the despotism of the company. All that is necessary for their support, is three hundred horse and four hundred soldiers, whose maintenance, including the pay of the agents, costs them 760,000. livres.*

THE company are amply reimbursed for this expence by the advantages it secures them. The harbours of this state afford docks for the construction of all the small vessels and sloops employed in the company's service. They are sup‑

33,250 l.

plied

plied from hence with all the timber that is wanted in their several Indian settlements, and in part of their foreign colonies. Here too they load their vessels with the productions with which the kingdom is obliged to furnish them; consisting of five thousand lasts of rice, at forty-eight livres * a last; as much salt as they require, at twenty-eight livres sixteen sols † a last; a hundred thousand pounds of pepper, at nineteen livres four sols ‡ a hundred; all the indigo that is raised, at three livres § a pound; cadjang, for the use of their ships, at seventy-six livres sixteen sols ‖ a last; cotton yarn, from twelve sols to one livre ** a pound, according to its quality: and the small quantity of cardamom that is produced there, at a shameful price.

The island of Madura, which is separated from the ports of Mataram only by a narrow channel, is obliged, by a garrison of fifteen men, to furnish rice at a very low rate. This island, in common with the people of Java, labours under a still more odious oppression. The company's commissaries make use of false measure in order to procure a larger quantity of goods from the people that are to furnish them. This fraud, practised for their own private advantage, has not hitherto been punished; and there is no reason to hope that it ever will. Balambangan is the only district in the island of Java, that is not exposed to these iniquitous practices. The Dutch who slighted it, or

---

* 2 l. 2 s. † About 1 l. 5 s. 2 d. ‡ 16. 9 d. ¼. § About 2 s. 7 d. ¾
‖ About 3 l. 7 s. 2 d. ⅖. ** From about 6 d. to 1 s. 3 d.

accoun

IN THE EAST AND WEST INDIES.

account of its not furnishing any article of trade, have held no correspondence with it.

For the rest, the Dutch having abated the turbulency of the Javanese, by gradually undermining the laws that maintained it; and satisfied with having forced them to give some attention to agriculture, and with having secured to themselves a commerce perfectly exclusive, have not attempted to acquire any property in the island. Their territory extends no further than the small kingdom of Jacatra. The ravages committed by the Dutch when they conquered this state, and the tyranny that followed that conquest, had turned it into a desert. It still remains uncultivated and inactive.

The Dutch, those of them in particular who go to India to seek their fortunes, were hardly qualified to recover this excellent soil from its exhausted state. It was several times proposed to have recourse to the Germans; and by the encouragements of some advances, and some gratuities, to exercise their industry in a manner the most advantageous to the company. What these laborious people might have done in the fields, the silk manufacturers from China, and the linen-weavers from Coromandel might have executed in the workshops, for the improvement of manufactures. As these useful projects did not favour any private views, they continued to be nothing more than projects. At length the governors-general Imhoff and Mossel, struck with a scene of such great disorder, endeavoured to find out a remedy.

With this view they sold to the Chinese and the Europeans, at a small price, the lands which the government had acquired by oppreffive means. This management has not produced all the good that was expected from it. The new proprietors have feldom ventured to keep any thing upon their eftates but fheep and cattle, for which they have an eafy, certain and advantageous market. They would have applied themfelves to agriculture, which requires more care, greater pecuniary encouragements, and a greater number of hands, if the company did not infift on their furnifhing the commodities at the fame price they give for them in the reft of the ifland. At this prefent time there are no more than a hundred and fifty thoufand flaves, who are under the direction of a fmall number of free men. The produce of their labours confifts of two million weight of coffee, a hundred and fifty thoufand pounds of pepper, twenty-five thoufand pounds of cotton, ten thoufand pounds of indigo, ten million of fugar, and fix thoufand leques of areca. The two laft articles have been cultivated with more fpirit than the reft, becaufe private perfons, having the liberty to purchafe and export them, pay twenty per cent. dearer for them than the company.

THESE commodities, as well as all thofe that are produced in Java, are carried to Batavia, which is built on the ruins of the ancient capital of Jacatra.

A CITY which has become fo confiderble a mart, muft have received many fucceffive improvements. It is well built; the houfes though not magnificent, are pleafant, commodious, and well furnifhed; the ftreets are broad, running in ftrait lines, with rows of large trees on each fide,

and

IN THE EAST AND WEST INDIES. 245
and canals cut through them; they are always clean
though it has not been thought proper to pave them,
for fear of increafing the heat by too ftrong a reflection of the fun's rays. All the publick buildings
have an air of grandeur; and the generality of travellers look upon Batavia as one of the fineft cities
in the world.

THE number of inhabitants, including the fuburbs and liberties, does not exceed a hundred thoufand. The greateft part of them are flaves. Here
are likewife Malayans, Javanefe, free Macaffers, who
are all of them indolent; and Chinefe, who have the
exclufive exercife of all trades, are the only cultivators of the fugar-cane, and manage all the manufactures. The number of Europeans may amount to
ten thoufand; of thefe, four thoufand born in India,
are, to an inconceivable degree, degenerated. This
ftrange perverfion is probably owing to the generally received cuftom of committing the care of
their education to flaves.

THE corruptions at Batavia have, however, been
exaggerated. Diffolute manners are not more prevalent there than in other fettlements formed by
the Europeans in Afia. It is true, the people
drink to excefs; but the ties of marriage are held
facred. None but unmarried men keep concubines, who are generally of the rank of flaves.
The priefts have endeavoured to ftop the progrefs
of thefe connections, which are always fecret, by
refufing to baptize the offspring of them; but
they are become lefs rigid, fince a carpenter belonging to the company, who chofe his fon fhould

R 3 be

be of some religion or other, took it into his head to have him circumcised.

Luxury has maintained its ground more successfully than concubinage. The ladies, who are universally ambitious of distinguishing themselves by the richness of their dress, and the magnificence of their equipage, have carried their taste for finery to excess. They never stir out without a numerous train of slaves; and either ride in magnificent cars, or are carried in superb palanquins. They wear gold or silver tissues, or fine Chinese sattins, with a net of gold thrown over them; and their head-dress is loaded with pearls and diamonds. In 1758 the government attempted to reform these extravagancies, by prescribing a mode of dress suitable to each rank. These regulations were received with contempt, means were found to elude, or to purchase an immunity from them, and no change took place. It would, indeed, have been a strange singularity, if the use of precious stones had been discontinued in the country that produced them; and that the Dutch had regulated a species of luxury in India, which they brought from thence with a view of introducing, or increasing it in this part of the world. The force and example of an European government struggle in vain against the laws and manners of the climate of Asia.

The heats, which might naturally be expected to be excessive at Batavia, are allayed by an agreeable sea-breeze, which begins to blow every day at ten o'clock, and continus till four. The nights are rendered cool by land-breezes, which die away at day-break. It would contribute to make the air as pure as the sky is serene, if the canals were made somewhat deeper, and sluices were constructed. Disorders are not, however, very frequent here. The mortality that prevails among the soldiers and sailors, is rather owing to debauchery, bad provisions and fatigue, than to the inclemency of the climate.

NOTHING can be more agreeable than the environs one or two leagues round the capital. The country is interspersed with delightful villas, plantations that yield an agreeable shade, and gardens finely ornamented, and even disposed with taste. It is the fashion to live there all the year, and the people in office only come to Batavia to transact public business. These charming retreats formerly owed their tranquillity to forts erected at a certain distance from one another, to prevent the incursions of the Javanese. Since these people have contracted a habit of slavery, these redoubts serve as barracks for the refreshment of the recruits, after the fatigues of a long voyage.

BATAVIA is situated at the bottom of a deep bay, containing several islands of a middling size, which resist the impetuosity of the sea. It is properly speaking, a road; but is as safe a retreat from all winds, and in all seasons, as the best harbour. The only inconvenience is the difficulty of going, in stormy weather, aboard the ships that are obliged to anchor at a considerable distance. The ships undergo the necessary repairs at the small island of Onrust; which, though two leagues and a half distant, is one of those that chiefly con-

tribute

tribute to the goodnefs of the road. It forms an excellent dock, is well fortified, and never without three or four hundred European carpenters; and as veffels can eafily take in their lading there, magazines are erected for the reception of the larger kinds of merchandize intended for exportation. A pretty confiderable river, after fertilizing the fields, and refreshing Batavia, falls into the fea, for no other purpofe, as it fhould feem, than to ferve as a channel of communication between the town and the fhipping. The lighters that are continually meeting each other in this paffage, and formerly drew twelve feet water, are reduced to one-half: the fands and rubbifh have formed a bank, which, if fuffered to increafe, will prove an inconvenience, and occafion a very confiderable expence. It is well worth while, on account of the importance of Batavia, to pay a ferious attention to every thing that may contribute to the improvement and utility of its road, which is the moft important one in India.

ALL the veffels fent out by the company from Europe to Afia touch at Batavia; and except thofe that go directly from Bengal to Ceylon, they are laden in their return with all the articles of thofe rich fales, which create among us fo much furprize and admiration.

THE expeditions to the different fea-ports of India are hardly lefs; perhaps they are more confiderable. European veffels are employed in this fervice during the unavoidable ftay they are obliged to make in thefe remote feas.

THIS

IN THE EAST AND WEST INDIES.

This two-fold navigation is founded upon that which connects all the Dutch settlements with Batavia. Those that lie to the east are led from their situation, the nature of their merchandise, and their wants, to keep up a more frequent correspondence with it than the rest. But all of them are obliged to have pass-ports. Any ship belonging to a private person, that should neglect this precaution, which was taken to prevent fraudulent trade, would be seized by the sloops that are continually cruising in these latitudes. When they arrive at the place of their destination, they deliver to the company such of their commodities as they have reserved the exclusive trade of to themselves, and dispose of the rest to whom they please. The slave-trade, constitutes one of the principal branches of the commerce last mentioned, Six thousand of both sexes are annually carried to Batavia, where they are employed in domestic service, the cultivation of the lands, or manufactures. The Chinese, who cannot bring or invite over any of their country women, make their choice among the slaves.

To these articles of importation may be added those brought every year, by a dozen Chinese junks, from Emoy, Limpo, and Canton. Their cargo is valued at about three millions*, and consists of camphire, porcelain, silk and cotton stuffs, which are used in Batavia and the rest of the Dutch colonies; of unwrought silks, which are bought by the company when they are in any considerable quantity, or which, when they are but few of

* 131,250 l.

them,

them, are fold to thofe who chufe to fend them to Macaffar or Sumatra, where the great have pagnes made of them; of tea, which was formerly engroffed by the company, but is now given up to private traders, who fend it to Europe, where it is fold by the company, who deduct forty per cent. for the freight. This tea is generally bad, and of the coarfeft quality.

THE junks, which befides the aforementioned articles regulary bring two thoufand Chinefe to Java, who come thither in hopes of making their fortunes, carry back ftags' pizzles and the fins of the fhark, which are reckoned among the delicacies of the table in China. Another article they receive in exchange from Batavia is tripam, to the annual amount of two thoufand peculs. Each pecul, weighing a hundred and twenty-five pounds, fells from twelve to forty livres * according to its quality. It grows only two feet from the fea upon the barren rocks of the eaft, and of Cochin-china, from whence it is carried to Batavia, together with thofe birds' nefts fo much celebrated all over the eaft which are found in the fame places. A pecul of the laft-mentioned merchandife fells from 1,400 to 2,800 livres †, and the Chinefe carry away one thoufand. Thefe nefts are of an oval fhape, an inch high, three inches round, and weigh about half an ounce. They are formed by a fpecies of the fwallow; its head, breaft, and wings are of a fine blue, and its body milk white. They

* From 10s. 6d. to 1l. 15s. † From 61l. 5s. to 122l. 10s.

are compofed of the fpawn of fifh, or of a glutinous froth which the agitation of the fea leaves upon the rocks, to which they are faftened at the bottom and on the fide. When feafoned with falt and fpices, they make a nourifhing, wholefome, and delicious jelly, and are an article of the higheft luxury at the tables of the eaftern Mohammedans. Their whitenefs conftitutes their delicacy. The Chinefe likewife carry away calin and pepper, though the company referved the exportation of thofe articles to themfelves. Their principal agents pretend, for their own advantage, that thefe exportations are not prejudicial to the body which has intrufted its interefts to their management.

THE traffic of the Chinefe at Batavia, befides the merchandife they export from thence, brings them in fome ready money. This wealth is increafed by the confiderable fums that the Chinefe fettled at Java remit to their families, and by the fums fooner or later amaffed by thofe, who, content with their fortune, return to their own country, of which they feldom lofe fight.

THE Europeans are not fo well treated at Batavia as the Chinefe. None are admitted there as merchants, but the Spaniards. Their fhips come from Manilla with gold, which is the produce of that ifland; and with cochineal and piafters brought from Mexico. They take in exchange, linens for their own ufe and that of Acapulco; but the principal article is cinnamon, the confumption of which is much increafed by the general ufe of chocolate in the

new

new world, and the progress it is daily making in Europe. Since the English and French have failed to the Phillippines, the former branch of this trade has considerably declined; the latter suffered a change in the year 1759. Before that time, cinnamon was sold to the Spaniards at a moderate price; but, at present, they are expected to give the same that it bears in Europe. This innovation occasions a coolness between the two colonies. The consequences of this misunderstanding have not come to our knowledge.

ALL we know is, that the French hardly ever go to Batavia but in time of war. They purchase rice and arrack there for the use of their ships and their settlements, and make their payments for these commodities in silver, or bills of exchange.

THE English are oftener seen there. All their vessels coming from Europe to China put in at this harbour under pretence of taking in fresh water; but in reality with a view of vending the goods, which are the property of the ships company, consisting of cloths, hard-ware, glasses, arms, Madeira wines, and Portugal oils. This clandestine trade seldom exceeds a million of livres *.

BESIDES the English vessels sent from Europe, there are three or four belonging to the same nation, which are every year fitted out for Batavia from different parts of India. They have

* 43,750 l.

attempted

IN THE EAST AND WEST INDIES. 253

attempted to fell opium and linens there, but have been obliged to difcontinue this importation, which was too prejudicial to private intereſt to be permitted. Their trade is limited to the purchafe of fugar, which they export to all parts, and of arrack, prodigious quantities of which are confumed in their colonies. Arrack is a kind of brandy made of rice, fyrup of fugar, and cocoa-tree, which, after being fermented together, are diſtilled. This is one among other branches of trade which the Dutch by their induſtry have deprived the Portuguefe of. The art of making arrack, which was originally eſtabliſhed at Goa, has for the moſt part been transferred to Batavia.

ALL imported or exported commodities pay this city a tax of five per cent. The revenue ariſing from the cuſtoms is farmed at the rate of 1,828,000 livres *. The extent of the trade muſt not be eſtimated by this rule, which, however, is always the moſt to be depended upon. The people in office pay what they think proper, and the company pay nothing, as that would be paying to themfelves. Though they are here, as well as in other places, the only merchants in the ifland, the profits ariſing from the productions peculiar to Batavia, do not defray the expences of this celebrated mart, which amount to fix millions †.

ONE of the articles of this expence, which is undoubtedly very great, is the maintenance of

BOOK II.

The manner of conducting the affairs of the Dutch company in India, and in Europe.

* 79,975l.   † 262,500l.

of a council, which gives laws to all the settlements in India, and has the sole direction of affairs. This council is compoſed of the governor of the Dutch Indies, the director-general, five directors in ordinary, and a ſmall number of extraordinary counſellors, which laſt have no votes, and only ſupply the place of the deceaſed counſellors in ordinary, till ſucceſſors are appointed.

The power of nomination to theſe offices is veſted in the direction at home. They are open to all who have money, or are relations or retainers to the governor-general. On his demiſe, the directors in ordinary proviſionally appoint a ſucceſſor, who ſeldom fails to be confirmed in his employment. If the contrary happens, he is not admitted into the council; but may enjoy all the honours granted to the preſidents that retire.

The governor-general reports to the council the ſtate of all affairs in the iſland of Java: and each counſellor, that of the province intruſted to his care. The director has the inſpection of the cheſt and magazines at Batavia, which ſupply the reſt of the ſettlements. All purchaſes and all ſales are directed by him. The ſignature of the company is indiſpenſably neceſſary in all commercial tranſactions.

Though all points ought, ſtrictly ſpeaking, to be decided in the council by a majority of votes, the governor-general ſeldom fails to exerciſe an uncontrouled authority. This influence is owing to the care he takes to admit none
bu

IN THE EAST AND WEST INDIES. but perſons of inferior abilities, and to the intereſt they find in making their court to him, in order to advance their fortunes. If on any occaſion he meets with an oppoſition that thwarts his deſigns, he is at liberty to take his own meaſures, making himſelf anſwerable for the conſequences.

THE governor-general, like all the reſt of the officers, is appointed only for five years, but uſually holds his place during life. There have formerly been inſtances of governors-general who have retired from buſineſs, to paſs their days in tranquillity at Batavia; but the ill treatment experienced from their ſucceſſors, has, of late years, determined them to remain in their poſt till death. They formerly appeared in great ſtate, but it was laid aſide by governor general Imhoff, as uſeleſs and troubleſome. Though all orders of men may aſpire to this dignity, none of the army, and but few of the gown, have been known to obtain it. It is always filled by merchants, becauſe the ſpirit of the company is entirely commercial. Thoſe who are born in India have ſeldom ſufficient addreſs or abilities to procure it. The preſent preſident, however, has never been in Europe.

THE ſalary of this principal officer is but ſlender; he has no more than two thouſand livres* a month, and ſubſiſtence equal to his pay. The greateſt part of his income ariſes from the liberty allowed him, of taking as much as he pleaſes

* 87l. 10s.

from

from the magazines at prime coft, and from the liberty he affumes of trading to any extent he judges convenient. The income of the counfellors, members of the council, is likewife very confiderable, though the company allows them only four hundred livres * a month, and goods to the fame amount.

THE council meets but twice a week, unlefs when fome extraordinary events require a more ftrict attendance. They appoint to all civil and military employments in India, except thofe of the writer and ferjeant, which they thought might be left, without inconvenience, at the difpofal of the governors of the refpective fettlements. On his advancement to any poft, every man is obliged to take an oath, that he has neither promifed, nor given any thing to obtain his employment. This cuftom, which is very ancient, familiarizes people to falfe oaths, and proves no bar to corruption. Whoever confiders the number of abfurd and ridiculous oaths neceffary to be taken at prefent in moft countries, on being admitted into any fociety or profeffion whatever, will be lefs furprifed to find prevarication ftill prevails where perjury has led the way.

ALL connections of commerce, not excepting that of the Cape of Good Hope, are made by the council, and the refult of them alway falls under their cognizance. Even the fhips that fail directly from Bengal and Ceylon, only carry to Europe the invoices of their cargoes. Their

* 17l. 10s.

accompts,

IN THE EAST AND WEST INDIES.

accompts, as well as all others, are fent to Batavia, where a general regifter is kept of all affairs.

THE council of India is not a feparate body, nor is it independent. It acts in fubordination to the direction eftablifhed in the united provinces. Though this is, in the ftrict fenfe of the word, a direction, the care of difpofing of the merchandife twice a year, is divided between fix chambers concerned in this commerce. Their bufinefs is more or lefs, according to the funds that belong to them.

THE general affembly, which has the direction of the bufinefs of the company, is compofed of directors of all the chambers. Amfterdam nominates eight; Zealand, four; each of the other chambers, one; and the ftate but one. Hence we fee that Amfterdam, having half the number of voices, has only one to gain to enable it to turn the fcale, where every queftion is to be decided by a majority of votes.

THIS body, which is compofed of feventeen perfons, meets twice or thrice a year, during fix years at Amfterdam, and two at Middleburg. The other chambers are two inconfiderable to enjoy this prerogative. It having been found by experience, that the fuccefs frequently depended on fecret intrigues, it was propofed, about the middle of the laft century to chufe four of the moft able of the feventeen deputies, and to inveft them with authority to regulate all affairs in Europe and India, without

VOL. I.   S   the

the confent of their colleagues, and without being obliged even to afk their opinion.

It is true, their myfterious tranfactions, and the confequences of them, cannot long be kept a fecret. The fleet that returns at the end of the fummer, brings their books of accounts regulary from India. They are compared with thofe in Europe. The general balance of the company's accounts are always publifhed in May. Every perfon concerned knows what he as gained or loft. The gain is commonly confiderable.

The company's fund did not at firft exceed 12,919,680 livres *; Amfterdam furnifhed 7,349,830 †; Zealand, 2,667,764 ‡; Delft, 940,000 §; Rotterdam, 354,800 ‖; Horn, 533,736 **; Enchuyfen, 1,073,550 ††.

This fund was divided into fums of 6,000 livres ‡‡, which were called fhares.

Their numbers were two thoufand one hundred: fince 1692, however, the profits are divided into two thoufand one hundred and thirty. It was then that the company, which had always been protected by the houfe of Orange, and ftill ftood in need of its affiftance, made the ftadtholder a prefent of a revenue of thirty fhares for life.

The fhares fell for ready money, or upor credit, like merchandife. No other form is re quifite than to fubftitute the name of the buye for that of the feller in the company's books

---

* 585,236 l.   † 321,555 l. 1s. 3d.   ‡ 116,714 l. 13s. 6d.
§ 41,125 l.   ‖ 15,522 l. 10s.   ** 23,350 l. 19s.
†† 46,967 l. 16s. 3d.   ‡‡ 262 l. 10s.

IN THE EAST AND WEST INDIES.

the only title by which they are held by the proprietor. Avarice and the spirit of commerce have invented another method of acquiring a share in this traffic. Persons who have no stock to sell, and who do not intend to buy, enter into a reciprocal engagement that one of the parties shall deliver, and the other receive a certain number, at such a time, at a price agreed upon. On the day fixed, they compute the difference between the current price of the stocks and their value when the agreement was made; they settle the balance of the account in money, and the transaction is over. The desire of gaining, and the fear of losing by these speculations, is productive of great anxiety. They invent good or bad news; they favour or oppose the reports of others; they try to penetrate the secrets of the court, or to purchase those of foreign ministers. These clashing interests have often disturbed the public tranquillity. Matters have even been carried to such a height, that the public have been obliged to take measures to put a stop to the rage of stock-jobbing. The most efficacious method has been to declare all bargains of sale for time null and void, unless it appears, by the company's books, that the seller was a proprietor at the time the bargain was made. Men of honour hold themselves obliged to fulfil their engagements, notwithstanding this law: but it is natural to think that it must, and indeed it does, make these transactions less frequent.

The price of stocks, which may be looked upon as the true thermometer of the company, has often varied. Injudicious or unsuccessful treaties, fresh competitions, accidents unavoidably attending an extensive commerce, the tranquillity or the disturbances of India, and of Europe in particular, have occasioned these changes. For some years the standing price of stocks has been two hundred and forty per cent. more than their original value. They formerly rose as high as six hundred and fifty per cent. So considerable an advantage must have greatly enriched the original proprietors of these funds, and the families that inherit them; but the present purchasers seldom get more than three and a half per cent. interest for their money. This remarkable prosperity has no parallel in history. Let us try to explain the causes of it.

Causes of the prosperity of the company.

The earliest success of the company was owing to their having the good fortune, in less than half a century, to take more than three hundred Portuguese vessels. These ships, some of which were bound for Europe, and others for different sea ports in India, were laden with the spoils of Asia. This wealth, which the captors had the honesty not to meddle with, brought to the company immense returns, or served to procure them. Thus the sales were very considerable, though the exports were very modeate.

The decline of the maritime power of the Portuguese, encouraged the Dutch to attack the settlements belonging to that nation, and greatly

IN THE EAST AND WEST INDIES.

ly facilitated the conqueſt of them. They found the forts ſtrongly built, defended by a numerous artillery, and provided with every thing that government and the rich individuals of a victorious nation might naturally be ſuppoſed to have collected together for their protection. To form a juſt idea of this advantage, we need only conſider what it has coſt other nations to obtain permiſſion to fix in an advantageous ſituation, to build houſes, magazines, and forts; and to procure all the conveniences neceſſary for their ſecurity, or their commerce.

WHEN the company found themſelves in poſſeſſion of ſo many rich and well eſtabliſhed ſettlements, they did not give way to a graſping ambition. They were deſirous of extending their commerce, not their conqueſts. They can hardly be accuſed of any inſtances of injuſtice, except thoſe that ſeemed neceſſary to ſecure their power. The eaſt was no longer a ſcene of bloodſhed, as it had been at the time, when the deſire of diſtinguiſhing themſelves by martial exploits, and the rage of making proſelytes, gave the Portugueſe a menacing air wherever they appeared in India.

THE Dutch ſeemed to have arrived rather to revenge, and reſcue the natives of the country, than to enſlave them. They maintained no wars with them, but ſuch as were neceſſary to procure ſettlements upon their coaſts, and to oblige them to enter into treaties of commerce. It is true, theſe people received no advantage from them, and were deprived of a great part of their liberty; but in other refpects, their new mafters, rather lefs barbarous than the conquerors they difpoffeffed, left the Indians at liberty to govern themfelves, and did not compel them to change their laws, their manners, or their religion.

By their manner of pofting and diftributing their forces, they contrived to keep the people in awe, whom they had at firft conciliated by their behaviour. If we except Cochin and Malacca, they had nothing upon the continent but factories and fmall forts. The iflands of Java and Ceylon contained their troops and magazines: and from thence their fhips maintained their authority, and protected their trade throughout India.

This trade became very confiderable by the fpices falling into their hands, after the deftruction of the Portuguefe fettlements. The demand for this valuable article has been more or lefs extenfive, accoording to circumftances. At prefent they fell every year a hundred and fifty thoufand pounds of cloves in India, and three hundred and fifty thoufand in Europe: the price in both parts of the world is fixed at ten livres* a pound. Though the Dutch give no more than eight fols and a few deniers † a pound, it cofts them four livres fix fols ‡, on account of charges and deficiencies. India takes off no more than a hundred thoufand weight of nutmegs, whereas Europe confumes two hundred and fifty thou-

* 8s. 9d.   † About 8d. ½ or 9d.   ‡ About 3s. 9d.

fand,

IN THE EAST AND WEST INDIES.

fand. It is bought at the rate of two fols three deniers * a pound, and the neceffary expences bring it to two livres ten fols †. It fells for feven livres ten fols ‡, on this fide the Cape, and for no more than five livres twelve fols §, on the other fide. This difference will never induce any merchant to bring us the nutmeg; becaufe the nuts that are fent all over Afia are fhrivelled, have no oil in them, and often decay. Ten thoufand pounds of mace is fufficient for the fupply of India, a hundred thoufand for that of Europe. The prime coft is fixteen fols fix deniers ‖ a pound, it rifes to five livres eight fols **, and is fold every where at twelve livres fixteen fols ††. As for the cinnamon, the confumption of it in Europe does not exceed four hundred thoufand weight, and in India it does not amount to two hundred thoufand; the greateft part of which is fent to Manilla for the ufe of Spanifh America. It is every where fold by the company at prefent, at the rate of ten livres ten fols ‡‡ a pound, though it does not coft them twelve fols §§. That which they refufe to purchafe, as being too courfe, is made into oil. They make prefents of it to the powers of Afia wo do not chufe to purchafe it; and it fells here from about twenty to fifty or fixty livres ¶¶ an ounce. The fmell is fo ftrong, and at the fame time fo agreeable,

* About 1 d. ¾.   † 2 s. 2 d. ½.   ‡ 6 s. 6 d. ¾
§ 4 s. 10 d. ¼.   ‖ About 8 d. ¾   ** About 4 s. 8 d ½
†† About 11 s. 2 d. ¼   ‡‡ About 9 s. 2 d. ¼   §§ About 6 d. ¼
¶¶ 17 s. 6 d.—to 2 l. 12 s. 6 d.

that

that it would be commonly, if not univerfally ufed, if the Dutch did not afk fo high a price for it : it being more for their advantage to fell this fpice in its original form.

WE cannot conclude this important article without obferving, that in proportion as the company's profits have decreafed, they have raifed the price of fpices both in India and Europe. This though in itfelf a bad expedient, has not injured in any great degree the fale of cloves and nutmeg, for which there is no fuccedaneum. But the cafe has been otherwife in regard to cinnamon. A fpurious kind has, in feveral markets, been fubftituted for the genuine; and this branch of commerce is vifibly on the decline, and will continue to be more fo every day.

THE company have fpared no pains to preferve the exclufive trade of pepper, which they held for fome time. Though their attemps have not been quite fuccefsful, they have fo far gained their point, as to maintain a confiderable fuperiority over their competitors. The quantity they fell of this article in Europe amounts to five millions weight, and three millions five hundred weight in India. The company purchafe it, upon the whole, at thirty-fix livres * a hundred weight, and fell it to us at a hundred livres †, and from forty-eight to feventy-two livres ‡ to the people of Afia.

IN confequence of the fale of fpices, the greateft part of the India trade muft of courfe fall into

* 1 l. 11 s. 6 d. † 4 l. 7 s. 6 d. ‡ About 2 l. 12 s 6 d. on an average.

the

the hands of the Dutch. The neceffity of exporting them, gave the Dutch an opportunity of appropriating to themfelves feveral other branches of commerce. In procefs of time they became mafters of the coafting trade of Afia, as they were already of that of Europe. This navigation employed a great number of fhips and failors, who without caufing any expence to the company contributed to its fecurity.

By virtue of thefe fuperior advantages, they were enabled, for a long time, to prevent the attempts of other nations to interfere in the Indian trade, or to make them abortive. The produce of this rich country came to the Europeans through the hands of the Dutch; who never experienced thofe reftraints from their country, which have in later times been impofed every where elfe. The government, convinced that the proceedings of other nations neither ought, nor could be a rule to direct theirs, always gave the company leave to difpofe of their merchandife at the capital freely, and without referve. At the time this fociety was inftituted, the United Provinces had neither any manufactures nor crude materials to work upon. It was, therefore, no inconvenience, but rather a point of great policy, to allow, and even encourage, the citizens to wear linens and ftuffs imported from India. The various manufactures which were introduced into the republic, in confequence of the repeal of the edict of Nantz, might have induced them to lay afide the thoughts of purchafing their cloathing from so remote a country; but the fondness that prevailed in Europe at that time for French fashions, had given so advantageous an opening for the manufactures of the refugees, that they had not the least idea of departing from the ancient channel. Since the high price of labour, the necessary consequence of a redundancy of money, has lessened the manufactures, and obliged the nation to trade upon a frugal plan, India stuffs have had a greater run than ever. It was thought that fewer inconveniences would arise from enriching the Indians than the English or French, whose prosperity would not fail to hasten the ruin of a state, the opulence of which is only supported by the rashness, the disputes, or indolence of other powers.

This wise conduct has retarded the decline of the company; but the change is at last effected, notwithstanding the flattering illusions of an imaginary prosperity. A detail of facts will set this truth in a clear light.

We have seen that the original fund of the company, which has never been since augmented, was no more than 12,919,680 livres*. With this slender capital, they attacked the Spaniards and Portuguese in the Indian seas, gained conquests over these, then warlike nations, and over the people of Asia, whose numbers, at least rendered them formidable; they formed magazines, built cities, and erected forts without number; and established or supported their com-

* 565, 36².

merce

merce by force of arms. These amazing expences lasted from the first institution of the company till the year 1665, the æra when all their acquisitions were made, all their settlements formed. During this long and restless period, the annual returns amounted to twenty and three-fourths per cent.

The company had afterwards no occasion to send one fleet after another into the east, to assert the dominion of those seas, to raise new armies to subdue or awe their enemies, or to lavish their blood and treasure in securing their possessions. Their operations were only those of a brisk and advantageous commerce; and, consequently, their dividend, till the year 1728 increased to about three and twenty per cent. It has since that time gradually fallen to twenty, fifteen, and even lower. A further reduction will in all probability take place, and we shall now state the reasons upon which this conjecture is founded.

It is demonstrated, that at the closing of the books in 1751, the capital of the company in India did not amount to more than 71,000,000 livres*, the fleet that was on its way to Europe stood them in 19,200,000†, and the vessels fitted out for India in 3,000,000 of livres ‡. They had a debt of 14,000,000 of livres § in India, and were 22,400,000 livres ‖ in arrears in Europe. Consequently the stock of the com-

* 3,106,250 l. † 840,000 l. ‡ 131,250 L
§ 612,500 l. ‖ 980,000 l.

pany

pany, exclusive of their fortifications, did not exceed 56,800,000 livres*.

Of this sum, inconsiderable as it was, there were only 23,400,000 livres † in commercial effects; that is to say, ready money, merchandise, and good debts. The remainder consisted of bad debts to the amount of 3,000,000 ‡, and of doubtful ones to the amount of 6,600,000 livres §; 8,000,000 livres ¶ allotted for provision for the table; 1,400,000 ** for brass cannon; for iron ordnance, bullets, and balls, 500,000 ††; for muskets and ammunition 1,800,000 ‡‡; for plate 200,000 §§; for slaves 300,000 ¶¶; for cattle and horses 200,000 ***; and for goods entered from different parts of India for Batavia 11,200,000 livres †††.

It remains to examine what profits the company have been able to make with so weak a capital. Their gains, as far as it is possible to compute them, annually amount to 25,400,000 livres ‡‡‡, but their ordinary expences amount to 18,600,000 §§§, and their dividend, supposing it to be twenty-five per cent. to 3,330,000 ¶¶¶; consequently they have only 470,000 **** livres remaining, to defray the expences of war, the loss of their magazines by fire, or their vessels by sea, and all that train of evils which human prudence can neither foresee nor prevent.

* 2,485,000 l. † 1,023,750 l. ‡ 131,250 l.
§ 288,750 l. ¶ 350,000 l. ** 61,250 l.
†† 21,875 l. ‡‡ 78,700 l. §§ 8,750 l.
¶¶ 13,125 l. *** 8,750 l. ††† 490,000 l.
‡‡‡ 1,111,250 l. §§§ 813,750 l. ¶¶¶ 145,687 l. 10s.
**** 20,562 l. 10s.

IN THE EAST AND WEST INDIES.

This state of the matter must appear to those who see things at a distance to have so little probability, that we should not have ventured to warrant the truth of it, if we had not before us governor-general Moffel's correspondence with the direction. This discerning and able administrator considers the company as an exhausted body that is sustained by cordials: it is, as he expresses himself, a leaky vessel, that is kept from foundering only by the pump.

This deplorable situation, which will reduce the company to the necessity of borrowing money upon their capital, or of lessening their dividend still more, if any new misfortune should happen, must have had its causes, and those too very considerable. The most obvious of all is the multitude of petty wars which have followed each other without interruption.

The inhabitants of the Moluccas had scarce recovered from the astonishment into which they had been thrown by the victories gained by the Dutch over a people whom they looked upon as invincible, when they grew impatient of the yoke. The company, dreading the consequences of this discontent, made war upon the king of Ternate, to oblige him to consent to the extirpation of the clove-tree every where except in Amboyna. The islanders in Banda were utterly exterminated, because they refused to become their slaves. Macassar, in order to support their interests, kept up a considerable force for a long time. The loss of Formosa brought on the ruin of the factories of Tonkin and Siam.

Reasons of the decline of the company.

They

They were obliged to take up arms to support the exclusive trade of Sumatra. Malacca was besieged, its territory ravaged, and its navigation interrupted by pirates. Negapatan was twice attacked; Cochin was engaged in resisting the attempts of the kings of Calicut and Travancor; Ceylon has been a scene of perpetual disturbances; which are full as frequent, and still more violent at Java, where peace can never continue long, unless the company will give a reasonable price for the commodities they require. They have engaged in bloody contests with an European nation, whose power in India increases every day, and whose character is not that of moderation. All these wars have proved ruinous, more ruinous indeed, than might have been expected, because those who had the management of them only sought opportunities of enriching themselves.

These notorious dissensions have in many places been followed by odious oppressions; which have been practised at Japan, China, Cambodia, Arracan, on the banks of the Ganges, at Achem, Coromandel, Surat in Persia, at Bassora, Mocho, and other places. Most of the countries in India are filled with tyrants who prefer piracy to commerce, who acknowledge no right but that of power, and think that whatever is practicable, is just.

The profits accruing to the company from the places where their trade met with no interruption, for a long time counterbalanced the losses they sustained in others by tyranny or anarchy; but other European nations deprived them of this indemni-

indemnification. This competition obliged them to buy dearer, and to fell cheaper. Their natural advantages might, perhaps, have enabled them to fupport this misfortune, if their rivals had not determined to throw the trade carried on from India to India into the hands of private merchants. By this expreffion we are to underftand the operations neceffary to tranfport the merchandife of one country in Afia to another; from China, Bengal, and Surat, for inftance, to the Phillippines, Perfia, and Arabia. By means of this circulation, and by a multiplicity of exchanges, the Dutch obtained for nothing, or for a trifle, the rich cargoes they brought to Europe. The activity, œconomy and fkill of the free merchants drove the company from all the fea-ports where equal favour was fhewn. Their flag was feldom feen in the roads where eight or ten Englifh veffels appeared.

THIS revolution, which fo clearly pointed out to them what fteps they had to take, did not fet them right with refpect to a meafure that was deftructive to trade. They had been accuftomed to carry all their Indian and European merchandife to Batavia, from whence it was diftributed among the different factories who fold it to advantage. This cuftom occafioned expence and lofs of time, the inconveniences of which were not perceived while their profits were fo enormous. When other nations carried on a direct trade, it became indifpenfably neceffary to relinquifh a fyftem, not only bad in itfelf, but imcompatible with circumftances. The dominion of cuftom, however, ftill prevails;

prevails; and it was said to be owing to the company's apprehensions that their servants would make an ill use of any innovation, that they did not adopt a measure, the necessity of which was so fully demonstrated.

This motive was probably nothing more than a pretext which served as a cover to private interest. The frauds of the commissaries were more than winked at. The chief of them had for the most part been exact in their conduct. They were under the direction of admirals who visited all the factories, were invested with absolute powers in India, and, at the conclusion of every voyage, gave an account in Europe of their administration. In proportion as the government became less active, the agents, who were not so strictly watched, grew more remiss. They abandoned themselves to effeminacy, a habit of which is easily contracted in hot countries. It became necessary to increase the number of these agents: and no one made a capital point of correcting an abuse, which gave the people in power an opportunity of providing for their dependents. They went to Asia with a view of making a considerable fortune in a short time. Being prohibited from trading, their appointments not being sufficient to maintain them, and all honest ways of enriching themselves being shut against them, they had recourse to mal-practices. The company were cheated in all their affairs by factors who had no interest in their prosperity. These disorders grew to such a height, that it was proposed to allow a premium of

IN THE EAST AND WEST INDIES.

of five per cent. upon all commodities fold or bought, which was to be divided among all the servants according to their ranks. Upon these terms, they were obliged to take an oath that their account was just. This arrangement lasted but five years; it being found that corruption prevailed as much as ever: the premium and the oath were abolished; and from this period the agents ask any confideration for their trouble that their avarice dictates.

THE contagion, which at first infected the lower factories, gradually reached the principal settlements, and, at last, Batavia itself. So great a simplicity of manners prevailed there at first, that the members of the government usually dressed like common failors, and never wore decent cloaths but in their council-chamber. This modesty was accompanied with so distinguished a probity, that before the year 1650, not one remarkable fortune had been made; but this unheard-of prodigy of virtue could not be of long duration. We have seen warlike republics conquer and make acquisitions for their country, and fill the public treasury with the spoils of kingdoms. But we shall never see the citizens of a commercial republic amass riches for a particular body in the state, from which they derive neither glory nor profit. The austerity of republican principles must of course give place to the example of the people of the east. This relaxation of manners was more sensibly perceived in the capital of the colony, where the articles of luxury that came from all parts, and the air of magnificence it was thought necessary to throw round the adminiftration, introduced a tafte for fhew. This tafte occafioned a corruption of manners; and this corruption of manners made all methods of getting money alike indifferent. Even the appearance of decency was fo far difregarded, that a governor-general finding himfelf convicted of plundering the finances without mercy, made no fcruple of juftifying his conduct by fhewing a carte blanche figned by the company.

How could the conduct of the governors be remedied when their depravation could not be forefeen in the infancy of the republic, where a purity of manners and frugality prevailed? In thefe fettlements of the Dutch, the laws had been made for virtuous men; other manners required other laws.

These diforders might have been repreffed in their firft beginnings, if they had not naturally made the fame progrefs in Europe as in Afia. But as a river that overflows its banks collects more mud than water in its paffage, fo the vices which riches bring along with them, increafe fafter than riches themfelves. The poft of director, which was at firft allotted to able merchants, was, at length, vefted in great families, where it is held with the magiftracies, by virtue of which it was firft procured. Thefe families, engaged in political views, or in the fervice of adminiftration, confidered thefe pofts, which they had ravifhed from the company, only in the light of a confiderable income, or an eafy provifion for their relations; fome of them even as opportunities of making a bad ufe of their credit. The bufinefs of

receiving

receiving accounts, hearing debates and carrying on the moſt important tranſactions of the company, was left to a ſecretary, who, under the plauſible title of advocate, became the ſole manager of all the affairs. The governors, who met but twice a-year, in ſpring and autumn, at the arrival and departure of the fleets, forgot the habit and track of all buſineſs which requires a conſtant attention. They were obliged to repoſe an entire confidence in a perſon appointed by the ſtate to make extracts from all the diſpatches that arrived from India, and to draw up the form of the anſwers that were to be returned. This guide, who was ſometimes incapable, often bribed, and always ſuſpicious, frequently led thoſe whom he conducted to the brink of a precipice where he left them to fall.

The ſpirit of commerce ariſes from intereſt, and intereſt always occaſions diſputes. Each chamber wanted to have docks, arſenals, and magazines, for the ſhips it was to fit out. Offices were multiplied, and frauds were encouraged by ſo wrong a proceeding.

It was a maxim in every department to furniſh goods, as it had a right to do, in proportion to the number of its ſhips. Theſe goods were not alike proper for the places for which they were deſtined, and were either not ſold at all, or ſold to diſadvantage.

When circumſtances called for extraordinary ſupplies, a ſpirit of puerile vanity, which is afraid of betraying its weakneſs by confeſſing its wants, led them to avoid borrowing money in Holland, where they would have paid only an intereſt of three per cent. and to have recourſe to Batavia, where money was at fix, or more frequently to Bengal, or the coaft of Coromandel, where it was at nine per cent. and fometimes much higher. Abufes were multiplied on all fides.

The ftates-general, whofe bufinefs it was to examine, every three years, into the ftate of the company; to fatisfy themfelves that they kept within the limits affigned by their grant; to fee that juftice was adminiftered to the perfons concerned; and that the trade was carried on in a manner that was not prejudicial to the republic; fhould have put a ftop to thefe irregularities, and ought to have done it. Whatever their reafons might be, this was never accomplifhed. In confequence of this behaviour, they had the mortification to fee the proprietors unite in conferring upon the laft ftadtholder the fupreme direction of their affairs in Europe and India; without being aware of the danger that might refult from the influence that a perpetual prefident of the ftate muft have over a rich and powerful body. Notwithftanding this, the dividend is at this time larger, and the price of ftocks higher. A certain premature death has drawn a veil over the plan of reformation that had been concerted. Neceffity will oblige them to refume it, with fuch wife precautions, no doubt, as may prevent the abufe of that power, againft which they think themfelves bound to proteft.

Meafures that remain to be taken for the re-eftablifh-ment of the company's affairs.

The firft ftep muft be, to convince themfelves that the government of the company is too complicated even in Europe. A direction vefted in fo many chambers, and in fuch a number of directors,

rectors, muft be attended with infinite inconveniences. It is impoffible that the fame fpirit fhould operate every where alike, and that the tranfactions fhould be carried on without receiving a tincture from the oppofite views of the perfons who conduct them in different places, without concert or connection. Unity of defign, fo neceffary in the fine arts, is equally advantageous in bufinefs. It will be in vain objected, that it is the intereft of all democratical ftates to divide their wealth, and to make the eftates of the citizens as equal as poffible. This maxim, in itfelf true, is not applicable to a republic that has no territory, and maintains itfelf merely by its commerce. It will therefore be expedient that every article bought or fold fhould fall under one general infpection, and be brought into one port. The favings that would be made, would be the leaft advantage the company would receive from this alteration.

From this place, which would be the center of intelligence from all quarters, deputations might be fent to enquire into, and correct abufes in the remoteft parts of Afia. The conduct of the Dutch towards the Indian princes, from whom they have forcibly extorted an exclufive commerce, will be one of the firft objects of their confideration. They have, for a long time, behaved towards them with an infolent pride; have attempted to learn the fecrets of their government; and to engage them in quarrels with their neighbours; they have fomented divifions among their fubjects, and fhewn a diftruft mixed with animofity; they have obliged them to make sacrifices which they never promised; and deprived them of advantages secured to them by the terms of capitulation. All these intolerable acts of tyranny, occasion frequent disturbances, which sometimes end in hostilities. To restore harmony, which is a task that grows more necessary and more difficult every day, agents should be appointed, who to a spirit of moderation join a knowledge of the interests, customs, language, religion, and manners of these nations. At present, perhaps, the company may be unprovided with persons of this character: but it concerns them to procure them. Perhaps too they might find them among the superintendents of their factories, which they have every reason to induce them to abandon.

THE discerning part of the merchants of all nations unanimously agree, that the Dutch settlements in India are too numerous: and that by lessening their number, they would greatly reduce their expences, without confining their commerce. The company cannot possibly be ignorant of what is so generally known. One would be apt to think, they were induced to continue the factories that were chargeable to them, to prevent a suspicion that they were not in a condition to maintain them. But this weak consideration should sway them no longer. All that deserves their attention, is to make a due distinction between what it is convenient to part with, and advantageous to retain. They have before them a series of facts and experiments, which must prevent any mistake in an arrangement of such importance.

IN

In the subordinate factories, which they may think proper to continue for the advantage of trade, they will demolish all useless fortifications; they will dissolve the councils established from motives of ostentation rather than necessity; and they will proportion the number of their servants to the extent of their business. Let the company call to mind those happy times, when two or three factors chosen with judgment, sent out cargoes infinitely more considerable than any they have received since; when they raised amazing profits upon their goods, which, in process of time, have been diverted into the pockets of their numerous agents; and then they will not hesitate a moment to return to their old maxims, and to prefer a simplicity which made them rich, to an empty parade that ruins them. These disorders were owing to their own misconduct. The Europeans, settled in their colonies, lived in disgrace if they were not engaged in their service. Every expedient was tried to extricate themselves from a state of humiliation which it was impossible to endure. The superintendents suffered themselves to be corrupted; and employments were multiplied without necessity and without measure. Let them discountenance a prejudice, which in whatever light it is viewed, is unjust and prenicious; and the reformation we are pointing out will easily be accomplished.

It will be attended with greater difficulties in the large colonies. The company's agents there are a more numerous, reputable, and in proportion a more opulent body, and consequently less disposed to submit to any regulations. It is, however,

ever, neceffary to reduce them to order, fince the abufes they have either introduced, or winked at, muft fooner or later inevitably bring on the ruin of the interefts over which they prefide. The mif-management that prevails in the manufactories, magazines, docks, and arfenals at Batavia, and other large fettlements, is fcarcely to be paralleled. The mal-practices of the fuperintendents and fubordinate officers are fo notorious, that according to the moft favourable reprefentations, at leaft two-thirds might be faved if the buildings, works and repairs were executed by contract.

These arrangements would lead to others ftill more confiderable. At their firft rife, the company eftablifhed fixed and precife rules, which were not to be departed from on any pretence, or on any occafion whatfoever. Their fervants were mere machines, the fmalleft movements of which were wound up before-hand. They judged this abfolute and univerfal direction neceffary to correct what was amifs in the choice of their agents, who were moft of them drawn out of obfcurity, and had not the advantage of that careful education which would have enlarged their ideas. The company themfelves did not fuffer the leaft variation in their own conduct, and to this invariable uniformity they attributed the fuccefs of their enterprizes. The frequent misfortunes, which this fyftem occafioned, did not prevail with them to lay it afide; and they always adhered obftinately to their firft plan. In this they were not guided by reflection, but followed

followed a blind impulſe. At this time of the day, when they can no longer commit errors with impunity, it is neceſſary they ſhould make ſome alterations. Tired of maintaining a diſadvantageous ſtruggle with the free traders of other nations, they ſhould reſolve to leave the commerce from one part of India to another, to private perſons. This happy innovation would make their colonies richer and more powerful. They themſelves would reap more advantage from the cuſtoms that would be paid in their factories, than they receive from the faint efforts of an expiring commerce. Every thing, even the ſhips that are too old to be ſent to Europe, would turn to account. The navigators in theſe ſettlements would be glad to make uſe of them in thoſe calm ſeas.

PERHAPS the company might carry the plan of reformation ſtill further. Would it not be a proper ſcheme to reſign the trade of linens exported to Europe to individuals? Thoſe who are acquainted with their tranſactions, know very well that they gain no more than thirty per cent. by this article, which is always ſold to them at a dear rate by their agents, though it is bought with their own money. If we deduct from this profit, the averages, the intereſt of advance-money, the ſalaries of the commiſſaries, and the hazards at ſea, the remainder will be very trifling. Would not twenty per cent. freight, which the free merchants would readily give, be of greater advantage to the company?

THEY

They would then be releafed from the cares and reftraints of their prefent commerce, and the port of Batavia would be open to all nations, who would load their fhips with the merchandife of Europe; with the goods bought by the company, at a low price, of the India princes, with whom they carry on an exclufive trade ; and with the fpices deftined for all the fea-ports in Afia, where the confumption would neceffarily increafe. The facrifice they would make to the general freedom of trade, would be amply rewarded by the certain, eafy and advantageous fale of fpices in Europe. The progrefs of corruption would be ftopt by adhering to fo plain a rule of adminiftration; and order would be eftablifhed on fuch firm grounds, that it would require but little care to preferve it.

The neceffity of making the internal arrangements we propofe, is fo much the more urgent, as the company are in imminent danger of lofing the conftituent part of their power, and of having their fpice trade taken from them.

It is confidently reported, that the clove-tree is no longer to be found any where but at Amboyna; but this is a miftake. Before the Dutch got poffeffion of the Moluccas, properly fo called, all the iflands in this archipelago were covered with thefe trees: they ordered them to be pulled up, and continue to fend two floops, each having twelve foldiers on board, with orders to deftroy them wherever they make their appearance. But not to lay any ftrefs here upon the bafenefs of fuch avarice, which counteracts the

bounty

IN THE EAST AND WEST INDIES.

bounty of nature, thefe extirpators, with all their induftry, can only execute their commiffion upon the coaft. Were three hundred men to be continually employed in traverfing the forefts, they would not be able fully to anfwer the intention of their employers. The earth rebels againft this devaftation, and feems to refift the wickednefs of men. The clove fprings up under the inftrument that deftroys it, and mocks the unfeeling induftry of the Dutch, who wifh to fee nothing grow but for themfelves. The Englifh that are fettled at Sumatra have, for fome years, fent cloves to their mother-country, which they obtain from the inhabitants of Bali, who gather them in places where, it is pretended, they no longer exift.

It is equally a miftake that the nutmeg-tree is confined to Banda: it grows in New Guinea, and in the iflands that lie near that coaft. The Malays, the only people who held any correfpondence with thefe fierce nations, have carried the produce of this tree to Batavia; the precautions that have been taken to conceal the knowledge of this fact have only ferved the more fully to confirm it; and its truth is fupported by fo many atteftations, that it is impoffible to entertain a doubt of it.

If, however, the certainty of thefe facts fhould be called in queftion; if either habit or tradition fhould make it blieved that the Spaniards fettled at the Philippine iflands could not, with great advantage to themfelves, eafily procure the clove and nutmeg-tree; it muft on all hands be acknowledged, that, in thefe remote feas, an event has happened, which merits a ferious attention. The ftrait of Lombok has been difcovered by the Englifh: in confequence of this difcovery, they have penetrated as far as Saffara, which lies between New Guinea and the Molucca iflands. This ifland is found to be in the fame latitude, to have the fame foil, and the fame climate, with thofe that porduce the fpices, and they have formed a fettlement upon it. Is it credible that this active and perfevering nation will lofe fight of the only object they can propofe to themfelves from this fituation? or that they will be difcouraged by the obftacles they may meet with? Could we fuppofe the company fo little acquainted with the character of their rivals, their fituation would no longer be doubtful; it would be defperate.

SETTING afide this conteft between trading interefts, the Dutch have reafon to be apprehenfive of one of a flower and more deftructive kind. All circumftances, particularly their manner of conducting their forces both by fea and land, confpire to invite their enemies to attack them.

THE company have a fleet of about a hundred fhips, from fix hundred to a thoufand tons burthen. Twenty-eight or thirty are annually fent out from Europe, and a fmaller number returns. Thofe that are not in a condition to return, make voyages in India, where the feas, except thofe in the neighbourhood of Japan, are fo calm, that weaker veffels may fail in them with fafety. In times of profound peace the fhips fail feparately, but

on

on their return they always form two fleets at the Cape, which pafs by the Orcades, where two fhips belonging to the Republic wait to convoy them to Holland. In time of war this detour was contrived to avoid the enemy's privateers; and they continue to make ufe of it in time of peace, to prevent contraband trade. It was found difficult to procure failors who would encounter the cold blafts of the north, after being ufed to hot climates; but this difficulty was furmounted, by offering two months pay extraordinary. This cuftom has been continued even when contrary winds and ftorms drove the fleets into the channel. The chamber of Amfterdam attempted but once to fupprefs it; but they were in danger of being burnt by the populace, who, like the reft of the nation, difapproved of the arbitrary proceedings of the company, and lamented their exclufive privilege. The company's navy is commanded by officers who were originally failors or cabin-boys; they are qualified for pilots, and for working a fhip, but they have not the leaft notion of naval evolutions; not to mention, that from the defects of their education they can have no idea of the love of glory, or of inculcating it into that clafs of men who are under their command.

THEIR conduct is ftill worfe with regard to their land forces. Soldiers who have deferted from every nation in Europe may, indeed, be expected not to want courage; but their provifion and cloathing is fo bad, and they are fo much haraffed, that they have an averfion for the

the service. The officers, who, for the most part originally belonged to some low profession, in which they got a sum sufficient to purchase their posts, are incapable of infusing into them a military spirit. The contempt in which a people purely commercial hold those whose situation dooms them to an involuntary poverty, together with their aversion for war, contributes greatly to degrade and dispirit them. To these several causes of their inactivity, weakness, and want of dicipline, may be subjoined another, which is equally applicable both to the land and sea service.

THERE is not, perhaps, in the most slavish governments so dishonourable and iniquitous a mode of raising seamen and soldiers, as that which has, for a long time, been practised by the company. Their agents, called by the people *vendeurs d'ames* (kidnappers), who are always busy in the territories, and even beyond the boundaries of the republic, make it their employment to entice credulous men to embark for India, in hopes of making a considerable fortune in a short time. Those who are allured by the bait are enrolled, and receive two months pay, which is always given to their betrayer They enter into an engagement of three hundred livres*, which is the profit of the person that enlists them, who is obliged by this agreement to furnish them with some clothes worth about a tenth part of that sum. The debt i

* 13 l. 2 s. 6 d.

secure

secured by one of the company's bills, but it is never paid unless the debtor lives long enough to discharge it out of his pay.

A COMPANY which supports itself, notwithstanding this contempt for the military order, and with soldiers so corrupted, should enable us to determine the progress which the arts of negociation have made in these latter ages. It has ever been necessary to supply the want of strength by treaties, by patience, by moderation, and by artifice; but republicans should be well informed, that such a state can only be a precarious one, and that political measures, how well soever they may be combined, are not always able to resist the torrent of violence and the necessity of circumstances. The company should have troops composed of citizens, which is by no means impossible. It never can inspire that public spirit, that enthusiasm for glory which it has not itself. In this respect it is the same with a company as with a governmet, which ought to form its troops upon those principles only that are the basis of its own constitution. Oeconomy and the desire of gain are the principles of administration adopted by the company. These are the motives that should attach the soldier to their service. As he is engaged in commercial expeditions, he should be assured of a reward proportioned to the means he hath exerted in forwarding their success, and his pay should be made out to him in stock. Then personal interests, far from weakening the general intentions, will only serve to strengthen them.

IF

If thefe reflections fhould not prevail upon the company to alter this important part of their adminiftration, let them at leaft be awakened by the profpect of the dangers that threaten them. If they were attacked in India, they would be deprived of their fettlements there in lefs time than they have employed in wrefting them from the Portuguefe. Their beft towns have neither covert ways nor glacis, nor outworks, and would not hold out a week. They are never ftocked with provifions, though they are always filled with warlike ftores. There are not more than ten thoufand men, whites and blacks, to defend them, and their fhould be double that number. Thefe difadvantages would not be compenfated by the refources of the navy. The company has not a fingle veffel of the line in all its ports, and it would be impoffible to arm the merchantmen as fhips of war. The largeft of thofe that return to Europe have not one hundred men; and if the men difperfed in all the fhips that fail to India were collected, there would not be a fufficient number to form one fingle fhip's crew. Any man accuftomd to calculate probable events would not fcruple to fay, that the power of the Dutch might be annihilated in Afia, before the ftate could come to the affiftance of the company. The only bafis upon which this apparently gigantic Coloffus is fixed, is the Molucca iflands. Six men of war and fifteen hundred land forces would be more than fufficient to fecure the conqueft of them, which might be effected either by the French or the Englifh

If

IN THE EAST AND WEST INDIES.

If the French should form this enterprize, their squadron might sail from the isle of France, and bear down upon Ternate, where a commencement of hostilities would give the first intelligence of its arrival in those seas. A fort without outworks, and which might be battered from the ships, would not make much resistance. Amboyna, which formerly had a rampart, a bad ditch, and four small bastions, has been so frequently subverted by earthquakes, that it cannot be in a condition to put a stop to an enterprising enemy for two days. Banda has its peculiar difficulties. There is no bottom round these islands, and there are such violent currents, that if two or three channels which lead up to it were missed, the vessels would be unavoidably carried away under the wind. But this might be easily prevented by the pilots of Amboyna. There is nothing more to attack than a wall without a ditch, or a covert way, defended only by four bastions in bad condition. A small fort erected upon an eminence that commands the place, could not defend itself four and twenty hours.

All those who have seen the Moluccas, and examined them attentively, agree, that they would not hold out one month against the forces we have mentioned. If, as it is probable, the garrisons, which are not half so numerous as they ought to be, and exasperated with the manner in which they are treated, should refuse to fight, or should make but a feeble resistance, the conquest would be more rapid. To secure it as firmly as it deferves, it would be neceffary to take poffeffion of Batavia; a circumftance not fo difficult as it may feem to be. The fquadron, with the foldiers that were not left in garrifon, and as many of the Dutch troops as fhould have joined the conqueror, with a timely reinforcement of eight or nine hundred men, would infallibly accomplifh this enterprife, of which we fhall be convinced if we have a juft idea of Batavia.

THE moft common obftacle to the befieging of maritime places is the difficulty of landing; which is by no means the cafe at the capital of Java. Governor-general Imhoff, who was apprized of this circumftance, attempted in vain to remedy it, by conftructing a fort at the mouth of the river which embellifhes the city. If thefe works, erected at a great expence by perfons of no fkill, had even been brought to perfection, they would not have improved the fituation much: the landing, which would have been made impracticable in one place, would always have been open by means of feveral rivers that empty themfelves into the road, and are all navigable by floops.

THE troops being once formed upon land would find nothing but an immence city without a covert way, defended by a rampart, and by fome low and irregular baftions, furrounded by a ditch formed on one fide by a river, and on the other by fome marfhy canals, which might eafily be filled with running water; it was formerly defended by a citadel; but Imhoff, by building between the city and this fortrefs fome extenfive

and

IN THE EAST AND WEST INDIES.

and high barracks, intercepted the communication. He was afterwards told of this blunder, and could think of no better way of rectifying it, than to demolish two half baftions of the fortrefs, looking towards the city. Since that time they have been joined to each other.

But if the fortifications were as perfect as they are bad; if the artillery, which is immenfe, were directed by men of judgment; if even Cohorn or Vauban were fubftituted in the room of thofe unfkilful perfons, who have now the charge of their works, the place could not hold out. It would require at leaft four thoufand men to defend it, and their are feldom more than fix hundred. Neither indeed are the Dutch fo ignorant as to place their confidence in fo feeble a garrifon: they depend much more upon the inundations they are able to raife by opening the fluices that confine feveral fmall rivers. They imagine that thefe inundations would retard the operations of the fiege, and would deftroy the befiegers by the diftempers they would occafion. With a little more reflection they would difcover, that the place muft furrender, before thefe drainings had taken effect.

The plan of conqueft that France might form, would equally fuit the intereft of Great Britain; with this difference, that the Englifh would in the firft place make themfelves mafters of the Cape of Good Hope, an excellent harbour, which they are in want of for their voyages to India.

The Cape may be attacked in two places: the firft is Table Bay, at the extremity of which
the

the fort is situated. It is an open road, where the violence of the sea is broken only by a small island, and is so bad in the months of June, July, August, and September, that in 1722 twenty-five ships were lost there, and seven in 1736. Though all navigators prefer it in the other seasons of the year, on account of the accommodations they find there, it is probable that a landing would not be attempted here, because the two sides of the harbour are covered with batteries, which it would be hazardous, and, perhaps, impossible to silence. False Bay would undoubtedly be preferable, which though at thirty leagues distance from the former by sea, is yet no more than three leagues from the capital on the land side. The landing would be effected quietly in this place of security, and the troops would gain, without opposition, an eminence which commands the fort. As this citadel, in other respects confined, is only defended by a garrison of three or four hundred men at most, it might be reduced in less than a day's time by a few bombs. The inhabitants of the colony dispersed throughout an immense space, and separated from each other by deserts, would not have time to come to its relief. Perhaps, they would not if it were even in their power. We may be allowed to suppose that the oppression under which they groan, may make them wish for a change of government. The loss of the Cape would, perhaps, render it impossible for the company to convey

vey to India the succours necessary for the defence of their settlements, or would at least make those succours less certain and more expensive. The English, on the contrary, would draw great conveniences, and even immense advantages from this conquest, if the spirit of monopoly, which reason and humanity will always oppose, could once be laid aside.

THE British colonies of North America have iron, wood, rice, sugar, and various other articles of consumption, which the Cape is entirely without. They might be conveyed thither, and wines and brandy received in exchange. The soil and climate of this part of Africa are so favourable to the cultivation of the vine, that an immense extent of land may be allotted to it. If a regular consumption could be established, we should soon see a space of two hundred leagues covered with vineyards. Toleration, and the mildness of the government; the prospect of a comfortable situation would attract cultivators from all quarters. They would soon be in a condition to furnish wholesome and agreeable liquors in plenty to British America, and, perhaps, the metropolis itself might one day be supplied from the same plentiful source with wine, which it unwillingly purchases from France.

IF the republic of Holland should not consider as imaginary the dangers to which our love of the general good of nations makes us apprehend her commerce may be exposed, she ought to omit no precaution to prevent them. She must constantly keep in mind, that the company, from its beginning to the year 1722, has received about

fifteen

fifteen hundred ships, the freight of which amounted in India to 70?,366,000 livres*, and has been sold in Europe for double that sum: that by sending 6,000,000 of livres † into India, annual returns of 40,000,000 ‡ are procured, only the fifth part of which at most is consumed in the united provinces; that at the renewal of each grant, the company has given considerable sums to the republic; that it has assisted the state whenever it has stood in need of assistance; that it has raised a multitude of private fortunes, which have prodigiously increased the riches of the nation; in short, that it has doubled, perhaps trebled the activity of the metropolis, by furnishing it with frequent opportunities of forming great enterprises.

The company usually pay to the state duties of import for all the merchandise they receive from India. By a regulation of the 10th of July 1677, they are annually to pay 32,000 livres § in lieu of the duties of export. They obtained the renewal of their grant in 1743, with this formal stipulation, that the republic should receive three per cent. upon the dividend. It is thought, however, that the government have a right to derive greater advantages from an exclusive privilege of such importance.

It has always been acknowledged by all nations, whatever the form of their government might be, that the estates acquired in any country ought to contribute to the expences of government.

---

* 30,772,262 l. 10s.   † 262,500 l.   ‡ 1,750,000 l.
§ 1,400 l.

The reason of this grand maxim is evident to all capacities. Private fortunes are so essentially connected with the prosperity of the public, that when the latter is injured the former must suffer of course. Thus, when the subjects of a state serve it with their fortunes or their persons, they do nothing but defend their own private interest. The prosperity of the country is the prosperity of each citizen. This maxim, which is true in all governments, has a particular propriety when applied to free societies.

FURTHER than this, there are bodies of men, whose interest, either from the nature of those bodies, their extensive relations, or the variety of their views, are more essentially connected with the common interest. Of this kind is the India company in Holland. The enemies to its trade are enemies to the republic; and its security is established on the same basis with that of the state.

IN the opinion of men of the best discernment, the national debt has sensibly weakened the United Provinces, and affected the general welfare, by gradually increasing the load of taxes. The republic can never be restored to its original splendor, till it is released from the enormous burthen under which it groans; and this relief can only be expected from a company, which it has always encouraged, protected and favoured. To place this powerful body in a situation to render the highest services to the country, it will by no means be necessary to reduce the profits of the proprietors; it will be sufficient

sufficient to bring it back to those principles of œconomy and simplicity, and to that plan of administration, which laid the foundation of its early prosperity.

<small>Former good conduct of the Dutch, and their present degeneracy.</small>

A REFORMATION so neceffary will admit of no delay. This confidence is due to a government which has always endeavoured to maintain a great number of citizens within itself, and to employ only a small part of them in its diftant settlements. It is at the expence of all Europe that Holland has continually increased the number of its subjects: the liberty of confcience allowed there, and the moderation of the laws, have attracted all persons who were oppreffed in feveral other places by a spirit of intoleration and the feverity of government.

THE republic has procured means of fubfiftence to all perfons who have been willing to fettle and work among them: we have feen at different times the inhabitants of a country ruined by war, feeking fecurity and employment in Holland.

AGRICULTURE could never be a confiderable object in Holland, although the land is cultivated to as great a degree of perfection as poffible. But the herring fifhery fupplies the place of agriculture. This is a new method of fubfiftence, a school for feamen. Born upon the waters, they plough the fea, from whence they get their food: they grow familiar with ftorms, and learn without rifque to overcome dangers.

THE traffic of transport which the republic continually carries on from one European nation

IN THE EAST AND WEST INDIES.

tion to another, is alſo a kind of navigation, which, without deſtroying men, ſupplies them with ſubſiſtence by labour.

In ſhort, navigation, which depopulates a part of Europe, peoples Holland. It is as it were the produce of the country. Her ſhips are her landed eſtates, which ſhe makes the moſt of, at the expence of the ſtranger.

The elegant accommodations of life are known in Holland without being an object of purſuit: the refinements of behaviour are adopted with moderation; thoſe of caprice they are unacquainted with. A ſpirit of order, frugality, and even avarice prevails throughout the nation, and has been carefully kept up by the government.

The colonies are conducted by the ſame ſpirit. They are peopled in general with the ſcum of the nation, or with foreigners; but rigid laws, an equitable adminiſtration, an eaſy ſubſiſtence, and uſeful labour ſoon infuſe morals into theſe men, who were exiled from Europe, becauſe they had none.

The ſame deſign of preſerving the population prevails in the military ſyſtem; the republic maintains a great number of foreign troops in Europe, and ſome in the colonies.

The ſailors in Holland are well paid; and foreign ſeamen are conſtantly employed either on board their trading veſſels, or their men of war.

For the purpoſes of commerce, it is neceſſary that harmony ſhould be preſerved at home, and peace abroad. No people, except the Swiſs,

take

take more care to keep on good terms with their neighbours; and they endeavour, ſtill more than the Swiſs, to encourage peace among them. The republic preſerves unanimity among her citizens, by very excellent laws, which preſcribe the duties of every ſtation, by a ſpedy and diſintereſted adminiſtration of juſtice, and by regulations admirably well adapted to the merchants. She has ſhewn the opinion ſhe entertains of the neceſſity of good faith by her obſervance of treaties, and has endeavoured to inculcate the ſame principle among individuals.

IN a word, we know of no nation in Europe that has conſidered better what its united advantages of ſituation, ſtrength, and population allow it to undertake, or that has known and followed more effectually the means of increaſing both its population and its ſtrength. We know of none, which having ſuch objects as an extenſive commerce and liberty, mutually attracting and ſupporting each other, hath conducted itſelf in a better manner for the preſervation of both the one and the other.

BUT how are theſe manners already changed and degenerated from the purity of a republican government! Perſonal intereſts, which become laudable by being combined, are now totally ſelfiſh, and corruption is become general. There is no patriotiſm in that country, which above all others in the univerſe ſhould inſpire its inhabitants with more ſtedfaſt attachments. In reality, what patriotic ſentiments might we
not

not expect from a nation that can say to itself, This land which I inhabit, has been fertilized by me; it is I who have embellished, who have created it. This threatening sea, which deluged all our plains, rages in vain against the powerful dikes I have opposed to its fury. I have purified this air which stagnant waters had filled with fatal exhalations. It is by my means that superb cities stand now upon the slime and mud, over which the ocean once rolled its waves. The ports I have constructed, the canals I have digged, received the productions of the whole universe, which I dispense at pleasure. The inheritances of other nations are only possessions which man disputes with man; that which I shall leave to my posterity, I have ravished from the elements which conspired against my territory, and am now the master of it. It is here that I have established a new arrangement of nature, a new system of manners. I have done every thing where there was nothing. Air, land, government, liberty, all these are my works. I enjoy the glory of the past; and when I cast a look into futurity, I see with satisfaction that my ashes will rest quietly on the same spot where my fore-fathers saw the breaking of storms.

What motives these for idolizing one's country! Yet there is no longer any public spirit in Holland: it is a whole, the parts of which have no other relation among themselves than the spot they occupy. Meanness, baseness and dishonesty characterise now the conquerors of Philip. They make a traffic of their oath, as of their merchandise;

chandife; and they will foon become the refufe of the univerfe, which they had aftonifhed by their induftry and by their virtues.

Ye unworthy members of the government, under which ye live, fhudder at leaft at the dangers that furround you! Thofe who have flavifh fouls are not far removed from flavery. The facred fire of liberty can only be kept up by chafte hands. Ye are not now in the fame ftate of anarchy, as when the fovereigns of Europe all equally oppofed by the nobles in their refpective ftates, could not carry on their defigns either with fecrecy, unanimity or rapidity; as when the equilibrium of the feveral powers was merely the effect of their mutual debility. At prefent, power grown more independent, confirms thofe advantages to a monarchy which a free ftate can never enjoy. What have republicans to oppofe to fuperiority fo formidable? Their virtues; but ye have loft them. The corruption of your manners, and of your magiftrates, encourages every where the detractors of liberty; and, perhaps, your fatal example is the means of impofing a heavier yoke on other nations. What anfwer would you wifh us to make to thofe men, who, either from the prejudice of education or the want of honefty, are perpetually telling us; This is the government which you extol fo much in your writings; thefe are the happy confequences of that fyftem of liberty you hold fo dear. To thofe vices which you have laid to the charge of defpotifm, they have added another,

ther, which furpaffes them all, the inability to ſtop the progreſs of evil. What anſwer can be given to ſo ſevere a ſatire on democracy?

INDUSTRIOUS Hollanders! ye who were formerly ſo renowned for your bravery, and are at preſent ſo diſtinguiſhed by your wealth, tremble at the idea of being again reduced to crouch under the rod you have broken, and which ſtill hangs over you. Would you learn how the ſpirit of commerce may be united and preſerved with the ſpirit of liberty? View from your ſhores that iſland, and thoſe people, whom nature preſents to you as a model for your imitation. Keep your eyes conſtantly fixed upon England: if the alliance of that kingdom has been your ſupport, its conduct will now ſerve you as an inſtructor, and its example as a guide.

BOOK

BOOK III.

Settlements, Trade, and Conquests of the English in the East Indies.

<small>BOOK III.

Sketch of the ancient state of the English commerce.</small>

WE know nothing either of the period in which the British isles were peopled, nor of the origin of their first inhabitants. All we can learn from the most authentic historical records is, that they were successively visited by the Phœnicians, the Carthaginians, and the Gauls. The traders of these nations used to go there to exchange earthen vessels, salt, all kinds of iron, and copper instruments, for skins, slaves, hounds, and bull-dogs, and especially for tin. Their profits were just what they pleased in their dealings with savages equally ignorant of the value of what they sold or bought.

A LOOSE speculation would lead us to imagine, that islanders have been the first civilized people among mankind. Nothing puts a stop to the excursions of people living on a continent: they may get their livelihood and avoid fighting at the same time. In islands, war, and the inconveniences of a too limited society, should sooner make laws and treaties necessary. But whatever is the reason of it, we generally see the manners and the government

ment of iflanders formed later and more imperfectly than others. All the traditions refpecting Britain, particularly confirm this affertion.

THE Roman empire was not fufficiently durable, and too eagerly difputed, to improve in any confiderable degree the induftry of the Britons. Even the fmall progrefs that hufbandry and the arts had made during this period, was loft as foon as that haughty power had determined to abandon this conqueft. The fpirit of flavery which the fouthern inhabitants of Britain had contracted, deprived them of the courage neceffary to refift at firft the overflowings of their neighbours the Picts, who had faved themfelves from the yoke by flying towards the north of the ifland, and prevented them afterwards from being able to oppofe the more deftructive, more obftinate and more numerous expeditions of plunderers that poured in fwarms from the more northern parts of Europe.

ALL nations were affected with this dreadful plague, the moft deftructive, perhaps, that ever was recorded in the annals of the world; but the calamities which Great Britain particularly experienced are inexpreffible. Every year, feveral times even in a year, her countries were ravaged, her houfes burnt, her women ravifhed, her temples ftripped, her inhabitants maffacred, put to torture, or enflaved. All thefe misfortunes fucceeded each other with inconceivable rapidity. When the country was fo far deftroyed that nothing remained to glut the avidity of thefe barbarians, they feized on the land itfelf. One nation fucceeded another.

another. One troop fupervening, expelled or exterminated the one that was already eftablifhed; and this fucceffion of revolutions conftantly kept up indolence, miftruft and mifery. In thefe difpiriting times, the Britons had fcarce any commercial connection with the continent. Exchanges were even fo rare amongft them, that it was neceffary to have witneffes for the fale of the leaft trifle.

It might have been expected that the union of the two kingdoms would have put a ftop to thefe calamities; when William the Conqueror fubdued Great Britain a little while after the middle of the eleventh century. His followers came from countries rather more civilized, more active, and more induftrious, than thofe they came to fettle in. Such a communication ought naturally to have rectified and enlarged the ideas of the conquered people. The introduction of the feudal government occafioned fo fpeedy and fo complete a revolution in matters of property, that every thing was thrown into confufion.

The minds of men were fcarcely fettled, and the conquerors and the conquered had but juft begun to confider themfelves as one and the fame people, when the abilities and ftrength of the nation were engaged in fupporting the pretenfions of their fovereigns to the crown of France. In thefe obftinate wars, the Englifh difplayed military talents and courage; but after feveral great efforts, and confiderable fuccefs, they were forced back into their ifland, where domeftic troubles expofed them to frefh calamities.

DURING

IN THE EAST AND WEST INDIES.

During thefe different periods, the whole commerce was in the hands of the Jews and the bankers of Lombardy, who were alternately favoured and robbed, confidered as ufeful perfons, and condemned to death, expelled and recalled: thefe tumults were increafed by the audacity of the pirates, who being fometimes protected by the government, with which they fhared their fpoils, attacked all fhips indifcriminately, and frequently fank their crews. The intereft of money was at fifty per cent. Leather, furs, butter, lead, and tin were the only things exported from England at a very moderate rate, and thirty thoufand facks of wool, which returned annually a more confiderable fum. As the Englifh were then totally unacquainted with the art of dying this wool, and manufacturing it with elegance, the greateft part of this money returned. To remedy this inconvenience, foreign manufacturers were invited, and the people were prohibited from wearing any cloaths that were not of home manufacture. At the fame time, the exportation of manufactured wool and wrought iron was forbidden; two laws altogether worthy of the age in which they were inftituted.

Henry VII. permitted the barons to difpofe of their lands, and the common people to buy them. This regulation diminifhed the inequality which fubfifted before between the fortunes of the lords and their vaffals; it made the latter more independent, and infpired the people with the defire of enriching themfelves, and with the hope of enjoying their riches. There were many

many obstacles to this wish, and this hope; some of which were removed. The company of merchants established at London was prevented from exacting in future the sum of one thousand five hundred and seventy-five livres* from each of the other merchants in the kingdom, desirous of trading at the great fairs of the low countries. In order to fix a greater number of people to the labours of husbandry, it was enacted, that no person should put his son or daughter out to any kind of apprenticeship, without being possessed of a rent of twenty-two livres ten sols † in landed property: this absurd law was afterwards mitigated.

UNFORTUNATELY that law which regulated the price of all sorts of provisions, of woollens, of workmen's wages, of stuffs, and of cloathing, was maintained in its full force. Other impediments even were thrown in the way of commerce, on account of some pernicious combinations that were set on foot. The loan of money at interest, and the profits of exchange were strictly prohibited, as usurious in themselves, or calculated to introduce usury. The exportation of money in any kind of coin was forbidden; and, in order to prevent foreign merchants from carrying it clandestinely away, they were compelled to change into English merchandise the entire produce of the goods they had brought into England. The exportation of horses was likewise prohibited; and the people were not sufficiently enlightened to discover that

* 63l. 18s. 1d. ¾   † Near 20s.

such

such a prohibition would necessarily cause the propagation and improvement of the species to be neglected. At length corporations were established in all the towns; that is to say, the state authorised all persons of the same profession, to make such regulations as they should think necessary for their exclusive preservation and success. The nation is still oppressed with a regulation so contrary to general industry, and which reduces every thing to a kind of monopoly.

Upon considering such a number of strange laws, we might be induced to think that Henry was either indifferent about the prosperity of his kingdom, or that he was totally deficient in understanding. Nevertheless, it is certain that this prince, notwithstanding his extreme avarice, often lent considerable sums of money, without interest, to merchants who had not property sufficient to carry on the schemes they had planned: besides, the wisdom of his government is so well confirmed, that he is accounted, with reason, one of the greatest monarchs that ever filled the throne of England. But, notwithstanding all the efforts of genius, it requires a succession of several ages before any science can be reduced to simple principles. It is the same thing with theories as with machines, which are always very complicated at first, and which are only freed in the course of time by observation and experience, from those useless wheels which served merely to increase their friction.

The knowledge of the succeeding reigns was not much more extensive upon those matters we are treating

treating of. Some Flemings, fettled in England, were the only good workmen in that country; they were almoft always infulted and oppreffed by the Englifh workmen, who were jealous without emulation: they complained that all the cuftomers went to the Flemings, and they raifed the price of corn. The government adopted thefe popular prejudices, and forbad all ftrangers to employ more than two workmen in their fhops. The merchants were not better treated than the workmen, and thofe even who were naturalized, were obliged to pay the fame duties as aliens. Ignorance was fo general, that the cultivation of the beft lands was neglected, in order to convert them into pafture lands, even at the time that the number of fheep, which might be in one flock, was reftrained by the laws to two thoufand. All mercantile correfpondences were confined in the low countries. The inhabitants of thefe provinces bought the Englifh commodities, and circulated them through the different parts of Europe. It is probable that the nation would not have made any confiderable figure for a long time, without a concurrence of favourable circumftances.

THE Duke of Alva's cruelties drove feveral able manufacturers into England, who carried the art of the fine Flemifh manufactures to London. The perfecutions which the Proteftants fuffered in France fupplied England with workmen of all kinds. Elizabeth, impatient of contradiction, but knowing and defirous of doing what was right, at once defpotic and popular, with the advantages of a good underftanding, and of being properly obeyed, availed

availed herself of the fermentation of people's minds, as prevalent throughout all her dominions as through the rest of Europe; and while this fermentation produced among other people nothing but theological disputes, and civil or foreign wars; in England, it gave rise to a lively emulation for commerce, and for the improvement of navigation.

The English learned to build their ships at home, which they bought before of the merchants of Lubec and Hamburgh. They were soon the only persons who traded to Muscovy by the way of Archangel just discovered; and they presently became competitors with the Hanse towns in Germany, and in the north. They began to trade with Turky. Several of their navigators attempted, though in vain, to discover a passage to India by the northern seas. At length Drake, Stephens, Cavendish, and some others, reached that place, some by the south sea, and others by doubling the Cape of Good Hope.

The success of these voyages was sufficient to determine the most able merchants of London to establish a company in the year 1600; which obtained an exclusive privilege of trading to the East Indies. The act which granted this privilege, fixed it for fifteen years: it declared, that if it should prove injurious to the state, it should be annulled, and the company suppressed, by giving two years previous notice to its members.

This clause of reserve was owing to the displeasure the commons had lately shewn on account of a grant, the novelty of which might possibly offend them. The queen had returned to the

First voyages of the English to India.

house, and had spoken on this occasion in a manner worthy to serve as a lesson to all sovereigns.

"Gentlemen," said she to the members of the house commissioned to return her thanks, " I am
" extremely sensible of your attachment, and of the
" care you have taken to give me an authentic
" testimony of it. This affection for my person had
" determined you to apprize me of a fault I had
" inadvertently fallen into from ignorance, but in
" which my will had no share. If your vigilance
" had not discovered to me the mischiefs which my
" mistake might have produced, what pain should
" I not have felt—I, who have nothing dearer to
" me than the affection and preservation of my peo-
" ple? May my hand suddenly wither, may my
" heart be struck at once with a deadly blow, be-
" fore I shall ever grant particular privileges that
" my subjects may have reason to complain of!
" The splendour of the throne has not so far daz-
" zled my eyes, that I should prefer the abuse of
" an unbounded authority to the use of a power
" exercised by justice. The brilliancy of royalty
" blinds only those princes who are ignorant of the
" duties that the crown imposes. I dare believe
" that I shall not be ranked among such monarchs.
" I know that I hold not the scepter for my own
" proper advantage, and that I am entirely devoted
" to the society, which has put its confidence in
" me. It is my happiness to see that the state has
" hitherto prospered under my government;
" and that my subjects are worthy that I should
" yield up my crown and my life for their sakes.
" Impute

"Impute not to me the improper meafures I may
"be engaged in, nor the irregularities which may
"be committed under the fanction of my name.
"You know that the minifters of princes are
"too often guided by private interefts, that truth
"feldom reaches the ears of kings, and that obliged
"as they are, from the multiplicity of affairs they
"are laden with, to fix their attention on thofe which
"are of the greateft importance, it is impoffible
"they fhould fee every thing with their own eyes."

THE funds of this company were, at firft, far from being confiderable. Part of them was expended in fitting out a fleet of four fhips which failed in the beginning of the year 1601; and the reft was fent abroad in money and merchandife.

LANCASTER, who commanded the expedition, arrived the year following at the port of Achen, which was at that time a celebrated mart. Intelligence was received of the victories gained by the Englifh over the Spaniards at fea; and this intelligence procured him a very diftinguifhed reception. The king behaved to him in the fame manner as if he had been his equal; he ordered that his own wives richly habited, fhould play feveral airs in his prefence, on a variety of inftruments. This favour was followed by all the compliances that could be wifhed for to facilitate the eftablifhment of a fafe and advantageous commerce. The Englifh admiral was received at Bantam in the fame manner as at the place where he firft landed; and a fhip which he had difpatched to the Molucca iflands, brought him a confiderable cargo
of

of cloves and nutmegs. With thefe valuable fpices, and the pepper he took in at Java and Sumatra, he returned fafe to Europe.

THIS early fuccefs determined the fociety who had intrufted their interefts in the hands of this able man, to form fettlements in India ; but not without the confent of the natives. They did not wifh to begin with conquefts. Their expeditions were nothing more than the enterprifes of humane and fair traders. They made themfelves beloved: but they gained nothing by this good impreffion, except a few factories, and were in no condition to fuftain the attempts of their rivals, who were very formidable.

THE Portuguefe and Dutch were in poffeffion of large provinces, well fortified places, and good harbours. By thefe advantages their trade was fecured againft the natives of the country, and againft new competitors; their return to Europe was rendered eafy; and they had opportunities of getting a good fale for the commodities they carried to Afia, and to purchafe thofe they wanted at a moderate price. The Englifh, on the contrary, expofed to the caprice of feafons and of people, having no ftrength, or place of fecurity, and deriving their fupplies from England only, could not carry on an advantageous trade. They found how difficult it was to acquire great riches without great injuftice, and that if they would furpafs or even equal the nations they had cenfured, they muft purfue the fame conduct.

THE plan of forming lafting fettlements, and of attempting conquefts, feemed too great to be accomplished by the forces of an infant society: but they flattered themselves that they should meet with protection, because they thought themselves useful. They were disappointed in their expectations. They could obtain nothing from James I. a weak prince, infected with the false philosophy of his age, of a subtile and pedantic genius, and better qualified to be at the head of an university than to preside over an empire. By their activity, perseverance, and judicious choice of officers and factors, the company provided those succours which were refused them by their sovereign. They erected forts, and founded colonies in the islands of Java, Poleron, Amboyna, and Banda. They likewise shared the spice-trade with the Dutch, which will always be the most certain branch of eastern commerce, because the objects of it are become necessary articles of life. It was of more importance at the time we are speaking of, because the luxury which arises from caprice had not then made so much progress in Europe as it has done since, and because there was not that prodigious demand for India linens, stuffs, teas, and Chinese varnish, that there is at present.

THE Dutch, who had driven the Portuguese from the spice-islands, never intended to suffer a nation to settle there, whose maritime force, character, and government, would make them formidable rivals. They had many advantages on their side, such as powerful colonies; a well exercised navy, firm alliances, a great fund of wealth, a knowledge of the country, and of the principles and

Disputes between the English and Dutch.

and details of commerce, which the English wanting, were attacked in all possible ways.

The first step their rival took was to drive them from the fertile places where they had formed settlements. In the islands where their power was less established, they endeavoured, by accusations, equally void of truth and decency, to make them odious to the natives of the country. These shameful expedients not meeting with all the success the Dutch expected, those avaritious traders resolved to proceed to acts of violence. An extraordinary occasion brought on the commencement of hostilities sooner than was expected.

It is a custom at Java for the new married women to dispute with their husbands the first favours of love. This kind of contest, which the men take a pride in terminating immediately, and the women in protracting as long as possible, sometimes lasts several weeks. The king of Bantam having overcome the resistance of a new bride, made public entertainments in celebration of his triumph. The strangers in the harbour were invited to these festivals. Unhappily for them, the English were treated with too much distinction. The Dutch looked with a jealous eye upon this preference, and did not defer revenge a moment. They attacked them on all-sides.

The Indian ocean became, at this period, the scene of the most bloody engagements between the maritime forces of the two nations. They fought out, attacked, and combated each other with the spirit of men who chose to conquer or die. Equal courage appeared on both sides, but
there

there was a disparity in their forces. The English were on the point of being overcome, when some moderate people in Europe, which the flames of war had not reached, endeavoured to find out the means of accommodating their differences. By an infatuation, which it is not easy to explain, the very strangest of all was adopted.

In 1619 the two companies signed a treaty, the purport of which was, that the Molucca islands, Amboyna, and Banda, should belong in common to the two nations: that the English should have one third, and the Dutch two thirds of the produce at a fixed price: that each, in proportion to their interest, should contribute to the defence of these islands: that a council composed of skilful men of both parties, should regulate all the affairs of commerce at Batavia: that this agreement, guaranteed by the respective sovereigns, should last twenty years; and that if any differences should arise during this interval, that could not be settled by the two companies, they should be determined by the king of Great Britain and the States-general. Among all the political conventions preserved in history, it would be difficult to find a more extraordinary one than this. It had the fate it deserved.

The Dutch were no sooner informed of it in India, than they devised means to render it ineffectual. The situation of affairs favoured their designs. The Spaniards and the Portuguese had taken advantage of the disputes between their enemies, to regain the settlements in the Moluccas.

luccas. They might fortify themfelves there; and it was dangerous to give them time. The Englifh commiffaries concurred with them in opinion, that it would be beft to attack them without delay; but added, that they were not at all prepared to act in concert with them. This declaration, which was expected, was regiftered; and their affociates embarked alone in an expedition, all the advantages of which they referved to themfelves. The agents of the Dutch company had only one ftep further to go, to get all the fpices into the hands of their mafters, which was, to drive their rivals from the ifland of Amboyna. The method by which they fucceeded in their project was very extraordinary.

A JAPANESE, in the Dutch fervice at Amboyna, made himfelf fufpected by his imprudent curiofity. He was feized, and confeffed that he had entered into an engagement with the foldiers of his nation to deliver up the fort to the Englifh. His comrades confirmed his account, making the fame confeffion. Upon thefe unanimous depofitions, the authors of the confpiracy, who did not difavow, but even acknowledge it, were loaded with irons: and the ignominious death which all the criminals were condemned to fuffer, put an end to the plot. This is the account given by the Dutch.

THE Englifh have always confidered this accufation as the fuggeftion of an unbounded avarice. They have maintained that it was abfurd to fuppofe, that ten factors and eleven foreign foldiers could

could have formed the project of seizing upon a place, which was garrisoned by two hunder men: that even if these unhappy men had thought it possible to execute so extravagant a plan, would they not have been discouraged by the impossibility of obtaining succours to defend against them an enemy who would have besieged them on all sides? To make a conspiracy of this kind probable, it requires stronger proof than a confession extorted from the accused by extremity of torture. The torments of the rack never afforded any other proof, than that of the courage or weakness of those whom barbarous custom condemned to it. These considerations, strengthened by several others, almost equally convincing, have made the story of the conspiracy of Amboyna so suspected, that it has generally been considered as a cloak to cruelty and avarice.

THE ministry of James I. and the whole nation, were at that time so engaged in ecclesiastical subtleties, and the discussion of the rights of king and people, that they were not sensible of the insults offered to the English name in the East. This indifference produced a caution which soon degenerated into weakness. These islanders, however, maintained the bravery of their character better at Coromandel and Malabar.

THEY had established factories at Mazulipatam, Calicut, and several other ports, and even at Delhi. Surat, the richest mart in these countries, tempted their ambition in 1611. The inhabitants were

Disputes of the English with the Portuguese.

disposed

disposed to receive them; but the Portuguese declared, that if they suffered this nation to make a settlement, they would burn all the towns upon the coast, and seize all the Indian vessels. The government was awed by these menaces. Middleton, disappointed in his hopes, was obliged to abandon the place, and return through a numerous fleet, to which he did more damage than he received.

CAPTAIN Thomas Best arrived in these latitudes the year following, with a very considerable force. He was received at Surat without any opposition. The agents he carried out with him had scarce entered upon their employments when a formidable armament from Goa made its appearance. The English admiral, reduced to this alternative, either of betraying the interests he was intrusted with; or of exposing himself to the greatest danger in defending them, did not hesitate what part he should take. He twice attacked the Portuguese, and notwithstanding the great inferiority of his squadron, gained the victory each time. However, the advantage the vanquished derived from their position; their ports, and their fortresses, always made the English navigation in Guzarat very difficult. They were obliged to maintain a constant struggle against an obstinate enemy that was not discouraged by defeats. No tranquillity was to be obtained, but at the price of new contests and new triumphs.

The English form connections with Persia.

THE news of these glorious successes against a nation which had hitherto been thought invincible, reached as far as the capital of Persia.

IN THE EAST AND WEST INDIES.

THIS vaft country, fo celebrated in antiquity, appeared to have been free at the firft inftitution of its government. The monarchy rofe upon the ruins of a depraved republic. The Perfians were long happy under this form of government: their manners were as fimple as their laws. At length the fovereigns were infpired with the fpirit of conqueft. At that time the treafures of Affyria, the fpoils of many trading nations, and the tribute arifing from a vaft number of provinces, brought immenfe riches into the empire, which foon occafioned a total alteration. The diforders rofe to fuch a pitch, that the care of the public amufements feemed to engage the chief attention of government.

A PEOPLE totally devoted to pleafure could not fail in a fhort time to be reduced to flavery. They were fucceffively brought into that ftate by the Macedonians, the Parthians, the Arabians, and the Tartars, and towards the clofe of the fifteenth century by the Sophis, who pretended to be the defcendents of Aly, author of the famous reformation, by which Mohammedifm was divided into two branches.

No prince of this new race made himfelf fo famous as Schah-Abbas, furnamed the Great. He conquered Candahar, feveral places of importance upon the Black Sea, part of Arabia, and drove the Turks out of Georgia, Armenia, Mefopotamia, and all the countries they had conquered beyond the Euphrates.

THESE victories produced remarkable changes in the interior adminiftration of the empire. The

great

great men took advantage of the civil broils to make themselves independent; they were degraded, and all posts of consequence were given to strangers, who had neither the power nor inclination to raise factions. The army having taken upon themselves to dispose of the crown at their pleasure; they were restrained by foreign troops, whose religion and customs were different. Anarchy had inclined the people to sedition; and to prevent this, the towns and villages were filled with inhabitants chosen out of nations whose manners and character bore no resemblance to those of the ancient inhabitants. These arrangements gave rise to a despotism the most absolute, perhaps, that any country ever experienced.

It is a matter of astonishment that the great Abbas should have combined some views of public utility with this government, which was naturally oppressive. He patronized the arts, and established them in the capital, and in the provinces. All who came into his dominions, if they possessed talents of any kind, were sure of being well received, assisted, and rewarded. He would often say, that strangers were the best ornaments of an empire, and added more to the dignity of the prince than the pomp of the most refined luxury.

While Persia was rising from its ruins by the different branches of industry that were every where established, a number of Armenians, transplanted to Ispahan, carried the spirit of commerce into the heart of the empire. In a little time, these traders, and the natives of the country who
followed

IN THE EAST AND WEST INDIES.
followed their example, spread themselves over the East, into Holland, England, the Mediterranean and the Baltic, and wherever commerce was carried on with spirit and advantage. The Sophi himself bore a part in their enterprises, and advanced them confiderable sums, which they employed to advantage in the most celebrated marts in the world. They were obliged to return the capital on the terms agreed upon, and if they had increased it by their industry, he granted them some recompence.

THE Portuguése, who found that part of the Indian trade with Asia and Europe was likely to be diverted to Persia, imposed restraints upon it; they would not suffer the Persians to purchase merchandise any where but from their magazines: they fixed the price of it; and if they sometimes allowed it to be taken at the places where it was manufactured, it was always to be carried in their own bottoms, charging all expences of freight and exorbitant customs. This stretch of power displeased the great Abbas, who being informed of the resentment of the English, proposed to unite their maritime strength with his land forces, to besiege Ormus. This place was attacked by the combined arms of the two nations, and taken in the year 1622, after a contest that lasted two months. The conquerors divided the spoil, which was immense, and afterwards totally demolished the place.

THREE or four leagues from hence there was upon the continent a harbour called Gombroon, or Bender-Abassi. Nature seemed not to have designed it should be inhabited. It is situated at the foot of a ridge of mountains of an excessive height; the air you breathe seems to be on fire; fatal vapours are continually exhaling from the bowels of the earth; the fields are black and dry, as if they had been scorched with fire. Notwithstanding these inconveniences, as Bender-Abassi had the advantage of being placed at the entrance of the Gulph, the Persian monarch chose to make it the center of the extensive trade he intended to carry on with India. The English joined in this project. A perpetual exemption from all imposts, and a moiety of the product of the customs, were granted them, on condition they should maintain, at least, two men of war in the Gulph. This precaution was thought necessary to frustrate the attempts of the Portuguese, whose resentment was still to be dreaded.

From this time Bender-Abassi, which was before a poor fishing town, became a flourishing city. The English carried thither spices, pepper, and sugar, from the markets of the east; and iron, lead, and cloths, from the ports of Europe. The profits arising from these commodities were increased by the very high freight paid them by the Armenians, who were still in possession of the richest branch of the Indian commerce.

These merchants had, for a long time, been concerned in the linen trade. They had never been supplanted either by the Portuguese, who were intent only on plunder, or by the Dutch, whose

IN THE EAST AND WEST INDIES.

whofe attention was totally confined to the fpice trade. They might, neverthelefs, be apprehenfive, that they fhould not be able to withftand the competition of a people who were equally rich, induftrious, active, and frugal. The Armenians acted then as they have ever done fince: they went to India, where they bought cotton, which they fent to the fpinners; the cloths were manufactured under their own infpection, and carried to Gombroom, from whence they were tranfported to Ifpahan. From thence they were conveyed into the different provinces of the empire, the dominions of the Grand Signior, and into Europe, where the cuftom has prevailed of calling them Perfian manufactures, though they were never made but on the coaft of Coromandel. Such is the influence of names upon opinions, that the vulgar error, which attributes to Perfia the manufacture of India, will in a feries of ages, perhaps, pafs with the learned in future times for an inconteftable truth. The infurmountable difficulties which errors of this kind have occafioned in the hiftory of Pliny, and other ancient writers, fhould induce us to fet a high value on the labours of the literati of this age, who collect the works of nature and of art with a view of tranfmitting them to pofterity.

In exchange for the merchandife they carried to Perfia, they gave the following articles, which were either the produce of their own foil, or the fruits of their induftry.

SILK,

SILK, which was the principal commodity; and was prepared and exported in great quantities.

CARAMANIAN wool, which nearly refembles that of the Vicuna. It was of great ufe in the manufacture of hats, and of fome ftuffs. It is a remarkable circumftance in the goats which fupply it, that in the month of May the fleece falls off of itfelf.

TURQUOISES, which were more or lefs valuable, according as they were procured from one or other of the three mines that produce them. They were formerly an article of the drefs of our ladies.

GOLD brocades, which fold at a higher price than any of thofe which are the produce of the moft celebrated manufactures. Some of them were made to be worn on one, and others on both fides. They were ufed for window-curtains, fkreens and magnificent fophas.

TAPESTRY, which has fince been fo well imitated in Europe, and has for a long time been the richeft furniture of our rooms.

MOROCCO leather, which, as other fkins, is brought to a degree of perfection that cannot be equalled any where elfe.

SHAGREEN, goats hair, rofe-water, medicinal roots, gums for colours, dates, horfes, arms, and many other articles, of which fome are fold in India, and others carried to Europe.

THOUGH the Dutch contrived to get all the trade of India into their hands, they viewed the tranfactions of Perfia with a jealous eye. They
thought

IN THE EAST AND WEST INDIES.

thought the privileges enjoyed by their rivals in the road of Bender-Abaffi, might be compensated by the advantage they had in having a greater quantity of spices, and entered into a competition with them.

THE English, haraffed in every mart by a powerful enemy resolutely bent on their destruction, were obliged every where to give way. Their fate was hastened by those civil and religious diffentions, which drowned their country in blood, and extinguished all sentiment and knowledge. India was totally forgotten, while the most important interests were at stake; and the company, oppressed and discouraged, were reduced to nothing at the time that the death of Charles I. afforded so instructive and dreadful a lesson.

CROMWELL, enraged at the favours the Dutch had shewn to the unfortunate family of the Stuarts, and at the asylum they had afforded to the English who had been proscribed; and piqued that the republic of the United Provinces should pretend to the dominion of the sea; proud of his success, and sensible of his own strength, and of that of the nation under his command, resolved at the same time to inspire respect for his country, and to avenge himself. He declared war against the Dutch.

OF all the maritime wars which have been recorded in history, none were conducted with more knowledge, or were more famous for the skill of the commanders, and the bravery of the sailors; none have abounded with so many

BOOK III.

Decline of the English in India.

obstinate

obstinate and bloody engagements. The English gained the superiority, and owed it to the size of their ships, in which particular they have since been imitated by other European nations.

The protector, whose voice was law, did not exert himself as far as he might in favour of India. He contented himself with providing for the security of the English trade, procuring a disavowal of the massacre at Amboyna, and insisting upon an indemnification for the descendents of the unhappy victims who perished in that dreadful transaction. No mention is made in the treaty, of the forts taken from the nation by the Dutch, in the island of Java, and in several of the Moluccas. It was stipulated, indeed, that the island of Puleron should be restored: but the usurpers, seconded by the English negotiator whom they had corrupted, found means to elude this article so dextrously, which would and ought to have produced a rivalry in the spice trade, that the observance of it was never enforced.

Revival of the English trade in India.

NOTWITHSTANDING this neglect, as soon as the company had obtained from the protector a renewal of their privileges in 1657, and found themselves firmly supported by the publick authority, they shewed a spirit of resolution which they had lost during their late misfortunes. Their courage increased with their rights.

The success they met in Europe, accompanied them into Asia, Arabia, Persia, Indostan, the eastern parts of India, China, and all the markets where the English had formerly traded, were opened

opened to them. They were even received with more franknefs and lefs diftruft than they had experienced formerly. Their trade was carried on with great activity, and their profits were very confiderable: nothing was wanting to complete their fuccefs, but to gain admittance into Japan, which they attempted. But the Japanefe being informed by the Dutch that the king of England had married a daughter of the king of Portugal, refufed to admit the Englifh into their ports.

NOTWITHSTANDING this difappointment, the company's affairs were in a very flourifhing condition: they flattered themfelves with the pleafing hopes of giving a greater extent and fecurity to their affairs, when they found their career retarded by a rivalfhip, which their own fuccefs created.

SOME traders, fired with the relation of the advantages to be obtained in India, refolved to make voyages thither. Charles II. who though feated on the throne was nothing more than a private man of voluptuous and diffolute manners, gave them permiffion for a valuable confideration: while, on the other hand, he extorted large fums from the company, to enable him to perfecute thofe who encroached upon their charter. A competition of this nature would unavoidably degenerate into piracy. The Englifh thus becoming enemies to each other, carried on their difputes with a fpirit of rancour and animofity, which lowered them in the opinion of the people of Afia.

Misfortunes and mifconduct of the Englifh in India.

The Dutch wifhed to take advantage of fo fingular a conjuncture. Thefe republicans had for a long time been abfolute mafters of the Indian trade. They had feen with regret a part of it taken out of their hands, at the conclufion of the civil wars in England. They hoped to recover it by the fuperiority of their forces, when in 1664 the two nations entered into a war in all parts of the world; but the hoftilities did not continue long enough to anfwer thefe fanguine expectations. As the peace prevented them from having recourfe to open violence againft one another, they refolved to attack the fovereigns of the country to oblige them to fhut their ports againft their rival. The foolifh and defpicable behaviour of the Englifh increafed the infolence of the Dutch, who proceeded fo far as to drive them ignominioufly from Bantam in 1680.

So ferious and public an infult roufed the fpirit of the Englifh company. The defire of re-eftablifhing their character, gratifying their revenge, and maintaining their interefts, animated them to the moft fpirited exertions. They equipped a fleet of twenty-three fhips, with eight thoufand regular troops on board. They were ready to fail, when their departure was poftponed by the king's orders. Charles, whofe neceffities and licentioufnefs were unbounded, entertained hopes of receiving an immenfe fum to induce him to recall this armament. As he could not obtain it from his fubjects, he was refolved to receive it from his enemies. He facrificed

the

IN THE EAST AND WEST INDIES.

the honour and trade of his nation for 2,250,000 livres*, which were paid him by the Dutch, who were intimidated by thefe great preparations. The intended expedition never took place.

The company exhaufted by the expences of an armament, which had been rendered ufelefs by the venality of the court, fent their veffels to India without the neceffary funds to fupply the cargoes; but with orders to the factors, if poffible to take them upon credit. The fidelity they had hitherto obferved in their engagements procured them 6,750,000 livres †. Nothing can be more extraordinary than the method that was taken to pay them back.

Josias Child who from being a director was become the tyrant of the Company, is faid, unknown to his colleagues, to have fent orders to India, to invent fome pretence or other, to defraud the lenders of their money. The execution of this iniquitous project was intrufted to his brother John Child, who was governor of Bombay. This avaritious, turbulent, and favage man immediately proceeded to make feveral claims upon the governor of Surat, fome more ridiculous than others. Thefe demands meeting with the reception they deferved, he attacked all the veffels belonging to the fubjects of the crown of Delhi, and fingled out in particular the fhips from Surat, as being the richeft. He paid no regard to veffels that failed with pafsports from that crown, and carried his infolence fo far as to feize a fleet laden with provifion for

* 98,437l. 10s. † 295,312l. 10s.

the

the Mogul's army. This terrible pillage, which lafted the whole year 1688, occafioned incredible loffes throughout all Indoftan.

AURENGZEBE, who held the reigns of the empire with a fteady hand, did not lofe a moment in revenging fo great an outrage. In the beginning of the year 1689, one of his lieutenants landed with twenty thoufand men at Bombay, an ifland of confequence on the coaft of Malabar, which a princefs of Portugal had brought as her dowry to Charles II. and which that monarch had ceded to the compan in 1668. On the enemy's approach, the fort of Magazan was abandoned with fuch precipitation, that money, provifions, feveral chefts of arms, and fourteen pieces of heavy cannon were left behind. The Indian general, encouraged by this firft advantage, attacked the Englifh in the field, routed them, and obliged them to retire into the principal fortrefs, which he invefted, where he hoped foon to make them furrender.

CHILD, who was as daftardly in time of danger as he had been daring in his piracies, immediately difpatched deputies to the emperor's court, to fue for pardon. After many intreaties, and much fubmiffion, the Englifh were admitted into the emperor's prefence with their hands tied, and their faces towards the ground. Aurengzebe, who was defirous of preferving a connection which he thought would be ufeful to his fubjects, was not inflexible. Having delivered himfelf in the ftile of an incenfed fovereign, who could, and ought, perhaps, to revenge

IN THE EAST AND WEST INDIES.

venge himself, he yielded to their intreaties and submission. The banishment of the author of the troubles, and an adequate compensation for such of his subjects as had been plundered, was all the justice exacted on this occasion by the supreme will of the most despotic monarch that ever existed. On these moderate terms, the English were permitted still to enjoy the privileges they had obtained at different times in the roads belonging to the Mogul.

Thus ended this unhappy affair, which for several years interrupted the trade of the company, brought on an expence of between nine and ten millions *, occasioned the loss of five large vessels, and a greater number of small ones; destroyed many thousand excellent sailors, and ended in the ruin of the credit and honour of the nation; two particulars, the value of which can never be estimated too highly.

By changing their maxims and their conduct, the company might have flattered themselves with the prospect of being extricated from the abyss into which their own behaviour had plunged them. These hopes were soon dashed by a revolution which did not directly concern them. James II. a tyrannical and fanatic prince, but one who understood maritime affairs and commerce better than any of his cotemporaries, was deposed. This event put all Europe in arms. The consequences of these bloody quarrels are well known. Perhaps, it is not a matter of such universal notoriety, that the French privateers took

* On an average about 416,000l.

four

four thousand two hundred Englifh merchantmen, valued at fix hundred feventy-five millions of livres *, and that the greateft part of the veffels returning from India were included in this fatal lift.

These depredations were fucceeded by a fpirit of œconomy, which muft naturally haften the ruin of the company. The French refugees had carried the culture of flax and hemp into Ireland and Scotland. For the encouragement of this branch of induftry, it was thought proper to prohibit the wear of Indian linens, except Muflins, and thofe which were neceffary for the African trade. How could a body already exhaufted fuftain fo unforefeen, fo heavy a ftroke?

The peace which fhould have put an end to thefe misfortunes, filled up the meafure of them. A general clamour was raifed in the three kingdoms againft the company. It was not their decline that raifed them enemies; it only encouraged thofe they had already. They met with oppofition at their firft eftablifhment. Ever fince the year 1615, feveral politicians had declaimed againft the trade to the Eaft Indies. They afferted, that it weakened the naval ftrength by deftroying great numbers of men; and leffened the Levant and Ruffian commerce, without affording an equivalent advantage. Thefe clamours, though contradicted by judicious people, grew fo violent towards the year 1628, that the company, feeing themfelves expofed to the odium of the nation, applied to government. They

* 29,531,250l.

petitioned

IN THE EAST AND WEST INDIES.

petitioned that the nature of their commerce might be examined: that it might be prohibited, if it were contrary to the interest of the state; and if favourable to them, that it might be authorised by a public declaration. The opposition of the nation, which had been some time dormant, was renewed with more fury than ever, at the period we are speaking of. Those who were less severe in their speculations, consented to a trade with India; but maintained that it should be laid open to the whole nation. An exclusive charter was, in their opinion, a manifest encroachment upon liberty. According to them, government was established by the people with a view of advancing the general good : and it would be a crime against it to sacrifice public to private interests, by tolerating odious monopolies. They supported this useful and incontestable principle, by appealing to a recent instance. They urged, that during the rebellion, the private merchants who had got possession of the Asiatic seas, carried double the quantity of national goods that were formerly brought, and were enabled to sell commodities on their return at so low a price as to supplant the Dutch in all European markets. But those acute republicans, who were certain of their ruin, if the English should continue any longer to conduct their affairs on the principles of universal liberty, bribed some persons to prevail with Cromwell to form a separate company. These secret practices were countenanced by the English merchants concerned in that trade, who hoped for greater advantages in future; when being the only

only venders, they might impofe what terms they pleafed upon the confumers. The protector, deceived by the artful infinuations of both, renewed the charter, but for feven years only, that he might alter his conduct, if he found reafon to think he had taken a wrong ftep.

THIS ftep did not appear improper to every one. Several people were of opinion, that the trade to India could not be carried on with advantage, without an exclufive privilege: but many of them maintained that the prefent charter was infufficient, becaufe it had been granted by kings who had no right to grant it. They recited many acts of this kind which were abrogated by parliament in the reigns of Edward III. Henry IV. James I. and other princes. Charles II. indeed, obtained a verdict of this nature in the court of common pleas, but it was founded upon a frivolous pretence. This tribunal had the confidence to declare, *That the prince had authority to prevent his fubjects from holding commerce with infidels, left the purity of their faith fhould be contaminated.*

THOUGH the parties above-mentioned were actuated by private, and even oppofite views, they all united in the plan of making the trade free, or at leaft of procuring the reverfal of the company's charter. The nation, in general, were on their fide: but the body that was attacked, defended itfelf by its partifans, the miniftry, and all the dependents of the court, who made this a common caufe. Each party had recourfe to libels, intrigue and corruption. Thefe contending paffions produced one of thofe ftorms, the violence of which can

IN THE EAST AND WEST INDIES.

can hardly be felt any where but in England. The several factions, sects and interests maintained a furious combat; in which they all mingled without distinction of rank, age, or sex. Such a spirit of enthusiasm had never been raised by the greatest events. To keep up the zeal of their friends, the company offered to lend large sums on condition of obtaining their charter. Their adversaries made offers still more considerable to get it revoked.

The two houses of parliament, before whom this cause was heard, declared in favour of the private merchants. They obtained leave to carry on trade to India, either separately or in concert. They entered into an association, and formed a new company. The old one had permission to continue its voyages till the expiration of their charter, which was very near at hand. Thus England had two East India companies at the same time authorised by parliament, instead of one established by royal authority.

These two bodies shewed as much zeal for the destruction of each other, as they had shewn for their respective establishment. They had both experienced the advantages of trade; and viewed each other with all the jealousy and hatred, which ambition and avarice never fail to inspire. Their dissentions soon broke out with considerable violence in Europe, as well as in India. At last, the two societies made advances towards a reconciliation, and united their funds in 1702. From this period the affairs of the company were carried on with greater propriety, prudence and dignity. The

principles

principles of commerce, which were every day better understood in England, had a good effect on their administration, as far as the interests of their monopoly could allow. They made improvements in their former regulations, and formed new ones. They endeavoured to indemnify themselves for the profits they were deprived of by a strong competition, by procuring a larger sale for their commodities. Their privileges were less violently attacked, since they had received the sanction of the laws, and obtained the protection of parliament.

Their prosperity was overcast by some transient misfortunes. In 1702 the English had formed a settlement in the island of Pulocondor, which was dependent on Cochin-China. Their design was to take a share in the commerce of this rich kingdom, which had till then been too much neglected. An instance of excessive severity had given disgust to sixteen soldiers of Macassar, who were part of the garrison. On the 3d of March 1705, they set fire in the night to the houses belonging to the fort, and massacred the Europeans as they came to extinguish it. Thirty out of forty-five lost their lives in this manner; the rest were massacred by the natives, who were exasperated at the insolence of these strangers. By this accident the company lost the money their enterprise had cost them, together with the stock of their factories and the prospects they had entertained.

The misfortunes they met with at Sumatra in the year 1719 were not attended with the same fatal consequences. This large island had been frequented

quented by the English ever since their arrival in India, but they did not settle there till the year 1688. They drove the Dutch from Bencoolen, a considerable town on the western coast, built near a large and commodious bay; and took possession of it in lieu of them. The conquerors found the islanders inclined to treat with them; and these dispositions were at first improved with prudence. This circumspect behaviour did not last long. The company's agents soon abandoned themselves to that spirit of rapine and tyranny, which the Europeans usually carry with them into Asia. Clouds of discontent between them and the natives of the country began to gather by degrees. Distrust and animosity had risen to the highest pitch, when at the distance of a few miles from the coast, the foundations of a fort were discovered. On seeing this, the inhabitants of Bencoolen took up arms, and were joined by the whole country. All the buildings belonging to the company were instantly reduced to ashes, the English were routed, and obliged to embark with all the effects they could carry off. Their exile was not of long continuance. The fear of their falling again under the dominion of the merciless Dutch, who had a strong force upon the frontier, occasioned them to be recalled. This misfortune procured them the advantage of finishing fort Marlborough without opposition, where they still remain.

These disturbances were no sooner appeased, than new ones arose in Malabar and other countries. As the source of them all was in the avarice

Vol. I. Z and

and turbulent difpofition of the company's fervants, they put an end to them by giving up the unjuftifiable pretenfions that had occafioned them. Other objects of the moft interefting nature foon claimed their attention.

<small>War between the Englifh and French.</small>

ENGLAND and France entered into a war in 1744. The whole world became the fcene of their operations. In India, as well as in other places, each nation fuftained its character. The Englifh, ever animated with the fpirit of commerce, attacked and ruined that of their enemies. The French, adhering to their paffion for conqueft, feized upon the principal fettlements belonging to their rival. The event fhewed which of the two nations had acted with the greateft prudence. That which attended only to its own aggrandizement, fank into a total inactivity; -while the other, though deprived of the center of its power, carried its enterprifes to a greater extent.

A CESSATION of hoftilties between the two divided nations had no fooner taken place, than they engaged themfelves as auxiliaries, in the quarrels of the Indian princes. Soon after they again took arms on their own account. Before the end of this war, the French were driven out of the continent and feas of Afia. At the conclufion of the peace in 1763, the Englifh company found themfelves in poffeffion of the power, in Arabia, in the Perfian Gulph, on the coafts of Malabar and Coromandel, and at Bengal.

IN all thefe countries there is a difference in climate, manners, foil, productions, the fpirit of induftry, and the price of merchandife. Thefe particulars

IN THE EAST AND WEST INDIES.
ticulars ought to be exactly and thoroughly understood. We will give a short sketch of them. This description will be found to have a particular connection with the history of a nation, which has obtained a remarkable influence in those countries, and derives from thence the greatest advantages.

ARABIA is one of the largest peninsulas in the known world. It is bounded by Syria, Diarbeck and Irac-Arabi on the north, by the Indian Ocean on the south, by the Gulph of Persia on the east, and on the west by the Red Sea, which separates it from Africa. It is commonly divided into three parts; Arabia Petræa, Arabia Deserta, and Arabia Felix, which names denote the nature of the soil in each of these countries.

ARABIA PETRÆA is the most western and the the smallest of the three. It is for the most part uncultivated, and almost totally covered with rocks. In Arabia Deserta nothing is to be seen but dry plains, heaps of sand raised and dissipated by the wind, and steep mountains never embellished with verdure. Springs are so rarely found there, that the possession of them is always disputed with the sword. Arabia Felix owes its specious appellation less to its fertility, than to its vicinity to the barren countries that surround it. These different regions, though exposed to great heats, enjoy a sky constantly pure and serene.

ALL histories agree that this country was peopled at a very early period. It is thought that its first inhabitants came from Syria and Chaldea. We cannot find at what period their form of government began; whether their knowledge was derived

General trade of the Red Sea, and of the English trade there in particular.

rived from India, or whether they acquired it themselves. It appears that their religion was Sabeism even before they were acquainted with the people of Upper Asia. They had conceived sublime ideas of the divinity at an early period: they worshipped the stars as bodies animated by celestial spirits: their religion was neither cruel nor absurd; and though they were liable to those sallies of enthusiasm so common among the southern nations, they do not seem to have been tainted with fanaticism till the time of Mohammed. The inhabitants of Arabia Deserta professed a worship not quite so rational. Many of them worshipped, and some offered human sacrifices to the sun. It is a truth that may be collected from the study of history and the inspection of the globe, that the religious systems in barren countries, subject to inundations and volcanos, have ever had a tincture of cruelty, and have always been of a milder cast in countries more favoured by nature. They take their character from the climate where they are formed.

When Mohammed had established a new religion in his country, it was no difficult task to infuse a spirit of zeal into his followers; and this zeal made them conquerors. They extended their dominion from the western seas to those of China, and from the Canaries to the Molucca islands. They also carried along with them the usual arts, which they improved. The Arabians did not equally succeed in the fine arts; they shewed, indeed, some genius for them, but had not the least idea of that taste with which nature some time after

ter infpired the people who have become their difciples.

PERHAPS genius, which is the offspring of a creative imagination, flourifhes in hot countries, which abound with a variety of productions, grand fcenes, and furprizing events that excite enthufiafm: while tafte, which felects and reaps the produce of the fields that genius has fown, feems rather to belong to people of a fedate, mild, and moderate difpofition, who live under the influence of a temperate fky. Perhaps too this fame tafte, which is the effect of reafon refined and matured by time, requires a certain ftability in the government, united with a certain freedom of thinking, a gradual improvement of knowledge, which affording a greater fcope to genius, enables it to difcern more exactly the relation one object has to another, and to combine with happier art thofe mixed fenfations which give the higheft entertainment to men of elegant minds. Accordingly the Arabians, who were almoft conftantly forced into regions difturbed with war and fanaticifm, never enjoyed that temperature of government and climate which gives birth to tafte. But they introduced into the countries they conquered fciences which they had pillaged, as it were, in the courfe of their ravages, and all the arts effential to the profperity of nations.

No nation at that time underftood commerce fo well, or carried it to a greater extent. They attended to it even in the courfe of their conquefts. Their merchants, manufactures, and ftaples, extended from Spain to Tonquin; and other people at least those in the western part of the world, were indebted to them for arts and sciences, and all articles conducive to the convenience, the preservation, and the pleasures of life.

WHEN the power of the Caliphs began to decline, the Arabians, after the example of several nations they had subdued, threw off the yoke of these princes, and the country re-assumed by degrees its ancient form of government, as well as its primitive manners. At this æra, the nation being, as formerly, divided into tribes, under the conduct of different chiefs, returned to their original character, from which fanaticism and ambition had made them depart.

THE stature of the Arabians is low, their bodies lean, and their voice slender; but they have robust constitutions, brown hair, a swarthy complexion, black sparkling eyes, an ingenuous countenance, but seldom agreeable. This contrasted mixture of features and qualities, which seem incompatible, appear to have been united in this race of men, to constitute a singular nation, whose figure and character partake strongly of that of the Turks, Africans, and Persians, by whom they are surrounded. Grave and serious, they consider their long beards as marks of dignity; they speak little, use no gesture, make no pauses, nor interrupt one another in their conversation. They pique themselves on observing the strictest probity towards each other, which is the effect of that self-love, and that spirit of patriotism, which, united together, make any nation, clan or society, esteem and prefer themselves to the rest of the world. The more care-

fully

IN THE EAST AND WEST INDIES.

fully they preferve their phlegmatic character, fo much the more formidable is their refentment when once it is raifed. Thefe people have abilities, and even a genius for the fciences; yet they cultivate them but little, either from want of affiftance, or becaufe they have no occafion for them; chufing rather, no doubt, to fuffer natural evils, than the inconvenience of labour. The Arabians, at this time of day, afford no monument of genius, no productions of induftry, which intitle them to hold any rank in the hiftory of the human mind.

THEIR ruling paffion is jealoufy; that torment of impetuous, weak, and indolent minds. It might naturally be afked, whether this diftruft was owing to the high or low opinion they entertained of themfelves? It is faid to be from the Arabians that feveral nations of Afia, Africa, and even Europe itfelf, have borrowed thofe defpicable precautions this odious paffion prefcribes againft a fex, which ought to be the guardian, not the flave of our pleafures. As foon as a daughter is born, they unite by a kind of future thofe parts which nature has feparated, leaving juft fpace enough for the natural difcharges. As the child grows, the parts by degrees adhere fo clofely, that when they become marriageable they are obliged to be feparated by an incifion. Sometimes it is thought fufficient to make ufe of a ring. The married women, as well as the unmarried, are fubjected to this outrage on the virtue of the fex; with this difference only, that the ring worn by the young women cannot be taken off, whereas that of the

married

married women has a kind of padlock, of which the hufband keeps the key. This cuftom, which is known in all parts of Arabia, is almoft univerfally adopted in that part that bears the name of Petræa.

Such are the manners of the nation in general. The different mode of living among the people who compofe it, muft neceffarily have introduced fome peculiarities of character that are worth obferving.

The number of Arabians who inhabit the defert may amount to two millions. They are diftributed into feveral clans, fome of which are more populous and confiderable than others, but all independent of each other. Their government is fimple : an hereditary chief, affifted by a few old men, determines all debates, and punifhes the offenders. If he is hofpitable, humane, and juft, they adore him; if haughty, cruel, and avaricious, they affaffinate him, and appoint a fucceffor out of his own family.

These people encamp at all feafons of the year. They have no fettled abode, and fix at different places where they can be fupplied with water, fruits, and pafture. They find an infinite charm in this wandering life, and confider the fedentary Arabs in the light of flaves. They live upon the milk and flefh of their herds. Their habits, tents, cordage, and the carpets they fleep upon, are all made of the wool of their fheep, and the hair of their goats and camels. This is the employment of the women in each family; and there is not a fingle single artist in the whole desert. What they consume in tobacco, coffee, rice, and dates, is purchased with the butter they carry to the frontiers, and by the money arising from the annual sale of twenty thousand camels, at least, at forty-eight livres * a head. These animals, so useful in the east, were formerly carried to Syria. Most of them are now sent to Persia, the perpetual wars there having occasioned an extraordinary demand for them, and diminished their species.

These articles not being sufficient to supply the Arabs with what they wanted, they have contrived to raise a contribution on the caravans, which superstition leads to travel through their sandy regions. The most numerous of these, which goes from Damar to Mecca, procures a safe passage by the payment of a hundred purses, or a hundred and fifty thousand livres †, to which the Grand Signior is subjected, and which, by ancient agreement, is distributed among all the hords. The other caravans make similar terms with the hords, through whose territories they are obliged to pass.

Independent of this expedient, the Arabs inhabiting the most northern part of the desert have had recourse to plunder. These people, so humane, faithful, and disinterested towards each other, are savage and rapacious in their transactions with foreigners. While they preserve in their tents the character of beneficent and generous hosts, they commit continual depredations in the towns and villages of their neighbourhood. They

* 2l. 2s.   † 6,562l. 10s.

are

are good fathers, good hufbands, and good mafters; but all are enemies who do not belong to their family. They frequently carry their incurfions to a great diftance; and Syria, Mefopotamia, and Perfia, are not uncommonly the fcenes of their depredations.

THE Arabs, who devote themfelves to plunder, form a fort of fociety with the camels, to carry on trade or war, where the man is to have all the profit, and the animal the principal fatigue. As thefe two beings are to live together, they are brought up with a view to each other. The Arab trains his camel from its birth, to all the exercifes and hardfhips it is to undergo during the whole courfe of its life. He accuftoms it to travel far, and eat little. The animal is early inured to pafs its days without drinking, and its nights without fleep. He teaches it to draw up its legs under its belly, while it fuffers itfelf to be laden with burthens, that are infenfibly increafed as its ftrength is improved by age and by the habit of bearing fatigue. In this fingular plan of education, which princes fometimes adopt the more eafily to tame their fubjects, in proportion as the labour of the animal is doubled, its fubfiftence is diminifhed. The Arabians qualify the camels for expedition, by matches, in which the horfe runs againft him. The camel, lefs active and nimble, tires out his rival in a long courfe. When the mafter and the camel are ready and equipped for plunder, they fet out together, traverfe the fandy deferts, and lie in ambufh upon the confines to rob the merchant or traveller. The man ravages, maffacres, and feizes the prey : and the camel

IN THE EAST AND WEST INDIES.

camel carries the booty. If thefe adventurers are purfued, they make a precipitate retreat. The mafter robber mounts his favourite camel, drives the whole troop before him, travels three hundred leagues in eight days without unloading his camels, or allowing them more than an hour each day for reft, or a cake of dough for their fubfiftence. They fometimes remain the whole time without drinking, unlefs they happen to fee a fpring at a little diftance from the road, when they redouble their pace, run to the water with eagernefs, which makes them take at one draught, as much as is fufficient to quench their prefent thirft, and ferve them to the end of their journey. Such is the animal fo often celebrated in the Bible, the Coran, and the eaftern romances.

THE Arabs, who live in diftricts that afford fome flender pafture, and where the foil is proper for barley, breed the fineft horfes in the world. Thefe horfes are fent into all parts to improve and multiply the breed of thefe animals, which are every where inferior in fwiftnefs, beauty, and fagacity, to thofe of Arabia. Their owners live with them as with domefticks, on whofe fervice and affection they can rely: and it happens with them as with all other wandering people, thofe, in particular, who treat animals with kindnefs, that both the men and the animals partake, in fome meafure, of each other's manners and difpofition. Thefe Arabs are fimple, mild and docile: and the different religions that have prevailed in thefe countries, and the feveral governments of which they

have

have been the subjects or tributaries, have produced very little alteration in the character they derive from climate or from habit.

The Arabs settled near the Indian and the Red Sea, and those who inhabit Arabia Felix, were formerly a mild people, fond of liberty, and content with a state of independence, without dreaming of conquest. They were too much prejudiced in favour of the beauty of their sky, and of the soil that supplied their wants almost without culture, to be tempted to extend their dominion over different countries lying in another climate. Mohammed changed their ideas: but they retain no traces of the impressions he communicated to them. They pass their time in smoaking, taking coffee, opium, and sherbet. These gratifications are preceded or followed by exquisite perfumes that are burnt before them, the smoke of which they receive in their clothes, which are slightly sprinkled with rose water.

Before the Portuguese had interrupted the navigation of the Red Sea, the Arabs had more activity. They were the factors of all the trade that passed through the channel. Aden, which is situated at the most southern extremity of Arabia upon the Indian ocean, was the mart in these parts. The situation of its harbour, which opened an easy communication with Egypt, Ethiopia, India, and Persia, had rendered it, for many ages, one of the most flourishing factories in Asia. Fifteen years after it had repulsed the great Albuquerque, who attempted to demolish it in 1513, it submitted to the Turks, who did not long remain masters of it.

The

IN THE EAST AND WEST INDIES.

The king of Yemen, who poffeffed the only diftrict in Arabia that merits the title of happy, drove them from thence, and removed the trade to Mocha, a place in his dominions, which till then was only a village.

THIS trade was at firft inconfiderable; confifting principally in myrrh, incenfe, aloes, balm of Mecca, fome aromatics and medicinal drugs. Thefe articles, the exportation of which is continually retarded by exorbitant impofts, and does not exceed at prefent 700,000 livres*, were at that time more in repute than they have been fince: but muft have been always of little confequence. Soon after a great change enfued from the introduction of coffee.

THE coffee-tree is originally a native of upper Ethiopia, where it has been known time immemorial, and is ftill cultivated with fuccefs. M. Lagrenée de Mezieres, one of the moft intelligent agents that France ever had in the India fervice, had fome of the fruit in his poffeffion, and has made trial of it. He found it to be larger, rather longer, not fo green, and almoft as fragrant as that which was firft gathered in Arabia towards the clofe of the fifteenth century.

IT is commonly believed, that a Mollach, named Chadely, was the firft among the Arabs who made ufe of Coffee, to relieve himfelf from a continual drowzinefs which hindered him from attending punctually to his nightly devotions. His dervifes did the fame: and their example was followed by the lawyers. It was foon found out,

* 30,625 l.

that

that this liquor purified the blood by a gentle agitation, diffipated the crudities of the ftomach, and raifed the fpirits: and it was adopted even by thofe who had no occafion to keep themfelves awake. It paffed from the borders of the Red Sea to Medina and Mecca, and was introduced by the pilgrims into all the Mohammedan countries.

In thefe countries where there is lefs freedom of manners than in ours, where the jealoufy of the men and the clofe confinement of the women make fociety lefs lively, it was thought proper to encourage public coffee-houfes. Thofe in Perfia foon became infamous, where young Georgian women, dreffed like courtezans, acted obfcene plays, and proftituted themfelves for hire. When thefe offenfive irregularities were fuppreffed by order of the court, thefe houfes became places of genteel refort for the indolent, and of relaxation for the bufy part of the world. The politicians entertained themfelves with news, the poets recited their verfes, and the Mollachs delivered their fermons, which were ufually rewarded with fome charitable donations.

Affairs were not in the fame peaceable ftate at Conftantinople. The coffee-houfes were no fooner opened than they were frequented to excefs. People fpent their whole time in them. The grand Mufti, concerned to fee the Mofques abandoned, pronounced that the infufion of this plant was included in that law of Mohammed, which forbids the ufe of ftrong liquors. Government, which frequently aids the fuperftition of which it is fometimes the dupe, gave immediate orders that the

houfes

houses which had given such offence to the priests should be shut up; and enjoined the officers of police to put a stop to the use of this liquor in private families. The strong inclination they had for it still prevailed over all these severe regulations. Coffee continued to be drunk, and the places where it was to be had, soon grew more numerous than ever.

IN the middle of the last century, Kuproli, the Grand Vizir, went in disguise to the principal coffee-houses in Constantinople. He there found a number of mal-contents, who, thinking the affairs of government were in reality the concern of every private person, spoke of them with warmth, and arraigned with great boldness the conduct of the generals and ministers. He then visited the taverns, where wine was sold. They were full of plain people, chiefly soldiers, who, accustomed to consider the interests of the state as those of the prince, for whom they entertained a silent veneration, sung lively songs, talked of their amours, and warlike exploits. These last societies, which are attended with no inconveniences, he thought ought to be tolerated: but the first he considered as dangerous in an arbitrary state. He therefore suppressed them, and no attempts have since been made to revive them. This regulation, which was confined to the capital of the empire, has not discouraged the use of coffee, and has, perhaps, increased the consumption of it. It is publicly offered to sale in all the streets and markets ready made, and is drunk in every family at least twice a-day. In some it is always ready, it being the

custom

custom to offer it to all visitors, and reckoned equally unpolite not to offer it, or to refuse it.

At the same time that coffee-houses in Constantinople were shut, they were opened in London. This novelty was introduced there in 1652 by a merchant of the name of Edward, who returned from the Levant. The English grew fond of it; and it has since been introduced among all the nations of Europe, but is drank with more moderation than in those climates where religion prohibits the use of wine.

The tree that produces the coffee grows in the territory of Betelfagui, a town belonging to Yemen, situated upon a dry sand at the distance of ten leagues from the Red Sea. It is cultivated in a district fifty leagues long, and fifteen or twenty broad: the fruit is not every where in equal perfection. That which grows upon high ground is smaller, greener, weighs heavier, and is generally preferred.

It is computed that Arabia contains twelve millions of inhabitants, among whom, in general, coffee constitutes a favourite article in their entertainments. None but the rich citizens have the pleasure of tasting the berry itself. The generality are obliged to content themselves with the shell and the husk of this valuable production. These remains, so much despised, make a liquor of a pretty clear colour, which has the taste of coffee without its bitterness and strength. These articles may be had at a low price at Betelfagui, which is the general market for them. Here likewise is sold all the coffee which comes out of the country

by

IN THE EAST AND WEST INDIES.

by land. The reſt is carried to Mocha, which is thirty-five leagues diſtant, or to the nearer ports of Lohia or Hodeida, from whence it is tranſported in ſmall veſſels to Jodda. The Egyptians fetch it from the laſt mentioned place, and all other nations from the former.

THE quantity of coffee exported may be eſtimated at twelve millions five hundred and fifty thouſand weight. The European companies take off a million and a half; the Perſians three millions and a half; the fleet from Suez ſix millions and a half; Indoſtan, the Maldives, and the Arabian colonies on the coaſt of Africa, fifty thouſand; and the Caravans a million.

As the coffee which is bought up by the Caravans and the Europeans, is the beſt that can be procured, it coſts from ſixteen to ſeventeen ſols * a pound. The Perſians, who content themſelves with that of an inferior quality, pay no more than twelve or thirteen ſols † a pound. The Egyptians purchaſe it at the rate of fifteen or ſixteen ‡; their cargoes being compoſed partly of good and partly of bad coffee. If we eſtimate coffee at fourteen ſols ‖ a pound, which is the mean price, the profits accruing to Arabia from its annual exportation will amount to 8,785,000 livres §. This money does not go into their coffers; but it enables them to purchaſe the commodities brought from the foreign markets to their ports of Jodda and Mocha.

MOCHA receives from Abyſſinia, ſheep, elephants teeth, muſk, and ſlaves. It is ſupplied

* About 8d. ½   † About 6d. ½   ‡ About 8d.
‖ About 7d. ¾   § 384,343 l. 15s.

VOL. I.   A a   from

from the eastern coast of Africa with gold, slaves, amber, and ivory; from the Persian Gulph with dates, tobacco, and corn; from Surat with a vast quantity of coarse, and a few fine linens; from Bombay and Pondicherry with iron, lead, copper, which are carried thither from Europe; from Malabar with rice, ginger, pepper, Indian saffron, with coire, cardamom, and also with planks; from the Maldives with gum benzoin, aloes-wood, and pepper, which these islands take in exchange; from Coromandel, with four or five hundred bales of cottons, chiefly blue. The greatest part of these commodities, which may fetch six millions [*], are consumed in the interior part of the country. The rest, particularly the cottons, are disposed of in Abyssinia, Socotora, and the eastern coast of Africa.

None of the branches of business which are managed at Mocha, as well as throughout all the country of Yemen, or even at Sanaa, the capital, are in the hands of the natives. The extortions with which they are perpetually threatened by the government, deter them from interfering in them. All the warehouses are occupied by the Banians of Surat or Guzarat, who make a point of returning to their own country as soon as they have made their fortunes. They then resign their settlements to merchants of their own nation, who retire in their turn, and are succeeded by others.

The European companies, who enjoy the exclusive privilege of trading beyond the Cape of Good Hope, formerly maintained agents at Mocha. Notwithstanding it was stipulated by a solemn capitulation,

[*] 262,500l.

pitulation, that the imposts demanded should be rated at two and a quarter per cent. They were subject to frequent extortions: the governor of the place infisting on their making him presents, which enabled him to purchase the favour of the courtiers, or even of the prince himself. However, the profits they obtained by the sale of European goods, particularly cloths, made them to submit to these repeated humiliations. When these several articles were furnished by Grand Cairo, it was then impossible to withstand the competition, and the fixed settlements were therefore given up.

THE trade was carried on by ships, that sailed from Europe with iron, lead, copper, and silver, sufficient to pay for the coffee they intended to buy. The supercargoes, who had the care of these transactions, settled the accounts every time they returned. These voyages, which at first were pretty numerous and advantageous, have been successively laid aside. The plantations of coffee, made by the European nations in their colonies, have equally lessened the consumption and the price of that which comes from Arabia. In procefs of time, these voyages did not yield a sufficient profit to answer the high charges of undertaking them on purpose. The companies of England and France then resolved, one of them to send ships from Bombay, and the other from Pondicherry to Mocha, with the merchandise of Europe and India. They even frequently had recourse to a method that was less expensive. The English and French who traffic

from

from India to India, vifit the Red Sea every year. Though they difpofe of their merchandife there to good advantage, they can never take in cargoes from thence for their return. They carry, for a moderate freight, the coffee belonging to the companies who lade the veffels with it, which they difpatch from Malabar and Coromandel to Europe. The Dutch company, who prohibit their fervants from fitting out fhips, and who fend no veffels themfelves to the Gulph of Arabia, are deprived of the fhare they might take in this branch of commerce. They have alfo given up a much more lucrative branch, that of Jodda.

JODDA is a port fituated near the middle of the Gulph of Arabia, twenty leagues from Mecca. The government there is of a mixed kind: the Grand Signior and the Xeriff of Mecca fhare the authority and the revenue of the cuftoms between them. Thefe impofts are levied upon the Europeans at the rate of eight per cent. and upon other nations at thirteen. They are always paid in merchandife, which the managers oblige the merchants of the country to buy at a very dear rate. The Turks, who have been driven from Aden, Mocha, and every part of the Yemen, would long ago have been expelled from Jodda, if there had not been room to apprehend that they might revenge themfelves in fuch a manner as to put an end to their pilgrimages and commerce.

SURAT fends three fhips every year to Jodda, which are laden with linens of all colours, fhawls, cotton and filk ftuffs, frequently ornamented with gold

IN THE EAST AND WEST INDIES.

gold and silver flowers. The sale of these goods produces 10,000,000 of livres*. Two, and more frequently three vessels belonging to the English, sail from Bengal for the same destination. They are fitted out by the free merchants of that nation. Formerly their company had concerns there; at present these merchants have no associates but the Armenians. These united cargoes may be estimated at 7,200,000 livres †. They consist of rice, ginger, saffron, sugar, a few silks, and a considerable quantity of linens which are for the most part ordinary. These vessels, which may enter the Red Sea from the beginning of December till the end of may, find the fleet of Suez at Jodda.

THIS fleet commonly consists of fourteen or fifteen vessels laden with corn, rice and pulse, for the use of Arabia They carry out for Asia, Venetian glass, coral, and yellow-amber, of which the Indians make necklaces and bracelets. They arrive in October, and return together in February, with 6,500,000 weight of coffee, and with linens or stuffs to the value of 7,000,000 of livres‡. Though they have only two hundred leagues to return to their port, they employ two months in the voyage; being retarded by the north wind, which blows continually in this sea. Their ignorance is such, that though they are accustomed to cast anchor every night, they think themselves fortunate when they lose only one ship in six. If to these losses we add the

* 437,500l.   † 315,000l.   ‡ 306,250l.

great

great expence of equipment, the exceffive impofts demanded at Suez, and the unavoidable extortions of a government that oppreffes all induftry, we fhall be convinced that, in the prefent fituation of things, the correfpondence between Europe and India by this channel is impracticable.

The merchandife brought from Surat and Bengal, which the Egyptian fleet does not take off, is partly confumed in the country, and bought in great quantities by the caravans, which come every year to Mecca.

The Arabs had ever entertained an affection for this city. They fuppofed it to have been the refidence of Abraham, and they flocked from all parts to a temple, of which they believed he was the founder. Mohammed, who was a man of too much underftanding to attempt to abolifh a devotion fo generally eftablifhed, contented himfelf with rectifying the object of it. He banifhed the idols from this revered place, and dedicated it to the unity of God. Mohammed was not the meffenger of heaven; but he was an acute politician, and a great conqueror. To promote the concourfe of ftrangers to a city which he intended to make the capital of his empire, he commanded that all who embraced his law fhould once in their lives undertake a pilgrimage thither, on pain of dying reprobates. This precept was accompanied with another, which makes it evident, that he was not guided by fuperftition alone. He ordered that every pilgrim, of whatever country he was, fhould purchafe five pieces of of cotton, and get them confecrated, and made into handkerchiefs for himfelf, and all the perfons belonging to his family who were prevented by reafonable impediments from undertaking this holy expedition.

THIS policy might naturally be expected to make Arabia the center of a prodigious trade, when the number of pilgrims fhould amount to feveral millions. This zeal is fo much abated, efpecially on the coaft of Africa, in Indoftan and Perfia, in proportion to the refpective diftances of thofe places from Mecca, that the number is reduced to a hundred and fifty thoufand; the majority of whom are Turks. They carry away with them feven hundred and fifty thoufand pieces of linens; each ten ells in length, exclufive of thofe which many of them buy for fale. They are encouraged in thefe mercantile fchemes by the advantages they have in croffing the deferts, and in not being expofed to thofe oppreffive tolls which are fo deftructive in the fea-ports of Suez and Baffora. The money received from thefe pilgrims and from the fleet, and by the Arabs from the fale of coffee, is expended in India. The veffels from Surat, Malabar, Coromandel, and Bengal, annually carry away 14,400,000 livres *, and about the eighth part of this fum in merchandife. When thefe riches are divided among the trading nations of Europe, the Englifh have contrived to appropriate to themfelves the moft confiderable fhare of them.

* 630,000l.

BOOK III.

They have acquired the same superiority in Persia.

General view of the trade in the Persian Gulph, and that of the English in particular.

THE English nation had scarce been admitted into the empire of the Sophis, when, as we have observed, the Dutch resorted there in great numbers. The trade of these republicans was at first established on a very disadvantageous footing; but being, by the civil wars of England, soon delivered from a rival whose various privileges were not to be overbalanced even by the greatest œconomy, they were in a short time without competitors, and consequently acquired an authority to set what price they thought proper on the commodities they bought or sold. The connections of the Persians with the Dutch were formed on this destructive system; when the return of the English, who were soon after followed by the French, gave a new turn to affairs, and put them upon a more equitable footing.

AT the time when the three nations exerted their utmost efforts to gain the superiority, and these efforts turned to the advantage of the empire, they were harassed with a thousand oppressions, some more unjust and odious than others. The throne was continually filled with tyrannical or weak princes, whose cruelty and injustice weakened the correspondence of their subjects with other nations. One of these tyrants was so savage, that a great man of his court used to say, *That whenever he came out of the king's closet, he clapped both his hands to his head to feel whether it was still upon his shoulders.* When the successor of this tyrant was told

told that the finest provinces in the empire were invaded by the Turks, he answered coolly, *That their progress gave him very little disturbance, provided they would leave him the city of Ispahan.* The son of the latter was so meanly enslaved to the most frivolous observances of his religion, that he was stiled by way of derision, *Huffein the monk, or priest*: a character less odious, perhaps, in a prince, but much more dangerous to his people, than that of impiety, or defiance of the gods. Under these despicable sovereigns, mercantile affairs declined every day more and more at Gombroon. The Afghans destroyed them entirely.

THESE are people of Candahar, a mountainous country, lying north of India. They have sometimes been subject to the Moguls, sometimes to the Persians, but more frequently independent. Those that do not reside in the capital live in tents, after the manner of the Tartars. They are of low stature and ill made; but are strong, robust, skilled in the use of the bow, and in horsemanship, and inured to fatigue. Their manner of fighting is singular; a chosen band of soldiers, divided into two parties, fall upon the enemy without any order, only endeavouring to open the way for the army that follows them. As soon as the battle is begun, they fall back upon the flanks and towards the rear-guard, where their business is to prevent any person from giving way. If any soldier attempts to fly, they attack him with their sabres, and compel him to return to his post.

ABOUT

About the beginning of this century, this fierce people left their mountains, invaded Perfia, carried devaftation every where, and at length fubdued it, after a bloody conteft of twenty years. Fanaticifm ftill perpetuates the memory of the horrid outrages which they committed in the courfe of their conqueft. An infatiable zeal for the Turkifh fuperftition, and an unconquerable averfion for the fect of Ali, prompted them to maffacre thoufands of Perfians in cold blood. In the mean time, the provinces they had not entered, were ravaged by the Ruffians, Turks, and Tartars. Thomas Kouli-Khan drove thefe robbers out of this country, but fhewed himfelf ftill more barbarous than they were. His violent death gave rife to new calamities. Anarchy aggravates the cruelties of tyranny. One of the fineft empires in the world is become an extenfive fcene of defolation, and a lafting and fhameful monument of that deftructive inftinct that animates uncivilized people, and is at the fame time an inevitable confequence of the evils of defpotic government.

During this general confufion, the Englifh fales in Perfia confifted of no more than a hundred bales of woollen manufactures, two hundred thoufand weight of iron, and the fame quantity of lead. Thefe articles, taken together, brought them no more than from twelve to thirteen hundred thoufand livres * paid in money. This languid ftate of trade determined the company to

---

* 554,687ᴸ 10s.

follow

IN THE EAST AND WEST INDIES.

follow the example of their rivals, and to seek those advantages at Baffora, which they could not obtain at Gombroon.

BASSORA is a large city, built by the Arabs in the height of their profperity, fifteen leagues below the place where the Tigris and Euphrates meet, and at the fame diftance from the Perfian Gulph, into which thefe rivers empty themfelves. Its inhabitants are computed at fifty thoufand; confifting of Arabs, fifteen hundred Armenians, and a fmall number of families of different nations whom the hope of gain has attracted. Its territory abounds in rice, fruits, pulfe, cotton, and particularly in dates.

THE port of Baffora, as thofe who firft eftablifhed it forefaw, became a famous mart. The merchandife of Europe was brought thither, by the Euphrates, and that of India by fea. The tyranny of the Portuguefe intercepted this communication. It would have been opened again when their power declined, had not this unhappy country continually been the fcene of the difputes between the Arabs, the Perfians, and the Turks. This laft power being in quiet poffeffion of this harbour, have availed themfelves of the troubles of their neighbours to renew the trade. The mercantile bufinefs, which was before tranfacted at Gombroon, is at prefent centered at Baffora, which has recovered its credit and importance.

THIS change has not been effected without difficulty. At firft the people of the country would not permit the traders to come out of the river.

river. They forefaw, that if thefe foreigners were permitted to fettle in the city, they would not be fo much under their direction, and might lay up in their magazines fuch of their commodities as they could not fell during one moonfoon, with a view of difpofing of them with greater advantage at another time. To this maxim, which was the refult of an ill-judged avarice, were added others arifing from fuperftitious notions. It was deemed a violation of the refpect due to religion to permit infidels to inhabit a city, confecrated by the blood of fo many martyrs and faints of the Mohammedan perfuafion; a prejudice that feemed to have fome weight with the government; but thefe fcruples were foon overcome. Pecuniary confiderations were offered by the nations, and they were allowed to eftablifh factories, and even to difplay their refpective flags there.

REVOLUTIONS are fo frequent in Afia, that trade cannot poffibly be carried on in the fame continued track as it is in Europe. Thefe events, joined to the little communication between the different ftates, either by land or by fea, muft naturally occafion great variations in the quantity and value of commodities. Baffora, on account of its great diftance from the center of trade, is more expofed to this inconvenience than any other place. However, upon an average, we need not be under any apprehenfion of departing much from the ftricteft truth, when we venture to eftimate the merchandife annually brought there by way of the Gulph, at twelve millions.

IN THE EAST AND WEST INDIES.

millions*. Of this the English furnish four millions †, the Dutch two ‡, the Moors, Banians, Armenians and Arabs, furnish the remainder.

THE cargoes of these nations consist of rice, sugar, plain, striped and flowered muslins from Bengal, spices from Ceylon and the Molucca islands; coarse, white, and blue cottons from Coromandel; cardamum, pepper, sanders-wood, from Malabar; gold and silver stuffs, turbans, shawls, indigo, from Surat; pearls from Baharen, and coffee from Mocha; iron, lead, and woollen-cloth from Europe. Other articles of less consequence are imported from different places. Some of these commodities are shipped on board small Arabian vessels, but the greater part is brought by European ships, which have the advantage of a considerable freight.

THIS merchandise is sold for ready money; and passes through the hands of the Greeks, Jews, and Armenians. The Banians are employed in changing the coin current at Bassora, for that which is of higher value in India.

THE different commodities collected at Bassora are distributed into three channels. One half of them goes to Persia, whither they are conveyed by the caravans; there being no navigable river in the whole empire. The chief consumption is in the northren provinces, which have not been so much ravaged as those in the south. Both of them formerly made their payments in precious stones, which were become common by the plunder of India. They had afterwards recourse to copper

* 525,000l. † 175,000l. ‡ 87,500l.

utensils,

utensils, which had been exceedingly multiplied from the great abundance of copper mines. At last they gave gold and silver in exchange, which had been concealed during a long scene of tyranny, and are continually dug out of the bowels of the earth. If they do not allow time for the trees that produce gum, and have been cut to make fresh shoots; if they neglect to multiply the breed of the goats which afford such fine wool; and if the silks, which are hardly sufficient to supply the few manufactures remaining in Persia, continue to be so scarce; in a word, if this empire does not rise again from its ashes, the mines will be exhausted, and this source of commerce must be given up.

THE second channel is a more sure one, by the way of Bagdad, Aleppo, and other intermediate towns, whose merchants come to buy their goods at Bassora. Coffee, linen, spices, and other merchandise that pass this way, are taken in exchange for gold, French woollen-cloths, galls, and orpiment, which is an ingredient in colours, and much used by the eastern people to extirpate their hair.

ANOTHER much less considerable channel is that of Arabia Deserta. The Arabs, bordering upon Bossora, repair annually to Aleppo in the spring, to sell their camels. It is usual to give them credit for muslins, which they buy very cheap to the amount of six hundred thousand livres [*]. They return in the autumn, bringing woollen-cloths, coral, hard-ware, and some glass and mirrors from Venice. The Arabian caravans are never molested in their journey; nor are foreigners in any danger, if they take care to carry

[*] 26,250l.

along with them a perfon belonging to each of the tribes they may happen to meet with. This road through the defert would be univerfally preferred to that of Bagdad, on account of fafety, expedition, and the advantages of fale, if the Pacha of the province, who has eftablifhed tolls in different parts of his territory, did not ufe every poffible precaution to hinder this communication. It is only by eluding the vigilance of his deputies, that one can prevail upon the Arabs to carry with them fome goods, which will not take up much room.

BESIDES thefe exportations, there is a pretty large confumption, efpecially of coffee, at Baffora, and the territories belonging to it. Thefe articles are paid for in dates, pearls, rofe-water, dried fruits, and grain, when that is allowed to be difpofed of to foreigners.

THIS trade would be more extenfive, if it were freed from the fhackles that confine it. But the activity that might be expected from the natives of the country is continually damped by the oppreffions they labour under, efpecially at a diftance from the centre of the empire. The foreigners are no lefs oppreffed by governors, who derive from their extortions the advantage of maintaining themfelves in their office, and frequently of fecuring their lives. Were it poffible in fome meafure to affuage this thirft of gold, it would foon be renewed by the rivalfhip of the European nations, whofe fole aim is to fupplant one another, and who, to gain their ends, fcruple not to employ the moft execrable expedients. A ftriking inftance of this odious fpirit of jealoufy happened in 1748.

BARON

Baron Knyphausen managed the Dutch factory at Baſſora with extraordinary ſucceſs. The English found themſelves in eminent danger of loſing the ſuperiority they had acquired at this place, as well as in moſt of the ſea-ports in India. The dread of an event which muſt wound at the ſame time their intereſts and their vanity betrayed them into injuſtice. They excited the Turkiſh government to ſuppreſs a branch of trade that was uſeful to it, and procured an order for the confiſcation of the merchandiſe and poſſeſſions of their rivals.

The Dutch factor, who under the character of a merchant concealed the ſtateſman, inſtantly took a reſolution worthy of a man of genius. He retired with his dependents and the broken remains of his fortune to Karek, a ſmall iſland at the diſtance of fifteen leagues from the mouth of the river: where he fortified himſelf in ſuch a manner, that by intercepting the Arabian and Indian veſſels, bound for the city, he compelled the government to grant him an indemnification for the loſſes he had ſuſtained by its behaviour. The fame of his integrity and abilities drew to his iſland the privateers of the neighbouring ports, the very merchants of Baſſora and the Europeans who traded thither. The proſperity of this new colony was daily increaſing, when it was forſaken by its founder. The ſucceſſor of this able man did not diſplay the fame talents. Towards the end of the year 1765 he ſuffered himſelf to be diſpoſſeſſed of his iſland by the Arabian Corſair Mirmahana. The Company loſt an important poſt, and more

than

than two millions *, in artillery, provifions and merchandife.

By this event Baffora was freed from a rivalfhip that was prejudicial to its interefts; but an unforefeen and much more formidable one has fucceeded in its room, which is that of Mufkat.

Muskat is a city in Arabia, fituated on the weftern fide of the Perfian Gulph. The great Albuquerque made himfelf mafter of it in 1507, and ruined its trade, which he wanted to transfer wholly to Ormus. When the Portuguefe had loft this fmall kingdom, they were defirous of reviving the trade at Mufkat, of which they ftill kept poffeffion. Their endeavours proved ineffectual; and the merchants bent their courfe to Gombroon. They dreaded the infolence of the old tyrants of India; and were unwilling to rely upon their fidelity. No veffels entered the harbour except thofe brought in by the Portuguefe themfelves. It ceafed to be frequented by the fhips of every nation, after thefe imperious mafters were driven from it in 1648. Their pride prevailing over their views of intereft, made them no longer defirous of going thither: and they had ftill a fufficient degree of influence to prevent any fhips from entering the harbour, or going out of it.

The decline of their power tempted the inhabitants of Mufkat to the fame acts of piracy, to which they themfelves had fo long been expofed. They made defcents upon the coafts of their ancient oppreffors; and the fuccefs they met with encou-

* 87,500l.

encouraged them to attack the small Moorish and European vessels that frequented the Persian Gulph. But they were so severely chastised for their plunders by several nations, and especially by the English, that they were obliged to desist. From that period the city sank into a state of obscurity, which was prolonged for a considerable time by intestine broils, and foreign invasions. At length the government assuming a more regular form at Muskat, and in the whole country under the jurisdiction of its Iman, its commerce began to revive about the year 1749.

The articles of consumption in the country itself are rice, blue linens, iron, lead, sugar, and some spices; the returns for which are made in myrrh, incense, gum-arabic, and a small quantity of silver. This trade, however, would not be considerable enough to invite ships hither, if Muskat, which is situated pretty near the entrance of the Persian Sea, were not an excellent mart for the innermost part of the Gulph. All trading nations begin to give it the preference to Bassora; because it makes their voyage shorter by three months; they are free from any kind of extortion; and imposts are lowered to one and a half per cent. The merchandise, indeed, is afterwards to be carried to Bassora, where it pays a tax of three per cent. but the Arabs sail with so little expence, and have so many methods of eluding the tolls, that they will always find their account in disposing of their goods at Muskat. Besides this, the dates, which are produced at Bassora in greater plenty and perfection than any other article, and
are

IN THE EAST AND WEST INDIES. 371

are often spoilt on board large vessels that sail slowly, are conveyed with the utmost expedition in light barks to Malabar, and the Red Sea. There is a particular reason which will always determine the English, who trade for themselves, to frequent Muskat. They are there exempted from the five per cent. which they are obliged to pay at Bassora, as well as at all other places where their company have made settlements.

The company have never attempted to establish themselves on the island of Baharen; which we are at a loss to account for. This island, which lies in the Persian gulph, has often changed its masters. It fell with Ormus, under the dominion of the Portuguese, and was governed by the same laws. These conquerors were afterwards deprived of it, and it has since undergone a variety of revolutions. Thamas Kouli Khan restored it to Persia, to which it had belonged. This haughty usurper at that time conceived the plan of forming a most extensive empire. He wanted to make himself master of two seas, some coasts of which he already possessed: but finding that his subjects opposed his design instead of favouring it, he had recourse to one of those arbitrary acts which tyrants make no scruple of exercising, and transported his subjects in the Persian Gulph to the Caspian Sea, and those in the Caspian Sea to the Persian Gulph. He looked upon this double transmigration as the necessary means of breaking the connections which both these people had formed with his enemies, and of securing their fidelity, if he could not engage their attachment. His death put a period to his vaſt deſigns : and the confuſion into which his empire was thrown, afforded a fair opportunity to an ambitious and enterprizing Arab of taking poſſeſſion of Baharen, where he ſtill maintains his authority.

This iſland, famous for its pearl fiſhery even at the time when pearls were found at Ormus, Karek, Keſhy, and other places in the Gulph, is now become of much greater conſequence; the other banks having been exhauſted, while this has ſuffered no ſenſible diminution. The time of fiſhing begins in April, and ends in October. It is confined to a tract of four or five leagues. The Arabs, who alone follow this employment, paſs their nights upon the iſland or the coaſt, unleſs they are prevented by the wind from going on ſhore. They formerly paid a toll, which was received by the galliots on that ſtation. Since the laſt alteration, none but the inhabitants of this iſland pay this acknowledgment to their Scheik, who is not in a condition to demand them from others.

The pearls taken at Baharen, though not ſo white as thoſe of Ceylon and Japan, are much larger than thoſe of the former place, and of a more regular ſhape than thoſe of the latter. They are of a yellowiſh caſt; but have this recommendation, that they preſerve their golden hue; whereas the whiter kind loſe much of their luſtre by keeping, particularly in hot countries. The ſhell of both theſe ſpecies, which is known by the name of mother of pearl, is uſed in Aſia for various purpoſes.

IN THE EAST AND WEST INDIES.

THE annual revenue arifing from the fifhery in the latitude of Baharen, is computed at 3,600,000 livres*. The greateſt part of the pearls that are uneven, are carried to Conſtantinople, and other ports of Turky; where the larger compoſe part of the ornaments of the head-drefs, and the ſmaller are uſed in works of embroidery. The perfect pearls muſt be reſerved for Surat, from whence they are diſtributed throughout all Indoſtan. The women have ſo ſtrong a paſſion for luxury, and the ſale of this article is ſo much increaſed by ſu-perſtition, that there is not the leaſt reaſon to ap-prehend any diminution either in the price or the demand. There are none of the Gentiles who do not make it a point of religion to bore at leaſt one pearl at the time of their marriage. What-ever may be the myſterious meaning of this cuſtom among a people whoſe morality and politics are couched in allegories, or where allegory becomes religion; this emblem of virgin modeſty has proved advantageous to the pearl trade. The pearls that have not newly been bored make a part of drefs; but cannot have a place in the marriage ceremony, where one new pearl is at leaſt indifpenſable. They are accordingly always ſold five and twenty or thirty per cent. cheaper than thoſe which come from the Gulph, where they are taken. There are no pearls at Malabar; but it has riches of another kind.

MALABAR is, properly ſpeaking, a country ſituated between Cape Comorin and the river of Neticeram. But to make our narrative the bet-

* 157,500l.

General ſtate of the trade on the coaſt of Ma-labar; and that of the Engliſh in particular.

ter underſtood, by accommodating it to the notions generally received in Europe, we ſhall give this name to the whole track extending from the Induſt to Cape Comorin, including the adjacent iſlands, and beginning with the Maldives.

THE Maldives form a long chain of iſlands to the weſt of Cape Comorin, which is the neareſt part of the Terra Firma. They are divided into thirteen provinces, which are called atollons. This diviſion is the work of nature, that has ſurrounded each atollon with a barrier of rocks, furniſhing a better defence than the ſtrongeſt fortification againſt the impetuoſity of the waves, or the attacks of an enemy. The natives reckon the number of theſe iſlands at twelve thouſand; the ſmalleſt of which are nothing more than banks of ſand that are overflowed at high tides, and the largeſt very ſmall in circumference. Of all the channels that ſeparate them, there are only four capable of receiving ſhips. The reſt are ſo ſhallow, that they have ſeldom more than three feet water. It is conjectured, with probability, that all theſe different iſlands were formerly one, and that the force of the waves and currents, or ſome great natural event, has divided them into ſeveral portions.

IT is probable, that this Archipelago was originally peopled from Malabar. Afterwards the Arabians went there, uſurped the ſovereignty, and eſtabliſhed their own religion. At length the two nations were united into one; when the Portugueſe, ſoon after their arrival in India, reduced them to ſubjection. This tyranny was

IN THE EAST AND WEST INDIES.

of short continuance. The garrison which held them in slavery was exterminated, and the Maldives recovered their independence. Since this period they have fallen under the yoke of an arbitrary prince, who keeps his court at Male, and has resigned the whole authority to the priests. He is the sole merchant in his dominions.

An administration of this stamp, and the barrenness of the country, which produces nothing but cocoa-trees, prevents the trade from being considerable. The exports consist only of cowries, fish, and kayar.

Kayar is the bark of the cocoa-tree, of which cables are made, that serve for the Indian navigation. This is no where so good, and in such plenty as in the Maldives. A great quantity of it is carried, with some cowries, to Ceylon, where these commodities are exchanged for the areca nut.

The fish called in the country conplemasse, is dried in the sun. It is salted by dipping it several times in the sea, and cut into pieces of the thickness and length of a man's finger. Cargoes of it are annually brought to Achen, which are purchased with gold and benzoin. The gold remains in the Maldives; and the benzoin is sent to Mocha, where it procures in return about three hundred bales of coffee for the consumption of these islands.

Cowries are white and shining shells. The inhabitants fish for them twice a month; three days before the new moon, and three days after. This empolyment belongs to the women, who wade to the middle in water to gather them upon the fands. They are put up in parcels, each containing twelve thoufand. Thofe that are not circulated in the country, or carried to Ceylon are fent to the banks of the Ganges. A great number of veffels annually fail from this river, laden with fugar, rice, linen, and other lefs confiderable articles for the ufe of the Maldives, and return with a cargo of cowries valued at about 700,000 livres*. One part is circulated in Bengal, where it ferves as fmall coin. The reft is taken off by the Europeans, who ufe it with advantage in their trade with Africa. They buy it at fix fols† a pound, and fell it from twelve to eighteen‡ in their feveral capitals: it is worth thirty-five livres ‖ in Guinea.

THE kingdom of Travancor, which extends from Cape Comorin to the frontiers of Cochin, was not formerly in poffeffion of a greater fhare of opulence than the Maldives. It is probable that it owed the prefervation of its independency to its poverty, when the Moguls made themfelves mafters of Madura. The father of the prefent monarch added more dignity to his crown than any of his predeceffors. He was a man of great abilities. A neighbouring ftate had fent him two ambaffadors, one of whom began a long harangue, which the other was preparing to continue. *Be not tedious*, faid the prince, with an auftere brow, *life is fhort*. This prince formed a fmall body of troops of the French and Portuguefe deferters, which,

* 30,625 l.   † About 3 d.   ‡ Near 8 d. on an average.
‖ 1 l. 10 s. 7 d. ¼

in time of peace, performed the military duties in the citadel of Kotate, with as much regularity as our garrisons, and were of signal service in enlarging his dominions in time of war. The interior parts of his country were benefited by his conquests, a circumstance that rarely happens. He established in them some manufactories of coarse cottons, which were at first disposed of among the Dutch at Tutocorin, and were afterwards carried to the English factory at Anjengo.

THERE are two European settlements in the kingdom of Travancor: that of the Danes at Kolechey is nothing more than a small storehouse, where they might neverthelefs be regularly supplied with two hundred thousand weight of pepper. Such is their indolence, or their poverty, that they have made but one purchase, and that only of a very small quantity, these ten years.

THE English factory at Anjengo has four small bastions without ditches, and a garrison of a hundred and fifty black and white men. It is situated on a sandy point of land at the mouth of a small river, which, is three-fourths of the year choaked up with sand. Its village is well peopled, and full of manufactures. This settlement is, in general, more lucrative to the agents of the company, who buy pepper, large cinnamon, and very good kayar on their own account, than to the company themselves, who trade only for fifty thousand weight of pepper, and some linens of small value.

COCHIN was a place of great note when the Portuguese arrived in India. They made themselves

selves masters of it, and were afterwards dispossessed by the Dutch. The sovereign, at the time this place was taken from him, had preserved his dominions, which, in the space of twenty-five years, have been repeatedly invaded by the people of Travancor. His misfortunes have obliged him to retire under the walls of his ancient capital, where he lives upon a revenue of 14,400 livres*, which was stipulated to be paid him by ancient capitulations, out of the produce of his customs. In the same suburb is a colony of industrious Jews, who are white men, and ridiculously pretend to have been settled here since the time of the Babylonish captivity, but have certainly been in this situation a very considerable time. A town encompassed with fertile lands, and built upon a river that receives vessels of five hundred tons burthen, and communicates by several navigable branches to the interior parts of the country, may naturally be expected to be in a flourishing condition. If it is otherwise, the blame must lie on the oppressive nature of the government.

This oppressive spririt is at least as sensibly felt at Calicut: all nations are admitted thither, but none have any sway. The sovereign who resides there at present is a Bramin. This is almost the only throne in India that is filled by a person of this first class. In other places the crown is worn by the inferior classes; and even by persons of such obscure origin, that their domestics would

* 630l.

be diſhonoured and baniſhed from their tribes, if they condeſcended even to eat with their monarchs. Theſe people take care not to boaſt of ſupping with the king: this prejudice is not, perhaps, more ridiculous than any other. It humbles the pride of princes, and deprives courtiers of one ſource of vanity. Such is the influence of ſuperſtition, that it gives riſe to the univerſal prevalence of opinion. By ſuperſtition artifice divides the empire with power: when the latter has conquered and enſlaved the world, the former interpoſes and preſcribes laws in its turn: they enter into a league with each other, mankind fall proſtrate, and ſubmit to their chains. Accordingly the Bramins, who are the depoſitaries of religion and the ſciences throughout Indoſtan, are every where employed by the Rajahs as miniſters or ſecretaries of ſtate, and make what arrangements they think proper; but affairs are not the better managed on that account.

The adminiſtration of Calicut is bad in general, and that of the capital ſtill worſe. No police is eſtabliſhed, no fortifications are raiſed. The trade, which is clogged with a multiplicity of impoſts, is almoſt entirely in the hands of a few of the moſt abandoned and faithleſs Moors in Aſia. One of its greateſt advantages is, that by the river Baypore, which is only at two leagues diſtance, it has the means of being furniſhed with teak timber, which grows upon the plains and mountains in great abundance.

The territories that border upon Calicut, and belong to the houſe of Colaſtry, are little known,

except

except by the French colony at Mahé, which is gathering fresh strength, and that of the English at Tellecherrry, which has experienced no misfortune. The latter has a fort flanked with four baftions without ditches, a garrifon of three hundred Europeans, five hundred fipahis, and to the amount of about fifteen thoufand inhabitants. The company to which it belongs receives from it annually fifteen hundred thoufand pounds weight of pepper.

IF we except a few principalities that fcarce deferve mention, the ftates we have been defcribing properly conftitute the whole of the Malabar coaft, a country more agreeable than opulent. The exports are few, befides aromatics and fpices. The principal articles are fanders wood, India faffron, cardamum, ginger, baftard cinnamon, and pepper.

THE fantalum or fanders grows to the fize of a walnut-tree; the fruit, which in fome degree refembles a cherry, is of no value. The wood, which is better in Malabar than in any other place except Kanara, where it grows in ftill higher perfection, is either red, yellow, or white. From the two laft kinds an oil is extracted, with which the Chinefe, Indians, Perfians, Arabians and Turks anoint their bodies. It is likewife burnt in their houfes, and yields a fragant and wholefome fmell. The red fanders is leaft efteemed, and is fcarce ever ufed but in medicine.

THE Indian faffron, called by the phyficians curcuma, is a plant with leaves refembling thofe of the white hellebore; the flower is of a fine purple

IN THE EAST AND WEST INDIES.

ple colour, and the fruit has, like our chefnuts, a rough coat containing the feed, which is round like a pea. The root, which has a bitter tafte, and has long been efteemed of an aperient quality, was formerly ufed as a remedy for the jaundice. The Indians make a yellow die of it, and it is an ingredient in moft of their difhes.

THE cardamum is a grain generally ufed in Indian ragoûts: it propagates itfelf without fowing or planting. Nothing more is required than, as foon as the rainy feafon is over, to fet fire to the herb that has produced it. It is often mixed with areca and betel, and fometimes chewed afterwards. The fort moft efteemed, which is fmall, grows in the territory of Cananor; it is ufed in medicine chiefly to help digeftion, and to ftrengthen the ftomach.

GINGER is a plant whofe root is white, tender, and almoft as pungent to the palate as pepper. The Indians put it into their rice, which is their common diet, to correct its natural infipidity. This fpice, mixed with others, gives the difhes feafoned with it a ftrong tafte, which is extremely difagreeable to ftrangers. The Europeans, however, who come to Afia in low circumftances are obliged to accuftom themfelves to it. Others adopt it out of complaifance to their wives, who are generally natives of the country. It is here, as in all other places, much eafier for the men to conform to the tafte and foibles of the women, than to get the better of them. Perhaps too the climate may require this manner of living.

BASTARD

BASTARD cinnamon, known in Europe by the name of caffia lignea, is to be had at Timor, Java, and Mindanao; but that which grows on the Malabar coaſt is much ſuperior. The Dutch, deſpairing of being able to root up all the trees out of the foreſts that produce it, fell upon the expedient, during their ſuperiority in Malabar, of requiring the ſovereigns of the country to renounce their right of barking them. This engagement, which was never ſtrictly obſerved, has been leſs fulfilled ſince the nation that made it has loſt its authority, and the price of the cinnamon of Ceylon has been advanced in conſequence of that meaſure. The preſent produce at Malabar may be computed at two hundred thouſand weight. The ſmalleſt portion of it is brought to Europe, where it is ſold for good cinnamon by merchants who are not very honeſt; the reſt is diſpoſed of in India, where it is ſold at twenty and from thence to twenty-five ſols* a pound, though it coſts no more than ſix.† The trade is entirely in the hands of the free Engliſh merchants; it may admit of improvement, but will never be equal to that of pepper.

THE pepper-plant is a ſhrub whoſe root is ſmall, fibrous, and flexible; it riſes into a ſtem, which requires a tree or a prop to ſupport it. Its wood has the ſame ſort of knots as the vine; and when it is dry, it exactly reſembles the vine-branch. The leaves, which have a ſtrong ſmell and a pungent taſte, are of an oval ſhape; but they diminiſh towards the extremity, and terminate in a point.

* From 10d.½ to about 13d.   † About 3d.

From

IN THE EAST AND WEST INDIES.

From the flower-buds, which are white, and are sometimes placed in the middle, and sometimes at the extremity of the branches, are produced small berries resembling those of the currant-tree. Each of these contains between twenty and thirty corns of pepper; they are commonly gathered in October, and exposed to the sun seven or eight days. The fruit, which was green at first, and afterwards red, when stripped of its covering, assumes the appearance it has when we see it. The largest, heaviest, and least shrivelled, is the best.

The pepper-plant flourishes in the islands of Java, Sumatra, and Ceylon, and more particularly on the Malabar coast. It is not sown, but planted; and great nicety is required in the choice of the shoots. It produces no fruit till the end of three years; but bears so plentifully the three succeeding years, that some plants yield between six and seven pounds of pepper. The bark then begins to shrink; and the shrub declines so fast, that in twelve years time it ceases bearing.

The culture of pepper is not difficult; it is sufficient to plant it in a rich soil, and carefully to pull up the weeds that grow in great abundance round its roots, especially the three first years. As the sun is highly necessary to the growth of the pepper-plant, when it is ready to bear, the trees that support it must be lopped, to prevent their shade from injuring the fruit. When the season is over, it is proper to crop the head of the plant. Without this precaution there would be too much wood, and little fruit.

The

HISTORY OF SETTLEMENTS AND TRADE

THE pepper exported from Malabar, which was formerly entirely in the hands of the Portuguese, and is at present divided between the Dutch, English, and French, amounts to about ten millions weight. At ten sols a pound * it is worth five millions † : it is exported, with other productions, for half that sum. By the sale of these commodities the country is enabled to purchase rice from the Ganges and Canara, coarse linens from Mysore and Bengal, and several sorts of goods from Europe. The payments in money amount to little or nothing.

KANARA, a country bordering upon Malabar properly so called, was formerly more opulent. It was an almost inexhaustible granary of rice; but has been much on the decline since it submitted to the yoke of Heyder-Aly-Kan. The trade of this country, which was carried on with freedom at Mangalore the capital, is entirely engrossed by the conqueror, who will deliver his commodities to none but those who furnish him with arms, powder and ammunition. The Portuguese are the only people exempted from this law, who having been formerly masters of the province, have always retained one staple which supplies Goa.

THE commerce, that raised Venice from her canals, and Amsterdam from her marshes, had rendered Goa the center of the riches of India, and the most celebrated mart in the world. It is now reduced to nothing, though it is defended

* 5d.¼   † 218,750l.

by

IN THE EAST AND WEST INDIES. by two thoufand European foldiers, by a company of artillery, and by five thoufand fipahis, and that it is an annual expence to the ftate of thirteen or fourteen hundred thoufand livres *. Superftition, the Autos da Fé, and the monks, extinguifh all defire of feeing it reftored to its former ftate. Deprived of fo many fertile provinces, which implicitly obey its laws, it has nothing remaining but the fmall ifland on which it is built, and the two peninfulas that form its harbour.

NEAR a century ago a power was eftablifhed by fea and land to the north of Goa, the increafe of which was not forefeen by any body. The name of the founder of it was Konna Ji Angria. He made himfelf mafter of the fmall ifland of Severndroog, where he had ferved as a foldier, and built a light veffel on which he embarked as a pirate. At firft he confined his attacks to the Moorifh or Indian veffels trading upon that coaft. His fuccefs, experience, and the number of adventurers whom the fame of his courage and generofity invited to join him, enabled him to engage in the greateft enterprifes. By degrees he acquired a dominion extending forty leagues along the fea-coaft, or which ran up between twenty and thirty miles in the inland country, according to the natural difpofition of the places, and the facility of their being defended. His fuccefs and renown were, however, principally owing to his naval operations; which were continued with good fortune by his fucceffors. Thefe

* About 59,100l. on an average.

VOL. I. C c pirates

pirates being masters of the coast, attacked the flag of all nations without distinction. Besides a great number of small vessels, they took ships of the largest size from the European powers; the Derby and the Restoration belonging to the English, the Jupiter belonging to the French, and three Dutch vessels at one time, one of which carried fifty guns.

THE plans of the English were disconcerted by these depredations. They had viewed with pleasure the first attempts of these pirates, which threw the greatest part of the trade, and the whole navigation into their hands; because their ships were of greater force and better manned than those of the country. They could no longer boast this advantage, when the vessels belonging to Bombay, which traded upon the coast, were insulted, cargoes plundered, and the sailors taken prisoners. The precaution taken never to sail without a convoy was very expensive, and proved ineffectual. The convoys were often molested, and sometimes taken. These depredations determined the company in 1722 to join their forces with those of the Portuguese, who were equally exasperated against these pirates; and it was determined between them to destroy the place of their resort. The expedition was disgraceful and abortive. That which was undertaken by the Dutch, two years after, with seven men of war and two bomb ketches, met with no better success. At length the Marattas, upon Angria's refusing to pay a tribute which had long been customary, agreed

agreed to attack the common enemy by land, whilft the Englifh attacked them by fea. This confederacy obtained a complete conqueft. Moft of the harbours and forts were taken in the campaign of 1755. Geriah, the capital, furrendered the year following, and with it fell a power whofe profperity had been only founded on public calamities. By its ruin the power of the Marattas, which was formidable already, was unhappily increafed.

These people, who had been long confined within the limits of their mountains, have by degrees extended themfelves towards the fea, and at prefent poffefs the large fpace between Surat and Goa, where they equally threaten thefe two cities. They are famous for their incurfions and depredations on the coaft of Coromandel, the neighbourhood of Delhi, and on the banks of the Ganges; but the center of their greateft ftrength, and their fixed ftation is at Malabar. That fpirit of rapine, which they carry into the countries where they occafionally make inroads, is forfaken in the provinces they have conquered. One may venture to foretell that Bacaim, Chaul, Dabul, and many other places, which were fo long oppreffed by the tyranny of the Portuguefe, will regain their former importance under the government of the Marattas. The fate of Surat is an object of ftill greater confequence.

This town was for a long time the only feaport for the exportation of the manufactures of the Mogul empire, and the importation of whatever was neceffary to fupply its confumption. To fecure its allegiance, and provide for its defence, a citadel was built, the commandant of which had no authority over that of the town; care was even taken to chufe two governors, who, from their character, were not likely to unite in oppreffing trade. Some difagreeable circumftances gave rife to a third power. The Indian feas were infefted with pirates who interrupted the navigation, and hindered devout Muffulmen from making voyages to Mecca. The emperor thought the chief of a colony of Coffrees, who were fettled at Rajapour, would be the proper perfon to ftop the progrefs of thefe depredations, and therefore appointed him his admiral. Three lacks of roupees, or 720,000 livres *, were affigned him for his annual pay. This falary not being punctually paid, the admiral feized the caftle, and from that fortrefs laid the town under contribution. A fcene of general confufion enfued; and the avarice of the Marattas, which was always active, became more eager than ever. Thefe Barbarians, who had extended their ufurpations even to the gates of the place, had, for a long time, been allowed a third part of the duties, on condition that they fhould not moleft the inland trade. They contented themfelves with this contribution, fo long as fortune did not throw more confiderable advantages in their way. As foon as they perceived this ferment among the citizens,

* Between 30,000l. and 40,000l.

not

IN THE EAST AND WEST INDIES.

not doubting that one of the parties might be tranſported ſo far by reſentment as to open the gates to them, they drew their forces near to the walls. The traders finding their effects daily in danger of being plundered, called the Engliſh to their aſſiſtance in 1759, and aided them in taking the citadel. The court of Delhi confirmed them in the poſſeſſion of it, and in the exerciſe of the naval command, together with the appointments annexed to both commiſſions. This revolution reſtored tranquillity to Surat; but Bombay, which was the cauſe of it, acquired an addition of credit, wealth, and power.

THIS ſmall iſland, which is not more than twenty miles in circumference, was, for a long time, of little ſervice to the Engliſh. No man choſe to ſettle in a country, ſo unhealthy, as to give riſe to the proverb, *That at Bombay a man's life did not exceed two monſoons:* the unwholeſomeneſs of the air was attributed to the bad quality of the water, the low marſhy grounds, and to the offenſive ſmell of the fiſh uſed in manuring the roots of trees. Every poſſible remedy was uſed to remove theſe cauſes of mortality. The number of inhabitants in the colony increaſed in proportion as theſe deſtructive principles were diminiſhed: it is computed to amount at preſent to fifty thouſand Indians, born in the iſland, or induced to ſettle there by the lenity of the government. Of theſe, ſome are employed in the cultivation of rice, a greater number in that of cocoa-trees which cover the plains, and the reſt are engaged in navigation and other useful labours, which are continually improving.

Bombay was at first considered in no other light than that of an excellent harbour, which in time of peace served as a place of refreshment for the merchant-men frequenting the Malabar coast; and in time of war, as a winter station for the squadrons that government might send to India. This was a very valuable advantage in seas where there are so few good bays, and where the English have no other but this. The settlement has since been rendered much more useful. The company have made it the mart of all their trade with Malabar, Surat, and the Persian and Arabian Gulphs. Its situation has invited the English merchants to resort thither; and by their means trade is carried on with greater spirit. The tyranny exercised by the Angrias upon the continent has compelled some of the Banians to take refuge at Bombay, notwithstanding the aversion these people, who never drink spirituous liquors, must have for living in a place where the water is so bad. Some rich Moors have likewise removed hither in consequence of the disturbances at Surat.

It is not to be imagined, that such a number of men, who, with the advantages of industry and large capitals, were intent on amassing wealth, would remain inactive. From Malabar they furnished themselves with ship timber, and kayar for cordage: these were worked up by the Parsees from Guzarat. The sailors of the country, under the command of European officers,

IN THE EAST AND WEST INDIES.

officers, have been found able to navigate their ships. Surat furnishes the cargoes, partly on its own account, and partly on account of the merchants of Bombay. They send out annually two ships to Bassora, one for Jodda, one for Mocha, and sometimes one for China. The cargoes of all these ships are immensely rich. Other vessels of less consequence are dispatched from the colony itself.

The private ships of the company are destined for the factories they have established between Surat and Cape Comorin. The rupees of Bombay, which have been substituted instead of those at Surat throughout the coast, and in the interior parts of the country, give the company an advantage of five per cent. over all the nations that are their rivals. They likewise send cargoes to Bassora, Bender-Abassi, and Sindi, where the sale of their cloths is the principal object of their settlements. Thirteen or fourteen hundred bales are sufficient to supply the consumption. Their connections with Surat are still more advantageous; this place buys of them a large quantity of iron and lead, and some woollen-cloths; the ships are freighted back from hence with manufactures to a great amount.

The ships sent from Europe formerly sailed to the sea-port, where they were to take in their lading. They now put in at Bombay. This alteration owes its rise to the advantage the company have of transporting hither all the merchandise of the country without expence, since they have been invested with the dignity of admiral to the great Mogul, and in consequence of this appointment have been obliged to maintain a maritime force upon the coast.

THE detail into which we have entered, may incline the reader to suppose that the situation of the English at Malabar is equal to their wishes. It is nevertheless certain that they gain no more than 2,250,000 livres * from all the settlements they have upon this coast; whereas their annual expences exceed 6,000,000†.

IF the attention of the company had not been diverted by the great scenes in which they have been engaged on the coast of Coromandel and in Bengal, it is natural to believe their affairs would be in a better state at Malabar.

THE fortifications at Bombay would not have been enlarged, then reduced, then extended again, and in short altered at several different times. Had the plans been drawn by skilful engineers, and executed by honest workmen, those enormous expences, which have excited such a general indignation, might have been avoided.

THEY would have sent from the Ganges, or from Europe, a fund sufficient to purchase seven or eight rich cargoes every year, instead of three or four very slender ones furnished by a declining and almost deserted trade.

THE feeble state of the independent kingdoms of this continent, particularly towards the south, and the anarchy and war in which they are perpetually involved, would have suggested a plan conducive to the welfare of the inhabitants, and

* Not quite 100,000l. † Above 260,000l.

IN THE EAST AND WEST INDIES

to the interests of the nation, by whose influence it would have been procured.

IN a word, the company might have obtained the island of Salsette, which was offered to them by the Marattas, on condition of their assisting them, on a sudden emergency, with five hundred men against the subah of the Decan: and by this arrangement they would have freed themselves from the shameful necessity they are under of depending upon these people for subsistence.

THE fertile island of Salsette, which is twenty-six miles in length, and eight or nine in breadth, was taken by the Marattas from the Portuguese. Masters of this post, they threatened Bombay, which is only separated from it by a narrow channel fordable at low water. Now that the English have raised large fortifications, and placed a numerous garrison in their colony, which is become of greater importance, an invasion is impracticable. The Marattas themselves are convinced of it; but they think it is in their power to ruin this settlement even without attacking it. This, they affirm, would easily be done by refusing to furnish it with provisions from Salsette, and preventing its procuring them from the continent. Persons of observation, who are well acquainted with the situation of the places, find something more than probability in these ideas.

THE truth is, that ever since that wrong step was taken, though perhaps it was unavoidable, of putting into the hands of the Marattas all the ports which belonged to the Angrias, those

barbarians

barbarians have been daily augmenting their marine. Their ambition will increase with their power; and it is impossible that in process of time, their claims and those of the English should not interfere.

IF we might hazard a conjecture, we should not scruple to prophesy that the company's agents will be the authors of the rupture. Beside the propensity to raise disturbances, which is common to all that set of men, because confusion is favourable to their avaritious views: they are devoured with secret spleen at having no share in those immense fortunes, which are made on the Coromandel coast, and especially in Bengal. Their avarice, jealousy, and even their pride will incline them to represent the Marattas as turbulent neighbours, always intent upon the invasion of Bombay: to magnify the facility of dispersing these banditti, provided they have a proper force; and to give exaggerated ideas of the advantage of plundering their mountains filled with the treasures of Indostan, which they have been accumulating during a whole century. The company accustomed to conquest, and having no longer any urgent occasion for its troops on the banks of the Ganges, will adopt a plan that promises an accession of riches, glory, and power. If those who dread the spirit of ambition, should prevail with the company not to embark in this new enterprize, it will be forced into it by its servants; and however the event of this war may operate upon its interests, those who involve the company in it will

IN THE EAST AND WEST INDIES.

will be sure to be gainers. There is less reason to fear a misfortune of this kind on the coasts of Coromandel and Orixa, which extend from Cape Comorin to the Ganges.

GEOGRAPHERS and historians always consider these as distinct countries inhabited by two nations, whose language, genius, and manners have not the least resemblance. But as the commerce in both is nearly the same, and carried on in the same manner; we shall comprehend them both under the general name of Coromandel. The two coasts resemble each other in other respects. In both of them, there reigns from the beginning of May to the end of October an excessive heat, which begins at nine in the morning, and continues till nine in the evening. During the night it is always allayed by a sea-breeze, that blows from the south-east; and most commonly this refreshing gale begins at three in the afternoon. The air is less inflamed, though too hot the rest of the year. It rains almost continually during the months of November and December. This immense tract is covered with a parched sand for the extent of two miles, and sometimes only one mile.

THERE were many reasons why this country was at first neglected by the Europeans who came to India. It was separated by inaccessible mountains from Malabar, where these bold navigators endeavoured to settle themselves. Spices and aromatics, which were the principal objects of their attention, were not be found there. In

General trade of the coast of Coromandel, and that of the English in particular.

short,

short, civil diffensions had banished from it tranquillity, security and industry.

At that period, the empire of Bisnagar, to which this vast country was subject, was falling to ruin. The first monarchs of that illustrious state owed their power to their abilities. They headed their armies in war; in peace, they directed their councils, visited their provinces, and administered justice. Prosperity corrupted them. By degrees they fell into a habit of withdrawing themselves from the sight of their people, and of leaving the cares of government to their generals and ministers. This conduct paved the way to their ruin. The governors of Visapour, the Carnatic, Golconda, and Orixa, threw off their dependence, and assumed the title of kings. Those of Madura, Tanjore, Mysore, Gingi, and some others, likewise usurped the sovereign authority, but retained their antient stile of Naick. This great revolution had just happened, when the Europeans appeared upon the coast of Coromandel.

The foreign trade was at that time inconsiderable; it consisted only of diamonds from Golconda, which were carried to Calicut and Surat, and from thence to Ormus or Suez, whence they were circulated through Europe and Asia. Masulipatan, the richest and most populous city in these countries, was the only market that was known for linens; they were purchased at a great fair annually holden there by the Arabian and Malayan vessels that frequented that bay, and by caravans that arrived from distant diftant parts. The linens were exported to the fame places as the diamonds.

The fondnefs for the manufactures of Coromandel, which began to prevail here, infpired all the European nations trading to the Indian feas with the refolution of forming fettlements there. They were not difcouraged either by the difficulty of conveying goods from the inland parts of the country, where there was no navigable river; by the total want of harbours, where the fea, at one feafon of the year, is not navigable; by the barrennefs of the coafts for the moft part uncultivated and uninhabited; nor by the tyranny and fluctuating ftate of the government. They thought that filver would be induftrioufly fought after; that Pegu would furnifh timber for building, and Bengal corn for fubfiftence; that a profperous voyage of nine months would be more than fufficient to complete their ladings; and that, by fortifying themfelves, they fhould be fecure againft the attacks of the weak tyrants that oppreffed thefe countries.

The firft colonies were eftablifhed near the fhore. Some of them obtained a fettlement by force: moft of them were formed with the confent of the fovereigns, and all were confined to a very narrow tract of land. The boundaries of each were marked out by a hedge of thorny plants, which was their only defence. In procefs of time fortifications were raifed; and the fecurity derived from them, added to the lenity of the government, foon increafed the number

of

of colonists. The splendor and independence of these settlements several times raised the jealousy of the princes in whose dominions they were formed; but their attempts to demolish them proved abortive. Each colony increased in prosperity in proportion to the riches and the wisdom of the nation that founded it.

None of the companies that exercised an exclusive privilege beyond the Cape of Good Hope had any concern in the trade of diamonds; which was always left to private merchants, and by degrees fell intirely into the hands of the English, or the Jews and Armenians that lived under their protection. At present this grand object of luxury and industry is much reduced. The revolutions that have happened in Indostan have prevented people from resorting to these rich mines; and the anarchy into which this unhappy country is plunged, leaves no room to hope that they will be again attended to. The whole of the commercial operations on the coast of Coromandel is confined to the purchase of cottons.

The manufacturing of the white cottons bought there, differs so little from that of ours, that it would be neither interesting nor instructive to enter into a minute description of it. The process used in making their printed cottons, which was at first servilely followed in Europe, has since been rendered more simple and brought to greater perfection by our manufactures. The painted cottons, which are likewise bought there, we have not yet attempted to imitate. Those who imagine

we

we have been prevented from undertaking this branch merely by the high price of labour among us, are miftaken. Nature has not given us the wild fruits and drugs neceffary for the compofition of thofe bright and indelible colours, which conftitute the principal merit of the Indian manufactures; nor has fhe furnifhed us with the waters that ferve to fix them; and which are good at Pondicherry, but excellent at Madras Paliacaten, Maffulipatan, and Bimilipatan.

The Indians do not univerfally obferve the fame method in painting their cottons; either becaufe there are fome niceties peculiar to certain provinces, or becaufe different foils produce different drugs for the fame ufes.

We fhould tire the patience of our readers, were we to trace the flow and painful progrefs of the Indians in the art of painting their cottons. It is natural to believe that they owe it to length of time, rather than to the fertility of their genius. What feems to authorize this conjecture is, that they have ftopped in their improvements, and have not advanced a fingle ftep in the arts for many ages; whereas we have proceeded with amazing rapidity, and view with an emulation full of confidence, the immenfe fpace that ftill lies between us and the goal. Indeed, were we to confider only the want of invention in the Indians, we fhould be tempted to believe that, from time immemorial, they had received the arts they cultivate from fome more induftrious nation: but when it is remembered that thefe arts have a peculiar dependence on the materials, gums, colours, and productions of India,

we

we cannot but be convinced that they are natives of that country.

It may appear fomewhat furprizing that cottons painted with all colours fhould be fold at fo moderate a price, that they are almoft as cheap as thofe which have only two or three. But it muft be obferved that the merchants of the country fell to all the companies, a large quantity of cottons at a time; and that the demand for cottons painted with various colours makes but a fmall article in their affortments, as they are not much efteemed in Europe.

Though cottons of all forts are in fome degree manufactured throughout the whole country of Indoftan, which extends from Cape Comorin to the banks of the Ganges; it is obfervable, that the fine forts are made in the eaftern part, the common ones in the center, and the coarfe ones in the moft weftern parts. Manufactures are eftablifhed in the European colonies, and upon the coaft: they are more frequent at the diftance of five or fix leagues from the fea, where cotton is more cultivated, and provifions are cheaper. 'The purchafes made there are carried thirty or forty leagues further into the country. The Indian merchants fettled in our factories have always the management of this bufinefs.

The quantity and quality of the goods wanted are fettled with thefe people: the price is fixed according to the patterns: and, at the time the contract is made, a third or a fourth part of the money agreed for is advanced. This arrangement is owing to the neceffity thefe merchants

themfelves

themselves lie under of advancing money to the workmen by the partners or agents who are dispersed through the whole country; of keeping a watchful eye upon them for fear of losing what they have advanced; and of gradually lessening the sum by calling for the cottons as fast as they are worked off. Without these precautions, nothing could be depended upon in an oppressive government, where the weaver cannot work on his own account, either because his circumstances will not permit, or because he dares not venture to discover them for fear of exactions.

THE companies that have either success or good management constantly keep the stock of one year in advance in their settlements. By this method they are sure of having the quantity of goods they have occasion for, and of the quality they chuse, at the most convenient time: not to mention that their workmen, and their merchants, who are kept in constant employment, never leave them.

THOSE nations that want money and credit cannot begin their mercantile operations till the arrival of their ships. They have only five or six months, at most, to execute the orders sent from Europe. The goods are manufactured and examined in haste; and they are even obliged to take such as are known to be bad, and would be rejected at any other time. The necessity they are under of compleating their cargoes, and fitting out their vessels before the hurricanes come on, allow no time for nicety of inspection.

IT would be a mistake to imagine that the country agents could be prevailed upon to order goods to be made on their account, in hopes of felling them with a reasonable advantage to the company in whose service they are engaged. For besides that the generality of them are not rich enough to embark in so large an undertaking, they would not be certain of finding their account in it. If the company that employ them should be hindered by unforeseen accidents from sending the usual number of ships, these merchants would have no vent for their commodities. The Indians, the form of whose dress requires different breadths and lengths from those of the cottons fabricated for our use, would not purchase them; and the other European companies would be provided, or certain of being provided with whatever the extent of their trade required, and their money enabled them to purchase. The plan of procuring loans, which was contrived to remedy this inconvenience, never has been, or can be useful.

It has been a custom, time immemorial, in Indostan, for every citizen who borrows money to give a written instrument to his creditor. This deed is of no force in a court of judicature, unless it be signed by three witnesses, and bears the day of the month, and the year when it was made, with the rate of interest agreed upon by the parties. If the borrower fails to fulfil his engagements, he may be arrested by the lender himself. He is never imprisoned, because there is no fear of his making his escape. He would not even eat without obtaining leave of his creditor.

The Indians make a threefold division of interest; one of which is vice, another neither vice nor virtue,

virtue, and a third virtue : this is their manner of expreſſion. The intereſt that is vice, is four per cent. a month ; and the intereſt that is neither vice nor virtue, is two; the intereſt that is virtue, one. The laſt is, in their opinion, an act of beneficence that only belongs to the moſt heroic minds. Yet though the Europeans who are forced to borrow meet with this treatment, it is plain they cannot avail themſelves of the indulgence without involving themſelves in ruin.

The foreign trade of Coromandel is not in the hands of the natives. In the weſtern part, indeed, there are Mohammedans, known by the name of Chalias, who, at Naour and Porto-Nuovo, fend out ſhips to Achen, Merguy, Siam, and the eaſtern coaſt. Beſides veſſels of conſiderable burden employed in theſe voyages, they have ſmaller embarkations for the coaſting trade for Ceylon, and the pearl fiſhery. The Indians of Maſſulipatan turn their attention another way. They import white callicoes from Bengal, which they dye or print, and ſell them again at the places from whence they had them, at thirty-five or forty per cent. advantage.

Excepting theſe tranſactions, which are of very little conſequence, the whole trade is veſted in the Europeans, who have no partners but a few Banians and Armenians ſettled in their colonies. The quantity of callicoes exported from Coromandel to the different ſea-ports in India, may be computed at three thouſand five hundred bales. Of theſe the French carry eight hundred to Malabar, Mocha, and the iſle of France; the Engliſh twelve hundred

hundred to Bombay, Malabar, Sumatra, and the Philippine Iſlands; and the Dutch fifteen hundred to their ſeveral ſettlements. Except five hundred bales deſtined for Manilla, each of the value of 2,400 livres *, the others are of ſo ordinary a kind that they do not exceed 720 livres † at prime coſt: ſo that the whole number of three thouſand five hundred bales does not amount to more than 3,360,000 livres ‡.

COROMANDEL furniſhes Europe with nine thouſand five hundred bales; eight hundred of which are brought by the Danes; two thouſand five hundred by the French; three thouſand by the Engliſh; and three thouſand two hundred by the Dutch. A conſiderable part of theſe callicoes is dyed blue, or ſtriped with red and blue for the African trade. The others are fine muſlins, printed callicoes, and handkerchiefs from Maſſulipatan, or Paliacate. It is proved by experience, that one with another, each bale, in the nine thouſand five hundred, coſts only 960 livres §, conſequently they ought to bring in to the manufactory where they are wrought 8,160,000 livres ‖.

THE payments are not entirely made in ſpecie either in Europe or Aſia; we give in exchange, cloths, iron, lead, copper, coral, and ſome other articles of leſs value. On the other hand, Aſia pays with ſpices, pepper, rice, ſugar, corn, and dates. All theſe articles taken together, may amount to 4,800,000 livres **. From this calculation it follows, that Coromandel receives 6,720,000 livres †† in money.

* About 100 guineas.   † About 30 guineas.   ‡ Not quite 50,000l.
§ 42l.   ‖ Near 360,000l.   ** About 210,000l.   †† Near 300,000l.

The English, who have acquired the same superiority upon this coast that they have elsewhere, have formed on it several settlements. In 1757, they took possession of Madura, a considerable town, and tolerably well fortified: but they did not fix there with any commercial views. The cottons calculated for the eastern part of Asia, and for Africa, which are manufactured in the kingdom of which Madura is the capital, are, for the most part, carried to the Dutch factories on the coast of the pearl fishery. The only use the English make of this acquisition is to raise from it a revenue sufficient to overbalance the expences that are unavoidably incurred there.

TRICHINOPOLY, though totally destroyed by the cruel wars it has sustained, is of much more importance to them. This strong post is the key of Tanjore, Mysore, and Madura, and gives them great influence in those three states.

It was solely with the view of securing an easy communication with this celebrated fortress, that they seized upon Devi-Cottah in 1749, whose territory is no more than three miles in circumference. There is no kind of manufacture carried on, either upon the spot, or in the neighbourhood, the only produce being some wood, and a little rice. The defence of this factory costs about 40,000 livres [*]; an expence that takes away the whole profits of it. It would, notwithstanding, be a post of importance, if what has been advanced by some intelligent men be true, that the Coleroon might, at an easy expence, be put into a condition to receive the largest vessels. The coast of

[*] About 1,800l.

Coromandel would not then be without harbours; and the nation, masters of the only port in those parts, would have powerful means of improving their commerce, which their rivals would be deprived of.

In 1686, the English purchased Cudalore, with a territory extending eight miles along the coast, and four miles into the interior part of the country. This acquisition, which they obtained of an Indian prince for the sum of 742,500 livres*, was confirmed to them by the Moguls, who soon after made themselves masters of the Carnatic. Considering afterwards, that the fortress, which they found ready built, was more than a mile from the sea, and that the reinforcements destined for it might be intercepted; they built fort St. David within cannon-shot of it, at the mouth of a river, and on the verge of the Indian Ocean. Since that three hamlets have been erected, which, with the town and fortress, are computed to contain sixty thousand souls. Their employment is dying blue, or painting the cottons that come from the inland parts of the country, and manufacturing the finest dimities in the world, to the amount of 1,500,000 livres†. The plundering of this settlement by the French in 1758, and the demolishing of its fortifications, have done it no lasting injury. Its spirit seems rather increased, though St. David has not been rebuilt, and Cudalore is only put into a condition of making a tolerable resistance. A revenue of 144,000 livres‡ defrays all the ex-

---

* About 32,000l.   † About 60,000l.   ‡ About 6,300l.

penees

IN THE EAST AND WEST INDIES. 407

pences of this fettlement. Maffulipatan affords advantages of another kind.

BOOK III.

This town, which paffed from the hands of the French into thofe of the Englifh in 1759, is by no means what it was when the Europeans, at the conclufion of the fifteenth century, doubled the Cape of Good Hope. There are but a few cottons made or fold there, which, notwithftanding their beauty, cannot furnifh any confiderable branch of export. Accordingly the new poffeffors confider their conqueft not fo much as a market for buying, as for felling large quantities of goods. By means of the caravans which come from very diftant places to furnifh themfelves with falt; and by the intercourfe they have formed with the inland parts of the country; they have contrived to eftablifh a demand for their cloths in the moft remote countries of the Decan, and this trade is likely to flourifh ftill more. To this may be added the further advantage of drawing a revenue from the product of the falt, and that of the cuftoms, amounting to 1,320,000 livres*, of which 600,000 livres † only are annually expended upon the fettlement.

Vizagapatan is a fmall town, with little territory belonging to it, and not four thoufand inhabitants. Being fituated between Maffulipatan and Ganjam, it receives all the fine cottons that are made in that part of Orixa, amounting to five or fix hundred bales, which coft 480,000 livres ‡.

* Near 58,000l. † Little more than 26,000l. ‡ About 21,000l.

Dd 4　　　　　　　　　The

merchandife procured from all thefe places and from a few fubordinate factories that vary according to circumftances, is carried to Madrafs, which is the center of all the Englifh tranfactions on the coaft of Coromandel.

This town was built a hundred years ago by William Langhorne, in the country of Arcot, and by the fea-fide. As he placed it in the midft of a fandy tract, altogether dry, and where there was no water fit for drinking, but what was fetched from the diftance of more than a mile, people were curious to know what reafons could have determined him to make fo bad a choice. His friends pretended that his view was to draw thither all the trade of St. Thomas, which has actually been the confequence, while his enemies imputed it to a defire of continuing in the neighbourhood of a miftrefs he had in that Portuguefe colony. This fettlement has increafed fo much fince its firft eftablifhment, that it has been divided into three diftricts. The firft of thefe, known in Europe by the name of Fort St. George, and in India by that of the White Town, is occupied by four or five hundred Englifh, men, women, and children. It is defended only by a flight wall, and four ill-conftructed baftions. To the north lies the Black Town, which is larger, and ftill worfe fortified; and is the quarter where the Jews, Armenians, Moors, and the richeft Indians refide. Beyond this are the fuburbs, which are entirely defencelefs, and full of inhabitants. The three divifions of which the place is compofed, two hamlets which lie at a fmall diftance from it,

and

IN THE EAST AND WEST INDIES

and the whole territory, which is not more than fifteen miles in circumference, contain two hundred and fifty thoufand inhabitants, almoft all of them natives of India.

AMONG this vaft number, there are but few weavers. Fifteen thoufand artifts are employed in printing and painting the fine callicoes that are worn in Europe; and a confiderable quantity of common cottons deftined for the different fea-ports of Afia, particularly for the Philippine iflands. There are, perhaps, forty thoufand people occupied in arranging and felling coral and glafs-ware, with which the women in the interior parts of the country adorn their hair, or make necklaces and bracelets. Other branches of induftry infeparable from a large mart, employ a great number of hands. The inhabitants, who have defervedly gained the confidence of the company, travel through Arcot and the neighbouring country, to buy what goods they have occafion for. The moft confiderable among them lend money to the Englifh merchants, who though not of the company, have liberty to traffic in the different fea-ports of Afia; they enter into partnerfhip with them, or embark on their veffels goods for their own private account. The bufinefs carried on by the company and the private merchants taken together, has made Madrafs one of the moft opulent and important places in India.

BESIDES the profits accruing to the Englifh from the cottons they purchafe in this town, and from the cloths and other merchandife they vend there, the cuftoms, the duties upon tobacco and betel,

betel, and some other imposts, bring in a revenue of 1,200,000 livres*. The continuation of these advantages is secured by a garrison of a thousand Europeans, and of fifteen or eighteen hundred sipahis.

Such is the situation of the English company on the coast of Coromandel, considered merely as a mercantile body. Let us now examine it in a political light.

In 1751, the English undertook to make Mohammed-Ali-Khan nabob of Arcot. The execution of this great plan was attended with innumerable difficulties, which were at length surmounted, after a series of battles, defeats, victories and negotiations, that lasted several years. The new sovereign, who had still many enemies remaining, committed the safety of his person to the care of his protectors, by fixing his residence at Madrass; and placed his provinces under the cover of their arms, leaving to them the sole charge of defending them. To enable them to support the burden they had undertaken, and to reimburse them for the money they had advanced, it was stipulated, that they should enjoy the revenues of the country, which in times of the greatest prosperity amounted to 12,000,000 livres†, and are still at least 8,400,000‡. It is true we ought previously to deduct 2,880,000 ‖ for public expences, and as much more for their maintenance of the nabob; but there still remain 2,640,000 livres §, clear income to the company. By this managment,

---

* Above 52,000l. sterling.   † 525,000l.   ‡ Near 368,000l.
‖ 126,000l.   § 116,000l.

IN THE EAST AND WEST INDIES. 411

they keep the Carnatic, which is the moſt induſtri- ous country in this immenſe tract, in a ſtate of abſolute dependence.

To ſtrengthen their influence ſtill more on theſe coaſts, the Engliſh had long meditated a plan of making a large acquiſition of territory in the neighbourhood of Maſſulipatan. In 1767 they ſucceeded ſo far as to procure, from the ſubah of the Decan, the ceſſion of the provinces of Candavir, Elur, Montaſanagar, Rajamandry and Chicacol. From this prodigious acceſſion of revenue and territory, they were induced to think that the only employment they ſhould have, would be to enjoy the advantages of their ſituation; when they obſerved a ſtorm coming upon them, which might poſſibly endanger, if not totally deſtroy their proſperity.

HYDER-ALI-KHAN, a ſoldier of fortune, who had learned the art of war from the Europeans, had made great conqueſts, and rendered himſelf maſter of Myſore. Relying upon his ſtrength and his reputation, he ſummoned the ſubah of the Decan, and the nabob of the Carnatic to join with him in driving the Engliſh out of Coromandel, threatening, if they refuſed, to ravage all their provinces. The company thought both their credit and intereſt concerned in anticipating the deſigns of an enemy who announced his reſentment and projects in ſo high a ſtrain, and they ſent out an army againſt him in March 1767.

COLONEL WOOD, who had the command of it marched forward with confidence; when to his great aſtoniſhment he beheld, in front, an army

that

that he found punctually paid, and excellently well disciplined, consisting of thirty thousand foot and twenty thousand horse, with a considerable train of artillery. The war was carried on by artifice, a circumstance very desireable to Hyder, whose genius was subtile and fruitful in stratagems. He contrived to surprize his enemies in their camp, and carry off their provisions and baggage; he seized their best posts by procuring the most exact intelligence, drove their troops before him, vanquished, disheartened, and made them almost ready to revolt for want of pay; and at last alarmed them with the apprehension of seeing their capital besieged, plundered, and destroyed. The panic was becoming universal, when some timely succours arrived, which enabled the English general to regain his ground. On the 4th of October 1768, he found means to compel the Indians to a general engagement, which they had hitherto seemed desirous to avoid. This was, perhaps, the most obstinate and bloody engagement that had ever happened in this part of the world. At last, Wood remained master of the field where both sides had fought so bravely: but this was all the advantage he gained by his victory.

HYDER, though defeated, kept up a menacing countenance, and was still formidable. Terms of accommodation were proposed to him. He listened to them with no small indifference; and it was not without much negotiation, nor, if some accounts may be blieved, without considerable presents that he was prevailed upon to conclude a peace after having carried on the war for two years. This prince

con-

IN THE EAST AND WEST INDIES.

continues to be confidered by the Englifh rather as an enemy, againft whom it is neceffary they fhould be conftantly on their guard, than as an ally on whom they may depend. Some of the moft judicious among them are even of opinion, that unlefs their nation by fome means or other gets rid of a neighbour too ambitious, and too active for its repofe, it cannot fecurely rely on the power which a combination of fortunate circumftances has given it on the coaft of Coromandel. Let us take a view of its fituation in Bengal.

BENGAL is a vaft country of Afia, bounded by the kingdom of Afham and Arracan on the eaft; by feveral provinces belonging to the Great Mogul on the weft; by frightful rocks on the north, and by the fea on the fouth. It extends on both fides the Ganges, which rifes from different fources in Thibet, and, after feveral windings through Caucafus, penetrates into India, acrofs the mountains on its frontier. This river, after having formed in its courfe a great number of large, fertile, and well peopled iflands, difcharges itfelf into the fea, by feveral mouths, of which only two are known and frequented.

TOWARDS the fource of this river, was formerly a city called Palibothra. Its antiquity was fo great, that Diodorus Siculus makes no fcruple of affuring us that it was built by that Hercules to whom the Greeks afcribed all the great and furprizing actions that had been performed in the world. In Pliny's time, its opulence was celebrated through the whole univerfe; and it was looked upon as the general mart for the people

General trade of Bengal, and that of the Englifh in particular.

inhabiting

inhabiting both sides of the river that washed its walls.

The history of the revolutions that have happened in Bengal, is intermixed with so many fables, that it does not deserve our attention. All we can discover, is, that the extent of this empire has been sometimes greater and somtimes less; that it has had fortunate and unfortunate periods; and that it has alternately been formed into one single kingdom, or divided into several independent states. It was under the dominion of one master, when a more powerful tyrant Akbar, grandfather of Aurengzebe, undertook the conquest of it; which was begun in 1590, and completed in 1595. Since this æra Bengal has always acknowledged the Mogul for its sovereign. At first, the governor to whom the administration of it was entrusted, held his court at Raja-mahul, but afterwards removed it to Dacca. Ever since the year 1718, it has been fixed at Muxadavad, a large inland town two leagues distant from Cassimbuzar. There are several Nabobs and Rajahs subordinate to this viceroy, who is called subah.

This important post was occupied for a long time by the sons of the Great Mogul: but they so frequently misemployed the forces and treasure at their disposal, to raise disturbances in the empire, that it was thought proper to commit that province to men who had less influence, and were more dependent. True it is, the new governors gave no alarm to the court of Delhi; but they were far from being punctual in remitting the tribute they collected to the royal treasury. These abuses

IN THE EAST AND WEST INDIES. 415
abufes gained further ground after the expedition
of Kouli Khan; and matters were carried fo far,
that the emperor, who was unable to pay the Marattas what he owed them, authorifed them, in 1740,
to collect it in Bengal themfelves. Thefe banditti,
to the number of two hundred thoufand, divided
themfelves into three armies, ravaged this fine
country for ten years together, and did not leave
it till they had extorted immenfe fums.

DURING all thefe commotions, defpotic government, which unhappily prevails all over India, maintained its influence in Bengal; though a fmall diftrict
in the province that had preferved its independence,
ftill continues to preferve it. This fortunate fpot,
which extends about a hundred and fixty miles, is
called Biffenpour. It has been governed time immemorial by a Bramin family of the tribe of Rajah-
puts. Here the purity and equity of the antient political fyftem of the Indians is found unadulterated.
This fingular government, the fineft and moft ftriking monument in the world, has, till now, been beheld with too much indifference. We have no remains of ancient nations but brafs and marble, which
fpeak only to imagination and conjecture, thofe uncertain interpreters of manners and cuftoms that no
longer exift. Were a philofopher tranfported to
Biffenpour, he would immediately be a witnefs of
the life led by the firft inhabitants of India many
thoufand years ago; he would converfe with them;
he would trace the progrefs of this nation celebrated
as it were from its very infancy; he would fee the
rife of a government, which being founded in
happy

happy prejudices, in a simplicity and purity of manners in the mild temper of the people, and the integrity of the chieftains, has survived those innumerable systems of legislation, which have made only a transitory appearance upon the stage of the world with the generations they were destined to torment. More solid and durable than those political structures, which, raised by imposture and enthusiasm, are the scourges of human kind, and are doomed to perish with the foolish opinions that gave them birth, the government of Biffenpour, the offspring of a just attention to order and the laws of nature, has been established and maintained upon unchangeable principles, and has undergone no more alteration than those principles themselves. The singular situation of this country has preserved to the inhabitants their primitive happiness and the gentleness of their character, by securing them from the danger of being conquered, or of imbruing their hands in the blood of their fellow-creatures. Nature has surrounded them with water; and they need only open the sluices of their rivers to overflow the whole country. The armies sent to subdue them have so frequently been drowned, that the plan of enslaving them has been laid aside; and the projectors of it have thought proper to content themselves with an appearance of submission.

LIBERTY and property are sacred in Biffenpour. Robbery, either public or private, is never heard of. As soon as any stranger enters the territory he comes under the protection of the laws, which provide for his security. He is furnished with guides at free cost, who conduct him from place to to place, and are anfwerable for his perfon and effects. When he changes his conductors, the new ones deliver to thofe they relieve an atteftation of their conduct, which is regiftered and afterwards fent to the Raja. All the time he remains in the country he is maintained and conveyed with his merchandife, at the expence of the ftate, unlefs he defires leave to ftay longer than three days in the fame place. In that cafe he is obliged to defray his own expences, unlefs he is detained by any diforder, or other unavoidable accident. This beneficence to ftrangers is the confequence of the warmth with which the citizens enter into each other's interefts. They are fo far from being guilty of an injury to each other, that whoever finds a purfe, or other thing of value, hangs it upon the firft tree he meets with, and informs the neareft guard, who give notice of it to the public by beat of drum. Thefe maxims of probity are fo generally received, that they direct even the operations of government. Out of between feven and eight millions * it annually receives, without injury to agriculture or trade, what is not wanted to fupply the unavoidable expences of the ftate, is laid out in improvements. The Raja is enabled to engage in thefe humane employments, as he pays the Moguls only what tribute, and at what times, he thinks proper.

Though the reft of Bengal is far from enjoying the fame happinefs, it is neverthelefs the richeft and moft populous province in the whole empire. Befides its own confumption, which is neceffarily

---

* About 330,000l. on an average.

considerable, its exports are immenfe. One part of its merchandife is carried into the inland country. Thibet takes off a quantity of its cottons, befides fome iron and cloths of European manufacture. The inhabitants of thofe mountains fetch them from Patna themfelves, and give mufk and rhubarb in exchange.

RHUBARB, which begins to be cultivated with fuccefs in the highlands of Scotland, is not, as is commonly believed, a creeping plant; but grows in tufts at fome diftance from each other. There is no occafion to fow it, as the feed naturally falls to the ground, and produces a new plant.

MUSK is a production peculiar to Thibet. It is contained in a fmall bag of the fize of a hen's egg, which grows in the fhape of a bladder under the belly of a fpecies of goat, between the navel and the genitals. In its original ftate it is nothing more than putrid blood which coagulates in this bag. The largeft bladder yields no more than half an ounce of mufk. The fmell of it is naturally fo ftrong, that, for common ufe, it is neceffary to moderate it by mixing it with milder perfumes. The hunters, with a view of increafing their profits, contrived to take away part of the mufk from the bladders, and to fill the vacuity with the liver and coagulated blood of the animal mixed together. The government, to put a ftop to thefe fraudulent mixtures, ordered, that all the bladders, before they were fewed up, fhould be examined by infpectors, who fhould clofe them with their own hands, and feal them with the royal fignet. This precaution

precaution has put a stop to the frauds practised to reduce the quality of the musk, but not to those which are calculated to increase the weight of it; they contrive to open the bags artfully and pour particles of lead into them.

THE trade of Thibet is nothing in comparison of that which Bengal carries on with Agra, Delhi, and the provinces adjacent to those superb capitals, in salt, sugar, opium, silk, silk-stuffs, and an infinite quantity of cottons, and particularly muslins. These articles, taken together, amounted formerly to more than forty millions a year[*]. So considerable a sum was not conveyed to the banks of the Ganges; but it was the means of retaining one nearly equal, which must have issued from thence to pay the duties, or for other purposes Since the viceroys of the Mogul have made themselves nearly independent, and send him no revenues but such as they chuse to allow him, the luxury of the court is greatly abated, and the trade we have been speaking of is no longer so considerable.

THE maritime trade of Bengal managed by the natives of the country, has not suffered the same diminution, nor was it ever so extensive, as the other. It may be divided into two branches, of which Catek is in possession of the greater part.

CATEK is a district of some extent, a little below the most western mouth of the Ganges. Balasore, situated upon a navigable river, serves it for a port. The navigation to the Maldives, which the English and French have been obliged to abandon on ac-

[*] 1,750,000l

count of the climate, is carried on entirely from this road. Here they load their veffels with rice, coarfe cottons, and fome filk-ftuffs for thefe iflands, and receive cowries in exchange, which are ufed for money in Bengal, and are fold to the Europeans.

THE inhabitants of Catek, and fome other people of the Lower Ganges, maintain a confiderable correfpondence with the country of Afham. This kingdom, which is thought to have formerly made a part of Bengal, and is only divided from it by a river that falls into the Ganges, deferves to be better known, if what is afferted be true, that gunpowder has been difcovered there, and that it was communicated from Afham to Pegu, and from Pegu to China. Its gold, filver, iron and lead mines would have added to its fame, if they had been properly worked. In the midft of thefe riches, which were of very little fervice to this kingdom, falt was an article of which the inhabitants were fo much in want, that they were reduced to the expedient of procuring it from a decoction of certain plants.

In the beginning of the prefent century, fome Bramins of Bengal carried their fuperftitions to Afham, where the people were fo happy as to be guided folely by the dictates of natural religion. The priefts perfuaded them, that it would be more agreeable to Brama if they fubftituted the pure and wholfome falt of the fea to that which they ufed. The fovereign confented to this, on condition that the exclufive trade fhould be in his hands; that it fhould only be brought by the people of Bengal, and that the boats laden with it fhould ftop at the

frontiers

IN THE EAST AND WEST INDIES.

frontiers of his dominions. Thus have all thefe falfe religions been introduced by the influence and for the advantage of the priefts who teach, and of the kings who admit them. Since this arrangement has taken place, forty veffels from 5 to 600 tons burden each are annually fent from the Ganges to Afham laden with falt, which yields two hundred per cent. profit. They receive in payment a fmall quantity of gold and filver, ivory, mufk, eagle-wood, gum-lac, and a large quantity of filk.

THIS filk, which is fingular in its kind, requires no trouble; it is found on the trees where the filk-worms are produced, nourifhed, and undergo their feveral metamorphofes. The inhabitants have no other trouble but that of collecting it. The neg-lected cods produce a new generation; during the growth of which, the tree puts forth new leaves, which ferve fucceffively for the nourifhment of the young worms. Thefe revolutions are repeated twelve times in a year, but do not produce fo much in the rainy as in the dry feafons. The ftuffs made of this filk have a great deal of luftre, but do not laft long.

EXCEPTING thefe two branches of maritime trade, which, for particular reafons, have been confined to the natives of the country, all the reft of the veffels fent from the Ganges to the different fea-ports of India belong to the Europeans, and are built at Pegu.

PEGU is a country fituated on the Gulph of Bengal, between the kingdoms of Arracan and Siam. Revolutions, which are fo common in all the despotic empires of Asia, have been here more frequently repeated than in any other. It has alternately been the center of a great power, and a province to several states less extensive than itself. It is at present dependent upon Ava.

The only port of Pegu that is open to strangers is Syriam. The Portuguese, during their prosperity, were long in possession of it, and it was then in great repute. At present it is scarce frequented but by the Europeans settled on the coast of Coromandel and Bengal. The latter can only sell there some coarse cottons, nor would they visit it at all, except for the building or refitting of their ships; for which purpose they are furnished with all necessary materials (except iron and cordage) of an excellent quality, and at a moderate price. Since the disgust taken at the high rate of ship-building at Surat, Syriam is become a kind of general dockyard for all vessels employed in the country trade.

Their exports consist of teak timber, wax, ivory, some calin, and an excellent oil for the preservation of ships. The finest topazes, saphires, amethysts, and rubies, in the world, come from Pegu. They are seldom to be met with at Syriam, nor can they be had without resorting to the court, which is kept at Ava. The Armenians have for some time had such an ascendent, that they make the trade difficult to the Europeans, and even to the English, who are the only people that have formed a settlement at Pegu.

A still more considerable branch of commerce, which the Europeans at Bengal carry on with

with the reſt of India, is that of opium. Opium is the produce of a ſpecies of poppy, whoſe root is nearly as large as a man's finger, abounding, as well as the reſt of the plant, with a bitter juice. The ſtem, which is commonly pliable, and ſometimes rather hairy, is two cubits high, and produces leaves reſembling thoſe of the lettuce, oblong, indented, curled, and of a ſea-green colour. Its flower is in the form of a roſe. When the poppy is full of ſap, a ſlight inciſion is made at the top, from whence diſtil ſome drops of a milky liquor, which is left to congeal, and is afterwards gathered. This operation is repeated three times, but the produce gradually diminiſhes in quantity, nor is it of ſo good a quality. When the opium is gathered, it is moiſtened and kneaded with water or honey, till it acquires the confiſtence, viſcidity, and gloſſineſs of pitch when it is well prepared, and is then made into ſmall cakes. That which is rather ſoft, and yields to the touch, is inflammable, of a blackiſh-brown colour, and has a ſtrong fœtid ſmell, is eſteemed the beſt; on the contrary, that which is dry, friable, burnt, and mixed with earth and ſand, is thought good for nothing. According to the different manner of preparing it, and the doſes in which it is given, it ſtupifies, excites agreeable ideas, or occaſions madneſs.

PATNA, ſituated on the Upper Ganges, is the moſt celebrated place in the world for the cultivation of opium. The fields are covered with it. Beſides what is carried into the inland parts, there are annually three or four thouſand cheſts exported,

exported, each weighing three hundred pounds. It sells upon the spot at the rate of five or six hundred livres* a chest. This opium is not purified like that of Syria and Persia, which we make use of in Europe; it is only a paste that has undergone no preparation, and has not a tenth part of the virtue of purified opium.

An excessive fondness for opium prevails in all the countries to the east of India. The Chinese emperors have suppressed it in their dominions, by condemning to the flames every vessel that imports this species of poison, and every house that receives it. On the Malayan coast, at Borneo, the Moluccas, Java, Macassar, and Sumatra, the consumption is incredible. These people smoke it with their tobacco. Those who are going to perform some desperate action intoxicate themselves with this smoke. They then encounter indiscriminately every thing they meet; and rush with impetuosity upon the enemy, through the most imminent danger. The Dutch, who are in possession of almost all the places where opium makes the greatest havock, have been more intent on the profits arising from the sale of this article, than touched with compassion for its numerous victims. Rather than prohibit the use of it, they have authorized individuals to massacre all those who, being disordered with opium, appear in the streets armed. Thus it is that some systems of legislation introduce and keep up intoxicating and violent passions and opinions; and when once these have prevailed among the

* Between 24l. and 25l. on an average.

people,

people, nothing but death or tortures can put an end to them.

The Dutch company formerly carried on the trade of opium in their fettlements. They vended but little, becaufe four hundred per cent. was gained by fmuggling it. In 1743, they refigned this branch to a particular fociety, to which they deliver a certain quantity of opium at a fixed price. The gains of this fociety, which confifts of the principal members of the government of Batavia, are immenfe; no one venturing to expofe himfelf to their refentment by purfuing a contraband trade incompatible with their interefts. The coaft of Malacca, and part of the ifland of Sumatra, are fupplied with opium by the free Englifh merchants, who gain more by this merchandife than by the common cottons they bring to thefe different markets.

The Dutch alfo fend rice and fugar to the coaft of Coromandel, for which they are paid in fpecie, unlefs they have the good fortune to meet with fome foreign merchandife at a cheap rate. They fend out one or two veffels laden with rice, cottons and filk : the rice is fold in Ceylon, the cottons at Malabar, and the filk at Surat; from whence they bring back cotton, which is ufefully employed in the coarfer manufactures of Bengal. Two or three fhips laden with rice, gum-lac, and cotton ftuffs are fent to Baffora, and return with dried fruits, rofe-water, and a quantity of gold. The rich merchandife carried to Arabia is paid for intirely in gold and filver. The trade of the Ganges with the other

fea-ports

sea-ports of India brings twenty-eight millions * annually into Bengal.

Though this trade passes through the hands of the Europeans, and is carried on under their protection, it is not intirely on their own account. The Moguls, indeed, who are usually satisfied with the places they hold under the government; have seldom any concern in these expeditions; but the Armenians, who, since the revolutions in Persia, are settled upon the banks of the Ganges, to which they formerly only made voyages, readily throw their capitals into this trade. The Indians employ still larger sums in it. The impossibility of enjoying their fortunes under an oppressive government, does not deter the natives of this country from labouring incessantly to increase them. As they would run too great a risque by engaging openly in trade, they are obliged to have recourse to clandestine methods. As soon as an European arrives, the Gentoos, who know mankind better than is commonly supposed, study his character: and if they find him frugal, active, and well informed, offer to act as his brokers and cashiers, and lend or procure him money upon bottomry, or at interest. This interest, which is usually nine per cent. at least, is higher, when he is under a necessity of borrowing of the Cheyks.

These Cheyks are a powerful family of Indians, who have, time immemorial, inhabited the banks of the Ganges. Their riches have long

* 1,225,000l.

ago

IN THE EAST AND WEST INDIES. 427

ago procured them the management of the bank belonging to the court, the farming of the public revenue, and the direction of the money, which they coin afresh every year, in order to receive annually the benefit arising from the mint. By uniting so many advantages, they are enabled to lend the government, forty*, sixty †, or even a hundred millions ‡ at a time. When the government finds it impossible to refund the money, they are allowed to indemnify themselves by oppressing the people. That so prodigious a capital should be preserved in the center of tyranny, and in the midst of revolutions, appears incredible. It is not possible to conceive how such a structure could be raised, much less how it could be supported for so long a time. To explain this mystery it must be observed, that this family has always maintained a superior influence at the court of Delhi; that the Nabobs and Rajahs in Bengal are dependent upon it; that those who are about the person of the subah have constantly been its creatures; and that the subah himself has been maintained or dethroned by the intrigues of this family. To this we may add, that the different branches of it, and the wealth belonging to them being dispersed, it has never been possible to ruin above one half of the family at a time, which would still have left them more resources than were necessary to enable them to pursue their revenge to the utmost. The Europeans who

* 1,750,000l.   † 2,625,000l.   ‡ 4,375,000l.

frequent

frequent the Ganges have not been sufficiently alarmed at this despotism, which ought to have prevented them from submitting to a dependence upon the Cheyks. They have fallen into the snare, by borrowing considerable sums of these avaritious financiers, apparently at nine, but in reality at thirteen per cent. if we take into the account the difference between the money that is lent them, and that in which they are obliged to make their payments. The engagements entered into by the French and Dutch companies have been kept within some bounds; but those of the English company have been unlimited. In 1755 they were indebted to the Cheyks about eight and twenty millions *.

Such is the conduct of this considerable set of men, who are sole managers of the European trade at Bengal. The Portuguese, who first frequented this rich country, had the wisdom to establish themselves at Chatigan, a port situated upon the frontier of Arracan, not far from the most eastern branch of the Ganges. The Dutch, who, without incurring the resentment of an enemy at that time so formidable, were desirous of sharing in their good fortune, were engaged in searching for a port, which, without obstructing their plan, would expose them the least to hostilities. In 1603, their attention was directed to Balasore; and all the companies, rather through imitation than in consequence of any well concerted schemes, followed their ex-

* 1,225,000L.

ample.

IN THE EAST AND WEST INDIES.

ample. Experience taught them the propriety of fixing as near as poffible to the markets from whence they had their merchandife; and they failed up that branch of the Ganges, which feparating itfelf from the main river at Mourcha above Caffim-buzar, falls into the fea near Balafore under the name of the river Hughly. The government of the country permitted them to erect warehoufes wherever there was plenty of manufactures, and to fortify themfelves upon this river.

The firft town that is met with in paffing up the river is Calcutta, the principal fettlement of the Englifh company. The air here is unhealthy, the water brackifh, the anchorage not very fafe, and the neighbouring country affords but few manufactures. Notwithftanding thefe inconveniences, great numbers of rich Armenian, Moorifh, and India merchants, invited by the profpect of liberty and fecurity, have fixed their refidence here. The people have multiplied in proportion through a territory of three or four leagues in circumference, of which the company are the fole fovereigns. The fortrefs has this advantage, that the veffels bound to the European fettlements are obliged to pafs under its cannon.

Six leagues higher is fituated Frederic Nagore founded by the Danes in 1756, in order to fupply the place of an ancient fettlement, where they could not maintain their ground. This new eftablifhment has not yet acquired any importance, and there is all the reafon imaginable to believe, that it will never become confiderable.

CHAN-

CHANDERNAGORE, which lies two leagues and an half higher, belongs to the French. It has the difadvantage of being fomewhat expofed on the weftern fide; but its harbour is excellent, and the air is as pure as it can be on the banks of the Ganges. Whenever any building is undertaken that requires ftrength, it muft here, as well as in all other parts of Bengal, be built upon piles: it being impoffible to dig three or four feet deep without coming at water. This diftrict, which is hardly a league in circumference, has been crouded with manufactures ever fince the invafion of the Marattas obliged the natives of the country to retire hither for refuge. Here is a large manufacture of handkerchiefs, and ftriped muflins; which have, indeed, rather degenerated fince their removal. This active fpirit of induftry has not, however, made Chandernagore the rival of Calcutta, whofe immenfe riches enable it to undertake the moft extenfive commercial enterprizes.

At the diftance of a mile from Chandernagore, is Chinfura, better known by the name of Dougli, being fituated near the fuburbs of that antiently renowned city. The Dutch have no other poffeffions there, but merely their fort; the territory round it, depending on the government of the country, which hath frequently made it feel its power by its extortions. Another inconvenience attending this fettlement is a fand-bank that prevents fhips from coming up to it; they proceed no further than Tulta, which is twenty miles below

IN THE EAST AND WEST INDIES.

below Calcutta, and this of courfe occafions an additional expence to the government.

THE Portuguefe had formerly made Bandel, which is eighty leagues from the mouth of the Ganges, and a quarter of a league above the Hughly, the principal feat of their commerce. Their flag is ftill difplayed, and there are a few unhappy wretches remaining there, who have forgotten their country after having been forgotten by it. This factory has no other employment than that of fupplying the Moors and the Dutch with miftreffes.

EXCEPT in the months of October, November, and December, when the frequent and almoft continued hurricanes render the Gulph of Bengal impracticable; European fhips may enter the Ganges during the remainder of the year. Thofe that defign to go up the river, previoufly touch at Point Palmiras, where they are received by pilots of their own nation who refide at Balafore. The money they convey is put on board fome floops of between fixty and a hundred tons belonging to the harbour, which always precede the fhips. The paffage into the river Hughly lies through a narrow ftraight between two fand-banks. The fhips ufed formerly to come to an anchor at Culpy, but time has worn off the dread of thofe currents, quickfands, and fhoals that feemed to choke up the navigation of the river, and the fhips have been brought up to their refpective places of deftination. This boldnefs has occafioned many fhip-wrecks; but in proportion as more experience has been gained, and the fpirit of obfervation has been

carried

carried further, accidents of that kind have been lefs frequent. It is to be hoped that the example of admiral Watfon, who failed as high as Chandernagore in a feventy-gun-fhip, will not be forgotten; as a proper attention to it would fave a great deal of time, trouble and expence.

BESIDES this great channel, there is another by which goods may be brought from the places which furnifh them to the principal fettlement of each company. For this purpofe a number of fmall fleets are employed, confifting of eighty or a hundred veffels, and fometimes more. Thefe are manned with black or white foldiers, in order to check the infatiable avarice of the Nabobs and Rajas they meet with in their paffage. The goods purchafed in the higher parts of the Ganges, at Patna and Caffimbuzar, are carried down the river Hughly: thofe purchafed near the other branches of the Ganges, which are all navigable in the interior parts of the country, and communicate with each other, efpecially towards the lower divifion of that river, are conveyed into the Hughly by Rangafoula and Batatola, about fifteen or twenty leagues from the fea. From thence they are carried up the ftream to the principal fettlement belonging to each nation.

THE exports from Bengal to Europe confift of mufk, gum-lac, nicaragua wood, pepper, cowries, and fome other articles of lefs importance brought thither from other places. Thofe that are the immediate produce of the country are borax, faltpetre, filk, filk-ftuffs, muflins and feveral different forts of cottons.

THE

THE borax which is found in the province of Patna, is a saline substance, which the chymist in Europe have in vain attempted to counterfeit. Some of them take it for an alkaline salt, which is found completely formed in the rich country of Indostan; others will have it to be the produce of volcanoes, or subterraneous fires.

BE this as it may, the borax is of great use in the working of metals by facilitating their fusion and purification. This substance being quickly vitrified by the action of fire, attracts the heterogeneous particles that are intermixed with these metals, and reduces them to drofs. The borax is likewise absolutely necessary in the essaying of mines, and the soldering of metals. The Dutch alone have the secret of refining it, which is said to have been communicated to them by some Venetian families that came to seek that liberty in the united provinces which they did not enjoy under the tyranny of their own aristocratical government.

SALTPETRE is likewise the produce of Patna. It is extracted from a clay, which is either black, whitish or red. The manner of refining it is by digging a large pit, in which the nitrous earth is deposited, and diluted with a quantity of water, which is kept stirred till it comes to a consistency. The water having drawn out all the salts, and the grosser parts subsiding at the bottom, the more fluid particles are taken out and put into another pit not so large as the former. This substance having undergone a second purification, the clear water that swims on the top, and is totally impregnated

pregnated with nitre, is taken off, and boiled in caldrons; it is skimmed while it is boiling, and, in a few hours, a nitrous salt is obtained infinitely superior to any that is found elsewhere. The Europeans export about ten millions of pounds for the use of their settlements in Asia, or for home consumption in their respective countries. It is bought upon the spot for three sols * a pound, at the most, and is sold again to us for ten † at the least.

CASSIMBUZAR, which is grown rich by the ruin of Malda and Rajamahal, is the general market for Bengal silk, the greatest part of which is supplied from that territory. The silk-worms are brought up and fed there in the same manner as in other places; but the heat of the climate hatches them and brings them to perfection at all times of the year. A great quantity of silk and cotton stuffs are manufactured here, which are circulated through part of Asia: those that are made entirely of silk, are for the most part carried to Delhi. They are prohibited in France; and throughout the north of Europe, the consumption in these articles is almost entirely confined to a few armozeens, and a prodigious number of handkerchiefs. As for the unwrought silk, the quantity consumed in the European manufactures may be estimated at three or four hundred thousand pounds weight. It is in general of a very inferior quality, ill twisted, and takes no gloss in dying. It is of little use except for the woof in brocades; and is sold upon the spot from 272 to 288 livres ‡ a quintal. The

* 1 d. ½   † 5 d.   ‡ From 11 l. 18 s. to 12 l. 12 s.

companies

IN THE EAST AND WEST INDIES.

companies that have a capital, and induftry and ſkill fufficient to twift it in their own warehoufes, obtain it at a cheaper rate.

It would be a tedious and ufelefs tafk to enumerate all the places where ticken and cottons, fit for table linnen, or intended to be worn plain, painted or printed, are manufactured. It will be fufficient to mention Dacca, which may be looked upon as the general mart of Bengal, where the greateft variety of fineft cottons are to be met with, and in the greateft abundance.

This town is fituated in twenty-four degrees north latitude. The fertility of its foil, and the advantages of its fituation have long fince made it the center of an extenfive commerce. The courts of Delhi and Muxadavad are furnifhed from thence with the cottons wanted for their own confumption. They each of them maintain an agent on the fpot to fuperintend the manufacture of them; who has an authority independent of the magiftrate over the brokers, weavers, embroiderers, and all the workmen, whofe bufinefs has any relation to the object of his commiffion. Thefe unhappy people are forbidden, under pecuniary and corporal penalties, to fell to any perfon whatever a piece exceeding the value of 72 livres *: nor can they, but by dint of money, relieve themfelves from this oppreffion.

In this, as in all the other markets, the European companies treat with Moorifh brokers fettled upon the fpot, and appointed by the government.

* Three guineas.

They

They likewife lend their name to the individuals of their own nation as well as to Indians and Armenians living in their fettlements, who, without this precaution, would infallibly be plundered. The Moors themfelves, in their private tranfactions, frequently avail themfelves of the fame pretence, that they may pay only two inftead of five per cent.

A DISTINCTION is obferved, in their contracts, between the cottons that are befpoken, and thofe which the weaver ventures, in fome places, to manufacture upon his own account. The length, the number of threads, and the price of the former are fixed: nothing further than the commiffion for the latter is ftipulated, becaufe it is impoffible to enter into the fame detail. Thofe nations that make a point of having fine goods, take proper meafures, that they may be enabled to advance money to their workmen at the beginning of the year. The weavers, who in general have but little employment at that time, perform their work with lefs hurry than in the months of October, November and December, when the demand is preffing.

SOME of the cottons are delivered unbleached, and others half bleached. It were to be wifhed, that this cuftom might be altered. It is very common to fee cottons, that look very beautiful, go off in the bleaching. Perhaps the manufacturers and brokers forefee how they will turn out: but the Europeans have not fo exquifite a touch, nor fuch an experienced eye as to difcern this. It is a circumftance peculiar to India, that cottons, of
what

IN THE EAST AND WEST INDIES.
what kind foever they are, can never be well bleached and prepared but in the place where they are manufactured. If they have the misfortune to get damaged before they are shipped for Europe, they must be sent back to the places from whence they came.

AMONG the cottons purchased at Dacca, the plain striped and worked muslins are, beyond all comparison, of the greatest importance. Bengal is the sole country in India where they are made, as it produces the only cotton proper for that manufacture. It is planted at the end of october, and gathered in February; when it is prepared with all expedition, that it may be ready for the loom in the months of May, June, and July. This is the rainy season; and as the cotton shrinks more, and is less apt to break at this time, it is therefore the fittest for the purpose of manufacturing muslins. The artists who work at other seasons of the year, give the cotton its requisite degree of moistness, by dipping the part immediately under the warp into water. In this sense we are to understand what is said of fabricating muslins in water.

To whatever degree of fineness these cottons have been brought, it is certain it falls very short of the perfection of which they are capable. The practice of the government in obliging the best manufactures to work on its account, in paying them ill, and keeping them in a state of captivity, makes them afraid of displaying too much skill. A prevailing spirit of restraint and rigour stifles industry,

industry, which though the daughter of necessity, is at the same time the companion of liberty.

THE courts of Delhi and Muxadavad lay no great stress upon the embroidered work wrought upon muslins: and the people of the country, the Moors, Patans, and Armenians, who give large orders, follow their example, and take them as they find them. This indifference hinders the progress of the art of embroidery. The Europeans agree for embroideries as they do for muslins and other merchandise, with brokers authorized by the government, to which they pay an annual contribution for this exclusive privilege. These agents assign to the women the pieces designed for low embroidery, and those in chain-work to the men. The Europeans frequently content themselves with Indian patterns; at other times they send patterns for stripes and embroideries.

THE sum total of the purchases made in Bengal by the European nations amounted, a few years ago, to no more than twenty millions of livres*. One third of this sum was paid in iron, lead, copper, woollens, and Dutch spices: the remainder was discharged in money. Since the English have made themselves masters of this rich country, its exports have been increased, and its imports diminished, because the conquerors have carried away a greater quantity of merchandise, and pay for it out of the revenues they receive from the country. There is reason to believe, that this revolution in the trade of Bengal has not arrived at

* Above 8;0,0col.

IN THE EAST AND WEST INDIES.

its crisis, and that sooner or later it will be attended with more important consequences and effects.

To maintain their correspondence with this vast country, and their other Asiatic settlements, the English company have fixed upon St. Helena as a place of refreshment. This island which is only between twenty-eight and twenty-nine miles in circumference, lies in fifteen degrees fifty minutes south latitude, between Africa and America, and almost at an equal distance from those two quarters of the globe. It does not appear that the Portuguese, who discovered it in 1502, ever established a colony there; but it is certain that, agreeable to their usual method, they put on shore some cattle and poultry for the use of the ships that might touch there. These conveniencies invited the Dutch to form a small settlement upon the island, which they were afterwards dispossessed of by the English, who have been settled there ever since the year 1673.

Thouh St. Helena appears to be nothing but a large rock, beaten on all sides by the waves, it is nevertheless a delightful spot. The climate is more temperate than might be expected; the soil, which is only a foot and a half deep, is covered with citrons, palms, pomegranates and other trees, laden with flowers and fruit at the same time; while streams of excellent water, which nature has distributed better than art could have done, enliven the whole scence. Those who are born in this fortunate abode enjoy a perfect state of health; passengers are here cured of their disorders, particularly

cularly of the scurvy. Four hundred families composed of English, and of French refugees, cultivate vegetables, and breed cattle, which are of an exquisite flavour, and of great service to the ships crews that put in there. This settlement, which nature and art have united to render almost impregnable, has, however, one grand defect; the ships that return from India to Europe land there with ease and security, but the outward-bound ships cannot reach this asylum, being strongly repelled by winds and adverse currents. To avoid the inconveniences attending so long a voyage, when made without stopping, several of them put in at the Cape of Good Hope; others, particularly those bound to Arabia and Malabar, take in refreshments at the islands of Comora.

The use the English make of the islands of Comora.

THESE islands, that lie in the Mozambique channel, between the coast of Zanguebar and Madagascar, are five in number; the principal one, from which this small archipelago takes its name, is little known. The Portuguese, who discovered it in the course of their first expeditions, brought the name of Europeans into such detestation by their cruelties, that all who have since ventured to go on shore there have either been massacred or very ill treated. It has accordingly been quite forsaken. The islands of Mayota, Moeti, and Anjuan, are not more frequented, on account of the difficulty of approaching them, and the want of a safe anchorage. The English vessels put in at the island of Joanna.

HERE it is that, within the compass of thirty leagues, nature displays all her riches, with all

her

her simplicity. Hills that are ever green, and vallies that are always gay, every where present a variety of delightful landscapes. Thirty thousand inhabitants, distributed into seventy-three villages, share its productions. They speak the Arabic language, and their religion is a very corrupt sort of Mohammedism; their moral principles are more refined than they usually are in this part of the globe; the habit they have contracted of living upon milk and vegetables has given them an unconquerable aversion for labour. This laziness is the cause of a particular air of consequence, which consists, among persons of distinction, in suffering the nails to grow to an immoderate length. In order that this negligence may have the appearance of beauty, they tinge their nails with a yellowish red, which they extract from a shrub.

THESE people, born to be indolent, have lost that liberty which they, doubtless, came hither to enjoy from a neighbouring continent, of which they were the original inhabitants. An Arabian trader, not quite a century ago, having killed a Portuguese gentleman at Mozambique, threw himself into a boat, which chance conducted to Joanna. This stranger made such good use of his superior abilities, and the assistance of a few of his countrymen, that he acquired an absolute authority, which is still maintained by his grandson. The change in the government did not at all diminish the liberty and security enjoyed by the English, who landed upon the island. They continued to put their sick on shore without molestation,

tion, where the wholefomenefs of the air, the excellence of the fruits, provifions, and water, foon reftored them to health. They were only obliged to give a higher price for the provifions they wanted, for which the following reafons may be affigned.

THE Arabians having been induced to frequent an ifland governed by an Arab, have brought the Indian manufactures into vogue; and as the cowries, cocoa-nuts, and other commodities they received in exchange, were not fufficient to defray the expence of this article of luxury, the iflanders have been obliged to demand money for their goats and poultry, which they before exchanged for glafs beads, and other baubles of as little value. This innovation has not, however, made the Englifh defert a place of refrefhment, which has no other inconvenience than that of being at too great a diftance from our latitudes.

The Englifh company leave the country trade to private adventurers.

A SIMILAR inconvenience did not prevent the Englifh company from extending their trade very confiderably. The intercourfe carried on between one port of India and another was too confined, and of too little confequence, to engage their attention for any long time. They were foon fufficiently enlightened to perceive that it was not for their interft to continue this kind of commerce; and therefore invited the private traders of their own nation to embark in it. They lent them their affiftance, by taking a fhare in their expeditions, and granting them privileges on board their own fleets, and frequently even undertook to be the carriers of their merchandife at a low freight,

This

This generous behaviour reufulting from a national fpirit, and fo diametrically oppofite to that of other companies, quickly gave activity, ftrength, and credit, to the Englifh fettlements. Their free merchants were foon in poffeffion of a dozen brigantines, that were employed within the Ganges, or were difpatched from thence to Acham, Keda, Johor and Ligor. They fitted out an equal number of larger veffels from Calcutta, Madras, and Bombay, which frequented all the fea-ports in the eaft. Thefe veffels would have been ftill more numerous, had not the company exacted a duty of five per cent. in all the places where they had fettlements, and eight and a half per cent. upon all the remittances made by the free merchants to the capital. When their neceffities did not compel them to remit part of thefe unreafonable demands, thefe merchants lent their money upon bottomry, fometimes to other European merchants that wanted it, but moft frequently to the captains of fhips belonging to their own nation, who, not being ftrictly dependent upon the company, can traffic for others in the voyages they make for them.

AT its firft rife, this great body was ambitious of maintaining a maritime force. This was quite laid afide when they refumed their operations in the time of the Protector. Having nothing then in view but profit, they refolved to embark the goods on private bottoms; and what was then done through neceffity, has fince been continued through œconomy. There are merchants who furnifh them with fhips, completely rigged and victualled,

The company judge it improper to keep up their navy.

victualled, to carry out to India, and bring back to Europe, such a number of tons as they contract for. The time they are to stay at the place of their destination is always fixed. Those which happen to have no cargo to bring back, are usually hired by some free merchant, who engages to indemnify the owner. These are always the first sent home the following year, to prevent their rigging from being too much worn. In cases of necessity the company will equip them out of their own storehouses; but they require the payment of a stipulated rate of fifty per cent. advance on them.

The vessels employed in this navigation carry from six to eight hundred tons burden. At their departure the company occupy just so much room as is sufficient to hold their iron, their lead, their copper, their woollens, and Madeira wine, which are the only merchandise they send to India. The owners are allowed to store the remaining part of each vessel with the provisions necessary for so long a voyage, and any other articles which the society they are concerned for do not trade in. On their return, they have likewise a right to assign to any use they think proper a space equal to thirty tons, which, by their contract, is reserved to themselves: they may even take in the same articles as are embarked for the company. Till lately they used to pay the company thirty per cent. on the value of these commodies; but since the 21st of October 1773, this duty has been reduced to one-half. It was thought that this indulgence would dispose the owners and their agents more punctually

IN THE EAST AND WEST INDIES.

punctually to fulfil their engagements, and would put a stop to fraudulent importations. The spirit of humanity, which is more common in free states than in others, has in England given rise to a very commendable custom: the surgeon of each ship that arrives from India receives, besides his pay, twenty-two livres ten sols*, by way of gratuity for every man in the ship's company whom he brings back to Europe.

THE company, disengaged from the trouble necessarily attending the maintenance of a navy, as well as from the country trade in India, had no other object to take up their attention than the commerce carried on directly between Europe and Asia. They entered upon it with a capital of 8,322,547 livres 10 sols †; and, in 1676, having by fortunate events been enabled to make a division of cent. per cent. they thought it most for their interest to double their capital. This capital still kept increasing, till in 1702 the two companies that had so obstinately opposed each other, threw their wealth, their plans, and their hopes, into one common stock. It has since risen to seventy-two millions ‡ divided into shares, originally of 1,125 ‖, and afterwards of 2,250 livres §.

THE trade was, in the beginning, carried on with great spirit and success, notwithstanding the smallness of their stock. As early as the year 1628, the company employed twelve thousand tons of shipping, and four thousand seamen.

Capital of the company.

Extent of the company's trade.

---

* Near 20 shillings. † 364,111l. 9d. ¾. ‡ 3,150,000l.
‖ Not quite 5cl. § Not quite 100l.

Their

Their expeditions varied in an inconceivable manner; and were more or lefs confiderable, according to the ignorance or capacity of thofe who conducted them; the different ftates of peace or war, the profperity, or misfortune of the mother country, the fondnefs or indifference of the Europeans for Indian manufactures; and the different degrees of competition they met with from other nations. Since the beginning of the prefent century, thefe changes have been neither fo frequent, nor fo remarkable. The trade has been eftablifhed upon a more firm bafis, and the fales have rifen to feventy-eight millions *.

THE increafe of their trade would have been ftill greater, had it not been for the reftraints that were laid upon it. To enter into a detail of thefe would be too long and too minute a tafk. It will be fufficient to mention, that every fhip returning from India is obliged to unlade in England, and that thofe which bring prohibited goods are compelled to land them at the port of London. The cottons and ftuffs that come from thefe countries pay very high duties; thofe levied upon tea are ftill higher. If the government hoped, by laying on fo enormous a tax, to abate the exceffive fondnefs of the people for this liquor, its expectations have not been anfwered.

TEA whas introduced into England by the Lords Arlington and Offory, who imported it from Holland in 1666, and their ladies brought it into fafhion among people of their own rank. At that

* Above 3,400,000l.

time

IN THE EAST AND WEST INDIES.
time it fold in London for fixty-feven or fixty-eight livres * a pound, though it coft but three or four at Batavia. Notwithftanding the price was kept up with very little variation, the fondnefs for this liquor gained ground; it was not, however, brought into common ufe till towards the year 1715, when green tea began to be drunk, whereas till then no fort was known but the bohea. The fondnefs for this Afiatic plant has fince become univerfal. Perhaps, the phrenzy is not without its inconveniences; but it cannot be denied, that it has contributed more to the fobriety of the nation than the fevereft laws, the moft eloquent harangues of chriftian orators, or the beft treatifes of morality.

In 1766 fix millions of pounds of tea were brought from China by the Englifh, four millions five hundred thoufand by the Dutch, two millions four hundred thoufand by the Swedes, the fame quantity by the Danes, and two millions one hundred thoufand by the French. The fum total of thefe quantities amounts to feventeen millions four hundred thoufand pounds. The preference given by moft nations to chocolate, coffee, and other liquors, joined to a feries of obfervations carefully purfued for feveral years, and the moft exact calculations that can poffibly be made in fuch complicated cafes, inclines us to think that the whole confumption throughout Europe does not exceed five millions four hundred thoufand pounds. In this cafe, that of Great Britain muft be twelve millions.

* About 3l.

It

It is universally allowed, that there are at least two millions in the mother country, and a million in the colonies, which constantly drink tea. It is not unreasonable to suppose, that each individual of these consumes four pounds in a year; but should the quantity be something less, the deficiency is supplied by those who are less attached to it, and who for this reason have not been taken into the account. A pound of tea, which costs only thirty sols* in the east, constantly sells in England for six livres ten sols † including the duty: consequently the rage for this Asiatic plant costs the nation about seventy-two millions ‡.

To oppose the entries of the custom-house to this computation would argue either ignorance or artifice. It is true that the amount of the duties, which, according to this calculation, ought to be about 18,000,000 livres ||, is hardly half so much; but the contraband trade in this commodity carried on in England is notorious. The government itself is so thoroughly convinced of it, that, in order to lessen it, it has lately lowered the duty twenty sols § a pound. In all probability it would have been still more generous, had it not unfortunately been under the necessity of considering its customs as a resource of finance, rather than as the regulator of its commerce. This relaxation, which of itself is not sufficient to prevent the teas in the different ports of Europe from being smuggled into Great Britain, has been rendered more efficaci-

---

* About 1s. 4d. † Near six shillings. ‡ About 3,150,000l.
|| Near 790,000l. § 10d.

IN THE EAST AND WEST INDIES.

ous by the national acquisition of the isle of Man, which belonged to the Athol family.

Though most branches of the public revenue have been increased by an arrangement, which deprived the illicit trader of his most convenient market, the Indian company have been particularly benefited by it. As their commodities were subjected to higher duties than any others, the clandestine importation of them was more common, and was principally carried on by the isle of Man, which is extremely well situated to receive every thing that comes from the North. Tea was the favourite object of this contraband trade. The English company will not fail, in future, to provide as much stock as may answer their demands, and to secure to themselves the advantages which their rivals came to carry away from them even within the limits of their own empire.

The teas and other merchandise that arrive from India are paid for in money. The government, which is not ignorant of this, has limited the exportation of specie to 6,750,000 livres*. This unaccountable restriction, so unworthy a commercial people, neither has been or can be carried into execution. The sums registered are always much higher; but this indulgence does not prevent considerable sums from being clandestinely carried abroad without the knowledge of the custom-house officers. These fraudulent practices have increased in proportion as the trade has

* About 295,000 l.

become

become more extensive; and the money sent out of the kingdom has been long computed at one third of the profit arising from the sales.

This exportation of specie would have been more considerable, if the company had adhered to that article in their charter, by which it is provided, that they shall export in merchandise of their own nation, the value of the tenth part of what they take in money upon their vessels. They have constantly made a charge for much greater sums in tin, lead, and English cloths, without reckoning the profits made in India upon iron from Sweden and Biscay, and other articles taken from several countries of Europe.

Their advocates, in order to reinstate them in the good opinion of the public, which they have but seldom enjoyed, have frequently asserted, that this body occasioned as much money to be brought into the country, as they carried out of it. This plea caused such a warm altercation in the beginning of the present century, that the government thought the question not unworthy of its attention. It was found by consulting the registers, that from the end of December 1712 to the end of December 1717, there had been exported to India 52,563,037 livres 10 sols[*]. From all circumstances it appeared, that the money clandestinely carried out amounted, at least to one half; and that consequently there could be no mistake in estimating the amount of both these sums at 78,844,566 livres 5 sols[†]. The

[*] 2,299,632 l. 17 s. 9 d. ¾. [†] 3,449,449 l.

IN THE EAST AND WEST INDIES.

fums remitted home by the company, in the fame fpace of time, amounted to 75,058,391 livres 5 fols *. Thus, fuppofing thefe calculations to be juft, the confumption of the Afiatic productions in England for five years, fhould not have rifen fo high as 3,786,165 livres †: but there is reafon to believe that it rofe much higher; and that a great deal of merchandife apparently fold to foreigners, never ftirred out of the kingdom. The partiality that has lately prevailed in favour of Scotch and Irifh linens printed in England, and the increafe of the filk manufacture, by leffening the demand for contraband goods, muft of neceffity render the commerce of the Eaft more advantageous to the nation. Before the year 1720, Great Britain annually confumed three millions feven hundred and fifty thoufand yards of India cottons; but this confumption is greatly diminifhed.

It is not to be fuppofed, that any changes could happen in the connections of the Indian trade with the ftate in general, without producing fome alterations in the private fhares of the proprietors. Their profits have at certain periods been enormous; at others, very flender. The fhares have been regulated in conformity to thefe variations. The dividend, which, for a long time, had been no more than feven per cent. was, in 1743, raifed to eight. It was afterwards reduced to fix; in 1766 it rofe to ten, and fince that time to twelve and a half. This was more than the fituation of

Dividends of the proprietors.

* 3,283,8241. 12s. 1d. ½.   † About 165,645 l.

the company could afford; since, at this period, they had little more remaining than their original capital. It this be the case, how has it happpened that so small a capital should, in the opinion of the public, have acquired the value of 280,000,000*, which is the amount according to the price of the stock.

It is not impossible to answer this objection. The enthusiasm of the English is well known. It has repeatedly been excited by circumstances that would not have made the least impression on the most volatile and trifling people. An important event has had a powerful effect upon the whole nation. They have abandoned themselves with all the impetuosity of their character to the vast prospects that were opened to them by the recent conquest of Bengal.

Conquest of Bengal. Advantages drawn by the English from t... acquisition, and the conduct they have hitherto observed.

Should it be asked, if this astonishing revolution, which has had so sensible an influence, both upon the state of the inhabitants of this part of Asia, and upon the trade of the European nations in these climates, hath been the consequence and result of a series of political schemes?— If it be one of those events, of which prudence has a right to claim the merit? We shall answer, No. Chance alone has determined it: and the circumstances that have opened this field of glory and power to the English, far from promising them the success they have had, seemed on the contrary to threaten them with the most fatal reverse of fortune.

* Above 12,250,000l.

A PER

IN THE EAST AND WEST INDIES.

A PERNICIOUS cuftom had for fome time prevailed in thefe countries. The governors of all the European fettlements took upon them to grant an affylum to fuch of the natives of the country as were afraid of oppreffion or punifhment. As they received very confiderable fums in return for their protection, they overlooked the danger to which the interefts of their principals were expofed by this proceeding. One of the chief officers of Bengal, who was apprized of this refource, took refuge among the Englifh at Calcutta to avoid the punifhment due to his treachery. He was taken under their protection. The fubah, juftly irritated, put himfelf at the head of his army, attacked the place, and took it. He put the garrifon into a clofe dungeon, where they were fuffocated in the fpace of twelve hours. Three and twenty of them only remained alive. Thefe wretched people offered large fums to the keeper of their prifon, to prevail upon him to get their deplorable fituation reprefented to the prince. Their cries and lamentations were fufficient informations to the people, who were touched with compaffion; but no one would venture to addrefs the defpotic monarch upon the fubject. The expiring Englifh were told that he was afleep; and there was not, perhaps, a fingle perfon in Bengal who thought that the tyrant's flumbers fhould be interrupted for one moment, even to preferve the lives of one hundred and fifty unfortunate men.

ADMIRAL

Admiral Watson, who was juft arrived in India with his fquadron, and Colonel Clive who had fo remarkably diftinguifhed himfelf in the war of the Carnatic, did not delay to avenge the caufe of their country. They got together the Englifh who had been difperfed, and were flying from place to place; they went up the Ganges in the month of December 1756, retook Calcutta, made themfelves mafters of feveral other places, and gained a complete victory over the fubah.

Such a rapid and extenfive fuccefs becomes in a manner inconceivable, when we confider that it was only with a body of five hundred men that the Englifh was to ftand againft the whole force of Bengal. But if their fuperiority was partly owing to their better difcipline, and to other evident advantages that the Europeans have in battle over the Indian powers; the ambition of eaftern chiefs, the avarice of their minifters, and the nature of a government, whofe only fprings are fear and prefent intereft, were of ftill more effectual fervice to them: they had experience enough to take advantage of the concurrence of thefe feveral circumftances in their firft, as well as in every fucceeding enterprize. The fubah was detefted by all his own people, as tyrants generally are; the principal officers fold their intereft to the Englifh; he was betrayed at the head of his army, the greateft part of which refufed to engage; and he himfelf fell into the hands of his enemies, who caufed him to be ftrangled in prifon.

The

IN THE EAST AND WEST INDIES.

They difpofed of the fubahfhip in favour of
Jaffier-Ally-Khan, the ring-leader of the confpiracy;
who ceded to the company fome provinces, with
a grant of every privilege, exemption and favour,
to which they could have any pretenfion. But foon
growing weary of the yoke he had brought upon
himfelf, he was fecretly looking out for means to
get rid of it. His defigns were difcovered, and he
was confined in the center of his own capital.

Cossim-Ally-Khan, his nephew, was proclaimed in his ftead. He had purchafed that
ufurpation with an immenfe fum of money. But
he did not enjoy it long. Impatient of the yoke,
as his predeceffor had been, he gave fome tokens
of his difpofition, and refufed to fubmit to the
laws the company impofed upon him. Upon
this the war broke out again. The fame Jaffier-Ally-Khan, whom the Englifh kept in confinement, was again proclaimed fubah of Bengal.
They marched againft Coffim-Ally-Khan. His
general officers were corrupted: he was betrayed
and entirely defeated: too happy, that whilft he
loft his dignity, he ftill preferved the immenfe treafures he had amaffed.

Notwithstanding this revolution, Coffim-
Ally did not drop his hopes of vengeance. Full
of refentment, and loaded with treafure, he fet
out for the nabob of Bennares, chief vifir in the
Mogul's empire. He and all the neighbouring
princes re-united in oppofition to the common
enemy, who threatened them all equally. But
now the conteft lay no longer between them
and

and a handful of Europeans juft arrived from the coaft of Coromandel; they were to engage with the whole ftrength of Bengal, of which the Englifh were mafters. Elated with their fucceffes, they did not wait to be attacked; they fet out directly and made head againft fo formidable a league, marching on with all the confidence which Clive could infpire, a leader, whofe name feemed to have become the pledge of conqueft. However, Clive did not care to hazard any thing. Part of the campaign was fpent in negociations; but in time the treafures which the Englifh had already drawn from Bengal, ferved to enfure them new conquefts. The heads of the Indian army were corrupted; and when the nabob of Bennares was defirous of coming to action, he was obliged to fly with his men without ever being able to engage.

By this victory, the country of Bennares fell into the hands of the Englifh: and it feemed as if nothing could hinder them from annexing that fovereignty to that of Bengal: but either from moderation or prudence, they were content to levy eight millions by contribution: and they offered peace to the nabob on conditions which would render him incapable of doing them any hurt; but fuch as they were, he moft readily agreed to them, that he might regain the poffeffion of his own provinces.

In the midft of thefe calamities, Coffim-Ally ftill found means to preferve part of his treafures, and retired to the Cheyks, a people fituated in the neighbourhood of Delhi, from whence he

IN THE EAST AND WEST INDIES.

he made an attempt to procure fome allies, and to raife up a body of enemies to oppofe the Englifh.

WHILE matters were thus circumftanced in Bengal, the Mogul having been driven out of Delhi by the Pattans, by whom his fon had been fet up in his room, was wandering from one province to another in fearch of a place of refuge in his own territories, and requefting fuccour from his own vaffals, but without fuccefs. Abandoned by his fubjects, betrayed by his allies, without fupport, and without any army, he was allured by the power of the Englifh, and implored their protection; they promifed to conduct him to Delhi, and re-eftablifh him on his throne; but they infifted that he fhould previoufly cede to them the abfolute fovereignty over Bengal. This ceffion was made by an authentic act, and attended with all the formalities ufually practifed throughout the Mogul empire.

THE Englifh, poffeffed of this title, which was to give a kind of legitimacy to their ufurpation, at leaft in the eyes of the vulgar, foon forgot the promifes they had made. They gave the Mogul to underftand, that particular circumftances would not fuffer them to be concerned in fuch an enterprife; that fome better opportunity was to be hoped for; and to make up for all his loffes, they affigned him a penfion of fix millions * with the revenue of Illahabad, and

* 262, 500l.

Shah

Sha Ichanabad or Delhi; upon which that unfortunate prince was reduced to subsist himself in one of the principal towns of the province of Bennares, where he had taken up his residence. Thus the Mogul empire comes to be shared between two governing powers, one of which is acknowledged in the several districts of India, where the English company has any establishments and authority; the other in such provinces as border on Delhi, and in those parts to which the influence of that company does not extend.

The English, thus become sovereigns of Bengal, have thought it incumbent on them to keep up the shadow of ancient forms, in a country where they have the lead, and, perhaps, the only power that is likely to be secure and lasting. They govern the kingdom still under the name of a subah, who is of their nomination and in their pay, and seems to give his own orders. It is from him that all publick acts seem to proceed and issue, though the decrees are in fact the result of the deliberations of the council at Calcutta; so that the people, notwithstanding their change of masters, have for a considerable time been induced to believe, that they still submitted but to the same yoke.

If we should wish to know the amount of the public revenues of Bengal, we shall find at the period of its conquest, it was equal to fourscore millions.* The outgoings, either for the government, or defence of the province,

* 3,500,000l.

were

IN THE EAST AND WEST INDIES.

were stated at forty-one millions *; six millions †
were agreed to be given to the Mogul, and three
millions ‡ to the nabob; so that the remainder
to the company was thirty millions §. Their
purchases in the different marts of India should
absorb a great part of this sum; but still it has
been thought there must after all remain a surplus of several millions to be carried into Great
Britain.

This new arrangement of matters, without
having wrought any sensible change in the exterior form of the English company, has essentially changed their object. They are no longer
a trading body, they are a territorial power which
farm out their revenues in aid of a commerce
that formerly was their sole existence, and which,
notwithstanding the extension it has received, is
no more than an additional object in the various combinations of their present real grandeur.
The arrangements intended to give stability to
a situation so prosperous are, perhaps, the most
reasonable that can be. England has at present in India an establishment to the amount of
nine thousand eight hundred European troops,
and fifty-four thousand sipahis well armed and
well disciplined. Three thousand of these Europeans, and twenty-five thousand sipahis are dispersed along the borders of the Ganges.

The most considerable body of these troops
has been stationed in Bennares, once the source

* 1,797,750l. † 262,500l. ‡ 131,250l.
§ 1,312,500l.

of Indian science, and still the most famous academy of these rich countries, where European avarice pays no regard to any thing. This situation is chosen, because it appeared favourable for stopping the progress of those warlike people who might descend from the mountains of the north; and in case of attack, the maintaining of a war in a foreign territory would be less ruinous than in the countries of which the company is to receive the revenues. On the south, as far as it has been found practicable, they have occupied all the narrow passes by which an enterprising and active adversary might attempt to penetrate into the province. Dacca, which is in the center of it, has under its walls a considerable force always ready to march wherever their presence may be necessary. All the nabobs and rajahs who are dependent on the subah of Bengal are disarmed, surrounded by spies in order to discover their conspiracies, and by troops to render them ineffectual.

IN case of any unfortunate revolution which might oblige the victorious power to change its quarters, and abandon its posts, the English have constructed a fort near Calcutta called Fort William, which, in times of urgent necessity, would serve as a place of refuge for the army, should they be forced to retreat, and give time to expect the necessary reinforcements for the recovery of their superiority. This fort is a regular octagon with eight bastions, several counter-guards, and some half moons already begun, without a glacis, or covered way. The ditch of
this

IN THE EAST AND WEST INDIES.

this fort may be about one hundred and sixty feet broad, its depth nearly eighteen. On the side of the Ganges, the place is weakest, and the curtains are covered only with redans, over which there is a double battery raised on piles. The principal inconvenience of this citadel, whose construction cost twenty millions *, is, that it does not serve to protect Calcutta, which is now become the city of the greatest importance in India, since its population has amounted to six hundred thousand souls, since immense treasures have been accumulated there, and since it is become from a variety of incidents the theatre of a most extensive commerce. It must necessarily be that the wholesomeness of the air, and the advantage of a very fortunate position, has prevailed over every other consideration.

NOTWITHSTANDING the wise precautions taken by the English, they are not, and cannot be, without apprehensions. The Mogul power may gain strength, and wish to rescue one of its finest provinces out of the hands of a foreign oppressor. They have reason to fear that the barbarous nations may be again allured by the softness of the climate. The princes now at variance may, perhaps, put an end to their contests, and reunite in favour of their common liberty. It is not impossible but the Indians, who at present constitute the chief force of the victorious English, may one day turn upon them those arms of which they have been taught the use. The

* 875,000l.

grandeur

grandeur of the company, which is but imaginary, may, perhaps, moulder away without their being actually driven from what they poſſeſs. It is well known that the Marattas have their eyes continually turned towards this fine country, and are conſtantly threatening it with invaſion. Unleſs the English are ſucceſsful enough either by bribery or intrigue, to divert the ſtorm, Bengal will be the object of their pillage and rapine, whatever meaſures may be taken to oppoſe a light cavalry, whoſe alertneſs exceeds every thing we can ſay of it. The incurſions of theſe ravagers may be repeated; and then the company will have leſs tribute to receive, and their expences will be increaſed. Suppoſing, however, that none of the misfortunes we have ventured to foreſee, ſhould take place, is it likely that the revenues of Bengal ſhould always continue the ſame? This is at leaſt a matter of doubt. The English Company no longer export any coin, but even carry away ſome for the uſe of their factories. The agents of the merchants make immenſe fortunes, and even private perſons gain a tolerable competence, which they repair to the mother country to enjoy. The other European nations find in the treaſures of this ruling power accommodations, which make it unneceſſary to introduce new bullion. Muſt not all theſe combined circumſtances neceſſarily occaſion a deficiency in the finances of thoſe countries, which will ſooner or later be felt in the making up of the public accounts?

THAT

IN THE EAST AND WEST INDIES.

That period might indeed be at some distance, if the English respecting the rights of humanity were to rid those countries of the oppression under which they have continued to groan for so many ages. Then Calcutta, far from being an object of terror to the Indians, would become a tribunal always open to the complaints of those unhappy sufferers whom tyranny should dare to molest. Property would be held so sacred, that the treasure which has long been buried would be taken out of the bowels of the earth, to serve the purpose of its destination. Agriculture and manufactures would be encouraged to such a degree, that the exports would become from day to day more considerable, and the company by following such maxims as these, instead of being driven to the necessity of lessening the tributes which they found established, might possibly find means to bring about an augmentation consistent with the general satisfaction of the natives. Let it no be said that such a plan is chimerical. The English company itself has already proved the possibility of it.

The Europeans, who have acquired any territory in India, generally choose for their farmers the natives of the country, from whom it is common to exact such considerable sums in advance, that in order to pay them they are obliged to borrow at an exorbitant interest. The distress, which these greedy farmers voluntarily bring on themselves, obliges them to exact of the inhabitants, to whom they let some parcels of the land below their value, so considerable a rent, that these unfortunate

fortunate perfons quit their villages, and abandon them for ever. The contractor, ruined by this incident, which renders him infolvent, is difmiffed to make room for a fucceffor, who commonly meets with the fame fate; fo that it very frequently happens, that nothing but the firft fum depofited, or very littled more, is ever received from the eftate.

DIFFERENT fteps have been taken in the Englifh colonies, on the coaft of Coromandel. It was obferved that the villages had been formed by feveral families, who for the moft part were connected with each other; this has been the reafon why the cuftom of employing farmers has been abolifhed. Every land was taxed at a certain rent by the year, and the head of the family was fecurity for his relations and connexions. This method united the colonifts one with another, and created in them a difpofition as well as the power of affording each other a reciprocal fupport. This has occafioned the fettlements of that nation to rife to the utmoft degree of profperity they were capable of attaining; while thofe of her rivals were languifhing for want of cultivation and manufactures, and confequently of population.

WHY muft a mode of conduct which does fo much honour to reafon and humanity be confined to the fmall territory of Madrafs? Can it be true that moderation is a virtue that belongs only to a ftate of mediocrity? The Englifh company till thefe latter times had always held a conduct fuperior to that of the other fettlements. Their agents, their factors, were well chofen. The moft moſt part of them were young men of good families, already inſtructed in the rudiments of commerce, and who were not afraid, when the ſervice of their country called upon them, to croſs thoſe immenſe ſeas which England confiders but as a part of her empire. The company had generally taken their commerce in a great point of view, and had almoſt always carried it on like an aſſociation of true politicians as well as a body of merchants. Upon the whole their planters, merchants and ſoldiers had retained more honeſty, more regularity, and more firmneſs than thoſe of the other nations.

WHO would ever have imagined that this ſame company, by a ſudden alteration of conduct, and change of ſyſtem, could poſſibly make the people of Bengal regret the deſpotiſm of their ancient maſters? That fatal revolution has been but too ſudden and too real. A ſettled plan of tyranny has taken the place of authority occaſionally exerted. The exactions are become general and fixed, the oppreſſion continual and abſolute. The deſtructive arts of monopolies are carried to perfection, and new ones have been invented. In a word, the company have tainted and corrupted the public ſources of confidence and happineſs.

UNDER the government of the Mogul Emperors, the ſubahs, who had the care of the revenues, were, from the nature of the buſineſs, obliged to leave the receipt of them to Nabobs, Polygars, and Jemidars, who were a ſort of underſecurity to other Indians, and theſe ſtill to others; ſo that the produce of the lands paſſed on, and

VOL. I. H h was

was partly funk amidft a multitude of intermediate hands, before it came into the coffers of the fubah, who, on his part, delivered but a very fmall portion of it to the emperor. This administration, faulty in many refpects, had in it one favourable circumftance for the people, that the farmers never being changed, the rent of the farms remained always the fame; becaufe the leaft increafe, as it difturbed the whole chain of advantage which every one received in his turn, would infallibly have occafioned a revolt: a terrible refource, but the only one left in favour of humanity in countries groaning under the oppreffions of defpotic rulers.

It is probable that in the midft of thefe regulations there were many injuries and partial diftreffes. But, at leaft, as the receipt of the public monies was made upon a fixed and moderate affeffment, emulation was not wholly extinguifhed. The cultivators of the land being fure of laying up the produce of their harveft, after paying with exactnefs the rate of their farm, affifted the natural goodnefs of the foil by their labour; the weavers, mafters of the price of their works, being at liberty to make choice of the buyer which beft fuited them, exerted themfelves in extending and improving their manufactures. Both the one and the other, having no anxiety with regard to their fubfiftence, yielded with fatisfaction to the moft delightful inclinations of nature, or the prevailing propenfity of thefe climates; and beheld in the increafe of their family nothing more than the means of augmenting their riches. Such are evidently

the

the reasons why industry, agriculture, and population, have been carried to such a height in the province of Bengal. One would think they might still be carried further under the government of a free people, friends to humanity; but the thirst of money, the most tormenting, the most cruel of all passions, has given rise to a pernicious and destructive government.

THE English, become sovereigns of Bengal, not content to receive the revenues on the same footing as the ancient subahs, have been desirous at once to augment the produce of the farms, and to appropriate to themselves the rents. To accomplish both these objects, they are become the farmers to their own subah, that is, to a slave on whom they have just conferred that empty title, the more securely to impose upon the people. The consequence of this new plan has been to pillage the farmers, in order to substitute in their room the company's agents. They have also monopolized the sale of salt, tobacco, and betel, articles of immediate necessity in those countries, but they have done this under the name, and apparently on the account of the subah. They have gone still further, and have obliged the very same subah to establish in their favour an exclusive privilege for the sale of cotton brought from any other province, in order to raise it to an exorbitant price. They have augmented the duties, and, to coclude all, have obtained an edict, which has been published, to forbid all Europeans, except the English, from trading freely in the interior parts of Bengal.

WHEN we reflect on this cruel prohibition, it seems as if it had been contrived only to deprive of every power of mischief that unfortunate country, whose prosperity, for their own interest, ought to be the only object of the English company. Besides, it is easy to see that the avarice of the members of the council at Calcutta has dictated that shameful law. Their design was to ensure to themselves the produce of all the manufactures, in order to compel the merchants of other nations, who chose to trade from one part of India to another, to purchase these articles of them at an exorbitant price, or to renounce their undertakings.

BUT still in the midst of this overbearing conduct, so contrary to the advantage of their constituents, these treacherous agents have attempted to disguise themselves under the mask of zeal. They have pretended, that as they were under the necessity of exporting to England a quantity of merchandise proportioned to the extent of her commerce, the competition of private traders was prejudicial to the purchases of the company.

UNDER the same pretence, and in order to extend this exclusion to the foreign settlements while they appear to respect their rights, they have of late years ordered more merchandise than Bengal could furnish. At the same time the weavers have been forbidden to work for other nations until the English orders were completed. Thus the workmen, not being any longer at liberty to choose among the several purchasers, have been forced to deliver the fruits of their labour at any price they could get for them.

LET

IN THE EAST AND WEST INDIES.

Let us confider too how thefe workmen have been paid. Here reafon is confounded; we are at a lofs for excufes or pretexts. The Englifh, conquerors of Bengal, poffeffors of the immenfe treafures which the fruitfulnefs of the foil, and the induftry of the inhabitants had collected, have debafed themfelves fo far as to alter the value of the fpecie. They have fet the example of this meannefs unknown to the defpotic rulers of Afia; and it is through this difgraceful act that they have announced to the natives their fovereignty over them. It is true that fuch an operation, fo contrary to the principles of trade and public faith, could not laft long. The company themfelves found the pernicious effects of it, and were refolved to call in all the bafe coin, in order to replace it with other money, exactly the fame as that which was always current in thofe countries. But let us attend to the manner in which fo neceffary an alteration was conducted.

They had ftruck in gold rupees to the amount of about fifteen millions * nominal value, but which reprefented in fact but nine millions †; for four-tenths, or fomething more was alloy. All who were found to poffefs thefe gold rupees of falfe alloy, were enjoined to bring them into the treafury at Calcutta, where they fhould be reimburfed for them in filver rupees; but inftead of ten rupees and a half of filver, which each gold rupee ought to be worth according to its rate, they gave them but fix; fo that the amount of the alloy became the clear lofs of the creditor.

* 656,250 l.   † 393,750 l.

An oppression so general must necessarily be attended with violence; and consequently it has been necessary several times to have recourse to force of arms to carry into execution the orders of the council at Calcutta. These forces have not been employed against the Indians alone; tumults have also broken out, and military preparations been made on all sides, even in the midst of peace. The Europeans have been exposed to signal acts of hostility, and particularly the French, who, notwithstanding their being so reduced, and so weak, have still excited the jealousy of their former rivals.

If to the picture of public distresses we were to add that of private extortions, we should find the agents of the company, almost every where, exacting their tribute with extreme rigour, and raising contributions for them with the utmost cruelty. We should see them carrying a kind of inquisition into every family, and sitting in judgment upon every fortune; robbing indiscriminately the artizan and the labourer, imputing it as a crime that he is not sufficiently rich, and punishing him accordingly. We should view them selling their favour and their credit, as well to oppress the innocent as to skreen the guilty. We should find in consequence of these irregularities, despair seizing every heart, and an universal dejection getting the better of every mind, and uniting to put a stop to the progress and activity of commerce, agriculture, and population.

IN THE EAST AND WEST INDIES.

It will be thought, without doubt, after thefe details, it was impoffible that Bengal fhould have frefh evils to dread. But, however, as if the elements, in league with mankind, had intended to bring all at once upon the fame people every calamity that by turns lays wafte the univerfe, a drought of which there never had been an inftance in thofe climates, came upon them, and prepared the way for a moſt dreadful famine in a country of all the moft fertile.

In Bengal they have two harvefts; one in April, the other in October. The firft, called the little harveft, confifts of the fmaller grain: the fecond, ftiled the grand harveft, is fingly of rice. The rains which commence regularly in the month of Auguft, and end in the middle of October, are the occafion of thefe different productions; and it was by a drought which happened in 1769, at the feafon when the rains are expected, that there was a failure in the great harveft of 1769, and the lefs harveft of 1770. It is true that the rice on the higher grounds did not fuffer greatly by this difturbance of the feafons, but there was far from a fufficient quantity for the nourifhment of all the inhabitants of the country; add to which, the Englifh, who were engaged before hand to take proper care of their fubfiftence, as well as of the fipahis belonging to them, did not fail to keep locked up in their magazine a part of the grain, though the harveft was infufficient.

They have been accufed of having made a very bad ufe of that neceffary forefight, in order to carry on the moſt odious and the moft criminal of all monopolies. It may be true that such an infamous method of acquiring riches may have tempted some individuals; but that the chief agents of the company, that the council of Calcutta could have adopted and ordered such a destructive scheme; that, to gain a few millions of rupees, the council should coolly have devoted to destruction several millions of their fellow creatures, and by the most cruel means; this is a circumstance we never can give credit to. We even venture to pronounce it impossible; because such wickedness could never enter at once into the minds and hearts of a set of men, whose business it is to deliberate and act for the good of others.

But still this scourge did not fail to make itself felt throughout the extent of Bengal. Rice, which is commonly sold at one sol [*] for three pounds, has gradually been raised till it came so high as to be sold at four sols [†] per pound, and it has even been up to five or six sols [‡]; neither indeed was there any to be found, except in such places where the Europeans had taken care to collect it for their own use.

The unhappy Indians were every day perishing by thousands under this want of sustenance, without any means of help and without any resource, not being able to procure themselves the least nourishment. They were to be seen in their villages, along the public ways, in the midst of our European colonies, pale, meagre, fainting, emaciated,

[*] ½.   [†] 1d.   [‡] About 3d.

consumed

IN THE EAST AND WEST INDIES.

confumed by famine; fome ftretched on the ground in expectation of dying, others fcarce able to drag themfelves on to feek for any nutriment, and throwing themfelves at the feet of the Europeans, intreating them to take them in as their flaves.

To this defcription, which makes humanity fhudder, let us add other objects equally fhocking; let imagination enlarge upon them, if poffible; let us reprefent to ourfelves infants deferted, fome expiring on the breaft of their mothers; every where the dying and the dead mingled together; on all fides the groans of forrow, and the tears of defpair; and we fhall then have fome faint idea of the horrible fpectacle Bengal prefented for the fpace of fix weeks.

DURING this whole time the Ganges was covered with carcafes; the fields and highways were choaked up with them; infectious vapours filled the air, and difeafes multiplied; and one evil fucceeding another, it was likely to happen, that the plague might have carried off the remainder of the inhabitants of that unfortunate kingdom. It appears, by calculations pretty generally acknowledged, that the famine carried off a fourth part; that is to fay, about three millions.

BUT it is ftill more remarkable, and ferves to characterife the gentlenefs, or rather the indolence, as well moral as natural, of the natives, that amidft this terrible diftrefs, fuch a multitude of human creatures, preffed by the moft urgent of all neceffities, remainded in an abfolute inactivity,

inactivity, and made no attempts whatever for their self-preservation. All the Europeans, especially the English, were possessed of magazines, and even these were not touched; private houses were so too; no revolt, no massacre, nor the least violence prevailed. The unhappy Indians, resigned to despair, confined themselves to the request of succour they did not obtain, and peaceably waited the relief of death.

Let us now represent to ourselves any part of Europe afflicted by a similar calamity. What disorder! what fury! what atrocious acts! what crimes would ensue! How should we have seen among us Europeans, some contending for their food with their dagger in hand, some pursuing, some flying, and, without remorse, massacreing one another! How should we have seen men at last turn their rage on themselves, tearing and devouring their own limbs, and, in the blindness of despair, trampling under foot all authority, as well as every sentiment of nature and reason!

Had it been the fate of the English to have had the like events to dread on the part of the people of Bengal, perhaps, the famine would have been less general and less destructive. For setting aside, as perhaps we ought, every charge of monopoly, no one will undertake to defend them against the reproach of negligence and insensibility. And in what crisis have they merited that reproach? In the very instant of time when the life or death of several millions of their fellow-creatures was in their power. One would

IN THE EAST AND WEST INDIES.

would think that, in such alternative, the very love of human-kind, that sentiment innate in all hearts, might have inspired them with resources. Might not the poor wretches expiring before the eyes of the Europeans with reason have cried out, " Is it
" then but for our ruin that you are fertile in
" expedients for your own preservation ? The im-
" mense treasures which a long succession of ages
" had accumulated in this country, you have made
" your own spoils; you have transported them into
" your own country; you have raised your contribu-
" tions on us; you have got your agents to receive
" them for you; you are masters of our inte-
" rior commerce; you are the sole managers of
" all our exported merchandise; your numer-
" ous vessels laden with the produce of our in-
" dustry and our soil, pass and repass to the en-
" riching of your factories and your colonies.
" All these things you regulate, and you carry
" on solely for your own advantage. But what
" have you done for our preservation ? What steps
" have you taken to remove from us the scourge
" that threatened us ? Deprived of all autho-
" rity, stripped of our property, weighed down
" by the terrible hand of power, we can only
" lift our hands to you to implore your assist-
" ance. Ye have heard our groans; ye have
" seen famine making very quick advances upon
" us; and then ye attended to your own pre-
" servation. Ye have hoarded up the small quan-
" tity of provisions which escaped the pestilence;
" ye have filled your granaries with them, and
distributed

"distributed them among your soldiers. But we,
"the sad dupes of your avarice, wretches in every
"regard, as well by your tyranny as by your in-
"difference, ye treat us like slaves, while you
"suppose we have any riches; but when it ap-
"pears we are but a set of beings full of wants,
"then you no longer regard us even as human crea-
"tures. Of what service is it to us that you have
"the management of our public forces entirely
"in your hands? Where are the laws and the
"morals of which ye are so proud? What then
"is that government whose wisdom you so much
"boast of? Have you put a stop to the pro-
"digious exports made by your private traders?
"Have ye changed the destination of your ships?
"Have they traversed the neighbouring seas in
"search of the means of subsistence for us?
"Have ye requested it of the adjacent coun-
"tries? Ah, why has Providence suffered you to
"break the chain which attached us to our ancient
"sovereigns? Less grasping, and more humane
"than ye are, they would have invited plenty from
"all parts of Asia; they would have opened every
"communication; they would have lavished their
"treasures, and have thought they did but enrich
"themselves while they preserved their subjects."

This last reflection, at least, was calculated to make an impression on the English, supposing even that every sentiment of humanity was extinguished in their hearts by the effects of depravity. The barrenness had been announced by a drought; and it is not to be doubted, that, if
instead

IN THE EAST AND WEST INDIES.

inftead of having folely a regard to themfelves, and remaining in an entire negligence of every thing elfe, they had from the firft taken every precaution in their power, they might have accomplifhed the prefervation of many lives that were loft.

It could not happen otherwife, than that an adminiftration fo faulty in itfelf fhould defeat the means of profperity attached to the poffeffion of thofe extenfive countries. The company, preffed by real neceffities, and finding only infufficient refources in thofe treafures which ferve to dazzle their imagination, has already been obliged to tear afide the veil which concealed their fituation from the eyes of all the world. According to a calculation, authenticated on the firft of January 1773, the total amount of the company's poffeffions in Europe, whether in arrears hereafter to be received, or in real merchandife now in their ftore-houfes, or even in immoveables, comes to the fum of 175,156,000 livres*: whereas their engagements amount to 207,430,000 livres†; fo that there is a deficiency of 32,274,000 livres‡. It is true, that the means of the company in India, that is to fay, their fpecie in the chefts of their different fettlements, outftanding debts due to them, the value of their wares, their civil and military preparations, their elephants, fhips and their cargoes at fea, form a capital of 143,939,000 livres ||. On the other hand, their debts are not lefs than the fum of 45,726,000 livres§; fo that upon the whole, of

---

* 7,663,075l.   † 14,075,062l. 10s.   ‡ 1,411,987l. 10s.
|| 6,297,331l. 5s.   § 2,000,462l. 10s.

their

their affairs in India, there is a balance in their favour of 98,213,000 livres *. From this muſt be deducted what the company owes in Europe, that is to ſay, 32,274,000 livres †, which reduces the ſum of the general account to 65,939,000 livres ‡; and as the amount of their ſtock is 72,000,000 livres ‖; it follows, that on their capital there is a real loſs of 6,061,000 livres §. So that, in caſe all the effects of the company, as well in Europe as in India, could be converted into money, a ſuppoſition extremely in their favour, the proprietors would not find their original depoſit. Doubtleſs it was not eaſy to ſuſpect their ſituation to be ſuch, when we find the ſales of the company have progreſſively riſen from 44,000,000 livres **, the amount of that in 1762, to 80,000,000 ††, according to the account of that of 1769. The trade of the company has been carried to ſuch a pitch, that the ſales for theſe laſt ten years, to 1771 incluſive, have produced the net ſum of 649,207,000 livres ‡‡. But is is neceſſary to remark, that during the above period the company paid for different duties, to which their goods are ſubject, to the amount of 170,665,000 livres ‖‖, that is more than five and twenty per cent. on the produce of the ſales. And ſtill this ſum, conſiderable as it is, is excluſive of an annual ſtipend of 9,000,000 livres §§; on which condition, government has given up to the company all territorial rights over Bengal.

* 3,798,068l. 15s. † 1,411,987l. 10s. ‡ 2,884,831l. 5s.
‖ 3,150,000l. § 265,168l. 15s. ** 1,925,000l.
†† 3,500,000l. ‡‡ 28,402,806l. 5s. ‖‖ 7,466,593l. 15s.
§§ 393,750l.

To make good engagements fo extenfive, and to diftribute at the fame time to the proprietors a dividend of 9,000,000 livres*, at the rate of twelve and a half per cent. the revenues of India ought to have been managed with great prudence and œconomy: then they might have been fufficient, as well for the purchafes the company make in India, as for thofe made in China, and they might have waved fending any fums to their fmall factories. It was with this confidence that the proprietors of flock enjoyed quietly their dividend, and even expected it to be raifed by the importation of money which had been announced to them. But fo far was the event from anfwering their large expectations, that the company's agents at Bengal, Bombay, and Madrafs, have continually drawn upon them to make good the infufficiency of the revenues. The draughts drawn by them during the laft five years, viz. from 1768 to 1772, both inclufive, amount to the fum of 49,250,000 livres†. Thefe draughts have made it unneceffary to fend out coin to India; but during the fome period they have been obliged to remit to China the fum of 20,000,000 livres‡. And even this remittance not having been anfwerable to the prodigious purchafes made for the company at Canton, the factory there have been obliged to draw on them for 7,780,000 livres ||. The company moreover, have exported to India, within the fame time, as much as 60,140,000 livres § of merchandife; fo that, bringing together all thefe fums it

* 393,75cl.   † 2,154,687l. 10s.   ‡ 875,000l.
|| 340,875l.   § 2,631,125l.

appears,

appears, that during thefe five years, which feemed likely to be the period of their greateft profperity, the company, whether by exportations abroad, or by draughts paid in Europe, has employed in trade 137,590,000 livres*, which makes the fum of 27,515,000 livres † *communibus annis.* However, notwithftanding this prodigious difference between the fpeculations and the real tranfactions, if the revenues of Bengal had not been fubject to depredations perhaps unparalleled, the company might have been enabled to fupport with eafe all their expences, and ftill continue a dividend of twelve and a half per cent. to the ftockholders. The proof of this will appear in the abftract of their commerce, calculated upon the receipts and difburfements of the laft years, on the experience of which it may be proper to ground our opinion of the actual ftate of things.

RECEIPT.

	Livres.
Produce of their fales, deducting difcount,	78,750,000 ‡
Produce of duties for the benefit of the company laid on private trade	560,000 ‖
Value of 500 tons of faltpetre wanted annually for the army	500,000 §
Total	79,810,000 **

* 6,019,562l. 10s.   † 1,203,78 1l.   ‡ 3,445,312l. 10s.
‖ 24,500l.   § 21,875l.   ** 3,447,937l. 10s.

DISBURSE-

IN THE EAST AND WEST INDIES. 481

BOOK III.

DISBURSEMENTS.

	Livres.
Amount of duties - - - - -	20,250,000 §
Freight and charges out - - - -	11,250,000 *
Value of goods annually exported -	11,250,000 †
Amount of bullion exported to China, and of the draughts the factory there draws annually on the company -	4,500,000 ‡
The impost of five per cent. on the rough produce of the annual sales, set at eighty-four millions -	4,200,000 ‖
Bills of exchange taken from different parts of India - - - - -	8,080,000 §§
Annual stipend to be paid to government on account of Bengal -	9,000,000 **
Annual dividend on the footing of twelve and a half per cent. per annum	9,000,000 ††
Interest of bills beyond what the company receives of government -	1,120,000 ‡‡

Total 78,650,000 ‖‖

IF, from the amount of the receipt stated at 79,810,000, livres §§, we deduct the latter sum of 78,650,000 livres ***, the surplus of the receipt will be 1,160,000 livres †††.

THIS state, the several articles of which having undergone the inspection of parliament cannot be called in question, serves to shew, that, even supposing a wiser administration, both at home and in India, the proprietors had no reason to expect any

§ 885,937l. 10s.   * 492,187l. 10s.   † 492,187l. 10s.
‡ 196,875l.   ‖ 183,750l.   §§ 353,500l.
** 393,750l.   †† 393,750l.   ‡‡ 49,000l.
‖‖ 3,440,937l. 10s.   §§ 3,491,687l. 10s.   *** 3,440,973l. 10s.
††† 50,750l.

VOL. I.   I i   advantage

advantage beyond the dividend of twelve and a half per cent. which had been fixed for them.

But, if we afcend from the particular intereft of the trading company to confiderations of more extent, what refources, what advantages, does not the commerce of India procure to the ftate? The amount of duties on the company's importations, the impoft of five per cent. on the grofs produce of their fales, the ftipend exacted by government on account of Bengal, form a tribute of 33,450,000 livres * paid annually to Great Britain out of the commerce and poffeffions of Afia. And fo long as the public treafure, affifted by this new branch of revenue, turns it to the improvement of the power and profperity of the kingdom, the annual mafs of riches is ftill increafed by the exports of the company's merchandife; by the charges of their navigation; by the benefit of the dividend at eight and a half above the common intereft ; by the draughts they pay, fince thefe draughts are the reprefentatives of the fortunes made by their agents in their fervice, and which they return home to enjoy. All thefe articles brought together conftitute nearly a total of 40,000,000 livres †, expended on the commerce of India to the advantage of the land and manufactures of England : and yet this fum of 40,000,000 livres ‡, together with the other of 33,450,000 livres §, received by the government, requires no more than an export of 2, or 300,000 in bullion ‖. Thus the public

---

* 1,463,437l. 10s.   † 1,750,000l.   ‡ 1,750,000l.
§ 1,463,437l. 10s.   ‖ About 109,000l. on an average.

IN THE EAST AND WEST INDIES. 483

treafury and the kingdom are equally enriched by the produce of a commerce, which, by the effect of a moſt extraordinary management, threatens with ruin the very proprietors who farm it out to their agents.

It is eafy to judge from the ſketch juſt given, that for a long time they muſt facrifice their dividends to clear away entirely that deficiency of 32,000,000 livres*, which has taken place in their affairs in Europe. But what will be attended with ſtill more difficulty will be, to revive in India the order and œconomy neceſſary for diſcharging the debt of 45,000,000 livres† contracted there on the company's account.

We muſt allow that the corruption to which the Engliſh have given themſelves up from the firſt beginning of their power, the oppreſſion which has fucceeded it, the abufes every day multiplying, the entire loſs of all principle; all thefe circumſtances together form a contraſt totally inconſiſtent with their paſt conduct in India, and the real conſtitution of their government in Europe. But this fort of problem in morals will be eafily folved, upon confidering with attention the natural effect of circumſtances and events.

Being now become abfolute rulers in an empire where they were but traders, it was very difficult for the Engliſh not to make a bad ufe of their power. At a diſtance from home, men are no longer reſtrained by the fear of being aſhamed to fee their countrymen. In a warm climate where

* 1,400,000l.   † 1,968,750l.

the body loſes its vigour, the mind muſt loſe ſome of its ſtrength. In a country where nature and cuſtom lead to indulgence, men are apt to be ſeduced. In countries where they come for the purpoſe of growing rich, they eaſily forget to be juſt.

Perhaps, however, in a ſituation ſo dangerous, the Engliſh would at leaſt have preſerved ſome appearance of moderation and virtue, had they been checked by the reſtraint of the laws: but there were none to direct or to bind them. The regulations made by the company, for the carrying on of their commerce, were not applicable to this new arrangement of affairs; and the Engliſh government, conſidering the conqueſt of Bengal but as a help towards increaſing numerically the revenue of Great Britain, gave up to the company for 9,000,000 livres * per annum the deſtiny of twelve millions of people.

Happily for this portion of our fellow-creatures, a revolution of a peaceable nature is at hand. The nation has been ſtruck with ſuch enormous exceſſes. She has heard the groans of ſuch a number of victims ſacrificed to the avarice and paſſions of ſome individuals. The parliament is already employed on this great object. Every detail of that adminiſtration is under their inſpection, every fact will be cleared up, every abuſe unveiled, and the reaſons of them inquired into and removed. What a ſight to be preſented to Europe! What an example to be left to

* 393,750 l.

poſterity!

posterity! The hand of liberty is going to weigh the destiny of a whole people in the scale of justice.

Yes, august legislators, ye will make good our expectations! Ye will restore mankind to their rights; ye will put a curb on avarice, and break the yoke of tyranny. The authority of law, which is not to be shaken, will every where take place of an administration purely arbitrary. At sight of that authority, the monopolist, that tyrant over industry, will for ever disappear. The fetters which private interest has riveted on commerce, ye will make to give way to general advantage.

You will not confine yourselves to this momentary reformation. You will carry your views into futurity; you will calculate the influence of climate, the danger of circumstances, the contagion of example; and, to prevent their effects, you will select persons without connexions, without passions, to visit these distant countries; issuing from the bosom of your metropolis, they are to pass through these provinces, in order to hear complaints, rectify abuses, redress injuries; in a word, to maintain and reunite the ties of order throughout the country.

By the execution of this salutary plan, you will, without doubt, have done much towards the happiness of these people; but not enough for your own honour. One prejudice you have still to conquer, and that victory is worthy of yourselves. Venture to put your new subjects into a situation to enjoy the sweets of property.

Portion out to them the fields on which they were born: they will learn to cultivate them for themselves. Attached to you by these favours, more than ever they were by fear, they will pay with joy the tribute you impose with moderation. They will instruct their children to adore, and admire your government; and succeffive generations will transmit down, with their inheritance, the sentiments of their happiness mixed with that of their gratitude.

THEN shall the friends of mankind applaud your success; they will indulge the hope of seeing prosperity once more revive in a country embellished by nature, and no longer ravaged by despotism. It will be pleasing to them to think that the calamities which afflicted those fertile countries are for ever removed from them. They will pardon in you those usurpations, which have been only set on foot for the sake of despoiling tyrants; and they will invite you to new conquests, when they see the influence of your excellent constitution of government extending itself even to the very extremities of Asia, to give birth to liberty, property, and happiness.

END OF THE FIRST VOLUME.

BOOKS Printed for and Sold by T. CADELL, in the STRAND, LONDON.

I. THE Hiftory of England, from the Invafion of Julius Cæfar to the Revolution: A new Edition, printed on fine Paper, with many Corrections and Additions, and a complete Index, 8 vols. Royal Paper, 7l. 7s.

II. The Hiftory of Great Britain from the Reftoration to the Acceffion of the Houfe of Hanover, by J. Macpherfon, Efq. the 2d Edition, 2 vols. with a Head of the Author. 2l. 5s.

III. Original Papers, containing the Secret Hiftory of Great Britain, from the Reftoration to the Acceffion of the Houfe of Hanover: To which are prefixed, Extracts from the Life of James II. as written by himfelf, publifhed from the Originals, 2 vols. 2l. 5s.

IV. The Hiftory of the Decline and Fall of the Roman Empire, by Edward Gibbon, Efq. vol. I. from the Reign of Trajan to that of Conftantine. 1l. 4s.

V. An Inquiry into the Nature and Caufes of the Wealth of Nations. By Adam Smith, LL. D. F. R. S. formerly Profeffor of Moral Philofophy in the Univerfity of Glafgow, 2 vols. 2l. 2s.

VI. An Effay on the Hiftory of Civil Society, by Adam Fergufon, LL. D. Profeffor of Moral Philofophy in the Univerfity of Edinburgh, 2d Edition. 15s.

VII. Another Edition, in 8vo. 6s.

VIII. Sketches of the Hiftory of Man, by Lord Kaimes, Author of the Elements of Criticifm, 2 vols. 2l. 2s.

BOOKS Printed for and Sold by T. CADELL.

IX. An Univerfal Dictionary of the Marine: Or, a copious Explanation of the technical Terms and Phrafes employed in the Conftruction, Equipment, Furniture, Machinery, Movements, and Military Operations of a Ship. Illuftrated with a Variety of original Defigns of Shipping, in different Situations; together with feparate Views of their Mafts, Sails, Yards, and Rigging. To which is annexed, a Tranflation of the French Sea Terms and Phrafes, collected from the Works of Meffrs. Du Hamel, Aubin, Saverion, &c. By William Falconer, Author of the Shipwreck, 3d Edition, 1l. 4s.

X. Commentaries on the Laws of England. By Judge Blackftone, 4 vols. 4l. 4s.

XI. Another Edition, in 8vo. 1l. 10s.

XII. Tracts, chiefly relating to the Antiquities and Laws of England. By Judge Blackftone, 1l. 1s.

XIII. The Works of Alexander Pope, Efq. with his laft Corrections, Additions, and Improvements, as they were delivered to the Editor a little before his Death: Together with the Commentary and Notes of Dr. Warburton. Adorned with Cuts. In 9 large vols. 8vo. 2l. 14s.

XIV. The fame, in 9 vols. fmall 8vo. 1l. 7s.

XV. The fame, in 9 vols. fmall 12mo. printed on a fine Writing Paper. 1l. 7s.

XVI. The Works of Mr. Thomfon, 4 vols. 12mo. with a Life of the Author. To which are added, fome Poems, never before printed. 12s.

www.ingramcontent.com/pod-product-compliance
Lightning Source LLC
Chambersburg PA
CBHW021423300426
44114CB00010B/625